ℒℴℐ

# Four Perspectives in Multicultural Education

**JOAN THROWER TIMM**

The University of Wisconsin Oshkosh

Wadsworth Publishing Company

I⟨T⟩P® An International Thomson Publishing Company

Belmont • Albany • Bonn • Boston • Cincinnati • Detroit • London • Madrid
Melbourne • Mexico City • New York • Paris • San Francisco • Singapore
Tokyo • Toronto • Washington

**Education Editor:** Sabra Horne
**Editorial Assistant:** Louise Mendelson
**Production Editor:** Jennie Redwitz
**Managing Designer:** Stephen Rapley
**Print Buyer:** Karen Hunt
**Permissions Editor:** Jeanne Bosschart
**Copy Editor:** Lee Motteler
**Compositor:** Margarite Reynolds, Wadsworth Digital Productions
**Cover:** Andrew Ogus
**Printer:** Malloy Lithographing, Inc.

Printed in the United States of America
1 2 3 4 5 6 7 8 9 10

For more information, contact Wadsworth Publishing Company.

Wadsworth Publishing Company
10 Davis Drive
Belmont, California 94002
USA

International Thomson Publishing Europe
Berkshire House 168-173
High Holborn
London, WC1V 7AA
England

Thomas Nelson Australia
102 Dodds Street
South Melbourne 3205
Victoria, Australia

Nelson Canada
1120 Birchmount Road
Scarborough, Ontario
Canada M1K 5G4

International Thomson Editores
Campos Eliseos 385, Piso 7
Col. Polanco
11560 México D.F. México

International Thomson
Publishing GmbH
Königswinterer Strasse 418
53227 Bonn
Germany

International Thomson Publishing Asia
221 Henderson Road
#05-10 Henderson Building
Singapore 0315

International Thomson Publishing Japan
Hirakawacho Kyowa Building, 3F
2-2-1 Hirakawacho
Chiyoda-ku, Tokyo 102, Japan

**Library of Congress Cataloging-in-Publication Data**

Timm, Joan Thrower.
    Four perspectives in multicultural education / Joan Thrower Timm.
        p.   cm.
    Includes bibliographical references and index.
    ISBN 0-534-50727-1 (pbk)
    1. Multicultural education—United States.   2. Pluralism (Social sciences)—United States.
I. Title.
LC1099.3.T56   1996                                                                    95-23218
370.19'6'0973—dc20

〰

*This book is dedicated to my grandchildren,*
*José Javier Aguilar and Mary Genevieve Aguilar*

ॐ

## *ACKNOWLEDGMENTS*

*I wish to thank Professors Jean Erdman, Richard Hammes, Anthony Koysiz,
and Shirley Wilbert, who reviewed portions of the manuscript
for this text and offered important suggestions.*

*I also wish to thank the reviewers whose comments provided valuable insights in the early
stages of this work: Jo Alexander, Auburn University; Arthur Anderson, Florida State
University; Denise Davis, University School; Mary Ann Flowers, Cleveland State
University; Teresa McCarty, University of Arizona; Pedro Noguera, University of California
at Berkeley; Sylvia Peña, University of Houston; Evelyn Reid, University of Toledo;
Francisco Rios, California State University, San Marcos; and Dan R. Whitmore, Texas
Woman's University. I further wish to express my gratitude to all those at Wadsworth
for their help with this project. Without their patient assistance,
this volume would never have been possible.*

*Finally, I thank my husband, Henry C. Timm,
for his unwavering faith and support in this effort.*

# Brief Contents

# Contents

## II   THE CULTURAL PERSPECTIVE

### 7   THE NATURE OF CULTURE                           133

# 1

⟨∞⟩

# What Is Multicultural Education?

It takes a whole village to raise a child.

AFRICAN PROVERB

I think the time has come when the American people realize that
we're in this together and that we sink or swim together. And I say to you
maybe ... that's the way it should be ... a test of our courage ... of our
compassion ... of our faith in ourselves and our faith in our country.

BILL MCKAY
CANDIDATE FOR THE U.S. SENATE IN *THE CANDIDATE*

Whenever people outside the field of education ask me what I teach and I reply "Multicultural Education," their response is often a look of surprise followed by the question "What is that?" The question is not altogether naive. In the view of the public, multicultural education is a mystery to some, perceived by others as contributing to our understanding of each other in a society that is increasingly diverse, and considered by still others as a threat to traditional mainstream American values and education.

Within the field of education, perceptions of multicultural education also depend upon the point of view of the speaker. A colleague of mine who teaches at a state university considers multicultural education to be the history and experiences of diverse groups. Another colleague, who also teaches at a university, perceives it as a way to help students develop an appreciation of their own heritage and that of others. Some educators view it as a way for students in teacher education programs to learn about diverse groups, which may help them in their own teaching in the future. Many teachers of my acquaintance view it as curricular content and sometimes teaching methodologies for working with diverse students. Teachers also consider it to be a way of helping diverse students to study, work, and learn together, and to appreciate each other in the process. Professionals in the field of multicultural education view it as a means of addressing inequities in American society that pertain to diverse groups. I believe that multicultural education is all of these things, but that it should also include theoretical cultural issues (in addition to cultural content) and considerations about cognitive development that all children share.

I came to the field of multicultural education from a graduate degree in human development—an interdisciplinary program that combined cultural anthropology with developmental psychology. Originally I taught courses in human development in cross-cultural perspective, which also included the historical contexts of diverse groups. Because I teach in a college of education, I also brought issues from educational psychology to my courses. When "multicultural issues" in education came to the purview of teaching programs, I began teaching courses in "multicultural education." Probably because of this background, I have believed for years that multicultural education encompasses a broad spectrum of concepts, all of which are important in order for students to develop an awareness of the way in which people's identity is inevitably derived from their culture and their history.

Identity is the theme of this text. My goal is to present the manner in which identity is construed through history, culture, and psychological development within a social context. Thus the perspectives are historical, cultural, psychological, and educational. The theme of identity and variations on it emerge quickly in the text and provide the conceptual framework for what follows. In the next section I will describe how these four perspectives relate to identity. Then I will offer a preview of the issues within the different perspectives.

## DELINEATING IDENTITY

The issue of defining one's identity, within the historical perspective, appears immediately (Chapter 2). All people living in the United States form a sense of who they are as individuals and as members of diverse groups within the context of the national society. Identity is thus perceived in terms of similarities and differences in relation to others. How people are treated also contributes to these perceptions. When individuals and members of diverse groups experience privilege or inequity in the American social system, they receive a message about ways in which others in positions of social power identify and view them (Chapter 3). In addition, the impact that educational practices have on diverse groups cannot help but affect students' perceptions about how others view them (Chapter 4). Women's changing perceptions about themselves and their role in American society have defined their identity over the years (Chapter 5). How members of diverse groups have been perceived (or identified) within the American legal system has impacted court decisions about them that have had far-reaching effects (Chapter 6).

Within the cultural anthropological perspective, culture has long been considered to be the most central factor in human experience by giving us language, values, attitudes, traditions, customs, knowledge, skills, and beliefs about the physical and spiritual world (Chapter 7). In other words, culture determines our identity. Popular culture reflects individual and diverse identity in its portrayal of a variety of American "myths" and images (Chapter 8). It may appear circular to comment here that people identify with the images in popular culture that in turn reinforce their self-image, but years of research have documented the powerful effect of these role models. (The fact that the portrayal of members of diverse groups may be based on stereotyped perceptions is a serious problem.)

Within the psychological perspective, educators have too long given students impressions of their abilities based on their performance or achievement without taking the students' cultural frame of reference into account. This practice obviously affects students' self-image. On the other hand, educators have also overgeneralized students within diverse groups and failed to consider individual differences within the same group (Chapter 9). Research in developmental psychology indicates that children's perceptions of their own identity as well as that of others are based upon cognitive developmental concepts that change with age. Research also reveals that prejudicial attitudes toward others are related to these perceptions (Chapter 10). The research in this area has been relatively ignored in the field of multicultural education.

Within the educational perspective, current political attitudes about multicultural education reflect different views about what it means to be an American—in other words, they reflect attitudes about American identity. One viewpoint considers this identity to be a national one and perceives identifying with diverse groups as being divisive to the society. Other viewpoints consider that it is possible to have an identity with diverse groups and still have a sense of "being an American" as well (Chapter 11). When it comes to the classroom (Chapter 12), diverse areas of focus present cultural information, address social issues, and facilitate relationships among members of diverse groups. Identity is thus important at both the personal (individual) and group level. Finally, language has long been considered a fundamental aspect of our identity. An immigrant recently arrived in the United States said to me, "Take away my language and you take away my culture, and then I don't know who I am." Bilingual education revolves around precisely this issue (Chapter 13).

## TOPICAL ISSUES

Part I of this text presents the historical perspective. It encompasses the history of diverse groups in the United States, including the different experiences that they have encountered, their education, and landmark court decisions that have impacted their lives. Sometimes teachers in the field of multicultural education assume that their students are familiar with the history of diverse groups when they enter multicultural education classes. I believe this assumption is questionable. I have discovered that the portion of my multicultural course that I devote to history from the point of view of diverse groups makes a noticeable difference in students' ability to understand and sympathize with groups other than their own. Over the years, literally hundreds of students have reported to me that either they have never been provided with the history of diverse groups, or the history courses they have had *presented the information from the European American point of view.* For example, one student commented:

> I never stopped to think what it must have been like to wake up one morning and be living in a whole different country. I mean it must have been a terrible shock to learn that you were no longer living in Mexico but you were now a *minority* living in United States territory. How would we like it if Canada suddenly decided to incorporate part of the United States?

I believe that knowledge of the experiences of diverse groups provides a broader understanding not only of the groups themselves but also of our nation's history taken as a whole. Therefore, I have devoted a sizeable portion of this text to the economic, social, and educational history of diverse groups.

Chapter 2, *The American Dilemma,* focuses on Americans' identities as individual, diverse, or national, and how these identities interrelate. It also reviews the foundations behind the American form of government, including the Iroquois Confederation. Chapter 3, *American Diversity,* reviews the various histories of diverse groups, including the impact of inequities in economic, political, and social power on these groups. Rather than separating the experiences of different groups into separate chapters, I have reviewed them together. Obviously, no groups have identical histories, but reviewing their past in the same chapter reveals a pattern of similar experiences. Chapter 4, *Diversity and American Education,* reviews education in the United States in reference to diverse groups as well as the privileges or inequities that members of these groups have encountered on the basis of race, ethnicity, and social class. It also examines a continuing hidden curriculum that results in unequal outcomes in education on the basis of social class. Chapter 5, *The Education of American Women,* reviews the history of education available to women, who have encountered discrimination based on a combination of gender, race, ethnicity, and social class. It also includes some historical background in regard to women's involvement in social issues in the United States. Much of this information is apparently new to students. One of my students remarked:

> I thought that women's interest in politics began in the 1960s. I never heard of the Grimke sisters or the convention in Seneca Falls before this course.

Chapter 6, *The Law and American Education,* examines landmark court decisions that were directly related to educational issues or that impacted education for minority groups in diverse ways. Many of these decisions continue to affect school policy in the United States today.

Part II presents the cultural anthropology perspective. Chapter 7, *The Nature of Culture,* examines ways of viewing culture that recognize differences and yet identify issues, accruing to the human condition, that members of diverse groups share. It examines both material and nonmaterial culture. Chapter 8, *Popular Culture: American Myths and Icons,* reviews ways in which films and television reflect American cultural values, portray diverse groups, and depict public leaders' roles in the United States. It also considers the long-standing involvement of education with popular culture.

Part III analyzes the psychological perspective. Chapter 9, *Cultural Styles or Learning Styles?* examines the ways in which culture influences learning and considers the possibility of multiple intelligences. It also addresses the concept of learning styles and the problems associated with them. Finally, it reviews the relationship between students' diverse backgrounds and their approach to learning situations. Chapter 10, *The Development of Prejudice,* reviews different theories about how prejudice develops and examines the relationship between cognitive developmental level and a developmental sequence in children's changing perceptions about themselves and members of other groups. These perceptions have been found in the thinking of children from all racial groups.

Part IV deals with the educational perspective. Chapter 11, *Politics and Multicultural Education,* reviews the current public controversy over multicultural education. It examines three conflicting political viewpoints: the politically conservative, the liberal, and the radical. I believe it is crucial for students of multicultural education to be familiar with these views in order for them to know the issues involved. Chapter 12, *The Multicultural Classroom: Putting It All Together,* offers a schema for multicultural education that includes three areas of focus: cultural information, social issues, and interpersonal relationships. It also (a) includes criteria for educators and teachers to consider in selecting materials for multicultural education; (b) offers some suggestions for combating bias; (c) presents some ways to help students recognize stereotypes as a way of combating them; and (d) discusses procedures that enhance students' cognitive ability to take other points of view. Chapter 13, *Bilingual Education,* describes the history of conflicting attitudes toward non-English languages in the United States. It reviews language development in a first language and the implications of that development for learning a second language. It also reviews approaches to language instruction in the United States, including different bilingual education programs. Chapter 14, *Toward the Future,* looks ahead to the diverse world of the twenty-first century, which is only the blink of an eye away.

Part V presents *The Sultan's Jester,* a multicultural comedy that was adapted from *Tales from the Arabian Nights* for community and school audiences. It is appropriate for elementary, middle, and high school productions. Cast members may also range in age. I have included it in this text because I believe it offers an example of the fact that humor about human foibles may bring a new dimension into multicultural education. The human condition is not an easy one, and a smile may help us to recognize that we are all in this situation together.

# PART I

# The Historical Perspective

# 2

## The American Dilemma

Where Do We Come From?
What Are We?
Where Are We Going?

The questions at the beginning of this chapter (in English translation) constitute the title of a masterpiece (*D'ou Venon Nous? Que Sommes Nous? Ou Allons Nous?*) by the French painter Paul Gauguin. This painting depicts women of Tahiti: an old woman, some in the bloom of youth, and some as children. The image is clear: the past, present, and future converge and the whole of Tahitian culture is contained in that moment in time. The questions apply not only to the Tahitians but also to Gauguin, who, as an immigrant to Tahiti, was searching for his own place in their world.

The questions of the painting just as easily apply to Americans today. How does our past influence us? Who are we? What is our future? The underlying issue for Gauguin was that of identity, and it is the same for us. How do we see ourselves—both individually and collectively? How does our identity influence our views about each other? How does it affect our behavior? How does it shape our values?

The answers to these questions depend upon one of three perspectives to which we refer at any given moment, for Americans have at least three distinct frames of reference by which we psychologically define our identity. Our first frame of reference is our view of ourselves as individuals, and includes our understanding of what that view means in terms of our relationships with others. Our second frame of reference derives from our diverse groups, which include race, ethnicity, gender, and socioeconomic status. Our third frame of reference is our country or nation as a whole, the United States of America.

Psychologically, our individual identity develops over time. Our awareness of ourselves and others becomes more complex as we grow from childhood into adulthood. For example, young children do not understand a national frame of reference beyond very concrete objects or events. To a six-year-old child, the Fourth of July means firecrackers and a picnic. (Perhaps it means this to some adults too!) Older children and adolescents, however, understand that it commemorates Independence Day, and whether or not the historical event is important to them personally, they at least understand what happened in 1776.

This chapter explores the three frames of reference common to Americans: individual, diverse, and national. These not only influence our sense of who we are both personally and collectively, but affect our actions toward each other as well.

To address the question of who we are as individuals, five historical views of individualism will be considered along with the values contained within them. To address the question of who we are collectively, the basic types of diversity will be reviewed. To address the question of who we are and where we have come from as a nation, the philosophical values underlying the creation of our Republic will be reviewed along with the contribution of the Iroquois Confederation to our federal government. To address the question of where we are going as a society, the concept of pluralism will be explored.

# INDIVIDUALISM

In historical terms, the political philosophy known as individualism has examined the relationship of individuals to each other and to their society. Individualism has been defined as "a doctrine that the interests of the individual are or ought to be ethically paramount" or "a conception that all values, rights, and duties originate in individuals" (Merriam-Webster, 1993, p. 593). This definition implies that personal interests are primary, but there is mention here of "duties" as well. Indeed, in the best interpretation of individualism, the notion of personal responsibility to others is fundamental.

The concept of individualism has recently been rejected by some advocates of multicultural education, primarily because some political conservatives place a high value on it. Conservatives tend to view individualism primarily in economic terms, speak of opportunity, and take the position that success is possible for everyone. Sleeter (1994) has pointed out that those who object to this view of individualism do so because it does not take into account social inequities regarding race, gender, or socioeconomic level. Fair enough, but objecting to the concept of individualism primarily on the basis of politically conservative interpretations overlooks the variety of interpretations about individualism in American society. Ironically, some conservatives disregard the different varieties of individualism as well. The current political views in the United States about these issues in relation to multicultural education are reviewed in Chapter 11.

## Types of Individualism in American Culture

The concept of individualism in American culture is complex. The term carries with it different historical connotations that are not readily apparent. There are several types of individualism, each of which contains its own interpretation of freedom, success, and justice in American life (Bellah et al., 1985).

**Protestant Individualism**   The first type of individualism is Biblical in origin and traces its existence in America from the Puritans who settled in New England. We may consider it Protestant individualism. The beliefs in this form of individualism originated in Europe during the Protestant Reformation. These beliefs included an emphasis on a personal and direct relationship with God, individual salvation through faith, and an emphasis on good works. In this view, individuals were seen as being responsible for their behavior and accountable for it directly to God. Members of the clergy were not viewed as being necessary to this personal relationship with God. The focus on good works was taken directly from the Biblical Scriptures (Bellah et al., 1985). Success in this world was interpreted as a sign of being in favor with God. This focus on good works became known as the **Protestant work ethic.**

John Winthrop, the first governor of the Massachusetts Bay Colony, articulated this viewpoint. He envisioned true freedom (or moral freedom) "to [be] that only which is good, just and honest" (Bellah et al., 1985, p. 29). In other words, Winthrop perceived an ethical component in the idea of freedom. For him, success in the society was linked to an ethical community. Justice was a matter of moderation, involving a view for others' needs and, therefore, an understanding of the reasons for their actions. While ethics have been ignored in some views of freedom, the centrality of ethics, interestingly, has reemerged recently in discussions of what a pluralistic society should be. I shall return to an issue of ethics later in this chapter.

The values of Protestant individualism appeared later in the views of both utilitarian individualism and economic individualism. It is not uncommon for some Americans to suggest that those with economic hardships may not have tried hard enough, or they have done something wrong that created those circumstances. This conclusion overlooks factors such as discrimination, unequal opportunities, or simple bad luck. As examples, a student who cannot afford to enroll in an educational program leading to a professional career, a factory worker who is not hired because of quotas, or a business executive who loses retirement benefits by being laid off because of company downsizing or mergers may be judged to be failures by some people even though their fortunes are determined by circumstances beyond their control.

**Republican Individualism**   The second type of individualism, Republican individualism, focuses on issues of political equality. This view of individualism derives from the political views of the philosopher John Locke and a doctrine known as natural rights. Thomas Jefferson expressed an American philosophy reflecting this point of view. For him, the political ideal was a society that was self-governing by its citizens. Jefferson believed that "men" acted as independent individuals whose "natural" condition included life, liberty, and ownership of property. A community of "political men" formed a government to ensure everyone's rights. Each person, however, had an equal responsibility to respect the rights of others. This viewpoint was fundamental to the American concept of government. In Jefferson's view, individual freedom meant freedom from "arbitrary" government action, but it also required education for participation in government. Success within the society involved active involvement on the part of every citizen. Justice was seen as deriving from the legal system (Bellah et al., 1985). Thus, Jefferson's view of government included not only political, but ethical considerations as well. In the eighteenth century, however, this perception of individualism did not include diverse groups in its understanding of citizenship but was originally limited to White males. Since then, legal and social reforms have extended participatory citizenship to diverse groups of people.

**Utilitarian Individualism**   The third type of individualism, utilitarian individualism, is similar to Republican individualism in its belief in "the pursuit of happiness" referred to in The Declaration of Independence. Utilitarian individualism, however, places a heavy emphasis on economic opportunity. The ability of an individual to succeed through hard work and personal initiative lies at the heart of this view. Benjamin Franklin expressed the central value of utilitarian individualism. Like Jefferson, Franklin envisioned a society that (a) provided the opportunity for ordinary citizens to advance; (b) protected their rights; and (c) provided equal or just treatment under the law. Economic opportunity was particularly important to Franklin, who was the son of an artisan and not from an economically advantaged family.

By the end of the eighteenth century, some Americans believed that general social good would result in a society open for individuals to pursue their own interests. We recognize this view in The American Creed, which blends political freedom with a faith in a capitalistic economic system. According to this view, "the greatest good comes to the greatest number of people when persons pursue their individual economic self interests" (Garcia, 1991, p. 16). We may conclude that in this type of individualism, freedom is seen as the right to pursue one's dreams. Success is judged in economic terms. Justice is perceived as fair opportunity. In spite of expressive individualism, which followed in the nineteenth century, utilitarian individualism continued as a powerful influence in American thought. It remains with us today and serves as the basis for the modern view of economic individualism. It may be important to point out here the fact that this utilitarian view of individualism was constructed on European, male, and upper socioeconomic perspectives. It is also significant that this view laid the foundations for legal policies in relation to economic individualism that followed later.

**Expressive Individualism**   The fourth type of individualism is expressive individualism. By the mid-nineteenth century, views of utilitarian individualism so prevailed in America that some people, men and women alike—including writers, social thinkers and members of the clergy—began to react against the idea of a life dedicated primarily to material gains.

The poet Walt Whitman lyrically expressed the views of this new individualism in his book, *Leaves of Grass.* In Whitman's view, freedom was the right to express personal feelings and to explore one's own various identities. Success did not involve material gain but rather a refined intellectual and sensual life (Bellah et al., 1985). Justice was assumed to be noninterference on the part of others. The modern derivative of this view is the notion that everyone is free to "do his or her thing" so long as it does not infringe on the rights of others. Success is a matter of individual interpretation. For example, a corporate executive of my acquaintance recently resigned his position in order to buy an eighteen-wheel "rig" because being a truck driver offered him the freedom of being on his own, which he did not enjoy in the corporate hierarchy. He has explained that he is able to go where he chooses and to spend his spare time visiting interesting places instead of writing reports every night until midnight. He is now happier than when he followed his friends' interpretation of "success."

**Economic Individualism**   Economic individualism derived from the material focus in utilitarian individualism and continued to influence American thought in the nineteenth and twentieth centuries, in spite of the values of expressive individualism. In this view, freedom implies individual rights to compete economically with as little regulation as possible. Success is measured primarily in economic terms. This view, interestingly enough, contains elements of the old Protestant view of success as reflecting good works and God's favor. Today this view emphasizes individual participation, competition, and personal rights in America's capitalistic free market economy. Justice is perceived as noninterference by government, but justice is also perceived as equity of individual rights.

There are benefits and problems in the values of economic individualism. On one hand, individuals are free to compete in the marketplace but, on the other hand, in a corporate context this freedom brings with it possibilities for the exploitation of others. Exploitation, unfortunately, is by no means a new phenomenon in the United States. Chapter 3 reviews the experiences of diverse groups in relation to economic and political power in American society. There have been demands, however, "that economic transactions—from equal treatment of women and people of color in employment, pay, and benefits to health and safety for everyone—are to be governed by rules of due process and fairness" (Apple, 1992, p. 42). This development has brought with it a larger social frame of reference for equity and justice that applies across groups and has occasioned a new intergroup consciousness in America.

A new concept in economic individualism has emerged recently which is a redefinition of our personal rights in the American economy. Perceptions of equal rights in the marketplace are no longer limited to those expressed by Ben Franklin that the society should provide opportunities for personal economic advancement. Lears (1984) has described this ethos as shifting from a work ethic involving saving, civic responsibility, and a morality of self-denial to a new set of values focusing on apolitical passivity, leisure, compulsive spending, and the fulfillment of individual material desires. The concept of equal rights in the marketplace now includes the notion that people not only have an equal right to economic opportunity, but also an equal right to consumer goods. The idea of the necessity of material luxuries is reinforced daily in media advertising.

**Mythic Individualism**  The final type of individualism is mythic individualism (Bellah et al., 1985), which reflects these values in popular culture. Because of the extent of mythic individualism in films and television, I have chosen to defer an analysis of these popular depictions of individualism to a separate chapter concerning popular culture. Chapter 8 examines how the various views of individualism and their interpretations of freedom, success, and justice are pervasive in our entertainment.

## Individualism in Perspective

Most Americans embrace several of these philosophies of individualism simultaneously. We believe in equal political rights, equal economic opportunity, and the right to live and express ourselves as we choose. There is a danger, however, in placing extreme value on autonomy, which in and of itself may become self-indulgent and indifferent to the needs and even the rights of others. Deriving our values primarily from an individual perspective leads to self-absorption and self-interests. Placing too heavy a value on personal desires is also ultimately detrimental to our perceptions of our responsibilities in the society. Two other frames of reference, namely our diverse groups of origin and our national perspective, are needed in order to avoid egoism and to broaden our identity.

## DIVERSITY OF ORIGIN

Diversity of origin is the most easily recognized frame of reference contributing to Americans' identity. We all belong to several diverse groups simultaneously, and many of our views and actions come about as a result of these memberships. The fact that we can identify with more than one group, or shift out of one reference group and into another within the same moment, makes our behavior sometimes seem not only complex, but inconsistent. We may describe these groups in terms of both horizontal and vertical diversity in American society.

### Horizontal Diversity

Horizontal diversity includes race, ethnicity, and gender, or variables that are determined before birth. It is important to note here that ethnicity refers to national (or tribal) origin and that all racial groups in America contain ethnic variations within them. In the case of African Americans, tribal origins have been lost among the descendants of former slaves, but ethnic variation is identified among later immigrants of African origin. For example, a student of mine is the daughter of an immigrant from Kenya, and she is proud of this national heritage.

**Horizontal Socialization**   Horizontal socialization refers to the process by which children are instructed in the knowledge, customs, traditions, and values of their particular group of origin. All societies instruct children in their cultural traditions and values, but in the United States, with its variety of racial and ethnic differences, these diverse viewpoints are more complex in relation to each other than in more homogenous societies. Traditional cultural expectations about gender-related roles are also included here.

### Vertical Diversity

Vertical diversity includes differences in socioeconomic status and educational level that occur in all horizontal groups. We are, of course, born into a family that has a certain economic status and a particular level of education, but we may have some control over this status through our own efforts. Our socioeconomic status and education, however, also depend on the availability of equal opportunity and freedom from discrimination and prejudice on the part of those in positions of social, economic, and legal power.

The final frame of reference for determining our identity is age. Age may be considered a form of vertical diversity, because the young generally have less power than older members of the society. Age is unique because it is the only frame of reference in which we may be a member of all of its subgroups if we live long enough. As we grow from childhood into youth and finally adulthood, we acquire more privileges and responsibilities. This situation is not unique to America. There is an age-status hierarchy in all societies. With advanced age, however, power usually decreases and discrimination increases. We are all familiar with stories of the difficulty even middle-aged people have finding employment if they have lost their jobs. An irony in American politics is the fact that a person who would be considered too old to become the chief executive officer in a large corporation is not considered too old to be president of the United States! Age influences our behavior, but it also affects what other people expect of us in terms of whether or not they judge our actions to be appropriate. For example, a cartoon that once appeared in a national magazine showed a group of people at a football game, with one woman looking at another. The caption read: "*He* (referring to the man sitting next to her) *hasn't changed a bit since we were in college—that's the problem.*"

**Vertical Socialization**   Vertical socialization is the process by which children are instructed in the diverse expectations that parents and others have for their behavior in reference to age and social class. Like horizontal socialization, all societies instruct children in their cultural expectations for age behavior and that if they do not conform to these expectations, their behavior is judged by others as not being appropriate. For example, after their education is completed, young adults are expected to go to work. An example in reference to socioeconomic status is the fact that in the past women in the middle class were not often expected to work outside of the home, but women in the working class were expected to do so.

### Diversity and Multicultural Education

Diversity has been the focus of most multicultural educational programs that include an emphasis on cultural content, intergroup relations, and classroom strategies. The problem with focusing primarily on diverse origins, however important, is that it tends to emphasize differences and to overlook similarities of experiences across groups. Both perspectives are needed for a clearer picture of American society. Both the differences and similarities in the experiences of diverse racial and ethnic groups are reviewed in Chapter 3 and Chapter 4.

## AMERICAN SOCIETY

The third frame of reference for Americans' identity is the nation itself, and the place of both individuals and diverse groups within it. In a vague way, most citizens of the United States see themselves as "Americans," but are often unable to articulate what that means. The answer is often couched in terms of personal rights, economic opportunities, or patriotic clichés. A responsible discussion about our national frame of reference must be based on perceptions that extend beyond these generalized and vague impressions of what being an "American" involves. There was an assumption in the minds of those who established our Republican form of government over two hundred years ago that American citizenship carries with it not only rights, but responsibilities as well. These responsibilities are sometimes viewed as inconvenient or not "individually" important, but in fact they are the foundation upon which our government and national unity depend. To what extent do we identify with these responsibilities?

## THE FOUNDATIONS
## OF THE UNITED STATES GOVERNMENT

The concept of representative government is not new. Every student who has studied European history is aware that officials were elected in Athens in the fifth century, B.C., and in ancient Rome as well. Some non-European societies enjoyed representative government as well. In Greece and Rome, this privilege of governance was limited to free, property-owning males. Signed in the year 1215, the Magna Carta was "the most important instrument of English constitutional history, issued by King John...under compulsion by the Barons" (Columbia-Viking, 1953, p. 588). Its purpose was to insure the Barons' feudal rights by guaranteeing that the king could not encroach on their privileges (or rights). It also guaranteed freedom of the church and towns by protecting the rights of subjects. The Magna Carta became the symbol of the supremacy of constitutional government over the power of kings. The heritage of the Magna Carta may well be the most important contribution that British culture carried to the American colonies.

### Republican Democracy

In the eighteenth century, the political philosophy of natural rights, described above under Republican individualism, contained within it the concept of a community of citizens who formed a government to ensure everyone's rights. Implied in this concept was also the notion of **correlative responsibility,** or an obligation on the part of every citizen to respect and protect the rights of others. Individual political participation in this form of government was seen as fundamental to its success. Becker (1955) has pointed out that:

> [There] is, to be sure, no Bill of Responsibilities in our [Federal and state] constitutions, but a careful reading of them will disclose the *annoying fact* [italics mine] that for every right to freedom that they confer they [also] impose, implicitly if not explicitly, a corresponding obligation or responsibility. (p. 4)

Thus, freedom and responsibility are two sides of the same coin, inextricably linked together. In Becker's view, we can preserve our rights and freedoms only by a "far more serious and intelligent attention to public affairs" (1955, p. 25). Sometimes Americans do not welcome their part in the political system. We talk about our freedom but tend to overlook our responsibilities. Without both faith and participation in the democratic process by its citizens, the cohesion of our society is in jeopardy. Thomas Jefferson realized this and believed that equality of educational opportunity was essential for ensuring an informed citizenry that would participate in the political process (Beck et al., 1968). Chapter 4 reviews how education for citizenship became a fundamental goal in public education following the American Revolution.

Today, Thomas Jefferson is generally regarded as the statesman who first articulated the values of life, liberty, and the pursuit of happiness in the relation of individuals to their government. He expressly referred to these values in the Declaration of Independence. At least some credit, however, should go to Thomas Paine, for it was Paine who most aroused the American public's sentiment for independence from England.

An immigrant from England, Thomas Paine arrived in Philadelphia on November 30, 1774. At that time, the city was filled with discussions of politics—"in taverns and coffee houses, homes and workshops" (Foner, 1976, p. 71). Debate was heated between those in opposition to England and those who favored reconciliation, in spite of the military skirmishes between colonists and the English in New England and the South. Paine, with Benjamin Franklin's help, became editor of the *Pennsylvania Magazine*. In January 1776, Paine published *Common Sense*. This little pamphlet changed political debate in America by its argument in support of a Republican form of government. Until its publication, Republicanism had been basically a vague form of radical political thought, but Paine "literally transformed the political language ... and made it [Republicanism] a living political issue and a Utopian ideal of government" (Foner, 1976, p. 75). In this pamphlet, Paine (a) denounced the legitimacy of the idea of a monarchy and the principle of hereditary rule; (b) considered and rejected prevailing popular arguments for reconciliation with England; and (c) urged the establishment of a Republican form of government in America.

*Common Sense* electrified the colonies. Its impact was nothing short of phenomenal. At a time when the average pamphlet was published in one or two editions, totaling a few thousand copies, this pamphlet had twenty-five editions eventually totaling 150,000 copies. Its success was due in part to the fact that it was written in plain language, clear and direct, without the stuffiness of most other pamphlets. It was read by all types of people, including educated politicians, farmers, and tradesmen. It made "sense" to ordinary Americans and galvanized them not only into the idea of national independence from England, but also to the idea of a Republican form of government. Within six months, the Declaration of Independence was signed.

The success of *Common Sense* was also due to three other factors. First, it fit with the experience of the colonists, especially in New England, where town meetings and elections had already set a precedent for more direct participatory government. Second, it referred to the *diverse origins* of the colonists and denied the idea that England was the sole "parent" of America. Third, the time was right. Americans were ready for Paine's appeal to material interests and colonists' hopes for a new society with opportunities that were different from those in Europe (Foner, 1976).

Perhaps the most important lessons to be learned from the public reaction to Paine's pamphlet were that the average citizen was able to understand the nature of politics and processes of government (Foner, 1976) and that citizens do care about their government if they see hope in the process. In other words, what is required for a Republican form of government to be successful is not only participation by its citizens, but a feeling that their participation matters. Without this, power can indeed fall into the hands of self-serving officials, as Thomas Jefferson once feared (Pangle & Pangle, 1993).

## The Iroquois Confederation

Most Americans are aware of the fact that our United States government was based on the English view of rights derived from the Magna Carta and the eighteenth-century political philosophy of natural rights, but the form of our government may, in fact, also be modeled after an alliance of tribes that had been formed by a group of Native Americans before the Europeans landed in the Western Hemisphere. This alliance, known as the *Iroquois Confederation*, was based on the idea of cooperation among diverse nations, with a central and duly elected council of representatives that considered problems common to all. It is important to point out here that this concept extended beyond the idea of elected officials to include the notion of cooperation among equal tribes or nations. The way in which this remarkable arrangement came into being deserves a closer look.

**History of the Confederation**    Although it may appear to the reader that perhaps the history of the Iroquois Confederation would be better placed in this volume within the context of Native American history, I have included it here because its development apparently influenced some of the American Founding Fathers in their formulation of our federal government. The history of the Confederation was handed down among the Iroquois from generation to generation. In the nineteenth century, a European American, Lewis Henry Morgan, recorded Iroquois history from direct accounts, and the Iroquois also started to write their own story (Graymont, 1988).

The Iroquois league began with a group of Native Americans who called themselves "Houdenosaunee" (hoo-dee-noh-SHAW-nee), or "People of the Longhouse." Early French explorers called them the "Iroquois." The Iroquois tribes included five separate nations: the Mohawk, Oneida, Onondaga, Cayuga, and Seneca. These tribes lived in what is now north and central New York State, not far from Lake Ontario. They had long made war, not only on common enemies but on each other, over many years of attack and counterattack.

Finally, a courageous Onondaga leader, **Hayenwatha** (or Hiawatha),[1] tried to convince another Onondaga leader, Tadodaho,[2] to consider more peaceful ways, but his efforts were rejected. After a series of personal sorrows, Hayenwatha departed and traveled eastward to the land of the Mohawks. It is important to point out here that in the nineteenth century, Henry Wadsworth Longfellow confused historical accuracy with fantasy in his famous poem, "The Song of Hiawatha." In writing this poem, he referred to the work of Henry Rowe Schoolcraft, a government agent who had written down some legends of the Ojibwa Indians, including a tale of a god-hero named Nanabozho. Schoolcraft had also obtained some information about Hayenwatha, and in error had applied his name to Nanabozho in his "The Hiawatha Legends." Thus, Longfellow wrote his poem on the legends of Nanabozho, but believed he was writing about a hero named Hiawatha. The fame of his poem obscured the historical achievements of Hayenwatha or Hiawatha, the great Iroquois leader (Graymont, 1988).

At the time that Hayenwatha arrived in the land of the Mohawks, another man, **Deganawidah,** an outsider from the Wendot tribe, was living with the Mohawks because he could not convince his native Wendot tribal members to give up their warlike ways. Deganawidah had come to the Mohawks with a plan for peace among tribes. The two men joined together to promote peace. They proposed a confederation of nations. The first treaty agreed upon was between the Mohawks and the Oneidas. It was this treaty that led to the Great League of Peace. The Onondagas, Cayugas, and Senecas followed in joining the alliance, which became known as the Iroquois Confederation. The date of the league is estimated to be sometime before 1500 A.D., although some have placed it earlier. Years later, in the 1700s, the Tuscarora also joined the league (Graymont, 1988).

Deganawidah chose the pine tree as a symbol for the confederation. The tree had four roots, the Great White Roots of Peace, which spread north, south, east, and west. Atop the tree he placed an eagle to warn of approaching danger. Under the tree, a hatchet was buried, symbolizing the end of warfare among the tribes. Today, the expression "bury the hatchet" refers to putting aside grievances. The tree was planted in Onondaga territory, where the Great Council of the Confederation met. Figure 2.1 illustrates this **Tree of Peace,** as well as a wampum belt known as the Hiawatha Belt (Graymont, 1988) or Aiionwatha Belt (Schaaf, no date). The pine tree in the center of this belt stands for the Iroquois Confederation, and the squares symbolize the tribes.

**The Governing Form of the Confederation**  Deganawidah and Hayenwatha based the governing form of the confederacy on the clan structure of the various tribes. Each clan had a certain number of chiefs and governed itself, but each clan also joined with other clans in governing the individual tribes. When this concept was applied to the confederacy, the clan chiefs became confederacy chiefs, but the confederacy did not interfere with the independence of the tribal governments. A Grand Council was formed of representatives from the various tribes. This council consisted of the Elder Brothers (the Mohawk and Seneca) and the Younger Brothers (the Oneida, the Cayuga, and later the Tuscarora). A single elder (an Onondaga) presided. The *women* of each of the various clans nominated a chief who held office so long as he was judged to be fulfilling his office with responsibility. Recall (or impeachment) was possible if it became clear that a chief statesman did not have the welfare of the people in mind or disobeyed the law (Schaaf, no date). Thus, a system of "checks and balances" was created.

Johansen (1982) has reported that Benjamin Franklin, after meeting with representatives of the six Iroquois nations in the summer of 1754, was so impressed with the Iroquois Confederation's centralized and dispersed form of governance

**FIGURE 2.1** The Iroquois Confederation Tree of Peace

*Courtesy of Meewha Lee.*

that he proposed it as a model for a union among the diverse colonies in the Albany Plan of Union. Franklin believed that the lesson to be learned from the wisdom of the Iroquois was that peace was possible through responsible representative government. In his view, one government should be formed in America that would be administered by a president and a council elected by the different colonies. It should be pointed out here that the framers of the United States Constitution were familiar with both the British parliamentary system and the Iroquois Confederation. In writing the United States Constitution, the Founding Fathers established a bicameral legislature, with the Senate and the House of Representatives (similar to the Council of Elder Brothers and Younger Brothers), as well as an executive branch or presidency. They also provided for impeachment of officials for misconduct in office. One of the most important concepts established by the Constitution was that of a dual level of government, which separated federal and state authority in a manner similar to that of the Great Council and local tribes of the Iroquois. It should be mentioned here that the Iroquois Confederation continues today in New York State.

In the new young Republic, the great Tree of Peace became the **Tree of Liberty.** The watchful eagle became the nation's symbol. And on the reverse side of our one dollar bill, an eagle holds in one claw thirteen arrows symbolizing the thirteen original colonies held together by the new federal union. In the other claw, the eagle holds an olive branch of peace.

## Government and Diverse Groups

It was James Madison who first addressed the issue of "factions" in American society. Madison viewed factions as "the great threat ... to successful and popular government" (Nicgorski, 1992, p. 25). He believed that government should protect the liberty of all, but at the same time balance or monitor the interests of diverse groups in order to prevent any one group from interfering with the liberty of others. As a federalist, he was concerned with the interrelationship of the issues that concern us in this chapter: namely, personal liberty, diversity, and national unity. His insight into the relationship between liberty and the interests of diverse groups was expressed in a powerful metaphor in "The Federalist Papers" (Number 10; in Bellah et al., 1987):

> Liberty is to faction what air is to fire, an aliment [sic] without which it instantly expires. But it could not be a less folly to abolish liberty, which is essential to political life, because it nourishes faction than it would be to wish the annihilation of air, which is essential to...life (p.380).

Madison recognized the inevitability of different interest groups within a society, but he also realized the possibility that, if left unchecked, their diverse interests could fracture the society. He further recognized that economics provided a basis for factions because of unequal distribution of property.

One might conclude that Madison opposed the idea of factions in society. In fact, he believed that factions are inevitable in all societies. He proposed a safeguard by suggesting that the effects of diverse self-interest might be limited by increasing the factions and enlarging the territory. To him, increasing diversity

decreased the possibility that an ill-intentioned or an unduly self-interested majority could dominate the other factions. Madison's fear was justified in light of the
influence of powerful self-interest groups that have in fact curtailed economic,
legal, and social equity for both individuals and diverse groups in the United States.

## The American Government in Practice

Leaders like Franklin, Jefferson, and Madison realized that the relationship between individual citizens and the governing process such as that acted out in
small New England town meetings was unworkable with large numbers of citizens. In other words, America was too big for this direct participation. In establishing our Republic, they assumed that issues of public concern would be made
available and understood by every citizen. As idealistic as the concept of our Republic was, there were difficulties in achieving and maintaining the process that
the Founding Fathers envisioned. Theoretically, our constitutional representative
government meant that the will of the people would be transmitted to elected
officials. Wolff (1970) has pointed out that in fact, however, individuals' relations
to their government were mediated through institutions that were more accessible, including state and local governments, political pressure groups, and diverse
ethnic and religious voluntary associations. State and local governments were
supposed to make it easier for Americans to relate to their local representatives
than to officials in Washington, but as the population grew, it became increasingly difficult for individuals to be in direct contact with state officials as well. It
is not hard to understand why some Americans have given up on the political
process and focus their attention on attaining the material pleasures of economic
individualism. Political pressure groups have proliferated ever since the eighteenth century, to the extent that in our time professional lobbyists are paid by
special groups, particularly with economic self-interests, to make their concerns
known to elected officials at the national, state, and local levels. We might wonder what Madison's view of today's political lobbyists would be. Voluntary organizations are perhaps today the only arena directly available to people from diverse
groups to make their values, needs, and frustrations heard. Often, however, the
voices of these groups are dismissed by those in political power as outside the
mainstream, too radical, or simply self-interested (Wolff, 1970).

The problem of making our concerns heard at both the national and state
level is serious. To what extent do our elected officials consider their priorities
in terms of their responsibilities? To what extent do lobbyists seriously consider
alternative viewpoints beyond those of the interest groups they are paid to serve?
To what extent do voluntary organizations heed the concerns of other groups?
As idealistic as our Republican form of government was, Madison was right to
worry about the dangers of conflicting interests. Our government is subject to
individual indifference, political expediency, and the self-interest of different
factions. An amazing example of this danger occurred in 1994 when the United
States Senate failed to pass the Old Faithful Protection Act. This act, which
passed the House of Representatives, was intended to outlaw geothermal development in a limited area near Yellowstone National Park. Such development
threatens the park's geothermal features, including hot springs and geysers like

Old Faithful. Paul Pritchard (1994), president of the National Parks and Conservation Association, expressed the problem as follows:

> Who and what do our legislatures serve? How can they turn their backs on the health of Old Faithful—one of America's most enduring symbols? Certainly the short-sighted needs of certain constituencies cannot justify this action.... It is a sad commentary on our...nation's priorities.... Future generations are unlikely to forgive us. (p. 4)

If some of our elected officials are so indifferent to a national natural treasure—which, once destroyed, can never be repaired—we might well share Madison's concern about their responsibility toward America's people also.

## THE AMERICAN DILEMMA

In the *Odyssey*, the Greek hero Odysseus faced the challenge of steering his ship through the strait of Scilla (modern spelling), located between Italy and Sicily. On one side of the strait, the monster Scylla lay in wait for unwary sailors. On the other side, the whirlpool Charybdis endangered ships that came too close. The challenge we face in America today is a similar one, and it may be equally perilous. On one hand we must find a way to respect the rights, viewpoints, and values of both individuals and our many diverse groups without, as Power (1992, p. 13) has expressed it, "dissolving into relativism." On the other hand, we must avoid attempts to ignore or discount our differences in what Nicgorski has referred to as a "melt down" (1992, p. 16) into a melting pot of uniformity and conformity. The motto of the United States, "e pluribis unum" (out of many, one), originated out of the blend of thirteen separate colonies into a national political state. The "pluribis" in that motto suggests that diversity is a fundamental part of our democratic process.

Recognizing the limits of our individual and diverse perspectives, however, does not necessarily give us guidelines for reconciling these points of view on a day-to-day basis. If every one of us voted in every election, participated in community meetings, and even ran for public office, these actions would not guarantee that we would understand or *care* about each other more. We need to find a way to control personal indifference, embrace our diversity, and maintain cohesion as a society. We need to find a process that would serve as an amalgam or glue to hold us together without sacrificing our diverse qualities.

## PLURALISM

One interpretation of pluralism is that it refers to diverse groups. Banks has reported that the pluralist regards ethnic groups as providing diverse peoples with their language, lifestyles, values, and *"with a sense of identity"* (1994, p. 123; italics mine). Therefore, in the field of education, it is important for teachers to know that students' differences are related to their ethnic groups and to their social class. Indeed, both are important. In applying this view of pluralism in the classroom, the curriculum would emphasize viewpoints relevant to diverse groups. It is important to point out that the focus here is on *groups,* not individuals.

Pluralism, however, may also be defined as *the holding of two or more viewpoints simultaneously,* in which people consider the viewpoints of others in addition to their own. The emphasis here is on both individual viewpoints and those of diverse groups.

In relation to this interpretation, Diller (1992) has described a form of pluralism known as an **ethics of care.** There are four processes involved in this ethics of care: (a) a pluralism of coexistence; (b) a pluralism of cooperation; (c) a pluralism of coexplorers; and (d) a pluralism of coenjoyment. In a broad social context, **coexistence** combines tolerance with mutual respect for others, but does not extend to getting to know them. It represents a live-and-let-live view, basically one of noninterference, but also without cooperation for mutual goals. **Cooperation** assumes that common interests require us to work together in order to accomplish goals that diverse groups could not achieve alone. These goals may be economic, political, or social. They may occur at work or in voluntary organizations. **Coexploring** refers to a process of discovering who we are as members of diverse groups and as individual people. The process here requires reciprocal effort, but it is not easy. In order to do this, people must enter into another's cultural world. This process may be confusing and even uncomfortable at first, but it is necessary to understand each other's values and experience. This process also requires that members of diverse groups allow others to enter and learn about their culture. **Coenjoyment** calls on us to share our personal interests—those things that give us pleasure. In so doing, our individual uniqueness is also shared. Diller (1992) has stated that:

> We have all had the experience of trying to "make conversation" with someone who seems a mute dullard until we hit upon their area of real interest, and suddenly they transform themselves before our eyes into an animated, vital, even fascinating being. (p. 210)

There is a developmental sequence in these pluralisms whereby people move from merely tolerating each other to working together, to understanding and appreciating each other, to finding pleasure in each other's company. Finding pleasure in each other's company leads to a caring. The ethics of care, therefore, involves our emotions—how we *feel* about each other.

## Pluralism and the Future

Most of us do not come to care about others through abstract philosophical concerns about each other's "rights." We hear a lot about tolerance and cooperation, but these do not necessarily lead to caring about each other. We come to care about each other by sharing our lives. In the past, some of us have assumed that sharing our pain and sorrows would help us to learn to care—and sometimes it does. Perhaps we have overlooked the possibility and power of sharing our joys. There is a risk in sharing our joys, however, because in doing so we make ourselves vulnerable. We take the chance that others will not share our excitement or understand our enjoyment. We risk rejection, or possibly even ridicule.

Taking this risk has two conditions. We need to believe that the risk is worth taking—but who is going to do that first? You or me? We need to care as much about what the other person is feeling as we care about our own feelings. We need to want more than respectful coexistence and the achievement of common goals. We need to want to become friends. The focus in an ethics of care is on individuals in the sense of personal relationships, because friendships occur between people and not on the basis of groups. In embracing this focus on individual relationships, I do not mean to imply that I endorse the emphasis on individualism in American society that in the past has placed personal goals, interests, and success ahead of a recognition and concern for others' well-being. I mean quite the opposite, in fact. If we care about the uniqueness of individuals, then we will care about equity, fairness, and social justice for each and every person—won't we?

The pluralisms of coexistence, cooperation, coexploring, and coenjoyment may be used in education. Recently, a lot of attention has been given to cooperative learning and coexploring in the classroom. These are steps in the right direction, but perhaps students also need to learn to share their personal interests—their joys—with each other. As educators, we cannot all run for public office, always contact our elected officials with our concerns, hope to influence lobbyists very much, or even have time to join more than two or three volunteer organizations, but we can influence what happens in our classrooms. We can help students from diverse groups to become *friends.* There is hope in the process for America's future.


## CHAPTER SUMMARY

This chapter has explored three frames of reference—individual, diverse, and national—by which Americans define their identity.

There are several different views of individualism in American society. These are (a) Protestant; (b) Republican; (c) utilitarian; (d) expressive; and (e) economic. Each of these has its own set of values and its own interpretation of freedom, success, and social justice. The behavior of Americans is influenced by these views.

There are also different kinds of diversity. Horizontal diversity refers to race, ethnicity, and gender. These groups obviously cannot be changed. Vertical diversity refers to socioeconomic status and age. Membership in socioeconomic status may change for the better or worse with luck or opportunity. Hard work may improve a person's socioeconomic status, but work cannot guarantee equal opportunity. As we grow older, we move through different age groups, which have greater or lesser social power.

The national frame of reference includes an awareness of citizenship and its responsibilities in our Republic. This awareness also relates to state and local levels of governance. Our federal government was founded upon the social philosophy known as natural rights, but its organization was modeled after the Iroquois Confederation.

The danger of factions in the United States may hopefully be lessened by a process of pluralism, by which Americans may come to appreciate each other as members of diverse groups and as individual friends.

## IMPORTANT TERMS

Protestant individualism

Republican individualism

Utilitarian individualism

Expressive individualism

Economic individualism

Republican democracy

The Protestant work ethic

The Magna Carta

Ethics of care

Coexploring

Coexistence

Coenjoyment

Horizontal diversity

Horizontal socialization

Vertical diversity

Vertical socialization

The Iroquois Confederation

Tree of Peace

Tree of Liberty

Pluralism

## QUESTIONS FOR DISCUSSION

1. What are the major differences among the various views of individualism?

2. If Benjamin Franklin had not been familiar with the Iroquois Confederation, how might our federal government have been organized?

3. What other kind of horizontal diversity can you think of whereby people cannot change their group?

4. What other kind of vertical diversity can you think of whereby people may be able to change their group?

5. What kind of experience have you had with an ethics of care?

6. In addition to the Tree of Peace and the eagle, what other important symbols can you think of that the United States has adopted from Native Americans?

## NOTES

1. Different sources refer to this hero as **Hayenwatha** (Graymont, 1988), **Ayawentha** (Wall & Arden, 1990), **Hiawatha** (Graymont; Johansen, 1982; Schaaf; Wall & Arden), or **Aiionwatha** (Schaaf, no date).

2. The term **Tadodaho** is now an ancient title meaning presiding moderator of the fifty coequal chiefs making up the Grand Council of the Six Nations of the Confederacy. In Iroquois historical legend, Tadodaho was a ferocious Onondago wizard (Wall & Arden, 1990).

# REFERENCES

Apple, M. W. (1992). "Ideology, equality, and the new right." In F. C. Power & D. K. Lapsley (Eds.), *Education, politics, and values: The challenge of pluralism*. Notre Dame, The University of Notre Dame Press.

Banks, J. A. (1994). *Multiethnic education: Theory and practice*. (3rd edition). Boston: Allyn and Bacon.

Beck, C. E., Bernier, N. R., MacDonald, J. B., Walton, T. W., & Willers, J. C. (1968). *Education for relevance*. Boston: Houghton Mifflin Company.

Becker, C. L. (1955). *Freedom and responsibility in the American way of life*. New York: Vintage Books.

Bellah, R. N., Madsen, R., Sullivan, W. M., Swidler, A., & Tipton, S. M. (1985). *Habits of the heart: Individualism and commitment in American life*. New York: Harper and Row.

Bellah, R. N., Madsen, R., Sullivan, W. M., Swidler, A., & Tipton, S. M. (Eds.). (1987). *Readings on the themes of habits of the heart*. New York: Harper and Row.

*Columbia-Viking desk encyclopedia, The*. (1953). New York: The Viking Press.

Diller, A. (1992). "What happens when an ethics of care faces pluralism? Some implications for education." In F. C. Power & D. K. Lapsley (Eds.), *Education, politics, and values: The challenge of pluralism*. Notre Dame, The University of Notre Dame Press.

Foner, E. (1976). *Tom Paine and revolutionary America*. New York: Oxford University Press.

Garcia, R. L. (1991). *Teaching in a pluralistic society: Concepts, models, strategies* (2nd edition). New York: HarperCollins.

Graymont, B. (1988). *The Iroquois*. New York: Chelsea House.

Johansen, B. E. (1982). *Forgotten founders: How the American Indian helped shape democracy*. Boston: The Harvard Common Press.

Lears, T. J. J. (1984). From salvation to self realization: Advertising and the therapeutic roots of the consumer culture. In R. W. Fox & T. J. J. Lears (Eds.), *The culture of consumption: Critical essays in American history, 1880-1980*. New York: Pantheon Books.

Madison, James. *The federalist papers, Number 10*. In Bellah, R. N., R. Madsen, W. M. Sullivan, A. Swidler, & S. M. Tipton (Eds.), *Readings on the themes of habits of the heart* (1987, pp. 379-386). New York: Harper and Row.

Nicgorski, W. (1992). American pluralism: A condition or a goal? In F. C. Power & D. K. Lapsley (Eds.), *Education, politics, and values: The challenge of pluralism*. Notre Dame, The University of Notre Dame Press.

Pangle, L. S., & T. L. Pangle (1993). *The learning of liberty*. Lawrence, KS: University Press of Kansas.

Power, F. C. (1992). "Introduction: Moral education and pluralism." In F. C. Power & D. K. Lapsley (Eds.), *Education, politics, and values: The challenge of pluralism*. Notre Dame, The University of Notre Dame Press.

Pritchard, P. C. (November/December 1994). "Outlook: A tragic vote." *National parks*. Washington, DC: National Parks and Conservation Association.

Schaaf, G. (no date). *The great law of peace and the constitution of the United States*. Akwesasne, NY: Tree of Peace Society.

Sleeter, C. (1994). "An analysis of the critiques of multicultural education." In J. A. Banks & C. M. Banks (Eds.), *Handbook of research on multicultural education*, New York: Macmillan.

Wall, S., & Arden, H. (1990). *Wisdomkeepers: Meetings with Native American spiritual elders*. Hillsboro, OR: Beyond Words Publishing.

*Webster's tenth new collegiate dictionary* (1993). Springfield, MA: Merriam–Webster, Inc.

Wolff, R. P. (1970). "Beyond tolerance." In *A critique of pure tolerance*. Boston: Beacon Press.

# 3

∽

# American Diversity

Give me your tired, your poor,
Your huddled masses yearning to breathe free,
The wretched refuse of your teeming shore,
Send these, the homeless, tempest-tossed, to me:
I lift my lamp beside the golden door.

EMMA LAZARUS
"THE NEW COLOSSUS," STATUE OF LIBERTY INSCRIPTION
ELLIS ISLAND: NEW YORK HARBOR

The moving words on the previous page, inscribed as they are at the base of what is probably the most famous public monument in the world, bring to mind the image of countless European immigrants laying eyes on that icon for the first time. One imagines that each of these newcomers experienced feelings as turbulent as the ocean they had just crossed; feelings of hope, fear, optimism, concern; feelings that are only natural to those who have chosen to exchange their homeland for a new and unfamiliar nation. Perhaps, in that moment, suspended between two worlds—the old and the new—these immigrants felt their native identity more deeply and poignantly than ever before—just as they were about to exchange it for a new identity as an American.

Ellis Island was the nation's main immigration station between 1892 and 1943. It is now a national park commemorating all of America's immigrants, whether they came to this country from Europe, from Asia through ports of entry on the West Coast, or across borders on the north and south.

There are, of course, other ports of entry that have a different poignancy. Let the restored slave market in Charleston, South Carolina, stand in silent tribute to those who came not out of their own choice, but were forced to these shores by a cruelty that understood freedom to be a matter of power or luck, rather than a matter of human rights.

And long before the modern era, there were those who lived on the continents that Europeans named the "Americas." These indigenous peoples had developed rich and varied cultures before immigrant generations fractured their world.

This chapter examines these various peoples in the United States and how social power affected their lives. I have chosen to review African Americans, Asian Americans, European Americans, Latino Americans, and Native Americans in one chapter because the experiences they have shared become clearer than if their histories were to be separated into different chapters. Their diverse histories form our collective history. In calling the reader's attention to some of the similarities in their experience, I am not discounting the differences. Indeed, their histories are not identical. It is important to recognize the variations in experiences that America's diverse groups have encountered. In identifying the similarities as well, we may gain a perspective about American society that is overlooked by focusing only on the differences. A comprehensive review of the history of America's diverse peoples is beyond the scope of this text. What follows is an overview of their story.

## THE AMERICAN DREAM AND ECONOMICS

When one considers the history of the United States from the perspective of the "inalienable rights" of life, liberty, and the pursuit of happiness referred to in the Declaration of Independence, one is immediately confronted with the juxtaposition of the philosophical and ethical ideals of the Founding Fathers with a subsequent emphasis on economic considerations. The Native Americans had developed a symbiotic relationship with the land, but Europeans viewed the land as personal property or as a resource to be used without considering the consequences for the future. From the earliest days of colonization, an economic relationship developed between those who owned the land and its resources and those who provided the labor for their enterprises. This relationship between capital and labor has touched every racial and ethnic group in the United States, including men and women of all ages. From the point of view of employers, there was a need for labor for planting and harvesting, for assembly lines, for mining, and for construction. From the point of view of the workers, there was the hope of opportunity. They have been indentured servants, slaves, craftsmen, small businessmen, union workers, and recruited foreign laborers, all of whom have done the work of America but have not necessarily shared in the profits.

The contradiction between the political ideal of the American Dream, which is Republican democracy, and the economic basis of the American Dream, which is a free market economy, is perhaps the most profound struggle in American history. No racial group has escaped this contradiction, which involves political, economic, and social power. Members of all groups have experienced oppression and opposed that oppression. In order to create a more just society, we need to recognize the power that privileged members have exercised over the lives of those less privileged. Abuse of power is immoral in all situations. The following review of this power is necessary for the reader to understand the experiences of those who have been affected by it.

## MINORITY STATUS

Ogbu (1983) has defined minority status not in terms of the number of people within a group but in terms of power relationships. In his view, a minority is a group that occupies a position *subordinate in power* to other groups in a society. Differential status results from differences in economic, political, and social power. Ogbu has suggested a "typology" of minority status not based on race or ethnicity, but on differences in these types of power. In other words, the common experiences of the groups in this typology have been shared by people from diverse racial, ethnic, and cultural backgrounds.

### Autonomous Minorities

Autonomous minorities have distinct ethnic, religious, linguistic, and/or cultural identities. They may be victims of social prejudice but generally have not been subordinated politically or economically. Their cultural frame of reference encourages success within the context of American society. In many cases they have been economically and/or politically successful. Autonomous minorities may include individuals who have lived in the United States for generations, or more recent immigrants as well. According to Ogbu, groups in this category include the Amish, Jews, and Mormons.

## Immigrant Minorities

Immigrant minorities are those who have moved voluntarily from their native countries. At first they may be lacking in economic and political power, but their goal is to improve their situation in relation to previous circumstances in their homelands. There are exceptions, of course, because not all immigrants have been poor or lacking in education. For many immigrants, the American Dream was conceived more in terms of economic opportunity, expressed in the symbols of gold mountains and cities paved with gold, than in the rhetoric of the political philosophy of natural rights. When these people arrive, they may initially be discriminated against, but they believe that hard work will produce success. As the number of "successful" individuals within any particular group increases, economic power leads to political power. Social power or status follows. According to Ogbu, these voluntary immigrants also have the option of either returning to their homeland or emigrating elsewhere if their situation becomes intolerable or does not meet their expectations. Ogbu has identified the Chinese, Japanese, Filipinos, and Koreans as members of this group. I would add Europeans and modern Africans as well.

## Castes

Historically, castes have had virtually no power and members are born into them. Castes are incorporated into a society involuntarily and permanently. In the United States, castes have been delineated along racial lines. Members have been looked down upon by Whites. It is important to point out here that this racial distinction has not been true for all societies. In India, for example, the lowest social class was formerly a caste known as "untouchables," but its members were not racially distinct. In the United States, castes have suffered economic exploitation and have struggled for economic, political, and social equality. Assimilation into the mainstream may or may not be a goal. According to Ogbu, African Americans, Native Americans, and Mexican Americans are included in this category.

## Refugees

To Ogbu's categories I would add refugees. Refugees are not, strictly speaking, immigrants because they have not voluntarily left their homeland. They are dislocated persons, forced to emigrate by circumstances such as war or persecution. A refugee is someone seeking to enter the United States who is a victim of persecution in his or her own nation or who has a good reason to fear persecution on the basis of race, religion, nationality, membership in a particular ethnic group, or personal political opinions (Stewart, 1993). Many suffer from the psychological trauma of having lost their homes and/or having been persecuted, not only by enemies, but by their own countrymen. Refugees do not have the option of returning to their homeland, although they may relocate to still another country.

The status of refugees in their homeland varies because not all are poor or lacking in economic, political, or social power. For example, prior to World War II, Albert Einstein, a famous scientist and a Jew forced to flee Nazi Germany, was welcomed into America as the renowned person he was. His social and political influence was of no small consequence in America. Similarly, Thomas Mann, a Nobel prize-winning author and a Christian, was also forced into exile from Nazi Germany for philosophical and political reasons. On a lecture tour in Europe in 1933, Mann was warned that his life would be in danger if he returned home (Winston & Winston, 1971).

Thus, refugees may include both the famous and the obscure. Some lacked economic, political, and social power in their homeland. Some, however, were forced into exile by a regime in their country because they had this power, but all have sought refuge in the United States. A Hmong refugee reported to me that to him the most important thing about America is the "freedom to speak his mind," which he could not do in Laos. Today, refugees include those from Southeast Asia, Central America, and the Middle East.

Under the Refugee Act of 1980, those seeking to come to the United States in order to escape from poverty in their country may be denied admission unless they can prove that they are in danger of persecution (Stewart, 1993). A problem for immigration officials is in determining whether an individual is truly seeking refuge or just economic opportunity; in the latter case, he or she would be considered a voluntary immigrant, rather than a refugee, and therefore be counted under immigration quotas.

## Asylees

To Ogbu's categories I would also add asylees. By immigration standards, asylees are in a different category from refugees. Asylees are people already in the United States who have entered the country under temporary visas but who would face persecution in their homeland if they were forced to return. There is no quota for asylees, but the number permitted to adjust their status to refugee is limited to 10,000 per year (Stewart, 1993).

Obviously, immigrants, refugees, and asylees include people of diverse races, but they all must find work in the United States. In other words, they all encounter the power of the American market economy. As individuals within these categories gain economic success, political influence, and social status, these advances may help other members of their racial or ethnic group. Members of castes, however, have experienced discrimination not only on the basis of their social class, but on the basis of their race alone. For example, a Black professional friend of mine has told me of an experience from her childhood. She and her mother waited to be served in a restaurant for half an hour while White customers who came in later were served first. They lived in a Northern city. Her mother had a Ph.D.

## AMERICAN DIVERSITY

*Diversity.* That word is used often these days in reference to racial groups: African Americans, Asian Americans, European Americans, Latino Americans, Native Americans. To identify diversity in such broad racial categories is misleading, however, because it overlooks the fact that there are subgroups within these groups. In other words, there is diversity within diversity. In addition to differences in socioeconomic status, gender, and age, differences may also be ethnic.

### Ethnicity

The word **ethnicity** derives from the Greek word *ethnos*, which means "nation." Ethnicity, therefore, refers to differences in national origin. Like race, ethnicity also includes men and women, young and old, and differences in socioeconomic status. McInnis-Ditrich (1993) has suggested that ethnicity is a template by which people perceive their world and that this perspective is the result not only of culture, but of *historical struggle.*

One point of view in multicultural education has been an assumption that references to ethnicity imply an endorsement of **ethnicity theory.**[1] This view confuses ethnicity with ethnicity theory. It is important to point out here that a recognition of diverse ethnic backgrounds is not a priori an endorsement of ethnicity theory.

There are three aspects of ethnicity: (a) ethnic identification; (b) ethnic heritage; and (c) ethnic culture (Novak, 1973). Ethnic identification refers to a personal interpretation of where one "fits" in relation to diverse groups. In other words, it refers to the contribution that diversity contributes to personal identity. Ethnic heritage refers to a group's past history. Ethnic culture refers to the attitudes, values, knowledge, and rules about behavior that are associated with belonging to a particular group. These cultural issues are addressed in Chapter 7.

As Banks has written, "The degree to which a particular cultural, national, or racial group is ethnic varies over time, in different regions, with social class mobility, and with the pervasive sociopolitcal conditions within the society" (1994, p. 75). Banks has referred to a "resurgence" of ethnicity among Whites recently, which suggests that their "assimilation" into a generic American point of view may have been overestimated in the past.

A good example of the impact of "pervasive sociopolitical conditions within the society" in regard to ethnicity comes from many of my students. The 1990 census indicated that 53.8 percent of the people in Wisconsin are of German descent—more than any other state in the country (*The Key,* 1994, p. 5). The students in my multicultural education classes *always* ask what difference it makes where their immigrant ancestors came from. Their comment is "We are all Americans." There is a historical reason for this attitude dating back to World War I, when Germans were faced with divided loyalties because many of them were immigrants themselves, or the children of immigrants. Their focus on their American identity grew out of this dilemma and is reflected even in the way names of communities are pronounced. For example, the town of New Berlin is not pronounced

New Ber*lin* but New *Ber*lin. The first time I pronounced it incorrectly, I was corrected. My students' view is understandable in light of the attitudes that their parents and grandparents have passed down to them. When anyone focuses solely on "being American," however, it makes it harder to understand why ethnicity is important to other groups and the degree to which it contributes to their identity.

I would mention here that the loss of a group's ethnic frame of reference has also been attributed to the educational policy of **assimilation,** which has historically aimed at "Americanizing" the children of diverse groups. The example of these German Americans suggests that not only region or social mobility but also deliberate choice within the context of sociopolitical circumstances may in fact contribute to its loss.

## AFRICAN AMERICANS

African Americans' knowledge of their national (or tribal) origins has been lost to most because of the circumstances under which they arrived in the Americas, including the United States, the Caribbean, and Latin America. The search for African "roots" has been a dream of many Blacks.

It is a common error to assume that all African Americans in the United States today are the descendents of former slaves. This view is not accurate for two reasons. First, both native-born Africans and people of African origin are presently immigrating to the United States for a variety of reasons. Some are refugees fleeing political persecution in their native countries. Others are immigrants from the Caribbean and elsewhere. These newcomers report that not only Whites but also their Black compatriots in the United States assume that the newcomers, like themselves, are the descendants of slaves, unless their Jamaican or other accent is particularly noticeable. A Black immigrant of my acquaintance speaks of the surprised reaction he receives when he says that he is from Guyana. According to his report, the common response is "Isn't that somewhere on the west coast of Africa?" When he answers that Guyana is in South America, the reaction is usually total confusion. Apparently we need more geography lessons!

The second reason why it is an error to assume that all African Americans are descendants of slaves is that a tiny percentage of Blacks were not slaves. Before the Civil War, approximately 5 percent of all American Blacks lived in the North as so-called free colored (Model, 1990). What is not generally known is that 7 percent of those living in the South were free. Having at one time been slaves, they had either earned their liberty or had been granted their freedom. The remaining 93 percent of Southern Blacks were slaves (Model, 1990).

### The Colonial Period

In the early 1600s, very few workers in the South were from Africa. Most were White indentured servants from Europe. Gradually, the few Black servants were separated from White servants and served longer terms as indentured servants. Thus they became more valuable because of this longer servitude.

De facto slavery was practiced in Virginia by 1650. The requirements of managing large agricultural tracts led to the expansion of this practice into the Carolinas and Georgia. Africans were not the only ones who suffered. Poorer Whites found it increasingly difficult to buy small plots of land as wealthy colonists bought up large tracts. By the 1660s, White plantation owners became concerned over growing discontent among White servants and turned to Black labor. Slavery increased sharply by the end of the century. As a portent of the future, wealthy Whites allowed White servants to abuse Black servants physically (Takaki, 1993). Thus, the seeds of racism were being sewn among poorer Whites. In the 1700s, some wealthy Southern Whites were ambivalent about slavery. Thomas Jefferson, a slaveowner himself, both severely punished slaves and yet supported an effort in the Virginia legislature to emancipate them. He even considered expatriation, but recognized that it would not be "practical"—at least not all at once (Takaki, 1993). Although a few Northerners had slaves, slavery did not proliferate in the North for a variety of reasons. One was the prevalence of smaller farms, which enabled farmers to manage the necessary work either by themselves or with the help of perhaps one servant. Apprentices were common in small trades.

## The Young Republic

As the idea of independence from Great Britain grew in the colonies, slavery became a thorny issue. Charles Pinckney of South Carolina strongly upheld the interests of wealthy plantation owners in his state, while John Adams of Massachusetts vigorously opposed slavery. In the end, Adams was forced to concede because the vote of Southern delegates at the Second Continental Congress was essential to pass the Declaration of Independence. The issue of slavery was resolved for the time being—there would be slavery in the United States.

In the North, the absence of slavery did not mean the absence of discrimination. Segregation was enforced in public facilities such as theaters. Some states denied African Americans the right to vote, while others required that they be property owners, although Whites could substitute other qualifications such as paying taxes or serving in the militia.

Following the Purchase of the Louisiana Territory from France in 1805, White colonists began moving beyond the Mississippi River. The first state to be formed out of this huge territory was Louisiana, which entered the Union in 1812 as a slave state. In 1819, Missouri sought admission to the Union. A United States Congressman from New York demanded that it be a free state. Because Maine, which was then a part of Massachusetts, was seeking admission to the Union at the same time, the affair was settled by the Missouri Compromise of 1820, in which Missouri entered the Union as a slave state and Maine entered as a free state. Under this compromise, it was also agreed that a line (which was a continuation of the southern border of Missouri) should be extended westward across the entire breadth of the Louisiana Purchase.[2] This line ran across *Indian territory.* All future states north of the line would be free states; all future states south of it would be slave states. A bitter debate grew between the North and the South over this compromise. In 1854, it was replaced by the Kansas–Nebraska Act, which provided that people in these territories could decide for themselves whether or not they would have slavery there. Both territories were *north* of the line drawn in the Missouri Compromise. Proslavery and antislavery factions became embattled as the Abolitionist movement grew. It would take a Civil War, however, to resolve the issue of slavery once and for all.

## Emancipation

The Thirteenth Amendment to the Constitution in 1864, the Fourteenth Amendment in 1868, and the Fifteenth Amendment in 1869 granted freedom, citizenship, and the franchise, respectively, to former slaves. With citizenship and the right to vote, education for Blacks became an important issue. The education of African Americans is reviewed in Chapter 4. After emancipation, most Blacks in the South remained in agriculture and hoped that freedom would bring prosperity. Benefits of freedom were short-lived, however, and economic gains were small. Most Blacks did not have the resources to become landowners, and many dropped into the status of tenant farmers. Relatives often lived together or nearby, sharing resources and labor. During the latter part of the nineteenth century and early twentieth century, Southern Blacks, as well as poor Whites, began to migrate north in search of expanding job opportunities. Others moved into Southern cities. Female heads of families increased as men moved from place to place for work. Low wages for males forced women into the workforce. By 1890, approximately 40 percent of Black women were employed. Seeking employment, Black children often left home early (Model, 1990). In the twentieth century, Black families have borne the burden of governmental policies such as restricting welfare benefits to families in which a male is not present. Black leaders have criticized this policy as contributing to the breakup of Black families. Black women, therefore, have benefited from these programs, more than Black men.

## The Twentieth Century

As increasing numbers of Blacks moved north, they encountered competition for jobs from White workers, including new immigrants. Wages were low and did not compensate for the increased cost of living in urban areas. Blacks were overrepresented in menial jobs. Work on railroads became a popular, but menial, opportunity. In World War I, Blacks entered the armed forces, but they were segregated and usually assigned to menial work. After the war, economic recession meant increased competition for fewer jobs. Race riots broke out in the North.

In 1916, Marcus Garvey moved to Harlem from Jamaica. Far in advance of the 1960s, he began to develop an ideology of Black nationalism. He promoted an ideal of Black capitalism and sought support for his own shipping company. In 1922 he was arrested for fraud, which he claimed was actually committed by another. The government could not prove fraud on Garvey's part, but nevertheless he was sentenced to prison. Granted a Presidential pardon two years later, he was deported to Jamaica. His message of racial pride, however, was not forgotten (Takaki, 1993).

From the late 1900s to the Great Depression, Blacks perceived immigrants, especially Asians and Mexicans, as being competition for employment. The Great Depression brought a sharp increase in unemployment, and labor statistics show that Black men were usually the first to lose their jobs. In the 1930s, Democratic Party leaders heard the concerns of Blacks and sought to end discrimination in the workplace. Blacks responded by supporting President Franklin Roosevelt and abandoning the (Republican) party of Abraham Lincoln (Takaki, 1993).

World War II brought increased opportunity in the armed forces, but it was not until after the war that President Harry Truman fully integrated the armed services. After the war, an increase in educational level among second-generation European immigrants resulted in an increase in white-collar positions for them, but not necessarily for Blacks. Northern Whites showed increasing racism toward uneducated and unskilled Black workers, whose numbers mounted through increased migration from the South (Model, 1990). Racism in companies occurred when employers cut costs by automation, recruited unskilled workers from other immigrant groups, and relocated plants and subsidiaries overseas, where labor was cheaper. These practices have actually increased in the 1980s and 1990s.

In the 1960s, civil rights leaders like Martin Luther King, Jr. were joined by members of other races in the crusade to end segregation in public facilities and to enforce civil rights. These efforts resulted in the enactment of civil rights legislation in Congress. Not all Americans agreed with these changes. Three civil rights workers, Michael Schwerner, James Chaney, and Andrew Goodman, were murdered in Mississippi. Black leaders like Medger Evers, and even King, fell as martyrs to the cause.

In the 1960s Martin Luther King, Jr. had supported Cuban immigrants in their flight to the United States and had led a change in Black attitudes toward immigrants. In the 1970s, after the Vietnam War, Black leaders expressed support for Southeast Asian refugees on the basis of their struggle for freedom, in a common bond for human rights (Fuchs, 1990). By the 1980s, however, Blacks were once again expressing concern over competition with immigrants for jobs. Ambivalent views continue in the 1990s.

What does it mean to be Black in America? Perhaps Maya Angelou addresses this question most keenly in her book *All God's Children Need Traveling Shoes.* Seeking her roots, Angelou went to live in Africa, but repeatedly was reminded of her American attitudes. For example, she could not envision accepting a marriage proposal when it meant being a second wife in a household with another wife present. When she entered a village where she was "recognized" by her resemblance to another woman, she realized this could be the village of her "roots." She further realized, however, that she did not really belong there—either by language or experience. She was African, but she was also American. It was time to go home—to the United States.

## ASIAN AMERICANS

Asians have been in the United States for over 150 years. They include Chinese, Japanese, Filipinos, Koreans, and Southeast Asians. Discriminated against legally, economically, and socially, they have also been touted as the model minority. Although discriminatory exclusion laws were directed against them in the past, immigration was reopened to them in 1965. Today they represent the fastest growing minority in America.

### Chinese Americans

The Chinese were the first Asians to come to America. Although Hawaii was not yet a part of the United States, Chinese workers were employed on sugarcane plantations there as early as the 1830s. Shortly after the Mexican War and the acquisition of California, Aaron H. Palmer, an American policy maker, called for the importation of Chinese laborers. He also recommended the establishment of San Francisco as the center of U.S. trade with China (Takaki, 1989).

By the 1850s, American planters used Chinese laborers to set an example for other workers. Chinese migration to the west coast in the mid-nineteenth century also included merchants and small businessmen. These early immigrants arrived in America full of hope for their future. Some were searching for the "Gold Mountain" after the discovery of gold in California. Almost all of them were men, many of whom had left their wives in China. Cultural institutions in China dictated that a wife was expected to care for her husband's parents in their later years. The women were also left behind because of the expense of travel and because many of the men believed that they would return to China. Many never did return. Almost three times as many wives accompanied their husbands to Hawaii in comparison with those who came to the mainland, because the islanders encouraged the migration of Chinese women, if circumstances in China permitted them to leave.

At first Chinese men were welcomed in California, but a changing political mood, primarily over competition among prospectors for mining rights for gold, quickly gave way to a view of "California for Americans." In 1865, fifty Chinese workers were hired by the Central Pacific Railroad to help build the tracks for the intercontinental line, starting at Sacramento. Within two years, 12,000 Chinese were employed by the Central Pacific Railroad and represented 90 percent of its entire workforce. They were paid a dollar a day, with no provisions for room or board. They consistently out-performed the other workers. Leland Stanford, president of Central Pacific, described these laborers as "quiet, peaceful, industrious,...ready...to learn all the different kinds of work" (Takaki, 1989, p. 84). After the transcontinental railroad was completed, thousands of these men went to San Francisco, which became the main community of settlement for the Chinese.

The Chinese contribution to industrial and agricultural development in California is well known. Many joined the cigar or garment industries, where they were again underpaid. The laundry business became an enterprise so well recognized that it is a cultural stereotype. Many Chinese entered this trade because it cost little to start, it required a minimal knowledge of English, and its self-employment ensured against being laid off or shut out of other work.

During Reconstruction, following the Civil War, many White Southerners welcomed Chinese as cheap labor and a means to some economic recovery. New England and northeastern manufacturers also imported them to work for low wages in their factories. In spite of their conscientiousness, the Chinese were viewed with mixed feelings, even misgivings. They came to be seen as competition for employment by both native born and immigrant White Americans. They were considered to be a greater threat than Blacks and Native Americans because of a belief that they were hard working.

By the end of the nineteenth century, Blacks also came to view Chinese as competition in the labor force. In addition, because they were non-Christian as well as non-White, their image challenged White concepts about what it meant to be "American." The result of these fears was the Chinese Exclusion Act of 1882, which banned the entrance of Chinese laborers into the U.S. In 1884, Congress extended this act by raising fines. In 1888, the Scott Act nullified Certificates of Return, whereby 20,000 Chinese traveling outside the U.S. were denied reentry. In addition, Certificates of Residence had to be shown on demand and any Chinese in the States without one could be deported. In 1892, the 1882 Exclusion Act was extended for another ten years (Kingston, 1980). Following these acts, the Chinese population in America dropped over the next twenty years. Their situation was at an impasse when a natural disaster occurred.

On April 18, 1906, an earthquake struck San Francisco. The ensuing fires destroyed virtually all of the city records. Chinese men were now able to claim that they had been born in San Francisco, and that they, as citizens, could bring wives to America. Chinese women began arriving, and by 1924 their number had increased ninefold. Chinese "sons" also entered the country, many with false papers to prove family membership. In 1924, a new law prohibited the entry of aliens ineligible for naturalized citizenship. This law was clearly directed against the Chinese. By 1930, 80 percent of the Chinese population was still male in spite of the dramatic increase in Chinese women entering the country. As Chinese American children were born, however, a new population began to emerge.

For these young Chinese, an education was viewed as the key to success in America. They attended public school and learned English in the process. They earned a reputation for being model students. They viewed the United States, not China, as their home. Like the children of other immigrants, they felt the tug of living in two worlds. They adopted American ways and challenged traditional values and customs. They wanted more than their parents had had.

World War II brought the United States and China into a close alliance, and the distinction between Chinese and Japanese became important to Americans. The Chinese were accepted, politically at least, as friends. Chinese Americans served in the armed forces. The need for labor in the defense industries opened new doors of employment opportunities for both men and women. Chinese Americans began to feel as though they could make it in America. Congress repealed the Chinese Exclusion Act, partially because the Japanese were broadcasting anti-American propaganda to a radio audience of millions in Asia and the Pacific, and partially because China was our ally. At long last, naturalized citizenship was extended to Chinese immigrants.

Since the Korean and Vietnam Wars, new Chinese immigrants have generally been more highly educated than their predecessors. Arriving in families, these new Chinese are the third largest group of immigrants, after Mexicans and Filipinos. Most have settled in California and New York (Takaki, 1993). Children of these new arrivals feel the same tug between the old ways and the new that their predecessors felt a generation ago, and, like their predecessors, they have earned a reputation for academic industriousness to the point of a stereotype. Because social class differences among Chinese Americans have emerged, some of these children, like the children of other immigrants, wonder if they can make it in America.

## Japanese Americans

Japanese immigrants began arriving in Hawaii in the 1880s and on the mainland by the 1890s. Like the Chinese, they arrived with hope for the future. For over two hundred years, Japanese people had been forbidden by law from traveling to foreign countries. After U.S. Navy Commodore Matthew C. Perry sailed into Japan in 1853, enforcing the ban on travel became more difficult. After 1868, the government of Emperor Meiji initiated many reforms. In that same year, the Hawaiian consul general in Japan secretly recruited 148 Japanese laborers, and in 1869 John Schnell took forty Japanese to California to found a silk farm.

Under Emperor Meiji, Japan began modernizing as a protection against imperialist powers abroad. To finance industry, the government levied land taxes and lowered the price of rice. Farmers were adversely affected by both practices, and by 1884 many were forced to sell their property in order to pay their debts. Stories of opportunity in Hawaii enticed them to emigrate. Like the Chinese before them, these laborers expected to return home after working for a few years abroad. They dreamed of returning to Japan wealthy. In Hawaii, work on the plantations paid six times more than day labor in Japan. A short separation from their families seemed worthwhile. By 1894, 30,000 Japanese had gone to Hawaii. American wages were equally attractive; a laborer could earn the equivalent of two yen in a day, compared to two-thirds of a yen in Japan (Takaki, 1989).

Between 1885 and 1924, 200,000 Japanese workers entered Hawaii and 180,000 came to the United States. Most of these men were in their twenties and thirties. Because Japan had compulsory education, most had an average of eight years of school, which gave them a literacy rate 3.5 percent higher than European immigrants (Takaki, 1993). Japanese review boards screened these emigrants to be sure they were healthy and literate, in order to maintain Japan's national honor abroad. The government wished to avoid the lower-class image that Chinese laborers had brought to America. In April 1891, the Japanese Consul, Chinda Sutemi, warned in a confidential memo that the emigration of lower-class Japanese would provide a pretext to the American working class and politicians to exclude the Japanese. His warning undoubtedly was influenced by the Chinese Exclusion Act.

When the Japanese school system was reorganized in 1876 under Emperor Meiji, English had been introduced as a major school subject. Thus, not only were Japanese immigrants to the United States more educated than Chinese laborers, many of them were also more literate in *English* than some of their European counterparts.

In addition to the educational level of their emigrants, the Japanese government was also concerned about avoiding the other problems that had plagued the Chinese bachelor society in the United States: drinking, gambling, and prostitution. Therefore, the Japanese government encouraged the emigration of women. In 1908, in the famous Gentlemen's Agreement with the United States, Japan agreed to restrict the emigration of laborers, but continued to allow the parents, wives, and children of laborers already in the U.S. to emigrate. After this, contract laborers began to view their move to America as permanent and looked for their families to join them. In addition, the practice of picture brides, based on the custom of arranged marriages with relatives as go-betweens, continued until 1921 among families in Japan and men in America. This custom merely extended traditional arranged marriages to transoceanic distances.

In Hawaii, plantation owners welcomed Japanese women as workers both in the fields and in their homes. They also welcomed them because the Japanese men fared better when their wives were with them. Because Emperor Meiji had supported education for females and his government had required it, these women had an educational level similar to that of the men. After Hawaii became a U.S. territory in 1900, plantation owners sought to employ men with families. The Japanese represented 43 percent of the population in Hawaii by the 1920s. Their problems were related primarily to their status as laborers, but there was not a prevailing feeling of anti-Japanese bigotry in the islands.

Such was not the case on the mainland, where much of the prejudice against the Chinese was also directed at the Japanese. They were sometimes segregated in public places. In California in the 1920s, White workers saw the Japanese as a labor threat, although they represented only 2 percent of the population. There were also other economic opportunities that these **Issei,** or first-generation Japanese, turned to as they developed supportive communities among themselves. Some became self-employed shop owners. Most of their businesses were small, although not all. Many were farmers. Resourceful in their methods, in addition to ownership they obtained land through contract, sharing, and leasing. When the Alien Land Law in the 1920s made it illegal for aliens ineligible for citizenship to lease or acquire agricultural land, Japanese ownership of land declined. Many farmers continued to lease land, although they appeared to be managers for the owners, including some Whites who supported them. Takaki (1989) summarizes these overall events as follows:

> The Issei had initially come as sojourners and had kept their cultural and national ties to Japan. Necessity ... encouraged them to promote intergroup cooperation and assistance. But ... they encountered racism that drove them into ethnic enclaves and strengthened their sense of ethnic solidarity. They were scorned as 'strangers from a different shore.' (p. 210)

While the Chinese population remained relatively stable, the Japanese population in the United States almost doubled in the last twenty years of the nineteenth century. By the 1930s, it was divided between the Issei and the **Nisei,** or second generation, as a result of the proliferation of Japanese families in America. These Nisei were Americans by birth. Their parents worked to give them a higher education as the key to overcoming discrimination and expanding their opportunities for success. Although many of the immigrants had studied English in Japan, the English of their children was American English. These Nisei lived in two cultural worlds. Determined to prove themselves, they worked hard at school. Many were honor students. Those who graduated from college, however, encountered difficulty finding employment commensurate with their level of education. Their educational achievements did not protect them from racial discrimination.

In 1930, a group of professional Nisei gathered in Seattle and established the Japanese American Citizens League (JACL). By 1940 there were fifty chapters and 5,000 members nationwide. Their goals were to claim their identity as Americans, educate the rest of American society about the achievements of Japanese Americans, and meet a need for ethnic community. The Nisei did not want to abandon the culture of their parents. They hoped to embrace both worlds. They viewed patriotism as the key to opening the door of acceptance in American society, but within the next year, history was to overtake and frustrate these efforts.

After the Japanese attack on Pearl Harbor on December 7, 1941, the reactions that faced Japanese Americans living in Hawaii differed markedly from those living on the mainland. In Hawaii, the Japanese continued working and living as they had been doing, largely due to the efforts of General Delos Emmons, military governor of Hawaii, who resisted massive deportation of the Japanese to the mainland and who even attacked the credibility of reasons for deportation given by the War Department and the Justice Department. He also resisted mass evacuation, because removal of Japanese workers would have serious effects on the Hawaiian economy. Furthermore, the Hawaiian Japanese were in a situation where they could be more visible in their defense of the islands. Feeling that the Japanese had attacked their country at Pearl Harbor (that is, America), Nisei in the Hawaiian Territorial Guard protected power plants, reservoirs, and waterfront areas in the night following the attack (Takaki, 1989).

On the mainland, however, Japanese on the West Coast were to endure a severe disruption in their lives. Like German Americans during the First World War, Japanese Americans became victims of mass hysteria. High-level government officials in Washington did not all agree that they posed a serious threat to national security. Three days after the attack on Pearl Harbor, FBI director J. Edgar Hoover reported that almost all suspect individuals were in custody, including not only Japanese, but Germans and Italians as well. In February 1942, Hoover concluded that there was no justification for large-scale evacuation of the Japanese. Western Defense Commander, Lt. General John DeWitt, however, had asked for approval for search and seize operations two weeks after the Pearl Harbor attack. Although the Federal Communications Commission reported that there were no grounds for fearing that Japanese in the U.S. would make radio contact with Japan, the Army continued with its plans, assuming Japanese disloyalty. DeWitt had no confidence in their loyalty, including the Nisei born in the United States. His claim of military necessity for evacuation was based more on public pressure than on evidence of subversive activities.

Pressure for internment in relocation camps came from the press, American Legion posts, farming interests in California, and politicians responding to their constituencies. (In California, Japanese labor was not necessary for the stability of the economy, as it was in Hawaii.) U.S. Attorney General Biddle was opposed to evacuation. Nevertheless, on February 19, 1942, President Franklin Roosevelt signed Executive Order No. 9066, which directed the Secretary of War to prescribe military areas under the restrictions of the War Department. A military curfew for all enemy aliens, including all persons of Japanese ancestry, was instituted. On April 30, 1942, Civilian Exclusion Order No. 27 provided for all residents of Japanese ancestry to be evacuated from "vital" West Coast areas by May 7th. Entire families were instructed to bring bedding, toilet articles, clothing, and utensils. Most sold the rest of their possessions (Takaki, 1989). Three residents, one each from California, Oregon, and Washington, refused to obey the order on the grounds of their Constitutional rights. They were arrested, convicted, and imprisoned. Their convictions were upheld in the U.S. Supreme Court on the basis of military necessity (Korematsu v. United States, 323 US 214, 1944).

In all, 94,000 Japanese Americans from California and 25,000 from Washington and Oregon were forcibly removed and placed in internment camps. Evacuees were transported in special trains to a total of ten internment camps located in more remote areas of Arizona, Arkansas, California, Colorado, Idaho, Utah, and Wyoming. They were assigned to barracks, with families quartered in a single room. On February 1, 1943, President Roosevelt wrote to the Secretary of War that *all* citizens should have an opportunity to serve in the armed forces. Following this, all internees were required to answer a loyalty questionnaire. One of the purposes of this questionnaire was to identify Nisei for military recruitment. Not surprisingly, very few Nisei in the camps volunteered for service. In January 1944, the Selective Service started to reclassify Nisei draft status from IV-C (enemy aliens) to I-A (eligible for the draft). When Nisei protested on the basis that their internment was in violation of their Constitutional rights as citizens, the federal government responded by arresting the leaders of the protest. Eventually, a total of 33,000 Nisei served in the armed forces (Takaki, 1989). Many Nisei distinguished themselves in combat. Among them was Captain Daniel Inouye from Hawaii, who went on to become a United States senator.

Closing of the internment camps began before the war ended. Some Japanese returned to the West Coast, while others relocated in other parts of the country. Many of these Japanese Americans have suffered the shame of their internment ever since. In August 1988, Congress passed a bill apologizing to the survivors of these camps and allocating a sum of $20,000 to each of them as reparation. President Ronald Reagan, in signing the bill, referred to the wrong that the United States had committed against loyal Japanese Americans (Takaki, 1993).

Since World War II, a third generation of Japanese Americans, or **Misei,** have sought to fulfill their own hopes in America, primarily through education, but they too have encountered bigotry. In the 1980s, economic recession in the United States and prosperity in Japan added to their problems.

## Southeast Asians

The war in Vietnam resulted in hundreds of thousands of people from Southeast Asia being displaced from their homes for political reasons in their countries. Among them were **Cambodians, Laotian Hmong,** and **Vietnamese.** When many of them came to the United States, they were not immigrants but refugees fleeing for their lives or from political persecution. Like others before them, they tried to find a place in America. Unlike immigrants who came seeking economic opportunity, these Southeast Asians often left their homeland with little advanced warning and no time to plan. Most of them had no idea of their final destination. They fled to stay alive. Figure 3.1 shows the area of Southeast Asia, including Cambodia, Laos, and Vietnam, where these newcomers originated. Upon their arrival in America, both old and young experienced severe culture shock. Some suffered from post-traumatic stress. The following review describes the plight of the Cambodians and the Vietnamese. The Laotian Hmong are discussed more fully in Chapter 7, as an example of a people in cultural transition in the United States.

**The Cambodians**   Situated as it is between Thailand and South Vietnam, Cambodia was caught in the Vietnam War. In 1965 the Cambodian government allowed North Vietnamese to move military supplies through Cambodia. In 1975 the Khmer Rouge forces led by Pol Pot came to power and changed the name of the country to Kampuchea. They began to relocate the urban population to the country and embarked on a campaign of genocide against all Cambodians who had been aligned with the former Lon Nol government, which had been supported by the United States. Educated and professional people were massacred.

In 1979 hundreds of thousands of Cambodians fled to Thailand when Vietnamese troops invaded Cambodia and overthrew Pol Pot. Under the Khmer Rouge and during the Vietnamese invasion, families were torn asunder. In Thailand, survivors endured wretched conditions in relocation camps. Over one hundred thousand of the survivors settled in the United States (Takaki, 1989).

Some of these refugees were children and teenagers orphaned by the war. The effects of hunger, violence, poverty, family separation, and cultural loss have resulted in post-traumatic stress disorder (PTSD) for many of these young people. Fred Bemak and I have reported the case of Tu, a fifteen-year-old Cambodian refugee (Bemak and Timm, 1994). Tu's recollections vividly illustrate his traumatic experiences. Tu was born in a country village outside of Phnom Penh, the capital of Cambodia. He remembers people being killed randomly in the streets. As a child, he was captured and taken to a Khmer Rouge work camp for Cambodian children. When he was ten years old, he escaped and made his way home. One day his mother sent him on an errand. He remembers running through the streets. Fighting was everywhere, and there were dead bodies lying about. He returned home to find his dead mother sitting on the floor, riddled

**FIGURE 3.1** Southeast Asia

with bullets and covered with blood. He fled through the jungle and into Thailand, where he found shelter in a refugee camp.

Tu was one of the first unaccompanied Cambodian minor refugees to enter the United States in 1982. He described his plane trip to the United States as follows (Bemak & Timm, 1994):

> It was a big plane. I sat alone by the window. My feet were cold…I just had rubber sandals, no jacket, one pants [sic], one shirt. I was wide awake the whole trip. The plane stopped in Italy or somewhere. Then we went over big mountains with ice on them to London.… [Tu was then put on a plane to the United States.] I was still awake watching the ocean. I got scared when I saw the smoke trail. When the plane tilted I thought it would crash. (p. 49)

Tu was taken to a Midwestern city, where he entered the home of a single foster mother. Over the next ten years, he continued to suffer from post-traumatic stress disorder, with symptoms of aggressiveness, fear, lack of trust, and profound cultural disorientation. These problems in turn caused conflict with his foster mother and another foster child in the household. Tu's tragic story suggests that safe relocation in a new land may not erase the nightmare of war.

**The Vietnamese**   Vietnam had been a French protectorate since the late nineteenth century. During World War II, Ho Chi Minh began to lead the Viet Minh to fight for Vietnam's independence. The French were defeated in 1954. During that same year the Geneva Accords provided for French withdrawal from Southeast Asia. The Accords also divided Vietnam at the seventeenth parallel and provided for an all-Vietnamese election, which was to occur in 1956. During the year following the Accords, however, a new government under the leadership of Ngo Dinh Diem was formed in the south to counter Ho Chi Minh's government in the north, which was supported by communist China and the Soviet Union. Not surprisingly, the United States in turn supported the government in South Vietnam. Thus, Vietnam remained divided and the intended election never occurred.

In the 1960s, President John Kennedy sent United States forces to South Vietnam and President Lyndon Johnson further expanded American military involvement in Southeast Asia. The Vietnam War became perhaps the most controversial war in United States history. Images of fighting appeared daily in television news coverage. The war lasted until the South Vietnamese government collapsed in April 1975. When this happened there was panic in Saigon, the capital. The city was under heavy bombardment, and there were fires everywhere. Thousands of people were evacuated. Some jammed the airport, while others sought refuge on boats. Some of these were rescued by American ships. Flight from South Vietnam continued until the late 1970s. Many people who left by boat fell victim to pirates (Takaki, 1989).

There were 603 Vietnamese living in the United States in 1964, most of whom were students, teachers, and diplomats. In 1975, 130,000 Vietnamese refugees arrived in the United States, followed by others over the next ten years. By 1985 there were over a half a million Vietnamese in America. Today, 20,000 a year are allowed to enter the country to join family members who are already here. Many who came after the fall of the South Vietnam government were from urban areas, especially Saigon, and had a high school or college education. Almost two-thirds of them could speak English. They had worked both with the French and with Americans. They were, in other words, familiar with Western culture (Takaki, 1989). Nevertheless, many have suffered from post-traumatic stress disorder in the United States. They have also encountered racism from those who view them as competing for jobs. Many still hope to return to Vietnam someday, while others have decided to stay and adjust to a new life. There are intergenerational tensions between older and younger family members. The Vietnamese represent a culture in transition in the United States, similar to other recent Southeast Asian refugees.

## Other Asians

Other Asian Americans include Filipinos, Asian Indians, and Koreans. These three groups share some characteristics with the early Chinese and Japanese immigrants. For example, many were recruited by United States employers as a labor force. Many of them also originally planned to earn higher wages than were available to them in their native countries for a few years, and then return home.

**Filipinos**   Filipinos began arriving in Hawaii and then on the mainland after the United States acquired the Philippines from Spain at the end of the Spanish-American War (1898). Like other Asians, they also encountered little racism in Hawaii but faced White working-class hostility on the mainland. They had also hoped to return home after a few years.

**Asian Indians**   Originally from the Punjab province, the Asian Indians who entered the United States in the first decade of the twentieth century were almost all males with little or no education. Like the Chinese and Japanese before them, they arrived on the West Coast with the intention of making good wages and then returning to India. Restrictions on Asian Indian immigration began almost as soon as their immigration. In 1917 Congress prohibited immigration from India. It was not until after World War II that Indian students studying in the United States were able to relocate in America. Many took American wives (Takaki, 1989).

**Koreans**   Koreans first arrived in Hawaii in the early 1900s, and on the mainland in the 1920s. They were encouraged to emigrate by American missionaries in Korea. Some left as political refugees. Some women came as "picture brides." When Japan declared Korea a protectorate, the Japanese government made Korean emigration to Hawaii illegal. After the Japanese attack on Pearl Harbor, Koreans in both the United States and Korea looked to an Allied victory with the hope of independence from Japanese domination. During World War II, Koreans were sometimes confused with Japanese by Americans who identified them as enemy aliens, but Koreans became actively involved in the war effort. The Korean War brought both visibility (and sympathy) to Koreans in the United States. Before the Immigration Act of 1965, Korean Americans were very few, but since then their numbers have increased tenfold (Takaki, 1989). Like the Chinese, the new Korean immigrants are better educated than their original predecessors in America.

## EUROPEAN AMERICANS

A review of the history of diverse races in the United States must include that of European Americans. Europeans should not be considered as a homogenous group any more than African, Asian, Latino, or Native Americans, but space in this volume does not allow for a consideration of the wide variety of European ethnic groups. European Americans, like other groups, have been immigrants, refugees, asylees, and autonomous minorities. At least some mention, therefore, should be given to the struggle that many European Americans have encountered in regard to economic success, political influence, and social status.

European Americans have wielded these types of power over each other as well as over other racial groups. When the British overcame New Amsterdam and changed its name to New York, political and economic power followed their military victory over the Dutch. The "haves" of higher socioeconomic status have usually looked down on the "have-nots" who were not so fortunate. Not only were wealthy Southern planters condescending toward Africans; they were condescending toward White indentured servants and poorer White freemen as well. The English relocated French Huguenots from Canada to Louisiana. The sad story of these Huguenots was immortalized by Henry Wadsworth Longfellow in his poem "Evangeline." The Anglos in the Southwest were ambivalent about the Spanish ranchers who were in the territory first. Some Anglos discounted them, while others married into wealthy ranchers' families. It is important to point out here that these ranchers were the descendants of the original Castillian Spanish settlers.

The Irish were exploited in the coal mines of Pennsylvania. The Irish were also victims of anti-Catholic attacks. In the Philadelphia riots of 1844, Catholic churches and schools and Irish homes were burned. In St. Louis in 1854, Irish homes were destroyed in four days of riots. Sometimes sentiment against the Irish led to violence in which people were killed (Sarason & Davis, 1979). Once they gained economic and political power in Boston, however, the Irish in turn resisted the rise of political power by Italians.

Germans suffered from a wartime hysteria against them in World War I similar to that endured by the Japanese in World War II. German settlers in Milwaukee, however, were scornful of the Polish.

Europeans from southern and eastern Europe were keenly aware of economic inequities and lack of political influence. Jews suffered social discrimination even as they gained economic success and political influence. A higher proportion of Jews are in the professions and business in comparison with other European ethnic groups.

And so it went. Differential economic, political, and social power juxtaposed with the American Dream was true for most Americans for at least a portion of our diverse histories, except for those few who brought power with them from their nation of origin.


## LATINO AMERICANS

Choosing a name to refer to all Americans who are of Spanish and/or Latin American descent is not an easy task. In the case of African, Asian, European, or Native Americans, these inclusive designations are generally accepted terms. Like members of other racial groups who refer to themselves as "Japanese" or "Irish" or "Oneida," "Latins" also refer to themselves by national origin, such as Cuban or Mexican, but finding agreement on a term that includes all of them is another matter.

Earl Shorris, in his monumental book *Latinos* (1992), has articulated this problem of finding agreement on a collective term. In trying to find a term for *his* book, Shorris asked a woman of Mexican descent what she meant by the word *we*. She replied **"Mejicanos"** (Shorris, 1992). When he responded that there was a larger group, she insisted on her term:

> No other word was acceptable, not because there were no other nouns or adjectives available, but because any less specific, more encompassing word was damaging…what name should be given to the set of people who share—with many exceptions—a common language, some customs, and some ancestors?
>
> …There must be one name, a single word that is not objectionable. (p. xvi)

According to Shorris, in 1980 the U.S. Census Bureau was on the verge of choosing Latino as the correct word when someone said that it sounded too much like **Ladino,** the ancient Castillian now spoken by descendants of Spanish Jews who went into exile in the fifteenth century. Latino was, therefore, replaced by **Hispanic** in the census. Shorris (1992) also reported that:

> The battle was joined immediately on all sides. Political, racial, linguistic, and historical arguments were advanced.…
>
> *Geographically,* Hispanic is preferred in the Southeast and much of Texas.[3] New Yorkers use both Hispanic and Latino. Chicago…prefers Latino.[4] In California, the word Hispanic has been barred from the Los Angeles Times.…
>
> *Politically,* Hispanic belongs to the right…of center, while Latino belongs to the left of center. Politically active Mexican-American women in Los Angeles are fond of asking "Why HISpanic? Why not HERspanic?"
>
> *Historically,* the choice went from Spanish or Spanish-speaking to Latin American, Latino and Hispanic.
>
> *Economically,* …Hispanic belongs to the middle class. [Note: For some it may imply poverty.] (p. xvii, all italics mine)

Shorris finally settled on the term Latino/Latina for linguistic reasons because Latino has gender connotations in Spanish. I have chosen the term "Latino" for this text. I am sensitive to the nuances of this term and do not mean to suggest that the gender, regional, political, or economic implications are not important. I simply need a common designate, and the term "Latin American" generally refers to the peoples living in Mexico, Central, and South America.

Within the broad category of this term Latino, therefore, are people whose ancestors lived in the Southwest since its settlement by Spanish colonists, immigrants seeking economic opportunity, and refugees who have fled their native lands to escape political persecution and even death. Differences in national origin are important, as stated in the Mexican American woman's answer "Mejicano." Shorris (1992) has called attention to the fact that:

To many Latinos, drawing the distinctions among the nationalities constitutes a kind of game, like a quiz program. Everyone has a theory about everyone else. Some are amusing, all are accurate, and every nuance is important. (p. 63)

## Mexican Americans

Sixty percent of all Latino Americans in the United States are of Mexican origin (Portes, 1990). There are several distinct groups among them. The first group consists of the descendants of the original settlers of the Southwest. The region itself reflects its Spanish heritage with names like El Paso, San Antonio, San Diego, and Los Angeles. At the end of the Mexican-American War in 1848, the Mexican government was forced to make peace with the United States. In the Treaty of Guadalupe Hidalgo, Mexico accepted the Rio Grande as the Texas border and ceded a huge tract of land to the United States. In return, the United States paid Mexico $15 million (Takaki, 1993). This vast territory totaled over one million square miles and included part or all of the present states of Arizona, California, Colorado, Nevada, New Mexico, Utah, and Texas.[5] Including Texas, it amounted to one-half of Mexico's land. Figure 3.2 shows the portion of the United States that was acquired in this treaty.

The Spanish and Mexican residents of this area were incorporated into the United States at this time. Gradually, Anglo settlers exceeded those of Spanish/Mexican descent. In California, for example, Mexicans were the majority in 1870, but by 1890 they represented only 10 percent of the population (Fernandez and Chan, 1989). The descendants of the original ranchers are proud of their long residency in the Southwest. They were Spanish in origin, and the notion that social class differences were brought into the area by **Anglo American** settlers is not valid. Barrera (1984) has described the social class structure that existed among the Spanish settlers. There were landlords or ranchers called **patrones,** and there were the **peones** who worked for them. There were also semi-independent or small farmers, merchants, and artisans. This social class structure changed with the infusion of Anglo colonization. Accommodations were made between the patrones and those Anglos who made a distinction between the Castillian ranchers and the peones. In some cases, Anglos married into patrones' families. Not surprisingly, the areas with less Anglo American economic influence retained the older Spanish pattern longer. Gradually, a working class evolved out of the old peon class. During the 1910s and 1920s, this agricultural working class expanded rapidly, and by World War II, new employment opportunities became available due to labor shortages. Many of these workers, however, suffered from the same dual-wage system that Asians encountered on the West Coast. There was a "Mexican wage," which was lower than the wages paid to Anglo workers (Barrera, 1984).

The second group of Mexican Americans in the United States are the descendants of those who entered the country after the Mexican-American War until the end of World War II. In the late nineteenth and early twentieth centuries, railroad companies, ranchers, and industries recruited unskilled Mexican workers to fill their labor needs (Garcia, 1978). These workers retained a culture

**FIGURE 3.2** Mexican Land Acquired by the United States

that blended Spanish and Mexican Indian customs. Until 1924 there was free movement of contract laborers back and forth between Mexico and the United States. Unlike immigrants from other parts of the world, Mexicans could enter and leave without passports whenever they wished. As Takaki has pointed out, "For many Mexicans, the border was only an imaginary line—one that could be crossed and re-crossed at will" (1993, p. 334). In 1924 the Border Patrol was established, but free travel between the two countries was common until the end of World War II. Many of these workers remained in the United States with their families. They faced prejudice and stereotyped views about them on the part of Whites. Public schools aimed at Americanizing Mexican children and training them for skilled labor jobs. These goals helped to create intergenerational cultural tensions in the Mexican population, as the older generation retained more traditional customs (Garcia, 1978). After World War II, crossing the border became more highly regulated.

The third group of Mexican Americans in the United States is composed of more recent immigrants, including those seeking reunification with family members already in the U.S., other legal immigrants, and undocumented workers (or illegal aliens). Immigration reforms in the 1960s and 1970s curtailed the number of Mexicans who could legally enter the United States per year. In the 1990s, some legal immigrants are well-educated college graduates seeking career opportunities. These more highly educated newcomers have come to the United States because of the extensive economic and fiscal problems that have plagued Mexico for the past two decades. However, Portes (1990) reported that only 11 percent of all Mexican Americans have professional or managerial positions. Other less educated legal immigrants supply a large portion of the unskilled labor force in the Southwest. Some are migrant workers whose children attend school in any one place, on the average, less than three months during the school year. Disruptive relocations are the leading cause of migrant children's failure to complete their schooling. The challenge that faces educators is finding ways of ameliorating these disruptions. School administrators have discriminated against Mexican children by de facto segregation through gerrymandering of school districts. In 1973 the U.S. Supreme Court found this practice in violation of the Fourteenth Amendment (Keyes v. School District No. 1, Denver, 413 U.S. 189; see Chapter 6).

The issue of undocumented workers remains a problem. Official estimates of illegal entrants are probably not valid, due to the fact that after deportation many of the same individuals repeatedly reenter the United States. In 1982 the U.S. Supreme Court upheld the right of children of illegal immigrants to a public education, and cited employment of low-cost workers by U.S. companies as one reason for the illegal immigrant problem (Plyler v. Doe, 457 US 202, 1982; see Chapter 6). With this support for their education, perhaps the children of poorer Mexican workers will have a brighter future.

## Puerto Rican Americans

Christopher Columbus landed in Puerto Rico in 1493, during his second voyage to the new world. Figure 3.3 shows the area in the Caribbean that includes Puerto Rico and Cuba, and will give the reader an image of their geographic relationship to the United States.

European settlement of Puerto Rico began in 1508, under the command of Juan Ponce de Leon. By 1540, an agricultural economy had developed, and in 1582 the importation of African slaves began (Mirande, 1985). A mixing of Spanish, Indians, and Africans produced a unique population and culture (Morales, 1986).

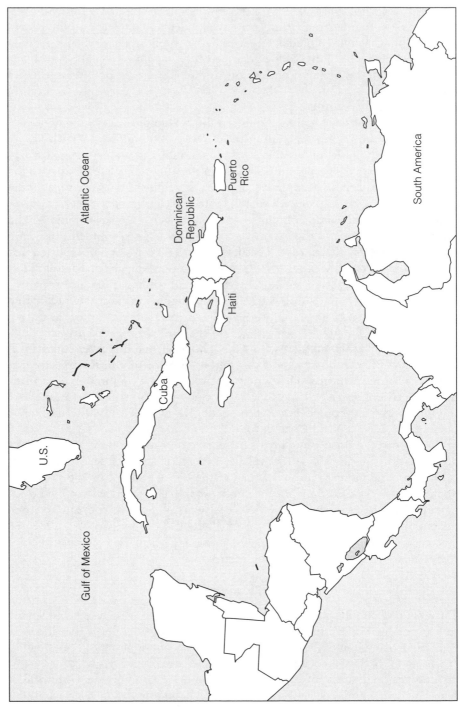

**FIGURE 3.3** The Caribbean

In 1868 Puerto Ricans led a failed revolt against Spain, but in 1897 negotiations with Spain resulted in autonomy for Puerto Rico. In 1898 the United States battleship *Maine* sank in the harbor at Havana, Cuba. The sinking was attributed to the Spanish, but it was later learned that it was caused by an explosion in a powder magazine. The United States government reacted by passing a resolution calling on Spain to abandon all claims on Cuba. Spain received this resolution as a declaration of war. The Spanish-American War escalated to the point where not only Cuba but Puerto Rico and the Philippines became involved (Spring, 1994). The United States invaded Puerto Rico and placed it under military rule. In 1899, under the Treaty of Paris, Spain ceded Puerto Rico to the United States.

In 1900 a civilian government was established by the Foraker Act (Fernandez and Chan, 1989). Thus, like some Mexicans before them, Puerto Ricans were "incorporated" into the United States. Soon after, American business investments on the island included industries such as sugarcane plantations and lumber mills. In 1917 the Jones Act gave United States citizenship to Puerto Ricans. They were, however, denied the right to vote in U.S. national elections. Because of their citizenship status, Puerto Ricans have not been considered immigrants (Shorris, 1992).

A slow migration to the U.S. mainland began in the 1920s, but increased after World War II as a result of unemployment in Puerto Rico, the advent of cheaper air travel, and labor recruitment by U.S. companies. In 1951, Puerto Rico's status changed from a territory to a U.S. commonwealth. During the 1950s and 1960s, there was a sharp increase in migration, particularly to New York City, partly as a result of more active recruitment by industries and politicians interested in keeping businesses in the U.S. Those who came to New York found that most employment was in low-paying, unskilled, or menial jobs in restaurants, hotels and hospitals, or in light manufacturing—the jobs that nobody else wanted. Most were dead-end jobs, such as machine operators in the garment industry. Today, there is an excess of "blue collar" or working-class laborers in proportion to job opportunities, but there is also a scarcity of Puerto Rican "white-collar" workers in proportion to available office-type jobs (Rodriguez, 1979). Only 14 percent of Puerto Ricans are employed in professional and managerial positions (Portes, 1990).

Education is mixed for Puerto Rican children, depending on the financial status of their families. Some are illegally employed minors, caught in the same danger of being in a permanent underclass as the children of Mexican laborers.

## Cuban Americans

Cuban immigration, like that of Puerto Rico, has its roots in political events involving the United States. The first wave of Cuban immigration began during the Cuban War of Independence from Spain (Portes, 1990). The United States intervened, and when the Spanish-American War ended, Cuba became a republic. The island was occupied by U.S. troops and governed by military authority from 1900 to 1902, and again from 1908 to 1909. Thus, politically and economically, the island became a protectorate of the United States. Americans invested in the sugar, iron, and nickel industries, but U.S. business never recruited Cuban labor as it did with Mexicans and Puerto Ricans. The Cuban upper class looked to the United States for political guidance and imitated American business patterns. As a result, strong feelings of anti-imperialism began to grow in the rest of the Cuban population.

The second wave of Cuban immigration to the U.S. occurred between 1959 and 1962 in response to the revolution against the Batista regime. Thirty-one percent of those leaving Cuba were professional, technical, and managerial workers; 33 percent were clerical or in sales; 7 percent were service workers; and 4 percent were agricultural workers. Thirty-six percent had completed high school or had some college education; only 4 percent had less than a fourth grade education (Shorris, 1992, p. 64). These exiles transformed Cuban communities in the United States. At first these refugees expected to return to Cuba once Fidel Castro's regime was overthrown. After the Cuban Missile Crisis in 1962, however, the U.S. government agreed to restrain Cuban groups on the mainland in their attempts to subvert Castro, in exchange for the removal of Soviet missiles from Cuba. Subsequently, Cubans in the United States became more concerned about making a new life here. There were wide educational and socioeconomic class differences between those who had arrived by 1962 and those who arrived in the late 1960s; of this later group, only 18 percent were professional, technical, and managerial, and the rest were laborers. By the late 1970s, the numbers of professional and managerial immigrants had dropped to 8.5 percent (Shorris, 1992).

Today, Cubans are located primarily in New York and Florida. Five percent of Latino Americans in the United States are Cuban. Twenty-two percent are professionals or have managerial positions (Portes, 1990). They are the most highly educated among Latinos in the United States. Four times as many Cubans have college degrees as Mexicans, and three times as many have college degrees as Puerto Ricans. It has been widely reported that Cubans own four of the ten largest banks in Miami and are entrepreneurs in a variety of businesses, including a television station and daily newspapers. The success of Cuban businesses is well known, but not all Cubans have reached this level of success.

Cubans are a proud people. Humor has helped them to survive their dislocation. Shorris (1992) has reported a Cuban joke about the poignancy of being an exile:

> [There was a] Cuban dog, a wretched little thing, with a short, ragged tail, thin haunches, and sorry, splayed paws. As it was walking down a Miami street it came across a group of large American dogs, with big tails and shiny coats. "Look at the bedraggled beast," the American dogs said. They laughed at the little Cuban and insulted him for being so small and powerless. The Cuban dog endured the insults for a few moments, then he said, "Go ahead, laugh. You see me as I am now, but in Cuba I was a German shepherd." (p. 65)

This story not only captures Cuban spirit, wit, and wisdom about the fleeting nature of power. It is also a story about the arrogance of members of another society in reference to newcomers among them.

## Other Latino Groups

These three groups, the Mexicans, the Puerto Ricans, and the Cubans, account for 79 percent of Latino Americans in the United States. The remainder come from the Caribbean and Central and South America. They come from the Dominican Republic; from El Salvador, Costa Rica, and Guatemala; from Argentina, Brazil, Chile, Colombia, Ecuador, and Peru. Some were refugees fleeing from persecution at home (Shorris, 1992; Burns, 1993). Differences among them besides nationality include variations in education and socioeconomic level.

# NATIVE AMERICANS

Of all the diverse groups in the United States, Native Americans are the most diverse of all. Although sharing some common values and philosophies, the variety of Native American nations ranged from the Penobscot on Northeastern shores to the Navajo in the Southwestern desert; from the Seminoles in Southeastern swamps to the Aleuts on the Northwestern coast; from those the French later called the Iroquois in the territory that was to become New York State to the Winnebago on the shores of Wisconsin. Native Americans are fiercely proud of their tribal nations. At a professional conference recently, a woman introduced herself with the words "I am Lakota." At another conference, a man identified himself as Seneca. "I am Chippewa" reported another. Figure 3.4 shows the variety and location of the major tribal groups prior to European colonization.

There is no possible way to review adequately the history or diversity among Native Americans in the space available. What follows is an attempt to capture some of their experiences that resulted from European settlement.

## European Colonization

The first impact of European contact on Native Americans was not war, but disease. With no immunity to common European illnesses, Native Americans died by the thousands along the East Coast and inland as Europeans moved westward. The second impact was relocation. In the seventeenth century the British created a "reservation" at Stockbridge, Massachusetts, after the defeat of the coastal tribes (Lurie, 1987). White settlements proliferated on the East Coast, and relationships with Native Americans were mixed. As the struggle for control of the eastern territories grew between the British and the French, both sides gained Indian support. The French had allies among the Hurons and Algonquins, while the British formed an alliance with the Iroquois. In return for this alliance, the Iroquois were assured that the flow of settlers into Iroquois territory would be controlled as much as possible (Johansen, 1982). The so-called French and Indian Wars ended at the Battle of Quebec in 1763. As a result, France lost vast territory in North America.

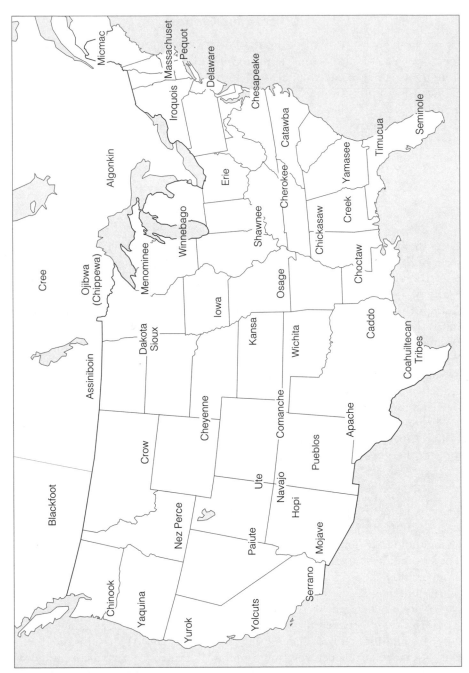

**FIGURE 3.4** Location of Some Native American Tribes or Tribal Groups Prior
to European Settlement

## Early Statehood

After the American colonies won their independence, Indian affairs became a federal rather than a state responsibility under Article I, Section 8 of the U.S. Constitution, which states:

> The Congress shall have power…to regulate commerce with foreign nations, and among the several States, and with the Indian tribes.

American policy toward Native Americans derived from British policy. The designation *Indian* is used in this section because it was the official term of the times. Today, Native Americans are again referring to themselves as American Indians. At first, the government was concerned with administering trade with the Indians, but as settlers moved west, federal treaties negotiated the sale of Indian land, with the Indians reserving small tracts as homelands under federal jurisdiction. In 1824, a special Indian Office was created to deal with the increasing amount of Indian business. Gradually enlarged, it was renamed the Bureau of Indian Affairs and transferred to the Department of the Interior in 1849. American law specified that Indian land was to be paid for, but the average price was about ten cents per acre. Few tribes sold all their land, but they did relinquish parcels and tried to hold out on reduced tracts in their old territories (Lurie, 1987).

## The Jacksonian Era

Andrew Jackson was elected president in 1828. Revered by Whites as an Indian fighter, he changed the fate of Native Americans for years to come. Jackson supported efforts in Georgia and Mississippi to abolish tribal units and to extend *state authority* over Indians. In 1832, when the Supreme Court ruled that states could not legally extend jurisdiction into Indian territory, Jackson refused to enforce the decision. Under the guise of protecting eastern tribes, Jackson sought to exercise "parental" control over his Indian "children." In January 1830, the Mississippi government abolished the sovereignty of the Choctaw Nation. Federal representatives met in September with Choctaws to negotiate a treaty for the purpose of acquiring their lands and removing them to a place west of the Mississippi River. The Choctaws refused, but the federal officials informed them that they had to accept or they would be destroyed. The treaty that did occur decreed that the Choctaws cede *all* of their land to the federal government and move west (Takaki, 1993).

Jackson's policies were not limited to the Choctaw. Where he was not able to buy out Indians, he used treaties to remove them. Such was the case with the Cherokee. In 1834, Jackson was not able to secure a treaty for the cession of Cherokee lands. The Cherokee had refused. The following year, Jackson sent the Reverend J. F. Schermerhorn to negotiate a new treaty stating that the Cherokee would cede their eastern territory and relocate west of the Mississippi in exchange for $4.5 million from the federal government. Although the treaty was signed in March by a pro-removal group within the Cherokee nation, it had to be ratified by the tribal council to be effective. The council rejected the treaty. Schermerhorn then made plans for another meeting in December in New

Echota, Georgia. John Ross, the leader who opposed removal, had been jailed. Thus, only a fraction of the tribe, with no tribal officers in attendance, signed the Treaty of New Echota. Andrew Jackson responded to the treaty as though it represented the will of the Cherokee people. To his credit, Major W. M. Davis, the officer appointed to enroll the Cherokees for removal, protested its legality when he discovered the treachery behind it. Ratification of the treaty resulted in White settlers moving into Cherokee territory. When the Cherokee continued to refuse to recognize the treaty, they were rounded up in 1838 by the United States Army, placed in detention camps, and 11,500 were forcibly marched in the middle of winter from their homeland in the Appalachian Mountains to Indian Territory, in what is now the state of Oklahoma. Over 4,000 died on this journey, which became known as the "Trail of Tears" (Foreman, 1972; Takaki, 1993).

Andrew Jackson also acted against the Seminoles. When he "counselled" them to migrate west in 1835, the Seminoles, under Osceola's leadership, responded with armed resistance. Even after he left the presidency in 1837, Jackson continued his campaign against the Seminoles. Ultimately, relocation of five Southeastern tribes (known as the Five Civilized Tribes) included the Cherokees, Chickasaws, Choctaws, Creeks, and Seminoles (Foreman, 1972).

## European Westward Expansion

Jackson's policy of relocation from the Southeast to areas west of the Mississippi could satisfy the desire of White settlers for more land for only a limited time. Indians in the Midwest had already encountered pressure to cede part of their lands as well. In Wisconsin, for example, the Chippewa, Ottawa, Potawatomi, Santee Sioux, and Winnebago ceded portions of their territories in the 1820s and 1830s (Lurie, 1987).[6] White settlers moved west of the Mississippi into the great northern and southern plains. The completion of the transcontinental railroad in 1869 marked the beginning of a new and accelerated era in westward expansion, not only for homesteaders but for industry as well. The story of westward expansion from a Native American point of view appears in Box 3.1.

Arapaho, Cheyenne, Dakotas, Kiowa, Pawnee, Sioux, and other tribes not only felt the presence of the White settlers, however. Dislocated from their territories, problems broke out among the tribes themselves. In 1873, a Pawnee hunting party was attacked by Sioux at Massacre Canyon. Over a hundred Pawnees died. Caught between their Sioux enemies and the possibility of federal protection, many Pawnees sadly made the choice for safety and migrated to a reservation in Kansas (Takaki, 1993). The world of the plains Indians was coming to an end.

After years of skirmishes and retaliations on the part of Whites and Indians alike, the final blow came at Wounded Knee. In 1890, a Paiute named Wovoka called for Indians everywhere to dance the Ghost Dance, for he believed that Christ had returned to earth as an Indian. Wovoka promised the restoration of Indian ways, Indian land, and the buffalo—a world without Whites. Among the Sioux, Ghost Dancing became extensive. Indian Bureau staff in Washington ordered the army to arrest the Sioux. A former Indian agent, Dr. Valentine McGillycuddy, advised pulling back the troops, saying that they had frightened

---

**BOX 3.1** The California Trail Reconsidered

---

The year was 1849. The place, the California Trail where it crossed the vast sagebrush and alkali desert of Nevada. To the hordes of fortune hunters hurrying from the East to the newly opened California gold mines, no part of their route seemed more dangerous than this inhospitable stretch. Not only were there few sources of water, but the desolate land was full of "treacherous savages"—bands of horseless Northern Paiute, Bannock, and Western Shoshone Indians. The whites compared them unfavorably with the bold, mounted, buffalo-hunting tribes of the Plains and referred to them contemptuously as "Diggers" because they dug with sticks for roots, a main component of the diet that had sustained them in their harsh Great Basin for ten thousand years.

In the travelers' diaries, journals, and letters—which served for generations afterwards as the prime source of what white men knew about these Indians—the writers described them as "wretched, degraded, and despicable," "the meanest Indians in existence," who hid from sight during the day but came out from among the desert vegetation after dark to sneak into the emigrants' camps along the trail and steal their food and livestock. At night the fearful, travel-worn whites had to mount guard, listening intently for every rustle and sound in the desert. When they heard a suspicious noise, they shot in the direction of its source, and at dawn they often found a dead Indian lying nearby. Sometimes it was the body of a young child, a woman, or a gnarled elder, and the travelers' stories circulated this information as proof that all "Diggers" were skulking thieves, no matter what their age or sex.

The Indians' side of what was going on was quite different. It never got into the history books, although in later years survivors, including the very articulate Sarah Winnemucca, who in 1849 had been a five-year-old Paiute child living along the Oregon Trail with her family, recalled poignant and terrible memories that cast a different light on those shots in the night.

What the whites had believed were "skulking" thieves and murderers in the darkness were in fact hungry and terrified Indian families trying to get safely across a road that the white men had unwittingly cut directly through territory where for centuries the Indians had lived, gathered food, and held their ceremonies. The bisecting road had crippled the Indians' freedom of movement across their lands, for they lived in mortal dread of the stream of trigger-happy white travelers who shot at them as if they were rabbits.

Attempting to get past them, from one part of their territory to another, to reach relatives or a desperately needed wild food source, Indian fathers and mothers hid anxiously with their children behind clumps of sage or other desert brush during the day, then at night directed the young ones to scamper silently across the road past the white men's camps and hide on the other side until all the elders, one by one, also got across.

If the whites had been careless with their livestock, some of the bolder young Indians, who naturally blamed the intruders for overrunning and destroying their food-gathering grounds and polluting their waterholes, saw no wrong in helping themselves to one or two of the emigrants' cows—as the Indians perceived it, an acceptable act of reciprocity. These, in short, were what the travelers cursed as "the meanest Indians in existence"—men, women, and children, trying to survive, but whom the whites occasionally heard in the night and killed.

In the history of the native American nations, the California Trail story is not unique. Ever since Europeans first arrived in the Western Hemisphere in 1492, their relations with Indians have been marked—even until today—by the stain of countless similar episodes in which groundless fears, prejudices, and misunderstandings have led to tragedy.

SOURCE: From D. H. Thomas, et al., *The Native Americans: An Illustrated History, 1993.* Reprinted by permission of Turner Publishing, Inc.

---

the Indians. Washington ignored his advice. Indian policemen went to Chief Sitting Bull's cabin and arrested him. Armed Sioux confronted them, and during the ensuing gunfire the police killed the chief. News of his death alarmed another group of Sioux, led by Chief Big Foot. In their attempt to escape, Big Foot and others, including women and children, were intercepted and taken by the U.S. Cavalry to a camp near a creek called Wounded Knee. On the morning of December 29, 1890, mounted soldiers surrounded the camp, told the Sioux to gather their men in the center of the camp, and ordered them to hand over their weapons. The Sioux did so, but the soldiers thought there were more hidden weapons and began searching the camp. The situation grew tense. When a shot was fired, the soldiers began shooting. The Sioux warriors tried to recover their confiscated weapons in order to defend themselves, but gunfire poured down on them from the ridge above the camp. When the Indians tried to flee, the soldiers pursued them, firing as they did so. Hundreds of Sioux men, women, and children died, along with some soldiers. A snow began falling and covered their bodies. "For Indian America, Wounded Knee violently symbolized the end of the frontier" (Takaki, 1993, p. 231).

## The Reservation System

Following Andrew Jackson's lead, the reservation system was expanded rapidly in the mid-nineteenth century. A patronizing attitude became part of federal policy. The term "ward" first appeared in 1831, during Jackson's presidency, when Chief Justice John Marshall explained the treaty responsibility of the federal government to protect Indian tribal lands. By the 1860s, the term meant that Indians were the responsibility of the Department of the Interior. Corruption permeated the administration of reservations. Indian Bureau officers interpreted their positions as *guardians* who could make decisions for Indian individuals as if they were children who needed guidance.

John Walker, known as the father of the reservation system, was Commissioner of Indian Affairs in the 1870s (Takaki, 1993). Although he advocated a "Peace Policy," he nevertheless held paternalistic views similar to those Marshall had expressed years earlier. At this time, the aim of the federal bureau was to repress Indian culture and to undermine traditional leadership and religion. The goal was to acculturate Indians to the ways of White culture (Lurie, 1987). Not surprisingly, Indians resisted. White officials viewed them as apathetic.

## The General Indian Allotment Act

To cope with Indian resistance to assimilation of White culture, the General Indian Allotment Act, otherwise known as the Dawes Act, was passed in 1887. It provided for a division of reservations into 160-acre tracts for each head of family, 80 acres for single adults over age eighteen, and 40 acres for single people under age eighteen. Larger tracts were allocated in western areas where grazing land was needed. These tracts could not be sold for twenty-five years. The federal expectation was that by that time the Indians would have broken their tribal ties and become individual farmers and ranchers. So-called surplus land left over after all the allotments had been made was bought by the government and opened to public sale. Between 1887 and 1934, Indian land was reduced from 140 million to 50 million acres nationwide (Lurie, 1987).

## The Twentieth Century

Although Indians were not eligible to be drafted in World War I, they enlisted in large numbers. Their heroism, along with newspaper reports of the appalling conditions on reservations, aroused public sympathy. In response, Congress granted full citizenship to all Indians in 1924. (Some were already citizens for a variety of reasons.) Although viewed by some Indians as long overdue, this action was viewed by other Indians as a further effort to deny their tribal status.

Also as a result of the reports of reservation conditions, a major investigation was conducted. Published in 1928 as the Meriam Report, this investigation produced some surprising conclusions in the context of its time—namely that the Indian people had managed to survive because they were able to maintain some community cohesion and tribal traditions—but the loss of Indian land brought about by allotment has been identified as a "primary cause of Indian despair, demoralization and poverty" (Lurie, 1987, p. 26). The Meriam report criticized the policies of the Indian Bureau that aimed at eradicating everything Indian.

In the depression of the 1930s, President Franklin Roosevelt appointed John Collier, Sr. as Commissioner of Indian Affairs. Collier conferred with Indian leaders to learn their opinions about what changes were needed. The result was the Indian Reorganization Act (IRA) in 1934. Under this Act, tribes could organize under their own constitutions and charters, elect their own governments, and enter into contracts with both the federal government and private businesses. Collier had also hoped to allow those tribes wishing to do so to take over some operations of reservations, but Congress deleted this from the Act. In its final form, the Act retained final power of federal superintendents over tribal decisions (Lurie, 1987).

Collier was criticized by some tribes for trying to impose bureaucratic concepts on Indian affairs. The Navajo were among the tribes who rejected the IRA. In their view, Collier appeared to be favoring a philosophy of Indian autonomy and was, like others before him, trying to manage their affairs.[7] Some Indians, however, credited Collier for understanding Indian grievances, halting the loss of Indian land, and trying to restore tribal lands (Lurie, 1987).

In 1946 the Indian Claims Commission (ICC) was established, allowing Indians to file long-standing claims through land settlement or payment. In practice, however, the Commission disallowed many of the claims. The ICC was terminated in 1978.

Indian affairs worsened during the 1950s. A double attack on the so-called Indian problem was aimed at *termination,* which would end reservations and federal protection of Indian property, and at *relocation,* which would move Indian populations from rural to more urban areas. Public Law 280 aimed at making law enforcement on reservations a state rather than a federal responsibility. Indian opposition, however, resulted in this law becoming effective in only a few states (Lurie, 1987).

In the 1960s, the Civil Rights Movement brought new determination to many minorities, but the Indian situation was somewhat different from that of other groups. The issue of desegregation, for example, brought hope to African

Americans, but it conveyed a threat to Indian peoples (Lurie, 1987). The reservations were not urban ghettos, which had been allowed to deteriorate by indifferent slumlords; the reservations were *Indian property*. Native Americans' determination took the form of a desire for noninterference by the federal government in Indian affairs. Philleo Nash, appointed by President John Kennedy as Commissioner of Indian Affairs, emphasized community development and making the relocation program voluntary. He recognized that Indian people wanted to explore their own alternatives for economic improvement. The threat of reservation termination declined by the mid-1960s. Interestingly, the relocation policy of the 1950s resulted in a heightened awareness of Indian identity and values among those in urban areas (Indians not living on reservations).

### Sovereignty and Treaty Rights

In the 1970s the American Indian Policy Review Commission published an extensive report that revealed conflicting opinions on the issue of **tribal sovereignty.** This important issue lies at the heart of legal, political, and economic conflicts between Native Americans and other groups, conflicts that continue in the 1990s.

The implication in Article 1, Section 8 of the U.S. Constitution is that the relationship of the United States government with the Indian tribes is one of negotiation. Although that concept has been both ignored and violated, in the Constitution Indian sovereignty was recognized. Theoretically, treaties were made on this basis. Conflicts between Indian peoples and others have generally occurred over Indian lands and resources. Conflicts have arisen with settlers, with business enterprises, including mining and logging interests, and with recreational and sporting interests, involving fishing and gaming privileges. Non-Indians become frustrated when they believe that Indians have what they interpret as special privileges. What they fail to understand is that these so-called privileges are the result of treaty negotiations aimed at preserving Indian rights over their own territory. The resolution of these conflicts remains at the federal level, with the result that state and local officials, with a few exceptions, do not have the authority to resolve them.

# DIVERSITY, SOCIAL POWER,
# AND THE FUTURE

The foregoing overview of the histories of diverse peoples in the United States suggests that they have indeed shared some common experiences in regard to economic, political, and social power. At the beginning of this chapter I mentioned that the European free market view of land was that of private ownership. Whether land was acquired by purchase, treaty, or staking a claim, the intent was the same. At different times in American history, those in positions of economic privilege and/or political influence have acquired land and enslaved, relocated, deported, and recruited different groups for the purpose of economic gain. Differential power has impacted all groups. Castes have encountered this power, not only on the basis of social class, but also on the basis of race.

Problems have not been limited to differences in privilege and power, however. Problems have also arisen from competition among workers themselves, particularly in economic hard times. Recently, there has been bitter competition between new immigrants and unskilled Americans seeking low-skilled and low-wage jobs.

Over the past few years there has been a rising sentiment against new immigrants, refugees, and those seeking political asylum in the United States. According to a report in *Time* magazine (*Time,* Fall Special Issue, 1993), 60 percent of those people responding to a poll were in favor of a law to reduce the number of legal immigrants allowed to enter the United States. The reason is economic. In good times there is less concern about immigrants creating competition for employment, whether they are African, Asian, Latino, or European.

On a popular television talk show recently, a White college graduate expressed deep anger over the arrival of a few Chinese laborers. "I worked four years for my education and paid thousands of dollars for it," he said. "Why should they come in and take a job away from me?" In saying this, he missed two crucial facts. First, the newcomers would have to study as long and hard as he had in order to compete for similar jobs, because he was not searching for a low-skill, low-wage position. Second, his forebears in their time had sought opportunity in America just as the newcomers were seeking it now.

Miss Liberty continues to hold her lamp beside The Golden Door. The important question is this: Do we believe in her promise not only of economic opportunity, but also of social justice?

## CHAPTER SUMMARY

Differences in economic, political, and social power have impacted the lives of diverse groups in the United States. Throughout American history, members of all of these groups have also suffered violence, even death, simply on the basis of their racial or ethnic groups.

African Americans have endured slavery, experienced discrimination in the workplace and public facilities, and struggled to attain civil rights.

Asian Americans have faced discrimination at work and in public facilities and have struggled to clarify their different ethnic identities in the eyes of other Americans. The Chinese were recruited for labor in the workforce, and also faced immigration barriers, deportation, and exclusion from American citizenship. Japanese American citizens endured relocation and public hysteria during World War II that violated their civil rights. Southeast Asian refugees have encountered prejudice due to a confusion on the part of other Americans about their role in the Vietnam War.

European Americans have faced discrimination in the workplace and in other arenas on the basis of their ethnic origin and social class.

Latinos have been recruited for low-wage employment and discriminated against in the workplace, faced deportation, and encountered confusion about socioeconomic differences among them.

Native Americans have been displaced, deprived of their land, endured enforced relocation, denied the privileges afforded to them by treaty rights in the U.S. Constitution, and suffered discrimination in the workplace.

## IMPORTANT TERMS

| | |
|---|---|
| Anglo American | Patrones |
| Ethnicity | Peones |
| Ethnicity theory | Anglos |
| Autonomous minorities | Issei |
| Immigrant minorities | Nisei |
| Castes | Misei |
| Refugees | The Chinese Exclusion Act |
| Asylees | Treaty rights |
| The Reservation System | Tribal sovereignty |
| Trail of Tears | |

## QUESTIONS FOR DISCUSSION

1. How might the experiences of diverse groups been different if there had been less emphasis on capital gain and more emphasis on profit sharing within a free market economy in the United States?

2. How might the experiences of diverse groups been different if the United States economy had been based on a different economic system?

3. What are some of the similar experiences that Chinese and Mexican immigrants have encountered?

4. What are some of the similar experiences that African Americans and Asian Americans have encountered?

5. Do you believe that the United States should or should not limit immigration in the future? Why do you believe this?

6. Has your family ever endured personally any of the differential power issues described in this chapter? How do you feel about that?

# NOTES

1. Ethnicity theory is based on White immigrant experience and assumes that groups lose their ethnicity as they become assimilated into mainstream American culture. It also assumes that non-Whites are not successful because they are not able to move beyond their group's frame of reference. The problems with this theory are (a) it overlooks the issues of economic, political, and social power in the control of privileged groups; (b) it assumes equity in the social system; (c) it discounts or ignores discrimination; (d) it disregards the degree to which ethnicity contributes to the identity of some groups, including European Americans.

2. This line is sometimes confused with the Mason-Dixon line, the boundary between Pennsylvania and Maryland.

3. Mexican Americans, whose families have resided in Texas for generations, refer to themselves as Tejanos (Shorris, 1992, p. 37).

4. A Mexican American has told me that "Latino" is commonly used in the upper Midwest.

5. Except for a small tract of land, Texas was already a part of the United States. Texas has its own unique history. Ruled by Spain and then Mexico, it was originally inhabited by Indians and wealthy Spanish ranchers. In 1822, Stephen F. Austin led a few American families into Texas. In 1820 his father had persuaded the Spanish government to give him a large tract of land for American settlers. When his father died, Austin promised the Mexican government, which now ruled Texas, that the settlers would (a) be Roman Catholic; (b) become Mexican citizens; and (c) obey Mexican laws. A land rush resulted, and by 1835 there were 20,000 colonists from the United States in Texas—more than there had been from Spain in three hundred years. Too late, Mexico tried to stop more settlers from entering Texas. In March 1836, the Americans revolted and declared Texas to be an independent nation. Mexico tried to crush the revolt and won two major battles, including the battle of the Alamo. In April 1836, General Sam Houston defeated the Mexican army at San Jacinto, and Texas became an independent nation. It was incorporated into the United States in 1845.

6. The Winnebago were tenacious. Pressured into selling the eastern portion of their Wisconsin lands 1832, some moved to an area in Iowa granted to them as partial payment for their ceded land; some joined the Omaha in Nebraska; some, however, either refused to leave or returned to Wisconsin on their own. In 1881 the government finally made a separate roll of "Wisconsin Winnebago" to delineate them from those in Nebraska.

7. For the Navajo, the issue centered on a reduction in the amount of sheep and other livestock, a stipulation that Collier advocated. For further details, see Takaki, 1993, pp. 238–45.

# REFERENCES

Angelou, Maya. (1987). *All God's children need traveling shoes.* New York: Vintage Books.

Banks, J. A. (1994). *Multiethnic education: Theory and practice.* (3rd edition). Boston: Allyn and Bacon.

Barrera, M. (1984). "Chicano class structure." In R. Takaki (Ed.) (1987), *From different shores: Perspectives on race and ethnicity in America,* New York: Oxford University Press.

Bemak, F., and Timm, J. (1994). "Case study of an adolescent Cambodian refugee: A clinical, developmental and cultural perspective." *International Journal for the Advancement of Counselling 17,* 47-58.

Burns, A. F. (1993). *Maya in exile: Guatemalans in Florida.* Philadephia: Temple University Press.

Fernandez, R., & Chan, A. (May 1989). "Inclusion and exclusion: Dual realities in American education." Paper presented at the Tenth Anniversary Green Bay Colloquium on Ethnicity and Public Policy—University of Wisconsin System Institute on Race and Ethnicity, Green Bay, WI.

Foreman, G. (1972). *Indian removal: The emigration of the five civilized tribes of Indians.* Norman: The University of Oklahoma Press.

Fuchs, L. H. (1990). "The reactions of Black Americans to immigration." In V. Yans-McLaughlin (Ed.), *Immigration reconsidered: History, sociology and politics* (293–314). New York: Oxford University Press.

Garcia, M. T. (1978). "Americanization and the Mexican immigrant." In R. Takaki (Ed.) (1987), *From different shores: Perspectives on race and ethnicity in America.* New York: Oxford University Press.

Johansen, B. E. (1982). *Forgotten founders.* Boston: The Harvard Common Press.

Kahl, J. A. (1968). *The measurement of modernism: A study of values in Brazil and Mexico.* Austin: University of Texas Press.

Kingston, M. H. (1980). *China men.* New York: Ballantine Books.

Lurie, N. O. (1987). *Wisconsin Indians.* Madison, WI: The State Historical Society of Wisconsin.

McInnis-Ditrich, K. (April 1993). "Hmong acculturation vs. assimilation: Why it matters in a multicultural society." Paper presented at the University of Wisconsin Series on Diversity, Oshkosh, WI.

Mirande, A. (1985). *The Chicano experience: An alternative perspective.* Notre Dame, IN: University of Notre Dame Press.

Model, S. W. (1990). "Work and family: Blacks and immigrants from South and East Europe." In V. Yans-McLaughlin (Ed.), *Immigration reconsidered: History, sociology and politics.* New York: Oxford University Press.

Morales, J. (1986). *Puerto Rican poverty and migration.* New York: Praeger.

"New faces: Immigrants to Wisconsin, 1970s to 1990s." (1994). Milwaukee, WI: *The Key* newspaper, Milwaukee Area Technical College.

Novak, M. (1973). "How American are you if your grandparents came from Serbia in 1888?" In S. TeSelle (Ed.), *The rediscovery of ethnicity* (1–20). New York: Harper and Row.

Ogbu, J. U. (1983). "Minority status and schooling in plural societies." *Comparative Education Review* 27 (2), 168–90.

Portes, A. (1990). "From south of the border: Hispanic minorities in the United States." In V. Yans-McLaughlin (Ed.), *Immigration reconsidered: History, sociology, and politics* (pp. 160–84). New York: Oxford University Press.

Rodriguez, C. E. (1979). "Puerto Ricans and the political economy of New York." In R. Takaki (Ed.) (1987), *From different shores: Perspectives on race and ethnicity in America.* New York: Oxford University Press.

Sarason, S., & Davis, J. (1979). *Educational public policy and social history.* New York: The Free Press.

Shorris, Earl. (1992). *Latinos.* New York: W. W. Norton.

Spring, J. (1994). *Deculturalization and the struggle for equality: A brief history of the education of dominated cultures in the United States.* New York: McGraw-Hill.

Stewart, David W. (1993). *Immigration and education: The crisis and the opportunities.* New York: Lexington Books.

Takaki, Ronald. (1989) *Strangers from a different shore.* Boston: Little, Brown and Company.

———. (1993). *A different mirror.* Boston: Little, Brown and Company.

Thomas, D. H., J. Miller, R. White, P. Nabokov, & P. J. Deloria. (1993). *The Native Americans: An illustrated history.* Atlanta: Turner Publishing, Inc.

*Time* (Fall 1993 Special edition). 142 (21), 10–12.

Winston, R., & Winston, C. (Trans.). (1971). *Letters of Thomas Mann.* New York: Alfred A. Knopf.

Zolberg, A. R. (1990). "Reforming the back door: The immigration reform and control act of 1986 in historical perspective." In V. Yans-McLaughlin (Ed.), *Immigration reconsidered: History, sociology and politics* (315–39). New York: Oxford University Press.

# 4

ဢ

# Diversity and American Education

Human history becomes more and more a race
between education and catastrophe.

HERBERT GEORGE WELLS

Public education in America has been shaped by philosophical traditions, political attitudes, and socioeconomic issues. The philosophical traditions are those of our Republican democracy that view education as preparation for citizenship. Political attitudes have involved those issues of power in regard to differential status that were discussed in Chapter 3. A continuing theme in American education has been that of inequities that resulted from the American economic system. On one hand American education has provided the means for social mobility and economic improvement, but on the other hand it has maintained social class, racial, and gender distinctions by channeling students into different programs. This theme will be examined throughout this chapter, which presents an examination of the differential education that children of diverse groups have received—the privileges they enjoyed, the obstacles they faced, and the discrimination they endured. The chapter begins with a historical summary of the foundations of American education. The experiences of African, Asian, European immigrant, Latino, and Native American students will be reviewed in that order. A "hidden curriculum," which continues today along social class lines, will be considered. Issues based on gender that affected the education of American women are examined in Chapter 5.

## AN OVERVIEW
## OF EARLY AMERICAN EDUCATION

In the days of the colonies, education followed the social class-oriented system of England. Education was not considered to be either a personal right or the responsibility of the state. The idea of free schools and universal education, supported by general taxation, was not envisioned by even the most progressive leaders. From the beginning, education reflected social class distinctions among Whites. The terms for the different types of schools may be confusing if the reader is not familiar with the history of American education. There were apprenticeships, dame schools, town schools, grammar schools, and academies. In New England, children of wealthier families received private education. Some attended **dame schools,** where neighborhood children were instructed in reading and writing in the teacher's house. Poorer children attended public **town schools,** as they became established. Poorer boys were often placed in **apprenticeships** to learn a trade, but they were also taught to read and write. Wealthier boys went to **grammar schools,** where they received a classical education as preparation for college. **Academies** developed in the eighteenth century and offered instruction in practical skills (Alexander & Alexander, 1985; Spring, 1994b). (The term "academy" was later used by elite preparatory schools to distinguish themselves from public institutions.)

In 1642 the first education law was enacted in Massachusetts; it required that there be schools in communities with fifty or more families (Beck et al., 1968). Five years later, Massachusetts enacted a law that required communities with fifty households to appoint a teacher for instruction in reading and writing, and further required communities of one hundred families to establish a grammar school. The purpose of this famous act, known as the **Old Deluder Satan Law,** was to ensure that all children should learn to read the scriptures in order to avoid falling prey to Satan's influence, and also to teach the laws of the land (Beck et al., 1968; Spring, 1994b). It is important to point out here that this education grew out of the Protestant religious belief in a direct relationship between individuals and the Deity (Chapter 2). Education was not yet perceived in terms of the responsibilities of citizenship; this idea came later, in conjunction with American independence from England.

Pauper school laws provided that if parents were too poor to pay, their children could be sent to pay schools for a free education. Other school laws were enacted in New Hampshire as early as 1680 and in Connecticut in 1700. Alexander & Alexander (1985) have reported the following:

> It was not until the eighteenth century that a new political philosophy developed that conceived of education as essential to the welfare of the state. Until then, the benefits of education were viewed as largely personal; the external values of education to society had yet to be realized. As the colonies began to struggle for independence from England, the concept of free public education gained momentum. Americans became obsessed with freedom and schools were viewed as the primary means by which freedom could be obtained and maintained. (p. 21)

Gradually the idea of schools based on religious values began to give way to a new concept of education that was uniquely American—that the purpose of education was to provide knowledge in accordance with democratic ideals. This view of education implied three considerations: (a) uniformity of access; (b) a means of pursuing a curriculum; and (c) some institutional organization by which a student could proceed from elementary to higher level instruction. Toward the end of the colonial period, more states enacted laws requiring towns to maintain schools for a period of time each year and imposed taxes for this purpose. These included Georgia in 1783, New York in 1795, and Delaware in 1796 (Alexander & Alexander, 1985). In the South, less attention was paid to the universal education of colonists. For the rich there were some private schools, but many wealthier families hired tutors, especially for their daughters. There were fewer nonprivate schools and apprenticeship possibilities for the poor than in New England (Spring, 1994b; Woody, I, 1966).

Harvard, the first American college, was founded in Cambridge in 1636. A private institution, its purpose was to educate ministers for the colony (Massachusetts). William and Mary followed in 1693 and Yale in 1701. College was not a possibility for most men, however, for financial and social class reasons. Colleges were closed to women until the nineteenth century.

As an alternative to the classically oriented curriculum of the colleges open to more affluent students, Benjamin Franklin had another idea. Born in 1706 in Boston, Ben Franklin had originally attended a grammar school to prepare him to be a minister, but because of family financial problems he was forced to change these plans. He attended another school and became an apprentice to his brother, where he learned printing. He moved to Philadelphia in 1723 and entered the newspaper business (Spring, 1994b). Franklin is known today for his statesmanship and wit ("Keep your eyes wide open before marriage and half fhut [shut] afterwards." *Poor Richard's Almanac,* 1738). He is also known for his idea about education, which was that it should be useful or practical. He established his famous academy in Philadelphia in 1751, thereby expanding the apprenticeship concept to a practically oriented curriculum (Beck et al., 1968). His vision was to be continued a hundred years later in 1862, when the Morrill Act provided land for the establishment of agricultural and technical colleges known as **Land Grant Colleges.** These institutions expanded educational opportunities for those who could not afford the private colleges and universities, and they met the practical needs of the nation as well.

By the end of the American Revolution, a shift in the responsibility for education from home, church, and apprenticeships to the public sphere was well in process. Thomas Jefferson became an advocate for a public educational system. His purpose was that of education for a democracy. His goal was to develop a literate and informed citizenry and, thereby, a literate and informed electorate. Among Jefferson's concerns were (a) equality of educational opportunity (for White students); (b) public support of bright but poor students to the highest level of their ability; (c) assurance of availability of education through the secondary level; (d) the creation of a public university; and (e) teachers who would report students' progress to their parents (Beck et al. 1968). Although his proposal was rejected in Virginia, Jefferson's hopes for such reforms as public scholarships, public high schools, and involvement of parents was ahead of his time.

In the nineteenth century, public education came to be regarded as essential to the responsibilities and duties of citizenship, narrowly defined with the franchise being generally limited to White males who, in many locations, were required to own property. In 1819 the governor of Kentucky called for a free system of schools. Although his plea was ignored, this idea became the basis of so-called **common schools,** or free schools. The democratic ideal of social equality provided further impetus to this concept. Horace Mann was a leader in the **Common School Movement,** which he believed would "do more than all things else to obliterate factitious distinctions in society" (1849; in Stevens & Wood, 1992, p. 136). In other words, he saw universal education as reducing conflict among different factions in America. However, Mann ignored this type of education for African American children.

By 1850, tax-supported, publicly controlled schools were proliferating in most northern and midwestern states. In the South, education of White children remained segregated by social class, with children of wealthier parents attending private schools. In 1851 a landmark court case regarding free public schools upheld the establishment of common schools for students between the ages of five and twenty-one (Commonwealth v. Hartman, Supreme Court of Pennsylvania, 17 Pa. 118). In 1852 Massachusetts enacted the first compulsory attendance law, thus helping to eliminate child labor abuses. In 1874 another landmark case extended free common schools through high school (Stuart v. School District No. 1 of Kalamazoo, Supreme Court of Michigan, 30 Mich. 69). By the end of the nineteenth century, free public schools had been extended through the secondary level, making education accessible—at least theoretically—to all children, including those of immigrants. In practice, however, selection policies based on race and socioeconomic status determined the education of children in America.

## THE IMPACT OF SOCIOECONOMIC STATUS ON EDUCATION

Socioeconomic considerations are entwined with the education of America's children. Although the expressed goals of education have been to prepare students to become responsible and informed citizens, another purpose has been to prepare them to become economically independent adults.

The colonial educational model, deriving from the English system, focused on preparing socioeconomically advantaged White males for higher education and careers in the professions. Those students who could not afford this education followed apprenticeships into skilled trades. In the nineteenth century, with the growth of common schools followed by public high schools, came the question concerning the purpose and relevance of education for larger numbers of students, as more immigrants entered the country. Bluntly put, the question for educators became *What kind of education for what kind of livelihood for what for kind of students?*

Joel Spring (1994a) has identified four critical issues that are related to equity in the education of children in the United States. These issues are access, quality, outcomes, and deculturalization. **Access** refers to whether or not school programs are open to students regardless of their race, ethnicity, gender, social class, handicap, or other factors. According to Fernandez and Chan (1989), whether a minority group is included or excluded from educational programs depends upon the social, economic, and political benefits to the larger society. Spring has interpreted these issues in relation to power (1994b) and viewed segregation in the United States as being "directly related to maintaining an inexpensive source of labor" (1994a, p. 42). **Quality** refers to equal resources and equal programs. Today, quality remains a problem based on the financial resources of schools in different communities. **Outcomes** refer to the result of the educational process across groups. In the view of Fernandez and Chan (1989), the status of true outcomes remains unclear. **Deculturalization** refers to the exclusion of the language and/or culture of minority students from school programs (Spring, 1994a). These four issues have impacted the education of students from all racial groups in the United States.

## AFRICAN AMERICANS

During the colonial period, African Americans were perceived as property, if they were indentured servants or slaves. Their education was usually limited to technical skills that would add to their economic value. Some slave owners did offer minimal literacy, related to teachings of the Bible, but after the American

Revolution, this practice ended for the most part (Fernandez and Chan, 1989). Southerners feared that educating slaves would provide them with "ideas." By the Civil War, approximately 5 percent of slaves were literate, and many of these were taught by other slaves (Spring, 1994a).

In the North, the Puritans were the first to offer an education. In 1750 Quaker schoolmaster Anthony Benezet established a night school for African Americans. A few "Africans" were educated through tutoring. One of these was Phillis Wheatley, a slave purchased in 1761 by "a gentleman of Boston" (Woody, I, 1966, p. 132). In a poem she addressed to students at "the University of Cambridge in New England," her words, "Improve your privileges while they stay" (Solomon, 1985, p. 5), foreshadowed civil rights sentiments two hundred years later. After the American Revolution and in the early nineteenth century, there were no laws excluding free Black children from public schools, but their attendance was low. By mid-century, most Black students were left out of the Common School Movement (Fernandez and Chan, 1989).

Interestingly, in 1798 and again in 1800, Black parents in Boston requested a separate school system for their children. The Boston School Committee rejected both requests on the grounds that if such schools were provided, similar facilities would have to be provided to other groups. In 1806, however, the School Committee did establish a school for Black students. This decision created an ambiguous situation whereby Black children could go to the regular public school or to the one created for them. By the 1820s, some parents reconsidered these segregated schools. A report in 1833 indicated that there were problems with the quality of teachers, quality of education, and physical conditions. The report concluded that segregated education was not a benefit to either race. The Black community increased demands for integrated education. In 1855 the Massachusetts governor signed a law requiring that students could not be refused admission to public schools because of race or religion (Spring, 1994a). The story of Black education in Boston in the first half of the nineteenth century reflects the issues of access and quality of education. The issue of de facto segregation reappeared in Boston a century later, with racially dominated neighborhoods resulting in largely "unbalanced" or segregated schools.

African American girls endured the double prejudice of racism and sexism in their pursuit of an education. White women who supported them were discriminated against as well. In 1831 Quaker Prudence Crandall admitted a Black girl to her teacher's preparatory school in Canterbury, Connecticut. When the community forced her to close her school, Crandall tried to open a teacher's training school for Black girls. She was supported by Abolitionists, but violence in the community forced her to leave town (Solomon, 1985).

White abolitionists opposed to slavery were in favor of education for African Americans. Black women worked for the education of their race. For example, African American Sarah Douglass, an abolitionist, opened a school for Blacks in Philadelphia in the 1820s. In her efforts she became a friend of Sarah Grimke, a *Southern* White abolitionist (Solomon, 1985).

In the South, most states prohibited education for slaves. An act passed by the General Assembly of North Carolina during the session of 1830–1831 is an example. Rothenberg (1995) has provided us with this document:

### An Act to Prevent All Persons from Teaching Slaves to Read or Write, the Use of Figures Excepted

Whereas the teaching of slaves to read and write has a tendency to excite dissatisfaction in their minds, and to produce insurrection and rebellion, to the manifest injury of the citizens of this State:

Therefore,

*Be it enacted by the General Assembly of the State of North Carolina, and it is hereby enacted by the authority of the same,* That any free person, who shall hereafter teach, or attempt to teach, any slave within the State to read or write, the use of figures except[ed], or shall give or sell to such slave or slaves any books or pamphlets, shall be liable to indictment in any court of record in this State having jurisdiction thereof, and upon conviction, shall, at the discretion of the court, if a White man or woman, be fined not less than one hundred dollars, nor more than two hundred dollars, or imprisoned; and if a free person of color, shall be fined, imprisoned, or whipped, at the discretion of the court, not exceeding thirty-nine lashes, nor less than twenty lashes. (p. 310)

The exception for "the use of figures" was based on the fact that some slaves' responsibilities included keeping records, such as the amount of crops produced and sales transactions. It should also be mentioned here that some Southern Whites, such as the Grimke sisters in Charleston, South Carolina, did teach slave children.

During and after the Civil War, former slaves organized schools. The first was Mary Peake, a Black teacher, who founded a school in Fortress Monroe, Virginia, in 1861. In the Zion School in Charleston, South Carolina, both the teachers and administrators were Black in 1866. Among Whites, opinion on Black education was divided. Plantation owners resisted because they wanted Black children as laborers. Others saw education for Blacks as being beneficial to industry. Southerners also supported industrial education for Blacks because it benefited the economy, offered cheap labor, and avoided the threat of labor unions. In the 1870s more Black children were enrolled in schools in the South than White children, but by the 1890s discriminatory laws had become a serious problem (Spring, 1994a).

Higher education for African Americans in the nineteenth century was severely limited. Oberlin College in Ohio led the way. From its establishment in 1833, it was also the first coeducational college in the United States. At Oberlin men and women, both Black and White, were enrolled, although there was gender segregation in some classes.

In the late nineteenth century, the question of relevancy in education became an issue for African Americans as it had for other students. It also became an issue among Black educators themselves. One educator who addressed the problem was Booker T. Washington. Born into slavery in 1856, Washington moved to West Virginia with his family after the Civil War. As a young man, he studied at Hampton Institute in Virginia. This experience affected him profoundly (Franklin, 1990). Best known for his founding of the Tuskegee Institute, Washington advocated vocational training for Blacks on the rationale of relevancy and job opportunities, similar to the views White educators held in regard to the children of poorer families in the North. Washington (in E. D. Washington, 1932) concurred with the idea of usefulness in education:

> If education is of any practical value it should serve to guide us in living, in other words, to fit us for the work around us and demanded by the times in which we live. It should aid us in putting the most into life in the age, country, and into the positions we are to fill. (p. 19)

W. E. B. Du Bois held a different point of view. Born in Great Barrington in western Massachusetts in 1868, Du Bois attended Fisk University. After graduation, he went on to graduate study at Harvard and became its first African American to earn a Ph.D. After traveling in Europe, he returned to the United States to teach the classics at Wilberforce College (Franklin, 1990). It is not surprising that Du Bois disagreed with Washington's focus on practical education. He sought a more liberal arts-oriented curriculum in higher education, whereby Blacks could be educated for potential upward economic, social, and political leadership, and not be limited to merely trained or skilled occupations. He viewed higher education as offering (in Foner, 1970, Vol. 2):

> ... a glimpse of the higher life, the broader possibilities of humanity, which is granted to the man who, amid the rush and roar of living, pauses four short years to learn what living means. (p. 87)

In spite of their different views, however, both Washington and Du Bois based their beliefs on their perceptions of what type of education would best serve the needs of African Americans.

By the end of the nineteenth century, precedence for segregated education for African Americans had been established in both the North and the South. Then, in 1896, the United States Supreme Court rendered a decision upholding segregation in public railway coaches that had a devastating impact on educational policy in America for almost sixty years. This case, Plessy v. Ferguson, is discussed in Chapter 6. It became the legal endorsement for a doctrine known as "separate but equal" for accommodations in public facilities including trains and buses, theaters, restaurants, restrooms, and even water fountains. After the Plessy v. Ferguson decision, segregation in public schools became public policy.

Other schools for African American students were financed by a combination of donations from Black citizens, private foundations, and government support. Julius Rosenwald, President of Sears, Roebuck and Company, established a fund for helping to build these schools with the intention of maintaining higher quality than was available in public segregated schools (Spring, 1994a). The first Rosenwald School was completed in 1914 in Lee County, Alabama, at a cost of $942. Poor local Blacks contributed $282; local White residents gave $360; the Rosenwald fund gave $300 (Anderson, in Spring, 1994a).

In 1954 the U.S. Supreme Court ruled against school segregation on the basis of race in the well-known case of Brown v. Board of Education of Topeka (347

US 483). Although the Brown decision legally ended segregation, enforcement of desegregation was another issue. The Brown decision is discussed in Chapter 6. Ten years after the Brown decision, the U.S. Congress passed the Civil Rights Act of 1964, followed by the Elementary and Secondary Education Act of 1965. Together these laws provided the regulatory mechanisms to enforce desegregation and the funding for compensatory programs for educationally disadvantaged students (Spring, 1994a).

Desegregation was resisted by communities not only in the South, but in the North as well. Ironically, strong resistance occurred in Boston, the city that had sought to protect both access and quality of education for African American children in the first half of the nineteenth century. Busing, a policy aimed at breaking down de facto segregation in racially dominated neighborhoods, resulted in violence by some White citizens in South Boston in the 1970s.

Today, the issue of segregation continues. A study conducted by Professor Gary Orfield, Harvard Project on School Desegregation ("Study finds school segregation increasing," 1994), indicates that public schools are becoming more segregated. In 1986, 63.3 percent of Black students attended schools in which the majority of students were minorities, but in 1991, 66 percent of Black students attended predominantly minority schools. In addition, three important findings appeared in this study: (a) The urban Northeast is the most segregated region in the nation; (b) Black students are "twice as likely" to attend segregated schools in the North than in the South; (c) Segregation by race is linked to poverty. Three-fifths of high-poverty schools in the United States have a majority of Black and Latino students attending them.

Ogbu (1988) has suggested that, historically, the caste system in the United States has been a more serious detriment to education for Blacks than social class discrimination or stratification because Black students know that their chances of access into mainstream jobs are limited. He has also called attention to the fact that "success" is related to the issue of Black *identity*. According to Ogbu, many Black students equate school learning with White culture and believe that in order to succeed they must "act White," which they interpret as working hard, getting good grades, being punctual, and speaking standard English. They fear rejection by their peers. They also may not believe that their efforts will be recognized later.

Interestingly, suggestions for the education of African American children have come full circle since the year 1806 in Boston. In some urban communities, educators have once again sought to establish separate schools from private funds and donations. Jawanza Kunjufu (1982, 1986) has repeated Ogbu's observations and described the dilemma that Black students face as a choice between being "popular or smart." (This may be a dilemma for other students, as well.) Kunjufu has advocated special academies for Black boys, whom he has described as being at the greatest risk in American education. In his view, such schools offer spiritual values, establish habits of self-discipline, and provide strong and positive adult male role models. These academies have been supported by some African Americans who perceive positive benefits in their programs, while others view them as being discriminatory against girls.

The majority of Black students attending nonpublic schools have been enrolled in Roman Catholic parochial institutions, which have been more effective in educating low-income Black students than the public schools (Greely, 1982). A few attend elite private preparatory schools, but access is curtailed by their family's economic resources or availability of financial scholarships, if they are needed.

A recent issue in Black education has been the development of an **Afrocentric** curriculum at the elementary, secondary, and college levels. Molefi Kete Asante has articulated the case for Afrocentric studies. Based on the work of Carter G. Woodson (1933), who viewed a traditional curriculum based on European culture as educating African Americans away from their own history, Asante has described African Americans as "marginalized" in American education and has seen a need for a new approach. In his view, education is a "social phenomenon whose ultimate purpose is to socialize the learner," and he claims that a White "supremicist-dominated society will develop a White supremacist educational system" (1991, p. 170). Asante (1991) has also asserted that:

> ... centricity refers to a perspective that involves locating students within the context of their own cultural references so that they can relate socially and psychologically to other cultural perspectives.... Afrocentricity is a frame of reference wherein phenomenon [sic] are viewed from the perspective of the African [American] person. (p. 171)

In Asante's view, different areas of curricular content may be adapted to an Afrocentric approach. Asante does not view an Afrocentric approach to education as being divisive for American society. Rather, he has described it as being beneficial for all Americans because Black children will not be "dislocated" and that White students may come to understand that their heritage is not threatened by the contributions of African Americans. Asante (1991) has also stated that:

> [i]f the curriculum were enhanced to include readings from the slave narratives; the diaries of slave ship captains; the journals of slave owners; the abolitionist papers; the writings of freedmen and freedwomen; the accounts of African American civil rights, civic, and social organizations; and numerous others, African American children would be different, White children would be different—indeed, America would be a different nation today. (p. 176)

In 1990 James Comer, an African American professor at Yale University, acknowledged a need for an educational approach that recognizes "the socioeconomically disadvantaged condition of Black children and the failure of educational institutions to respond appropriately and humanistically to the needs created by these conditions" (Comer & Haynes, 1990, p. 103). With these words, Comer concurs with both Kunjufu and Asante that Black children in American schools need to have their cultural heritage and their socioeconomic situation recognized and addressed by educators. The nation can only benefit from this approach.

## ASIAN AMERICANS

### Chinese Americans

Asian students have a reputation for being "model students," but they have not always been welcome in American schools. Early Chinese immigrants were, for the most part, men who initially planned to work in the U.S. for a few years and then return to China. By 1853, several church groups, including Presbyterians, Baptists, Methodists, Episcopalians, and Congregationalists, had opened mission- ary schools to offer some English language instruction to the Chinese. By 1876, some 5,500 California Chinese were enrolled in these classes (Fernandez and Chan, 1989).

In 1860 the California state superintendent recommended to the legislature that "Negroes, Mongolians, and Indians" be prohibited from attending public schools. In 1866 a state law provided for the establishment of separate schools (Cal. Stat. 1865–66, p. 398). By the 1870s, some Chinese language schools in San Francisco were operated by Chinese teachers. In 1877 there were approxi- mately 3,000 Chinese children who were denied a public education. In 1884 the Chinese Six Companies founded Chinese language schools whose curricu- lum also included Chinese culture and values (Fernandez and Chan, 1989).

The Chinese Exclusion Act of 1882 ended Chinese immigration to the United States, but the education of Chinese children continued. In 1884 Joseph and Mary Tape, immigrants who had been living in the U.S. for fifteen years, sought admission to the San Francisco public schools for their eight- year-old daughter. The principal denied their request, but a municipal court supported the Tape's petition and admitted the child on the grounds that she was an American citizen (born in the United States) and thus subject to equal protection under the Fourteenthth Amendment (Tape v. Hurley, 66 Cal 473, 1885). The state supreme court upheld the lower court's decision, but the Cal- ifornia assembly subsequently passed legislation to establish separate facilities for "Mongolians." Ironically, in spite of the judicial decisions supporting the Tape child's admission to public school, she was forced to attend the new Chi- nese school after all. The Tape case raises the issue of access for Asians in Amer- ican education. Here the California legislature effectively undercut two judicial decisions.

Other California schools followed San Francisco's example by establishing separate schools for Chinese students. Uneven segregation policies continued until World War II, when pro-Chinese nationalist sentiment affected American public opinion and educational policy. The repeal of the Chinese Exclusion Act in 1943 was a major outcome of national support for the Chinese. In 1974 the U.S. Supreme Court unanimously upheld another case involving Chinese stu- dents in San Francisco public schools. This case is discussed in relation to lan- guage issues in Chapter 6 (Lau v. Nichols, 414 US 563, 1974).

## Japanese Americans

The Japanese immigrants, arriving in Hawaii and on the West Coast of the United States in the second half of the nineteenth century, were better educated than the Chinese. In fact they were probably, as a whole, better educated than most immigrant groups. Ninety percent were literate in their native language. On the mainland their presence was viewed by some as competition for jobs, but not in Hawaii, where they were seen as an essential source of labor.

Japanese language schools were established in Honolulu in the 1890s and in California by World War I. These schools aimed at helping Japanese immigrants in assimilating into American society (Bell, 1935). The Japanese, like the Chinese, were affected by the bias in California against "Negroes, Mongolians, and Indians." In 1906 the San Francisco Board of Education established a separate school for Chinese, Japanese, and Korean children. Japanese parents then boycotted the school and tried to arouse public sympathy in Japan, where editorials appeared in Tokyo newspapers declaring that this segregation was an insult to the Japanese nation. The incident resulted in the U.S. Ambassador to Japan warning the American government of a developing international situation. Finally, President Theodore Roosevelt threatened to intervene. Segregation, however, did not end in other areas of public life for Japanese Americans (Spring, 1994a).

In 1924 Congress passed the National Origins Act, stopping all Asian immigration to the United States. During World War II, Japanese American residents on the West Coast were relocated in internment camps (Chapter 3), and the education of Japanese American children came under a federal agency.

More recent problems in the education of both Chinese and Japanese American students have resulted, ironically, from their generally high academic achievement. In the 1970s and 1980s, as more students sought admission to college, hidden quota admission policies came into effect. There is a stereotype of the Asian student as being the "model" student, which results in a "halo effect" in the classroom. While many do excel, the stereotype leads to an increased expectation on the part of teachers working with Asian students. As a result, teachers may overlook the needs of Asian students who do not meet the model or whose needs present new challenges, such as the recent Southeast Asian immigrant children.

## Recent Asian Immigrants

The war in Southeast Asia in the 1960s and 1970s resulted in the dislocation and relocation of thousands of refugees from Vietnam, Laos, Cambodia, and Thailand. These refugees, however, are more similar in some ways to former European immigrants for three reasons: (a) many (but not all) of them were poor; (b) many had little or no formal education in their own country; and (c) they do not share a common language like immigrants from Latin America, but speak different national languages. As a result, there is a significant lack of teachers who are prepared to work with these students. In my research with the Laotian Hmong in the United States, I heard countless stories of Hmong children with little knowledge of English being placed in classrooms with teachers who had no knowledge of Hmong. Many teachers assume that if a younger Southeast Asian child was born in the United States, he or she is familiar with English, but this is not a valid assumption because native languages are spoken at home. Furthermore, only a few children attend early childhood education programs. Many of them enter public schools with limited English skills (Timm, 1994). As they become more familiar with mainstream American culture, these students are undergoing a deculturalization process, with the result that they are now trying to live simultaneously in two cultural worlds.

## EUROPEAN MINORITIES

European immigrants are often overlooked in discussions of diverse groups, but many of their children faced the same educational problems as the children of minorities. The educational policies that affected their lives have reverberated throughout American education.

The fact is well known that large numbers of immigrants began arriving in the United States in the mid-nineteenth century. What is not so well known is the fact that between 1890 and 1920, immigrants made up between half and three-quarters of the population of cities like New York, Boston, Chicago, Cleveland, Milwaukee, St. Louis, and San Francisco (Fass, 1989). Many of these immigrants, with the exception of the Irish, were from eastern Europe, Poland, Russia, and Italy. They were different from the earlier English, Germans, and Scandinavians because they were less educated, less literate, and less skilled for the labor market. Their presence added a new challenge for American schools. Educators saw a need for socializing these children into American culture. A philosophy of **assimilation** was aimed at (a) providing to White males the skills necessary to be responsible voting citizens; (b) "Americanizing" the children into mainstream culture; (c) teaching English; and (d) inculcating the moral values of the Protestant work ethic. The shift for these students to English and American values constituted a loss of their European cultural heritage.

Socioeconomic status had a critical effect on the lives of these immigrant children and on other poor children as well. With the advent of the industrial age, many of them had worked in factories at menial tasks. By the 1870s, the enactment of child labor and truancy laws resulted in keeping children in school longer. While appearing to be concerned with their general welfare, these laws also had an economic purpose. If children were kept in school longer, more jobs would be available for adult workers. Most poorer immigrant children, however, dropped out of school by age fourteen (Fass, 1989). The task of making the education they did receive relevant to their lives was a challenge to educators. According to Fass (1989),

> if schools remained strictly academic and didactic, the children of immigrants would be denied schooling that made sense to their lives. Their all-too-brief exposure would provide nothing more than rudimentary literacy.... But, if the schools were to attend to the specific needs and probable goals of their students, how could these be judged without pre-defining their futures by an over-scrupulous adjustment to the present?... Schools could no longer ignore the populations they served. They had become more public than common...(p. 33)

Thus, at the same time that these immigrant students were being "assimilated" into American society, they were also perceived as being socially "different" from the children of more prosperous parents. Therefore, educators, while providing for these children's "needs," also decided their future place in the American social class structure.

The impact of socioeconomic status on the type of education that students received cannot be overestimated. It affected students' access to different types of educational programs, determined the quality of the education they received, and resulted in very different outcomes in terms of jobs available to them. Educators saw students in terms of the kind of occupations they would probably enter and planned courses according to different sets of standards in relation to their perceptions of students' needs. Furthermore, this selection process was regarded as appropriate for *all minorities, including women.* Thus, education based on socioeconomic considerations pertained to all students, but castes also encountered policies based on their race. Debates about the relevancy of education to students' lives continued into the twentieth century. Today, vocational and technical schools offer alternatives to four-year colleges.

# LATINO AMERICANS[1]

## Mexican Americans

After the Mexican War, and the incorporation of nearly half of Mexican land into the United States, Mexicans in the Southwest came under U.S. educational jurisdiction. The first concern of American educators was that of language. In 1854 the Texas legislature established public schools, and two years later passed a law requiring the teaching of English. In 1870 the legislature passed another law requiring English to be the language of instruction. In some communities, however, this requirement was not practiced. For example, in Brownsville, the first public school was opened in 1875 and because most of the students were Mexican who did not understand English, the rule for instruction in English was not enforced before the fourth grade (San Miguel, 1987). Attempts were also made to eliminate Spanish in California, where a mandate in 1855 required that instruction should be in English. There was an anti-Mexican bias among many school officials, which many Mexican Americans avoided by sending their children to Roman Catholic or other private Mexican schools; these schools aimed at maintaining the Spanish language, as well as Mexican culture and values (Spring, 1994a).

Early in the twentieth century, Mexican immigration increased dramatically. Data for Mexican immigration should be viewed cautiously, however, because there was a pattern of travel back and forth across the U.S.-Mexican border. This immigration was not only welcomed, but workers were actually recruited by farmers and industry as a source of cheap labor. (During World War II, Mexican immigrants were again welcomed into the United States as a means of alleviating the wartime labor shortage.)

There were basically three views regarding the education of Mexican immigrant children. First, White Americans did not agree among themselves about their education, but it is not surprising that farmers were opposed to the children attending school because it meant that they could not work as cheap labor. These farmers were more concerned with their personal economic advantage than they were about students' access to education. Educators, on the other hand, believed that education was important in order to assimilate these children into American culture and values. Compulsory attendance laws were not always enforced, which in the view of some educators deprived these children of the opportunity to advance in American society (San Miguel, 1987). A third view was that of Mexican parents, who were hesitant about sending their children to Anglo schools because (a) in some cases they needed the income from their children's wages, and (b) they feared the loss of their culture and language (Montejano, 1987).

The old question of what kind of education was "appropriate" to meet the socioeconomic needs of these children was a hidden agenda. The same issues that had been raised in regard to European minorities and African Americans after the Civil War were involved here. Were these children to be better served with a focus on literacy and training programs? What were the realistic expectations for their future? Could they hope to continue in academic programs leading to higher status occupations? Schooling for Mexican American students became focused on training skills, English literacy, health, and so-called American values (Carter and Segura, 1979).

Mexican Americans began to speak out. In 1929 a group of citizens formed the League of United Latin American Citizens (LULAC), which sought to integrate and respect both U.S. and Mexican culture and heritage. LULAC favored bilingual and bicultural education and fought against discrimination practices aimed at Mexican Americans. In the courts it challenged segregation and biased curricular materials (Garcia, 1989). By the time of the Civil Rights Movement, more organizations began to appear. The Mexican American Youth Organization (MAYO) was founded in 1967, and the Mexican American Legal Defense and Education Fund (MALDEF) followed in 1968. In the 1970s and 1980s, Mexican Americans sought programs that reflected pride in their heritage (Fernandez and Chan, 1989).

An important issue regarding Mexican American education was whether or not the children of undocumented workers (who have entered the country illegally) are entitled to education in the United States. In 1982 the U.S. Supreme Court determined that these children do in fact have the right to attend public school (Plyler v. Doe, 457 US 202). This case is discussed more fully in Chapter 6.

## Puerto Rican Americans

Events leading to the incorporation of Puerto Rico by the United States were reviewed in Chapter 3. The American occupation of Puerto Rico resulted in the development of a free public educational system there. The University of Puerto Rico was founded in 1903 (Fernandez and Chan, 1989). Previously, education had been primarily private and limited to children of upper-class families. The first U.S. Commissioner of Education was Martin Brumbaugh (1900–1901), whose policies set teachers' credentials and salaries along with a prescribed curriculum. American teachers were preferred, which meant that English-speaking teachers were sent to Puerto Rico to instruct Spanish-speaking children! The American educational policy in Puerto Rico focused on the learning of English, celebrating U.S. holidays, and conducting patriotic exercises.

It was not a simple matter to convert entire instructional programs to a different language literally overnight. Because the instruction offered in English was resisted by Puerto Ricans, modifications were made whereby Spanish was also spoken. Finally, a third approach was adopted, whereby Spanish was the language of instruction in elementary school but English continued to be taught, starting in the upper grades. Language, however, continued to cause friction. A Puerto Rican was not appointed as Commissioner of Education until 1921, when Juan B. Huyke took the post. Ironically, he strongly supported Americanization programs and resisted Spanish as the language of instruction. He banned school newspapers written in Spanish, required English to be spoken at teachers' meetings, and required students to pass an oral English exam as a graduation requirement from high school (de Montilla, 1971). Teachers began protesting the lack of information about Puerto Rico in the curriculum. Other protests led to the Padin Reform of 1934, which limited instruction in English to high school. In the 1930s, President Franklin Roosevelt urged a bilingual policy in Puerto Rico. In 1951 Puerto Ricans voted for Commonwealth status, which gave them more authority over their schools (Walsh, 1991).

Puerto Rican migration to the U.S. mainland was discussed in Chapter 3. As with other minorities, the educational opportunities of their children were affected by problems of access, quality, and outcomes in relation to their social class. Puerto Ricans have also encountered discrimination as perceived members of a caste.

## NATIVE AMERICANS

Early colonists from Europe looked with favor on educating the so-called Indians (a European designation) in order to bring Christianity to them. In 1636 the Plymouth Colony passed laws providing for teaching the Gospel. The colonists, however, were hungry for land and viewed the Indians as "a barrier to be removed" (Fernandez and Chan, 1989, p. 4). Ironically, the Pilgrims probably would not have survived their first winter if the nearby Native Americans had not helped them.

The education of Native Americans was a matter of military strategy during the American Revolution, when the Continental Congress gave $500 to Dartmouth College for the education of Indian youth. This measure was designed to conciliate Northeastern tribes in an attempt to prevent their attacks upon outlying settlements in New Hampshire (Weinberg, 1977). The military alliances among the French, English, American colonists, and the Indians interfered with the missionary efforts at education.

After the American Revolution, George Washington and other statesmen were concerned about the future of Native Americans. Spring (1994a) has described Washington's position as follows:

> Part of Washington's concern, and the concern of many other American leaders prior to the Civil War, was that the advance of European civilization in the United States was destroying most of the Native American population … this concern did not reflect a desire to limit the expansion of the European population but it did reflect a concern about protecting Native Americans from what were considered the worst aspects of European civilization—gambling, alcohol … and depraved sexual activities. (p. 5)

From the vantage point of the 1990s, this point of view seems more than a little paternalistic. Thus, federal policies in the nineteenth century supported missionary and manual labor schools in an attempt to protect Indians by making them Christians and farmers. In 1810 the American Board of Commissioners for Foreign Missionaries was founded to provide missionary teachers to Native Americans. In 1819 the Civilization Fund Act provided financial support for religious schools among the Indians. Interestingly, the Choctaws, Cherokees, and other southeastern tribes were in favor of these missionary schools, for they viewed them as a means of learning how to deal with both Whites and the federal government (Spring, 1994a).

Chapter 3 reviewed the events surrounding the treachery and treaties resulting in the relocation of the southeastern tribes to reservations in Indian Territory, now Oklahoma. These tribes, known as the Five Civilized Tribes, included the Choctaws, Cherokees, Seminoles, Creeks, and Chickasaws. After their relocation to the Southwest, the Choctaws thrived with their own government, economy, and schools. Choctaw schools aimed at teaching manual labor skills and instilling moral (Christian) values. The Choctaw educational system also recognized and rewarded merit by sending the best students to academies and the best academy graduates east to college (Spring, 1994a). The Cherokees also developed a school system and opened academies in 1851 that accepted both males and females. Thus, the Cherokee Nation developed an excellent school system of its own (Reyhner & Eder, 1989). Not all tribes fared so well.

During the Civil War, schools were closed throughout Indian territory because the federal government withheld funds. Following the Civil War until the 1920s, Indian education was under the control of federal officials (Weinberg, 1977). As the reservation system grew, a philosophy developed that advocated minimum contact between Indians and Whites. (In the preceding section on Asian American education, I mentioned the fact that California passed a law in 1866 that excluded "African, Mongolian, and Indian" children from White schools.) Manual labor schools were opened that focused on preparing students for agricultural vocations and various trades, as well as providing the basics in reading and writing English, and math. Teaching allegiance to the U.S. government became a major federal policy toward Native American children. An important part of their education was the **Indian Boarding School** concept, which removed children from their families and isolated them from the language, culture, and customs of their tribes (Spring, 1994a).

Off-reservation boarding schools began in 1879 with the founding of the Carlisle Indian School in Carlisle, Pennsylvania. Others followed. Students were punished if they spoke their native languages. Ironically, an interesting result of the common instruction in English was that the students in these boarding schools began to develop a cross-tribal identity that spawned a new Indian cohesiveness in the twentieth century (Lurie, 1987).

In the early twentieth century, more Indian students began attending public schools. In the 1920s, Native Americans began to speak out for different educational practices. In 1928 the Meriam Report recommended reform in both Indian administration and education. This report was based on an investigation at Johns Hopkins University that had been requested by the U.S. Secretary of the Interior, Hubert Work, and is known by the name of the principal investigator, Louis Meriam. The report criticized the early policies of the boarding schools, called for community day schools that did not separate Indian children from their families, and supported Native American cultures (The Meriam Report, in Meriam, 1928). American education now turned to repairing the damage that former federal policies had done.

In 1968 the enactment by Congress of Title VII of the Elementary and Secondary Education Act gave new support to bilingual education programs. The Indian Education Act of 1972 aimed at involving parents and tribes in the education of Indian children. In 1975 the Indian Self Determination and Educational Assistance Act gave authority to the tribes to contract with the Federal Bureau of Indian Affairs (BIA) to "administer part or all of any Indian program conducted by the Department of the Interior" (Fernandez and Chan, 1989, p. 41). These programs included health and education. Finally, the Native American Languages Act of 1990 aimed at preserving and practicing Native languages. In the 1990s, concerns in Indian education involve those students who are "at risk" for a variety of reasons, including limited financial resources.

The perspective that emerges from a review of Native American education is the similarity of four educational experiences that they have shared with other racial groups. These experiences are (a) problems of caste similar to those encountered by African and Latino Americans; (b) attempts at deculturalization shared by Asian, some European, and Latino Americans; (c) decisions on the part of educators in regard to the "relevancy" of their education on the basis of socioeconomic factors; and (d) problems of access, quality, and outcomes shared by all other groups.

## SOCIOECONOMIC STATUS
## AND THE HIDDEN CURRICULUM

Following American independence from England, public schools were intended to prepare citizens for their place in in the Republic and to provide them with the knowledge necessary to become self-supporting adults. The concept of tracking students in public schools into educational programs according to the "relevancy" of their lives came about in the nineteenth century, but it actually served the purpose of allocating human resources into a market economy. In the early twentieth century, a not-so-hidden curriculum appeared with a more business-oriented approach. According to Stevens and Wood (1992),

> The ability of an individual to succeed in society was enhanced by an education that stressed punctuality, the ability to follow orders…and an adaptation to a hierarchical, routinized, and standardized social system. Children were indoctrinated into such a system by the organization of the school itself, which came to mirror the industrial model. (p. 119)

Anyon has reported a **hidden curriculum** in American schools, based on the social class that the schools serve, which reflects this industrial model to a frightening degree. In Anyon's view, social class refers to the relationships between the capitalists, or those in positions of ownership of production (which obviously includes the stockholders of large corporations), and the workers who make it possible for the owners to gain profits. (There are, of course, professionals such as lawyers, physicians, clergy, and teachers who are neither directly involved in capital production nor in decision-making positions of controlling the nation's economy.) In an important and disturbing observational study, Anyon (1980) found four types of classrooms in four different types of schools whose student populations varied along social class lines. It is important to point out here that Anyon observed fifth-grade classrooms in all schools, thus controlling for age of students. The findings indicate that the old philosophy of preparing students for a future considered appropriate to their social class prospects continues in America.

### The Working-Class School

In the working-class school, the emphasis was on students' following directions. In the classroom, the teacher usually did not explain why the work was assigned or its purpose. The teacher often used worksheets. In math the focus was on using the right procedure, with little or no attempt by the teacher to relate the procedures to thinking processes. Language arts did not include creative writing but involved worksheets requiring short answers. Experiments were not used in science. Instead, the teacher lectured about the book! Work was mechanical, and orders were continuously given to the students. The focus was on conformity—on not "stepping out of line," both literally and figuratively speaking. Students' originality and reasoning skills were not valued. Clearly, this type of instruction prepares students for jobs involving routines and rote work.

### The Middle-Class School

In the middle-class school, the emphasis was on students getting the right answers. In the classroom, there was a focus on achieving good grades. Learning involved memorizing. Some attention was given to understanding procedures, as in math, for example. In social studies there was also a focus on students' understanding of the reading assignments. Language arts involved lessons in grammar. The teacher expressed a belief that the students would need to be able to write and speak properly in their future occupations. Lessons were based on the text, with little analysis of the relationships among ideas. Most assignments were not related to students' interests. Creative thinking was not involved. Clearly, this type of instruction prepares students for focusing on achieving a scholastic record of good grades required for college entrance and on getting the correct answers— a mindset to do well in a job later.

## The Affluent Professional School

In the affluent professional school, the emphasis was on students being able to express themselves and to apply the ideas they had learned. In the classroom, originality was valued. Math involved problems applied to everyday situations. In social studies, students wrote and acted in a play about an ancient culture. Social studies also involved current events. Creative writing was part of the language arts program. Science included hands-on experience. Whether or not students arrived at the right answers was not so important as their reasons. Negotiation between the teacher and students was used, rather than a focus on following rules. Clearly, this type of instruction prepares students for future careers in which they will need to be able to make their own decisions, to know the reasons for them, and to be responsible for them.

I am reminded here of an experience I had while teaching in a middle-class suburban school. When I negotiated with the students about their being able to talk with each other during lunchtime in the cafeteria, I was informed by other teachers that no one else in the school allowed the students to talk during lunch. When the students did not abuse the privilege, both the teachers and the principal expressed surprise.

## The Executive Elite School

In the executive elite school, the emphasis was on developing students' analytic skills and creative thinking. In the classroom, the focus was not on whether an answer was right or wrong but on *whether or not students agreed with an answer.* In math, the teacher asked if any student could *create* a formula for area. Word problems were common in math. Social studies involved independent projects and a critical analysis of history. Language arts focused on the interrelationships among parts of speech. Assignments included research reports and essays. There were very few rules. Students were in charge of their own behavior. Clearly, this type of instruction prepares students for positions that require a high level of self-confidence, which is necessary in positions of social, political, and economic leadership.

My college students report that they remember many of the procedures described in this review in their own educational experiences. They talk openly about still being afraid of saying the "wrong" answer in class. They report that many of their classes in school focused on memorizing information rather than on analyzing and interpreting it. Many express frustration over not having been allowed to explain their ideas or to offer suggestions.

## AMERICAN EDUCATION AND THE FUTURE

John Gatto, the New York State Teacher of the Year in 1991, has written a provocative critique of American public education. In *Dumbing Us Down: The Hidden Curriculum of Compulsory Schooling,* Gatto agrees that schools teach the lesson that "everyone has a proper place in the pyramid" (1992, p. 5). In Gatto's view, schools also have a hidden curriculum of developing emotional and intellectual dependency: "Individuality is a contradiction of class theory" (1992, p. 7). The implication here is that if individuality is respected, what becomes of the social class order? It is Gatto's contention that "schools are intended to produce…formulaic human beings whose behavior can be predicted and controlled" (1992, p. 26).

The issue of relevancy in American education extends far beyond the future career goals of our students. The question of relevancy applies to all diverse groups in the United States and to the nation as a whole. What kind of a society do we want our educational system to produce? Are our schools educating students for meaningful participation in public affairs and for mutual respect of diverse points of view? Teaching that there is one procedure or one right answer is devastating to the development of open-mindedness toward different ideas.

As we near the end of the twentieth century and look forward to a future in which the nation will be more diverse than ever before, we need to address the issue of waste—not only of our natural resources but also of our human potential. The past practice of allocating students on the basis of their social class, racial, or ethnic group into predetermined tracks is painful to consider. Surely we can do better. As John Gatto has stated, "We need to invent curricula where each kid has a chance to develop private uniqueness" (1992, p. 34).

I concur, with the hope that our students may have the opportunity to do so while at the same time recognizing the uniqueness of their own group and embracing that of other groups as well. We would all be richer for it.

## CHAPTER SUMMARY

American education began with social class distinctions in its preparation of students for their future work. Schools included dame schools, town schools, grammar schools, and, later, academies. Apprenticeships trained boys for various trades.

The education of African Americans varied by region. In the North, Black students attended public schools and some private schools. In the South, education was denied to slaves. After Emancipation, Black education faced choices about the relevancy of programs to students' future employment opportunities. A U.S. Supreme Court decision in 1896, Plessy v. Ferguson, resulted in segregated education in public schools until another decision in 1954, Brown v. The Board of Education of Topeka, rendered segregation on the basis of race illegal. Problems in segregation have continued, however. Currently an Afrocentric curriculum has been advocated by some Black educators as a means of providing pride in Black heritage.

Asian American students have encountered segregation from public schools. They have also gained the reputation of being model students due to the high academic achievement of many students. There is a danger of overgeneralizing this view to include students who may have special needs.

European immigrant children have encountered the issue of the relevancy of their education in regard to their future employment. Education has also aimed at assimilating immigrant children into American society. Discriminatory practices involving White European groups have been based on social class and students' ethnicity.

Latino students have encountered programs to assimilate them, including the learning of English. Mexican Americans who could afford it have chosen private Roman Catholic or Mexican schools as an alternative to public education. Puerto Rican Americans have encountered discrimination as a group.

Following enforced relocation from the East to Indian Territory, some Native American tribes established successful schools of their own, but these were subsequently closed under the federal policy of assimilating Native Americans into White society. Indian Boarding Schools, controlled by U.S. government agencies, removed students from their families and their tribes. In the twentieth century, reforms have resulted from Indian efforts.

Schools serving different social classes employ different hidden agendas in classroom procedures.

All groups have encountered three major issues—access, quality, and outcomes of their education—based on their racial or ethnic group, or socioeconomic status, or both.

## IMPORTANT TERMS

| | |
|---|---|
| Old Deluder Satan Law | Access |
| Land Grant Colleges | Quality of Education |
| Apprenticeship | Outcomes |
| Dame schools | Deculturalization |
| Town schools | Assimilation |
| Grammar schools | Afrocentric curriculum |
| Academies | Indian Boarding Schools |
| Common School Movement | Hidden curriculum |

## QUESTIONS FOR DISCUSSION

1. How did the earliest schools in the colonies set the pattern for later school programs?

2. What educational experiences did Asian, Latino, and Native American students share?

3. How were the educational experiences of Asian, Latino, and Native American students different?

4. What educational experiences did European immigrant children share with Asian and Latino students?

5. How did Booker T. Washington and W. E. B. Du Bois differ in their views about what type of education would best serve Black students' needs?

6. How did all groups encounter issues of access, quality, and outcomes?

# NOTES

1. Cuban American education is discussed in Chapter 13 in reference to bilingual education.

# REFERENCES

Alexander, K., & Alexander, M. D. (1985). *American public school law* (2nd ed.). St. Paul: West.

Anderson, G. (1988). *The education of Blacks in the South, 1860–1935.* Chapel Hill: University of North Carolina Press.

Anyon, J. (1980). "Social class and the hidden curriculum of work." *Journal of Education* 162 (1), 67–92.

Asante, M. K. (1991). "The Afrocentric idea in education." *Journal of Negro education* 60 (2), 170–80.

Beck, C. E., Bernier, N. R., MacDonald, J. B., Walton, T. W., & Willers, J. C. (1968). *Education for relevance.* Boston: Houghton Mifflin.

Bell, R. (1935). *Public school education of second generation Japanese in California.* Stanford, CA: Stanford University Press.

Carter, T. P., & Segura, R. D. (1979). *Mexican Americans in school: A decade of change.* Princeton, NJ: College Entrance Examination Board.

Comer, J., & Haynes, N. (1990). "Helping black children succeed: The significance of some social factors." In K. Lomotey (Ed.), *Going to school: The African-American experience.* Albany, NY: State University of New York Press.

de Montilla, A. N. (1975). *Americanization in Puerto Rico and the public school system from 1900 to 1930.* Rio Piedras, Puerto Rico: Editorial Universitaria.

Du Bois, W. E. B. (1970). In P. Foner (Ed.), *W. E. B. Du Bois speaks 1890–1919* (2 vol.). New York: Pathfinder Press.

Fass, P. S. (1989). *Outside in: Minorities and the transformation of American education.* New York: Oxford University Press.

Fernandez, R., & Chan, A. (May 1989). "Inclusion and exclusion: Dual realities in American education." Paper presented at the Tenth Anniversary Green Bay Colloquium on Ethnicity and Public Policy—University of Wisconsin System Institute on Race and Ethnicity, Green Bay, WI.

Foreman, G. (1972). *Indian removal: The emigration of the five civilized tribes of Indians.* Norman, OK: The University of Oklahoma Press.

Franklin, R. M. (1990). *Liberating visions: Human fulfillment and social justice in African-American thought.* Minneapolis, MN: Fortress Press.

Garcia, M. T. (1989). *Mexican Americans: Leadership, ideology, and identity.* New Haven: Yale University Press.

Gatto, J. T. (1992). *Dumbing us down: The hidden curriculum of compulsory schooling.* Philadelphia: New Society.

Greely, A. M. (1982). *Catholic high schools and minority students.* New Brunswick, NJ: Transaction Books.

Kunjufu, J. (1982). *Countering the conspiracy to destroy Black boys.* Chicago, IL: African American Images.

———. (1986). *Countering the conspiracy to destroy Black boys* (Vol. II). Chicago, IL: African American Images.

———. (no date). *Countering the conspiracy to destroy Black boys* (Vol. III). Chicago, IL: African American Images.

Lurie, N. O. (1987). *Wisconsin Indians.* Madison, WI: The State Historical Society of Wisconsin.

Mann, H. (1849). "Intellectual education as a means of removing poverty and securing abundance." In E. Stevens, Jr. & G. Wood (Eds.), (1992), *Justice, ideology, and education: An introduction to the social foundations of education* (2nd ed.), 133–36. New York: McGraw-Hill.

Meriam, L. (1928). *The problem of Indian administration.* Baltimore: Johns Hopkins Press.

Mirande, A. (1985). *The Chicano experience: An alternative perspective.* Notre Dame, IN: University of Notre Dame Press.

Montejano, D. (1987). *Anglos and Mexicans in the making of Texas, 1836–1986.* Austin: University of Texas Press.

Morales, J. (1986). *Puerto Rican poverty and migration.* New York: Praeger.

Ogbu, J. U. (1988). "Class stratification, racial stratification, and schooling." In L. Weis (Ed.), *Class, race, and gender in American education.* Albany, NY: State University of New York Press.

Reyhner, J., & Eder, J. (1989). *A history of Indian education.* Billings, MT: Eastern Montana College.

Rothenberg, P. S. (1995). *Race, class, and gender in the United States: An integrated study* (3rd ed.). New York: St. Martin's Press.

San Miguel, G., Jr. (1987). *Let all of them take heed: Mexican Americans and the campaign for educational equality in Texas, 1910–1981.* Austin: University of Texas Press.

Solomon, B. M. (1985). *In the company of educated women: A history of women and higher education in America.* New Haven: Yale University Press.

Spring, J. (1994a). *Deculturalization and the struggle for equality: A brief history of the education of dominated cultures in the United States.* New York: McGraw-Hill.

———. (1994b). *The American school: 1642–1993* (3rd ed.). New York: McGraw-Hill.

Stevens, E. Jr., & Wood, G. H. (Eds.). (1992). *Justice, ideology, and education: An introduction to the social foundations of education* (2nd ed.). New York: McGraw-Hill.

"Study finds school segregation increasing." (February/March 1994). *Education Alumni Bulletin,* Harvard Graduate School of Education 38 (2), 1, 6.

Timm, J. T. (1994). "Hmong values and American education." *Equity and Excellence in Education* 27 (2), 36–44.

Walsh, C. (1991). *Pedagogy and the struggle for voice: Issues of language, power, and schooling for Puerto Ricans.* New York: Bergin & Garvery.

Warren Button, H., & Provenzo, E.. (1989). *History of education and culture in America.* Englewood Cliffs, NJ: Prentice Hall.

Washington, B. T. (1932). In E. D. Washington (Ed.), *Selected speeches of Booker T. Washington.* Garden City, NY: Doubleday, Doran & Co.

Weinberg, M. (1977). *A chance to learn. The history of race and education in the United States.* New York: Cambridge University Press.

Woodson, C. G. (1933). *The miseducation of the Negro.* Washington, DC: Associated.

Woody, T. (1966). *A history of women's education in the United States* (Vol. I). New York: Octagon Books.

## KEY TO JUDICIAL REFERENCES

F.2d = Federal Reporter. St. Paul, MN:
West Publishing Company

US = United States Reports: Washington:
US Government Printing Office.

Cal., Mich., and Pa. refer to state volumes:
West Publishing Company

## JUDICIAL CASES

This reference system is standard in American legal documentation. The first number refers to volume number, and the second number refers to page number in the volume(s) indicated.

*Brown v. Board of Education of Topeka*, 347 US 483 (1954).

*Commonwealth v. Hartman*, Supreme Court of Pennsylvania, 17 Pa. 118 (1851).

*Danzl v. North St. Paul-Maplewood-Oakdale Independent School District No. 622*, U.S. Court of Appeals, Eighth Circuit, 706 F.2d 813 (1983).

*Lau v. Nichols*, 414 US 563 (1974).

*Plyler, Superintendent, Tyler Independent School District et al. v. Doe, Guardian et al.*, 457 US 202 (1982).

*Tape v. Hurley*, 66 Cal 473 (1885).

*Stuart v. School District No. 1 of the Village of Kalamazoo*, Supreme Court of Michigan, 30 Mich. 69 (1874).

# 5

⚭

# The Education
# of American Women

Prepare woman for duty and usefulness,
and she will laugh at any boundaries man may set for her.

SARAH GRIMKE
1853

The education of American women has been a different story from that of men's education. Women have encountered the problems of access, quality, and outcomes of education that were discussed in Chapter 4. Like males, many women encountered these issues on the basis of their race, ethnicity, socioeconomic status, or geographic area, but unlike males, many of them encountered these issues on the basis of their gender alone. For example, in higher education women were often denied the same education that was available to their brothers. Women of color have faced a triple jeopardy of discrimination on the basis of race, gender, and sometimes socioeconomic status.

This chapter examines the story of women's education from colonial times to the present. It reviews the innovations that followed American independence, the establishment of higher education for women in the nineteenth century, and the social questions about the purpose of education for women in the twentieth century.

## COLONIAL TIMES

Some of the Pilgrim women who arrived in Massachusetts in 1620 came with a distinct advantage—that of literacy. It has been estimated that one-third of the original female settlers and 45 percent of women born in the New England colonies could write (Lockridge, 1979). The attitude of Puritan New England about the education of women was limited, however (Woody, I, 1966). Daughters of well-to-do families were either taught at home or went to private "dame schools" where they were taught to read, write, and cipher in the teacher's home (Horowitz, 1993). As common schools were established by towns and villages, less affluent girls attended them. In some communities their attendance was limited to early morning or late afternoon, when the boys were not there (Woody, I, 1966). Girls did not go to the grammar schools that prepared a small number of boys for college. In the 1600s, the idea of a higher education for women would have been dismissed (Solomon, 1985). In the 1700s, girls could attend venture schools, the forerunners of academies, for a fee. By 1800, girls generally left school by age twelve or fourteen. In Connecticut and Massachusetts, "academies" were opened for girls in New Haven and Medford (Woody, I, 1966).

In the Middle Colonies, the education of girls was more equitable and varied by religious conviction. Among Quakers, elementary schools were open to both sexes. Among the Dutch, girls shared an elementary education with boys, although the Dutch Reformed Church believed in the supremacy of males in marriage. German congregations offered instruction in reading, writing, and religion to girls.

In the South, the plantation system resulted in tutorial instruction for wealthy girls, similar to that in England. Social accomplishments were emphasized. Among Quakers, elementary education was offered to girls on the same basis as boys. Poor children were "placed out" as apprentices (Woody, I, 1966).

In the eighteenth century, girls of wealthier parents along the East Coast attended private-venture schools where they studied literature, French, and the "needle arts." These "finishing schools" prepared young ladies for their place in polite society, but denied them the classical education available to their brothers. Less privileged girls did not share their social advantage. During the American Revolution, Abigail Adams, wife of John Adams, suggested that the new laws make provision for at least some liberal education for women and that the new society should include a place for them, but she also stressed the importance of education for domestic life (Woody, I, 1966). Even the male leaders, along with their less educated fellow country*men*, however, were not inclined to have women become too educated (Solomon, 1985).

After the American Revolution, education was viewed as important for preparing males for the responsibilities of citizenship. The U.S. Constitution had provided no rights to women but left decisions about voting, marriage, and property to state or local levels, where female suffrage was not granted except by an "error" in the law. Such was the case in New Jersey, where a 1787 law gave voting rights to everyone of proper age with property qualifications, which meant by default that women could vote. They did so until 1807, when a new law granted suffrage to free White males over twenty-one years old who also met a monetary requirement (Turner, 1916).

Although legal rights were denied to women, their education became viewed as important for the young republic. Women's education, however, depended upon male perceptions of women's roles in the new society. As wives, homemakers, and mothers, they were viewed as nurturing the future electorate. Academies proliferated in New England. Coeducational and single-sex institutions developed in the eastern part of the country. Derby Academy in Hingham, Massachusetts, admitted girls along with boys in the 1790s. Horowitz (1993) has reported that the impact of the new republic on women was profound:

> To women—not just unusual individuals, but potentially the sex as a whole—the entire world of thought and expression opened. While efforts to impose barriers along the way and to channel women's minds hardly ended at the turn to the nineteenth century, American women reached a new watershed from which they never turned back. (pp. 10–11)[1]

## THE NINETEENTH CENTURY

By the end of the colonial era, both men and women began to speak out in favor of more educational opportunities for women. Benjamin Rush, an early advocate of more advanced education, believed that American education should be different from that in England and France because women should be qualified to instruct their sons in democratic principles. In the early 1800s, DeWitt Clinton of New York was a strong advocate of high schools and teacher training institutions (Woody, I, 1966). The first high school for girls was established in Worcester, Massachusetts, in 1824. Clinton was correct in his view of a new need in American education.

As schools expanded westward with the frontier, the need for teachers became urgent and education became a career in which women were accepted. As women became the teachers of these schools, they needed additional education in order to be qualified. The early schools that prepared them became known as seminaries. (Male seminaries prepared young men for the ministry.)

## The Rise of Women's Seminaries

The **female seminary** offered a curriculum in history, philosophy, the natural sciences, and modern languages, but it did not offer the classical curriculum available to males. The average age of admission was early to middle teens. Emma Willard, born in 1787, sought and gained the support of DeWitt Clinton, and thereby pioneered the seminary movement in New York in the 1820s. Catharine Beecher's, founded in Hartford, Connecticut, in 1828, Zilpah Grant's, founded in Ipswich, Massachusetts, in 1828, and Mary Lyon's, founded in South Hadley, Massachusetts, in 1837, followed. Each brought high standards and new challenges to education for women. Today Emma Willard is an independent preparatory school (Horowitz, 1993).

Mary Lyon was born in 1797. Educated to be a teacher, she had taken her first teaching position when she was seventeen. By the mid-1830s, she had acquired considerable teaching experience, including a position at Zilpah Grant's seminary in Ipswich, but she realized that high tuition costs meant that less economically privileged women could not attend. She resigned from Ipswich in 1834 and turned her efforts to gathering support for a new school. A new seminary was proposed in western Massachusetts. She has been quoted as saying: "I may be fifty years in advance of the age, but the work is of God and must surely go on" (Solomon, 1985, p. 20). Several towns competed for the location of her school. South Hadley was chosen, provided it could raise $8,000 toward the costs. It did so, and construction began. Mary Lyon's "seminary" took the name "Mount Holyoke." Chartered in 1836, it opened its doors in 1837. Although it was a "seminary," it is sometimes credited as being the first college for women in the United States. It was not chartered as a college, but became one later.

Seminaries or academies appeared in other parts of country as well. In the South, the Moravians had established the first female academy in Salem, North Carolina, in 1802. Others followed in Charlotte, Nashville, Greenville, and Greensboro.

In the Midwest, seminaries or academies were founded in Detroit, Ann Arbor, Kalamazoo, Rockford, Beloit, Milwaukee, and Dubuque between 1833 and 1853 (Woody, I, 1966).

## The Rise of Women's Colleges

According to Woody (II, 1966), two conditions were necessary in order for true women's colleges to be achieved. First, seminaries and high schools needed to give better preparation to enable women to enter more advanced studies (than were offered in the common schools and town schools). Second, the advocates of colleges for women needed to gain the support of influential people in order to obtain financial backing. Between 1825 and 1875, experiments in advanced education for women gradually evolved into the attainment of colleges equal in course offerings to those available to men. Space does not allow for an intensive review of the many experiments in women's colleges, some of which succeeded and some of which did not. The overview that follows is intended to describe some innovative changes in women's education.

**The Northeast** In 1852 the Auburn Female University was chartered as "a real college for women." In 1855 it was relocated to Elmira and renamed Elmira Female College. Vassar, named for its founder, Matthew Vassar, was incorporated in 1861 and opened in 1865. Henry Fowle Durant founded Wellesley College, which opened in 1875. Smith opened the same year. Along with Wellesley, it finally offered to women an education on a level equal to that of the best men's colleges, such as Amherst and Harvard (Woody, II, 1966).

An interesting result of this type of higher education for women was their increasing independence of spirit and some financial independence for those who never married. A perception of personal individualism emerged for them. Solomon (1985) has described it this way:

> Individualism in old and new forms pressed the educated woman to be independent in seeking her own moral course. Independence was a double-edged ideal:while a young man was applauded, a young woman at best received ambivalent approval from family and society in her struggles to strike out on her own. (p. 30)

The fact remained, however, that many students who entered these colleges did have a socioeconomic advantage. Interestingly, the most "elite" eastern families preferred to educate their daughters privately or through travel abroad. The new nineteenth-century millionaires who had acquired wealth in industry were concerned about their daughters having "good" marriages—that is, marriages with other wealthy or even aristocratic families. Therefore, the women who attended these first women's colleges came more from the upper middle class and families of professionals such as doctors, lawyers, ministers, and moderately successful businessmen (Solomon, 1985). In other words, they came from families who were neither very rich nor poor, but whose decisions to send their daughters to college involved choices about personal costs and values about education for their daughters as well as their sons.

It is clear, however, that these women did enjoy a socioeconomic advantage. In the mid-nineteenth century, the White daughters of less affluent families or poor European immigrants, like their brothers, encountered the problems of access, quality, and outcomes. Questions educators raised about the "relevancy" of education to children's future lives were raised for girls as well as for boys, in regard to students' social class, race, and gender (Chapter 4). The women's colleges did not solve these problems for less advantaged girls. What the establishment of women's colleges did accomplish was the idea of access to an education equivalent to that available to males of similar social advantage. Some of these fortunate women excelled. For example, Sophonisba Breckinridge (Wellesley 1888) became the first woman to pass the bar exam in Kentucky, and Maud Wood (Park) (Radcliffe 1898) became the first president of the National League of Women Voters in 1920 (Solomon, 1985). Although access to these early women's colleges was in fact dependent on economic status, the issue of quality of education had been addressed for a few American women.

Admissions policies at these prestigious women's colleges were mixed toward African Americans in the nineteenth century. Smith, Radcliffe, and Wellesley admitted Black women, but Bryn Mawr and Barnard discriminated against them. More Black women entered these colleges in the twentieth century, but marriage data from the 1930s indicates that 58.5 percent out of 1,994 Black college graduates were not married at that time (Solomon, 1985, p. 179). White women had also faced this issue of perceived "eligibility" for marriage following their college education. Admissions for women of other racial groups were also mixed. Interestingly, women from foreign countries were attending these colleges by the turn of the twentieth century. Many women who attended these colleges, whether Black, White, or foreign students, assumed leadership roles in their careers and in their communities.

**The South**   At the end of the 1700s, women's education in the South had progressed more slowly, partly due to extensive devastation of the area during the American Revolution. In the early 1800s, education sought to prepare White women to be "ladies," thus reflecting an extensive social class (and racial) bias. Higher education for women in the South has generally been overlooked, but, in fact, it was important.

As early as 1807, Duncan Campbell of Georgia proposed a bill to the state legislature for the establishment of an institution for the education of females. The bill passed the House but was defeated in the Senate. In 1834 Daniel Chandler, Campbell's son-in-law, advocated educational opportunities for women similar to those for men. Two years later, the state legislature chartered the Georgia Female College at Macon. This college became the earliest institution *chartered as a college for women,* and opened in January 1839. The course of study, however, was not equal to that of some men's colleges. Girls were admitted as young as age twelve (Woody, II, 1966).

Institutions such as Mary Baldwin in Virginia, Agnes Scott in Georgia, and Randolph Macon in Virginia followed later. After the Catholic University of America refused to admit women in 1895, the College of Notre Dame in Maryland was founded in 1896, and Trinity College in Washington, D.C., followed in 1897 (Solomon, 1985).

**The Midwest**   A surprising new model of education occurred in 1833, when the militant Christian founders of Oberlin College in Ohio believed it was "God's College," wherein men and women, Black and White, would be educated together. Not all classes were coeducational, but it was a beginning. Age for admission was fourteen (Woody, II, 1966). Interestingly, some women faculty at Oberlin had studied under Mary Lyon and Zilpah Grant back in Massachusetts. Within a few years other Midwestern institutions followed Oberlin's lead.

Two Black women who were students at Oberlin should be recognized here. The first, Mary Eliza Church (Terrell), graduated in 1884. A civil rights and women's suffrage activist, she became president of the National Association of Colored Women from 1896 to 1901. The second, Anna Julia Haywood Cooper, was already widowed when she graduated in 1884. Author of *A Voice from the South by a Black Woman of the South* (1892), she worked for both Black advancement and equal rights for women (Solomon, 1985). Other Midwestern colleges included Wesleyan Female College at Cincinnati in 1842, and both Antioch and Oxford Female College in 1852 (Woody, II, 1966).

### Other Educational Opportunities

In the mid-nineteenth century, other types of schools, including public teacher training or normal schools, became educational alternatives for less affluent women. The first state-supported normal schools appeared in Massachusetts when the legislature approved funding in 1838. Schools were then established in Lexington, Barre, and Bridgewater (Woody, I, 1966). These schools were following the lead of the earlier seminaries that had focused on preparing women to be teachers. Some of these schools were part of larger universities. The first eight state universities to open their doors to women were Iowa (1855), Wisconsin (1867), Indiana, Kansas, and Minnesota (1869), and California, Michigan, and Missouri (1870). In Wisconsin, thirty women had entered the normal school for teacher training in 1863 and were allowed to take other courses as a result of low enrollments by men during the Civil War. In 1867 coeducation was stopped and a female college was established. The women boycotted this college and joined the men's classes! Cocducation was reestablished in 1873, and a year later President John Bascom supported this coeducation (Solomon, 1985).

It is clear that by 1900 women in the United States were being admitted into a wide variety of colleges, but the oldest prestigious men's colleges remained closed to them until the mid-twentieth century. In spite of women's achievements in higher education, the issue of outcomes in terms of real social opportunity remained unsolved.

## THE TWENTIETH CENTURY

In the early twentieth century, increasing numbers of women were attending college across the nation. By 1920 they totaled almost half of all college enrollments (Fass, 1989). Indeed, college enrollments increased in the 1920s for males as well. Among these students were those from more diverse ethnic and religious groups. This diversity caused some reactions at the prestigious older institutions, which developed selective admissions policies designed particularly to limit enrollments of Jewish students, male and female alike (Solomon, 1985).

In the 1920s and 1930s, more colleges and universities had followed the options initiated by the normal schools in the nineteenth century by offering to women alternative programs of study in subjects that did not focus on the liberal arts, such as home economics. Interestingly, these courses may have laid the groundwork for later programs in the 1940s and 1950s that were seen as "relevant" to women's roles as homemakers. A woman who graduated from a large midwestern university in the 1940s once remarked to me that she learned to bake a cherry pie in college.

In the early 1940s the majority of college students were women because of fewer male enrollments during World War II, following the pattern at the University of Wisconsin during the Civil War. By 1950, however, the proportion of female college students had fallen to 30 percent as a result of large enrollments by male veterans in the late 1940s (Fass, 1989). After the war the federal program known popularly as the "GI Bill" enabled literally millions of veterans to pursue an education they otherwise could not have afforded. (Women veterans also benefited from this program.) Admission to graduate schools also became more competitive, and many women were refused admission in favor of veterans. Women's roles in society once again were called into question at this time. What type of education was most relevant to women's lives?

Fass (1989) has described **"the female paradox"** in regard to higher education, which derived from the fact that women appeared to be receiving more education than they seemed to need:

> The female paradox was always latent in the nature of women's higher education in a society which continued to ascribe, though not entirely to confine, female roles to the family.... [T]he paradox of women's higher education penetrated to the very core of student culture as women students increasingly complained about the dissonance between their future lives and their studies. (p. 157)

This paradox was not new. In the nineteenth century, the founders of women's colleges acted against the prevailing views of women's education because they had believed in the equality of women's intellectual abilities and had therefore established these institutions, which offered courses in the liberal arts, the sciences, and the humanities. It was the conflict between a belief in the liberal arts and a view which held that programs for women should be more "relevant" to their lives that aroused a debate over women's education in the 1940s and 1950s.

This question of relevancy was really "What were women's lives about?" In the nineteenth century, some women who had attended the first women's colleges had gone on to careers in teaching and a few had gone on to graduate schools, but many of them had remained single. Those who married had submerged their possible career interests to those of their husbands. In the early twentieth century, as more women went to college, many of them worked for a short time after graduation and then married. By the 1920s and 1930s, women began to question the old dichotomy between marriage and careers and began to consider combining the two.

By 1944, a Radcliffe survey of graduates revealed three different groups: (a) those not married with careers; (b) those married without careers; and (c) those married and working, although perhaps with interruptions (Solomon, 1985).

The public image of college-educated women, however, continued to be that of wives and mothers at home, *in spite of their education*. In 1949 a *Fortune* magazine poll reported that 57 percent of parents thought colleges should provide professional preparation for their sons, and 46 percent thought colleges should provide preparation for family life for their daughters (Fass, 1989). In addition, women who had themselves attended liberal arts colleges began to express their confusion and frustration over the fact that their education had not emotionally prepared them to be homemakers. Educators interpreted these frustrations to mean that women wanted this domestic role. A so-called progressive view developed among educators that saw a need for programs relevant to women's roles and held that a liberal arts education did not prepare them for domestic responsibilities. The irony of this view was that it reaffirmed women's traditional roles as homemakers, and the formerly "radical" view in the nineteenth century of a liberal arts education for women was now called into question.

Interestingly, the greatest challenge to the traditional liberal arts came from the so-called progressive colleges, such as Sarah Lawrence and Bennington, which valued individualizing instruction to make it more relevant. For example, Constance Warren, President of Sarah Lawrence, supported programs that focused on family relationships and women's roles in the society. Thus educators, along with the general public, believed that women were more oriented toward marriage, and students seemed to reflect that view. Indeed, college women were under intense social pressure to follow the good family life portrayed in television programs. What was overlooked was the fact that men also had families, but educational programs for their roles were not considered. Fass has described the debates over women's education in the 1950s as "a case of the dog chasing its own tail" (1989, p. 178).

One woman who defended the place of a liberal arts education in the face of prevailing fashion was Margaret Clapp, President of Wellesley College. She maintained that women's interests were important, but also that institutions of higher learning had a responsibility to transmit knowledge accrued over centuries. According to Fass (1989),

> In the fifties, with issues of life adjustment ... all around, it was difficult to appreciate the degree to which Clapp's old fashioned position *provided the very vantage for the future progress and advancement of women.* (p. 179, italics mine)

Another factor also contributed to the advancements for women that followed in the 1960s and 1970s. In spite of the widespread belief that women's roles after college were centered in the home, the number of women in the workforce had actually been increasing since the years following World War I. By 1957, 22 million women were employed. The statistics for women in the 1950s reveal surprising information about their personal lives. Over half of them were married, although only a small percentage of them had young children under school age. Nearly one-quarter of them were widowed, divorced, or separated. More women with college degrees were working than those with only an elementary education. Finally, college-educated women were found to be more likely to return to employment in their mid-thirties and to remain working until their sixties. In other words, the prevailing assumption that college-educated women dropped out of the labor force to marry was inaccurate if one took into account what happened to these women later. They may have dropped out for a while when their children had not yet entered school, but they did not stay out.

The debate of career versus marriage did not address the fact that many women were combining employment with marriage. The popular television image of middle-class domestic life in the 1950s was more illusion than fact. Ironically, educational leaders were advocating so-called progressive college programs for women to prepare them for their roles as homemakers at a time when more women were remaining in or returning to the workforce. Many women were also entering graduate schools (or technical schools) after they were married (Fass, 1989). Therefore, an undergraduate degree in the liberal arts made sense because most graduate schools required it. (It should be pointed out here that in the field of professional education, some graduate schools of education accepted students from undergraduate teacher training programs, but others such as Harvard accepted candidates with liberal arts degrees.) Thus, liberal arts programs enabled women to continue their education and pursue career goals later in their lives. In the mid-1950s, Kate Hevner Mueller, a professor at Indiana University, not only recognized that women would work in the future, she viewed education as a catalyst for social change (Fass, 1989). That change was not far off.

Women in the 1960s began asking the same questions as other groups involved in the Civil Rights Movement: "What about us?" Today, some people have the impression that the women's movement of the 1960s and 1970s brought with it an interest in social and political issues and a demand for the right not to be limited to gender-related roles as homemakers. The women's movement did bring a renewed interest in social and political issues, but this impression is an oversimplification of women's previous involvement in these issues. The following review presents briefly why this view is a misperception of women's involvement in politics and the workforce.

## WOMEN AND SOCIAL ISSUES

Many women had been concerned with social issues ever since Abigail Adams reminded her husband, John, that the young American republic should include a place for women. Sarah and Angelina Grimke, the daughters of a Southern aristocratic family, had spoken openly against slavery in the early nineteenth century. These two remarkable women taught slave children and embraced abolitionist views. Sarah's *Letters on the Equality of the Sexes and the Condition of Women* in 1838 was a truly feminist tract on the equality of men and women. Other women abolitionists became politically active in the mid-nineteenth century. In 1840, elected women representatives from American antislave societies were refused seats at the International Anti-Slavery Convention in London. As a result, Lucretia Mott and Elizabeth Cady Stanton organized a convention in Seneca Falls, New York, in 1848. The *Declaration of Sentiments and Resolutions* enacted at that convention inaugurated the first women's movement in the United States

(Solomon, 1985). Twelve resolutions were passed in this declaration. Issues included a belief in equal access for women into various trades, professions, and commerce. Rothenberg (1995) has reported the resolutions verbatim. The most controversial resolution was the ninth, which initiated the suffrage movement. It read as follows:

> *Resolved,* That it is the duty of women of this country to secure to themselves their sacred right to the elective franchise. (p. 314)

Reactions to this resolution reverberated across the country for another seventy years.

Women in the nineteenth century also organized in support of the temperance movement. Interestingly, Giele (1995) has pointed out that both the women's temperance and suffrage movements grew out of the Protestant values and the Republican individualism that were reviewed in Chapter 2.


## WOMEN IN THE WORKFORCE

The predominant view of women as homemakers at mid-twentieth century may have been valid for some women in the middle class, but this image was not entirely accurate because many married women, as we have seen, did work. In fact, women in the working class had worked outside the home in the nineteenth century in factories and shops, on the farm, and as domestic servants. After the Civil War, as industrialization and urbanization created additional jobs for women, college-educated women and working-class women joined forces to form **The Women's Trade Union League.** In 1870, only 16 percent of all females over ten years old were in the labor force; by 1920 this had risen to 28 percent. The figures were higher for White ethnic minorities and Black women. By 1900, 25 percent of White women with foreign-born parents and 43 percent of Black women worked outside the home. In 1910 the census reported a sharp drop in domestic (servants) and agricultural occupations and a *doubling* from 24 percent to 49 percent in the number of women employed in manufacturing, trade, and clerical occupations. A few were in the professions (Giele, 1995).

Ironically, in the 1950s, the liberal arts programs that caused so much controversy by not preparing women for roles as homemakers, and leaving women frustrated over the relevancy of their college education, provided at the same time the basis for some women to continue into graduate schools, and thereby to enter professions dominated by men. Since the nineteenth century there had been women in the professions, but their numbers had been few. Admission to graduate schools had been very difficult. Howard University in Washington, D.C., had accepted both Black and White women by 1896, but other schools were not so accepting. For example, women did not gain access to Harvard Medical School until 1945 (primarily because of low male enrollments during World War II) or to Harvard Law School until 1950 (Solomon, 1985). After the wave of veterans declined in the mid-1950s, however, the number of women entering professional schools began to increase.

Who were these women whose educational goals foreshadowed the changes that were to come? Like the pioneers who had attended the first women's colleges in the nineteenth century, many of them who now pursued professional degrees had the support of their families behind them. Those who were married had husbands who did not share the prevailing social view that women's roles were more appropriately limited to domestic responsibilities. Some sought to improve their personal status from that of their working-class parents. None had the widespread support of peers or a publicly organized women's movement. By increasing the proportion of women in the professions, however, they became more numerous role models for the women who followed them.

## MODERN TIMES

It is clear from these examples that neither women's involvement in social issues nor working outside the home was a new idea in the women's movement in the 1960s and 1970s. What was new in the feminist movement were several other issues. These were (a) the realization of women's civil rights in political action; (b) a redefinition of the division of labor between the sexes, in which men were seen as sharing the nurturing role of child rearing and other homemaking responsibilities; (c) a focus on equal opportunity to enter a variety of careers that had formerly been viewed as "male" domain; (d) equity in salaries in comparison to males; and (e) equal opportunity for career advancement at work (Giele, 1995).

In education, women's demands for equal access to professional careers increased dramatically in the 1970s and 1980s. Enrollment statistics from graduate schools in the early 1990s show substantial increases in the number of women in the professions over the past twenty years. In 1970, 49 percent of women graduating from high school enrolled in college; in 1991, 67 percent did so. In 1970, women earned 40 percent of master's degrees; in 1991, they earned 53 percent. In 1970, women earned 13 percent of Ph.D.'s; in 1991 they earned 37 percent. In 1970 women earned 5 percent of law degrees; in 1990 they earned 42 percent. In 1970 women earned 8 percent of medical degrees; in 1990 they earned 34 percent. In 1970 they earned 1 percent of dentistry degrees; in 1990 they earned 31 percent (Ravitch, 1992). These figures reflect changing attitudes about women's role in the society on the part of admissions committees and administrators in higher education. Another advance over the past twenty-five years has been the origination of women's studies programs in colleges nationwide. And, finally, the oldest men's colleges, such as Yale and Princeton, opened their doors to women.

A recent report indicates that the issues of access, quality, and outcomes continue to pose problems for women (AAUW Report, 1992). Today, access in education refers to the opportunity to pursue any career a woman desires. Quality refers to adequate preparation for that career. Outcomes focus on equity and opportunity in employment on the basis of qualifications alone. If some women are attaining increasing access and quality in education, is equity in outcomes yet a reality? Currently, the concept of a "glass ceiling" suggests that women's advancement to upper-level positions in the professions and the corporate world continues to be limited. Lopez (1995) has suggested that there are "glass walls" that segregate women into staff and support positions in industry. How long will it take for equity of outcomes to be a reality in the future?

## CHAPTER SUMMARY

Women have encountered problems of access, quality, and outcomes in education not only on the basis of race and socioeconomic status, but also on the basis of their gender.

During colonial times, girls did not have the access to education that their brothers enjoyed. After the American Revolution, educational opportunities for girls improved as schools proliferated. A need to staff these schools resulted in the growth of female seminaries and normal schools to train women to become teachers.

In the nineteenth century, Emma Willard, Catharine Beecher, Zilpah Grant, and Mary Lyon were pioneers in women's higher education. State universities also began opening their doors to women by mid-century.

In the twentieth century, larger numbers of women attained a higher education, but questions about the appropriate type of education for women emerged after World War II. Starting in the late 1950s, a greater proportion of women pursued graduate degrees and entered the professions. Today, their enrollments in professional and graduate schools are closer to those of men.

## IMPORTANT TERMS

Female seminaries

The Women's Trade Union League

Normal schools

The Abolitionist Movement

The Suffrage Movement

The female paradox

The women's movement

Women's studies

The Temperance Movement

## QUESTIONS FOR DISCUSSION

1. Why do you think the view toward women's education was different in New England, the Middle Colonies, and the South? Why was it the same?

2. How was women's education affected by their fathers' attitudes about women's roles and responsibilities?

3. Why were the Grimke sisters especially courageous women?

4. Why was the convention in Seneca Falls, New York, the real beginning of women's movements in the United States?

5. Do you believe that Americans still have traditional views of "appropriate" careers for women? Why or why not?

6. What was the most surprising information to you in this discussion of women's education? Why were you surprised?

## NOTES

1. This may be an overly optimistic view of subsequent events. Women did go on to achieve significant advances in education, but even today professional journals continue to report gender bias in elementary and secondary school classrooms.

## REFERENCES

Birney, C. H. (1885). *The Grimke sisters: Sarah and Angelina Grimke: The first American women advocates of abolition and woman's rights.* Boston: Lee & Shepard.

Fass, P. S. (1989). *Outside in: Minorities and the transformation of American education.* New York: Oxford University Press.

Giele, J. Z. (1995). *Two paths to women's equality: Temperance, suffrage, and the origins of modern feminism.* Boston: Twayne.

Horowitz, H. L. (1993). *Alma mater: Design and experience in the women's colleges from their nineteenth-century beginnings to the 1930s.* Amherst: The University of Massachusetts Press.

Lockridge, K. A. (1979). *Literacy in colonial New England.* New York: W. W. Norton.

Lopez, J. A. (1995). "Women face glass walls as well as ceilings." In P. S. Rothenberg (Ed.) *Race, class, and gender in the United States: An integrated study* (3rd ed.). New York: St. Martin's Press.

Ravitch, D. S. (Fall 1992). "Do U.S. public schools really shortchange girls?" *Wellesley* 77 (1), 13, 35.

Rothenberg, P. S. (1995). *Race, class, and gender in the United States: An integrated study* (3rd ed.). New York: St. Martin's Press.

Solomon, B. M. (1985). *In the company of educated women: A history of women and higher education in America.* New Haven: Yale University Press.

The AAUW Report: How schools shortchange girls, 1992. Washington, D.C.: The American Association of University Women Educational Foundation.

Turner, E. R. (1916). "Women's suffrage in New Jersey." *Smith College Studies in History* 1 (4), 165–87.

Woody, T. (1966). *A history of women's education in the United States* (Vols. I & II). New York: Octagon Books.

# 6

⚭

# The Law and American Education

Education is perhaps the most important function
of state and local governments....
It is the very foundation of good citizenship....
Such an opportunity where the state has undertaken to provide it,
is a right which must be made available to all on equal terms.

BROWN V. BOARD OF EDUCATION OF TOPEKA
U.S. SUPREME COURT DECISION, 1954

comprehensive review of United States law in regard to diverse cultural groups is beyond the scope of this text. This chapter focuses on legal issues specifically concerning education. The chapter opens with a brief summary of federal and state powers. A more extensive examination follows of judicial milestones either directly regarding education or those whose implications were subsequently applied to school settings. The issues involved are segregation, gender discrimination, religion, language instruction, education of illegal immigrant children, and testing standards for teachers and students.

All these cases are relevant for multicultural education because they involved the rights of members of diverse groups. There are undoubtedly cases that the reader may believe should have been included here. This review is not exhaustive, but an attempt to include those cases that were landmark court decisions which set precedents for subsequent cases. In some places I have referred to the fact that decisions by the United States Supreme Court have sometimes involved more than one judicial case. This is standard procedure for the Supreme Court when different circuit courts of appeal decisions are at variance with each other, or when two or more circuit court cases have similar legal principles involved.

## FEDERAL AND STATE POWERS

Education is not specifically mentioned in the United States Constitution and is, therefore, assumed to be reserved to the states or to the people as implied in the Tenth Amendment, which states:

> The powers not delegated to the United States by the Constitution, nor prohibited by it to the States, are reserved to the States respectively, or to the people.

Since the establishment of the Republic, the federal government's role in education has been one of indirect support, and not one of control. The federal government, however, has been involved in educational issues. Following from the Tenth Amendment, Congress can involve itself in education through appropriation of funds, but does not have the power to legislate directly changes in education. Over the years this **categorical aid** approach has been used to bring about changes in education by providing supplementary assistance to meet specific national interests. One example of this approach was the Morrill Act, which provided land grants to the states for the establishment of agricultural and technical colleges.

The second area of federal involvement in education has been judicial. The Tenth Amendment assumes state powers, which "effectively places the burden on the federal government to justify in court its involvement in affairs that may have been presumed to be left to the states" (Alexander & Alexander, 1985, p. 57). U.S. district and circuit courts of appeal as well as the Supreme Court have become involved in cases when state laws have been challenged for violating individual rights. Almost all of these cases have been based on either the First or

Fourteenth Amendments, although a few have involved the Fourth, Fifth, Sixth, and Eighth Amendments. The First Amendment states:

> Congress shall make no law respecting an establishment of religion, or prohibiting the free exercise thereof; or abridging the freedom of speech, or of the press; or the right of the people to assemble, and to petition the government for a redress of grievances.

These individual rights of religion, speech, association, press, and assembly are the constitutional issues that have been "primarily responsible for the federal involvement in education" (Alexander & Alexander, 1985, p. 62). In American society, they have generally been regarded as the cornerstones of freedom.

Court cases based on the Fourteenth Amendment have primarily involved the due process and equal protection clauses. The amendment states:

> Section 1. All persons born or naturalized in the United States, and subject to the jurisdiction thereof, are citizens of the United States wherein they reside. No State shall make or enforce any law which shall abridge the privileges or immunities of citizens of the United States; nor shall any State deprive any person of life, liberty, or property, without due process of law; nor deny to any person within its jurisdiction the equal protection of the laws.

## JUDICIAL MILESTONES

The rights stated in the First and Fourteenth Amendments have had a significant impact on American society. Some judicial decisions based on them have had important consequences for American education.

### Segregation

In 1864 the Thirteenth Amendment granted freedom to former slaves. In 1868 the Fourteenth Amendment granted citizenship to "all persons born or naturalized in the United States and subject to the jurisdiction thereof." In 1869 the Fifteenth Amendment brought the voting franchise to all (male) citizens.

After the enactment of these amendments, education of African Americans became a public concern because of their rights as citizens. Public schools were expected to provide for the education of Black children. Even before the Civil War, separate schools had been established in the North. The Supreme Court of Massachusetts found that the "Boston school committee had power to provide for the instruction of [Black] children in separate schools established exclusively for them and to prohibit their attendance upon the other schools" (Roberts v. The City of Boston, 5 Cush. 198, 1850). Similar laws were enacted in Ohio, California, New York, and Kentucky. Because the due process and equal protection clauses of the Fourteenth Amendment forbade the states from abridging the privileges of citizens, such practices came under question and culminated in a Supreme Court decision that was to cloud the issue of racial equality under the law, with consequences for education, for years to come.

In 1896, the U.S. Supreme Court addressed the issue of segregation by race in railway carriages in Louisiana (Plessy v. Ferguson, 163 US 537). The Court did not regard the enforced separation of races as a denial of equal protection under the law. In the opinion of the Court:

> We cannot say that a law which authorizes or even requires the separation of the two races in public conveyances is unreasonable, or more obnoxious to the Fourteenth Amendment than acts of Congress requiring separate schools... in the District of Columbia, the constitutionality of which does not seem to have been questioned, or the corresponding acts of state legislatures.

To his everlasting credit, Justice Harlan dissented and wrote:

> Our constitution is color-blind, and neither knows nor tolerates classes among citizens. In respect of civil rights, all citizens are equal under the law.... In my opinion, the judgment this day rendered will, in time, prove to be quite as pernicious as the decision made by this tribunal in the Dred Scott case.
>
> The sure guaranty of the peace and security of each race is the clear, distinct, unconditional recognition by our governments, national and state, of every right that inheres in civil freedom, and the equality before the law of all citizens of the United States, without regard to race....
>
> I am of opinion that the statute of Louisiana is inconsistent with the personal liberty of citizens, White or Black, in that state and hostile to both the spirit and letter of the constitution of the United States.... For the reason stated, I am constrained to withhold my assent from the opinion and judgment of the majority.

In upholding segregated facilities in public railway coaches, the Court set a precedent for upholding segregated public schools, and the doctrine of "separate but equal" came under legal endorsement by the highest court in the land. It would be another fifty-eight years before the Supreme Court agreed with Justice Harlan's views.

In 1954 several cases from the states of Kansas, South Carolina, Virginia, and Delaware were collectively addressed by the Supreme Court (Brown et al. v. Board of Education of Topeka et al., 347 US 483). Here, Black minors sought to obtain admission to public schools in their respective communities on a nonsegregated basis. After reviewing the historical reasons for segregated schools, the Court turned to the effects of segregation on public education and concluded that segregation in public schools solely on the basis of race, even when physical facilities may be equal, does in fact deprive minority children of equal educational opportunities. In the opinion of the Court:

> To separate them from others of similar age and qualifications solely because of their race generates a feeling of inferiority as to their status in the community that may affect their hearts and minds in a way unlikely ever to be undone....
> We conclude that in the field of public education the doctrine of "separate but equal" has no place. Separate educational facilities are inherently unequal.

The Brown decision legally ended an era in public education in which segregation was endorsed through legal obfuscation of the intent of the Fourteenth Amendment. Compliance with the decision, however, was another matter. Perhaps the most dramatic example of enforcement of the Brown decision occurred in 1957 in Little Rock, Arkansas, where over a thousand federal troops had been deployed to defend the rights of Black students (Bennett, 1992). At 9:45 A.M. on the morning of September 15, soldiers escorted nine Black students into Central High School, in spite of public demonstrations of protest. The message was clear: local attempts to circumvent desegregation would be met with federal intervention. Another blatant example of resistance occurred in Prince Edward County, Virginia, where public schools were closed and private schools were operated with state and county funds. In 1964 the U.S. Supreme Court found this practice to be unconstitutional and ordered the reopening of public schools (Griffin v. County School Board of Prince Edward County, 377 US 218).

Both **de facto segregation** (segregation not by law or design but by circumstances such as racially unbalanced neighborhoods) and intentional segregation continued through a variety of local policies. Not all resistance to the Brown decision occurred in the South. In some northern communities, White parents accepted student integration but objected to their children being taught by Black teachers who had been reassigned to integrated schools.

The first Supreme Court case involving a major northern city was in 1973 (Keyes v. School District No. 1, Denver, 413 US 189). Parents of Denver school children had brought action against the school board for creating or maintaining racially and/or ethnically segregated schools through a variety of techniques including manipulation of school attendance zones, school site selection, a neighborhood school policy, and the use of mobile classroom units. The segregation involved both African American and Latino students. The district court ruled that one area of the city had in fact engaged in illegal segregation and ordered the school board to desegregate the schools in that area. The district court further concluded that a finding of racial segregation in one area of the city was "not material" to the issue of intention in other areas of the city and therefore did not impose on the school board a "duty" to eliminate segregation throughout the district.

The U.S. Supreme Court did not agree. In the opinion of the Court:

It is obvious that a practice of concentrating Negroes [sic] in certain schools by structuring attendance zones ... on the basis of race has the reciprocal effect of keeping other nearby schools predominantly White....

So also, the use of mobile classrooms, ... student transfer policies, ... the transportation of students, ... and the assignment of faculty and staff on racially identifiable bases, have the clear effect of earmarking schools according to their racial composition....

[I]t is both fair and reasonable to require that the school authorities bear the burden of showing that their actions as to other segregated schools within the system were not also motivated by segregative intent.

On this rationale, the Supreme Court in effect extended its rejection of **de jure segregation** (segregation by law) in the Brown case to include intentional segregation through gerrymandering of school districts and other means.

In 1971 the Supreme Court reviewed a case involving the issue of busing to overcome racial segregation (Swann v. Charlotte-Mecklenburg Board of Education, 402 US 1). The Court found that:

> all things considered being equal . . . it might well be desirable to assign pupils to schools nearest their homes. But all things are not equal in a system that has been deliberately constructed and maintained to enforce racial segregation. . . .
>
> We hold that pairing and grouping of noncontiguous zones is a permissible tool and such action is to be considered in light of the objectives sought. . . .
>
> [W]e find no basis for holding that the local school authorities may not be required to employ bus transportation as one tool of desegregation. Desegregation plans cannot be limited to "the walk-in school."

In the opinion of the Court, however, such busing practices need to take into account other factors including time and distances involved, the age of the students, and other issues that could "risk the health of children or impinge on the educational process."

## Gender Discrimination

In the courts, gender issues have revolved primarily around three issues: equal pay for equal skills, work, and effort; pregnancy; and hiring procedures. These will be examined in turn.

**Equal Pay**   The Equal Pay Act of 1963 amended the Fair Labor Standards Act of 1938, with the intention of eliminating discrimination in wages based on sex. The act specified that differential pay be based on a seniority system, a merit system, quantity and quality of production, or "any factor other than sex" (Alexander & Alexander, 1985, p. 643). In 1964 this act was included in the Civil Rights Act, which includes the categories of race, religion, and national origin in addition to sex. The Equal Pay Act, of course, applies to all employees, not simply to those in education. The Education Amendment of 1972 (Title IX), however, referred specifically to educational programs receiving federal funds. Some courts ruled that this amendment covered students but not school employees, but when the Supreme Court addressed this question in 1982, it extended the legal interpretation to include employees.

In 1982 two suits involving Connecticut schools came before the Supreme Court in the case of North Haven Board of Education v. Bell (456 US 512). In the first case, in North Haven, a tenured teacher filed a complaint in 1978 on the basis that she was not rehired after a year's maternity leave, and in Trumbull, a guidance counselor alleged that she had been discriminated against in job assignment, working conditions, and nonrenewal of her contract. After reviewing the evidence, the Supreme Court found that "no person" may be discriminated against on the basis of gender and "that Title IX's broad protection of person[s] does extend to employees of educational institutions."

**Pregnancy**  Employment policies concerning pregnancy have been addressed by Congress, which amended the Civil Rights Act of 1964 to prohibit discrimination on the basis of pregnancy, childbirth, or related medical conditions, but not including abortion unless the mother's life is in danger (Alexander & Alexander, 1985, p. 645). Women in business and education have been affected by this act.

In 1974 the Supreme Court reviewed the issue of mandating pregnancy leaves from work (Cleveland Board of Education v. LaFleur, 414 US 632). The trial actually involved two cases: one from Ohio and one from Virginia. In Cleveland, a school board policy required pregnant teachers to take maternity leave without pay, starting five months before the expected birth. Teachers were not allowed to return to work until the beginning of the next school semester following the date when the child reached the age of three months. A doctor's certificate of health was required to return to work, and teachers on maternity leave were not promised reemployment. Failure to comply with the mandatory leave constituted grounds for dismissal. In Chesterfield County, Virginia, a school board policy required pregnant teachers to take a maternity leave four months before the expected birth. Notice in writing was required six months prior to the expected birthdate. Teachers were eligible for reemployment upon submission of a physician's notice of health and upon assurance that caring for the child would "minimally" interfere with the job. In arriving at its decision, the Supreme Court stated:

> Public school maternity leave rules directly affect one of the basic civil rights ... the Due Process Clause of the Fourteenth Amendment requires that such rules must not needlessly, arbitrarily, or capriciously impinge upon this vital area of a teacher's constitutional liberty.

In addition to the issue of personal freedom, the Court addressed the issue of job competency:

> The provisions amount to a conclusive presumption that every pregnant teacher who reaches the fifth or sixth month of pregnancy is physically incapable of continuing....
>
> [T]he ability of any particular pregnant woman to continue at work past any fixed time in her pregnancy is very much an individual matter.... Thus, the ... presumption embodied in these rules ... is neither necessary [nor] universally true.

Finally, in regard to the issue of returning to work, the Court found that:

> [the] objectives unduly infringe upon the teacher's constitutional liberty....
>
> We conclude that the Cleveland return rule (three months after the birth) ... is wholly arbitrary and irrational, and hence violates the Due Process Clause.

Thus, the Court went a long way toward striking down discriminating regulations against women exercising their right to have children while they are employed.

**Hiring Practices**  The burden of proof of discrimination in hiring an applicant for a position lies with the applicant. In the absence of clear evidence, the claim of intentional discrimination cannot be supported. Such was the decision of a circuit court of appeals in 1983, in a case involving possible gender discrimination in the hiring of a male principal (Danzl v. North St. Paul-Maplewood-Oakdale Independent School District No. 622, US Court of Appeals, Eighth Circuit, 706 F.2d 813).

In 1979, twelve individuals applied for a high school principalship in the North St. Paul area. Out of four finalists, two applicants, one man and one woman, were selected as the leading candidates. Upon further queries by the committee with school personnel who knew the candidates, the male applicant was hired, primarily on the basis of his seven years' experience as a principal and one year's experience as a school superintendent, in comparison with the female applicant's five years' experience as an associate principal. The female candidate then filed a discrimination complaint in the district court that the school district had not hired her because of her sex. The district court found that she had been discriminated against, but the U.S. Court of Appeals found the district court to be in error when it shifted the burden of proof to the school district to prove it had not hired her for discriminatory reasons. In the words of the court:

> The initial burden (of proof) is on the plaintiff.... We have thoroughly searched the record in this case and have found nothing that supports the district court's finding of intentional discrimination.

In so deciding, the Court in effect ruled that the mere hiring of a male is not necessarily an indication of gender discrimination.

## Religion and Public Education

On first consideration, religion may not appear to be a cultural issue, but it is a subculture of its own, with different values, beliefs, and expectations about behavior within diverse groups. In the early days of the colonies, of course, the purpose of education was for religious ends. Indeed, the Old Deluder Satan Act in Massachusetts expressly stated its religious goals. As the focus in education shifted toward the more secular concerns of preparing citizens for participation in a democracy, some of our nation's Founding Fathers became concerned about the teaching of religion in public schools. They reasoned that if religion was to be taught in school, then the question arose as to whose religion should be taught, and the issue of indoctrination as a violation of personal liberty first appeared. The long history of religious strife and persecutions in Europe, resulting from the association of religion with the state, greatly influenced their views. The framers of the Constitution carefully avoided any mention of religion, but its omission ultimately resulted in the First Amendment, which made religious freedom explicit. Thomas Jefferson was a strong advocate for "a wall of separation between church and state." According to this doctrine, religion and religious instruction were viewed as a private concern. Logically, it follows that public tax funds should not be appropriated to support religion.

Of all the issues related to public education, religion remains one of the most emotionally charged and perhaps least understood in its relation to United States law. Perhaps the issue least understood by the general public is the fact that American public schools are *secular*—not simply nonsectarian. Being secular does *not* mean being "godless." It is merely a guarantee that the state or government will not encroach on individual religious beliefs (Pfeffer, 1967). There have been many court cases concerning religious issues in regard to education. They have involved three major issues: religion and the curriculum; prayer in public school; and religion and compulsory school attendance.

**Religion and the Curriculum**   From time to time, political activists in the United States have attempted to influence public policy in regard to specific religious beliefs, including bringing pressure on schools about curricular programs. A recurring battle has focused on the teaching of two specific viewpoints: the theories of evolution and creationism. The debate over Darwin's theory of evolution and the biblical account of creation has been reviewed in legislatures and courts. The famous "monkey trial" in Dayton, Tennessee, in July 1925, received national attention, primarily because it matched the famous lawyer Clarence Darrow against the politician William Jennings Bryan. Years later, there was a play and a movie (*Inherit the Wind*) made about this trial, in which a public school teacher, John Scopes, was convicted for teaching Darwinian theory, but who was later released on a technicality (*Columbia Viking Desk Encyclopedia*, 1953, p. 893). In this trial, a Tennessee statute that made teaching evolution a criminal offense was not overturned, but it was not enforced thereafter (Alexander & Alexander, 1985).

The debate over the teaching of creationism and Darwinian theory was to continue, however. In 1928 the State of Arkansas adopted a statute prohibiting the teaching of evolution, and for over thirty years official textbooks used in high school biology courses did not contain information on Darwinian theory. In 1965 biology teachers in the Little Rock school system adopted a text that did have a chapter on the theory of the origin of humans from lower-order species. Susan Epperson, a biology teacher, was confronted with this new textbook, but according to the state statute, just to make students aware of the existence of evolutionary theory would be grounds for dismissal and prosecution. When her case reached the Supreme Court in 1968 (Epperson v. State of Arkansas, 393 US 97, 89 S.Ct. 266), the decision was very different from that in the Scopes trial. In the opinion of the Court:

> There is and can be no doubt that the First Amendment does not permit the State to require that teaching and learning must be tailored to the principles or prohibitions of any religious sect or dogma.... It is clear that ... sectarian conviction was and is the law's reason for existence.

Thus the Arkansas statute fell because it conflicted with the First Amendment, which "does not tolerate laws that cast a pall of orthodoxy over the classroom."[1]

In 1987, a Louisiana statute that required "balanced treatment" of creation science and evolution was also struck down by the Supreme Court (Edwards v. Aguillard, 482 US 578). In this case, parents, teachers, and religious leaders challenged the constitutionality of the statute. Not only did it require schools to teach creation science along with evolution; it also *forbade* school boards to discriminate against those teaching creationism. The Supreme Court found the statute to be in violation of the First Amendment because its primary purpose was "to advance a particular religious belief... [and] it seeks to employ the symbolic and financial support of government to achieve a religious purpose." Again, the Supreme Court held firm on the separation of church and state in matters of curriculum.

**Prayer in Public School**  Another controversial debate involving religion has revolved around the issue of prayer in public schools. Two Supreme Court decisions aroused public confusion, relief, or anger, depending upon an individual's personal point of view.

Two cases involving state requirements that schools begin the day with readings from the Bible and recitation of the Lord's Prayer were heard together in the U.S. Supreme Court in 1963 (School District of Abington Township v. Schempp and Murray v. Curlett, 374 US 203, 83 S. Ct. 1560). In the case of Abington Township v. Schempp, the Schempp family had brought suit in Pennsylvania with the argument that the readings and prayer violated their rights under the Fourteenth Amendment, and therefore they sought to restrict this practice. The lower court in Pennsylvania found that this practice was intended as a religious exercise and was, therefore, in violation of the Fourteenth Amendment. In the case of Murray v. Curlett, Madalyn Murray had filed suit with her son William, a student in the Baltimore city schools, for the same practice to be cancelled. The lower court in Maryland found that the exercise was "sectarian," with the purpose of promoting moral values. The opinion of the Supreme Court, however, was that these religious exercises were in violation of the Constitution. The Court further stated:

> It is no defense to urge that the religious practices here may be relatively minor encroachments on the First Amendment....
>
> [I]t might well be said that one's education is not complete without a study of comparative religion or the history of religion and its relationship to the advancement of civilization. It certainly may be said that the Bible is worthy of study for its literary and historic qualities.... But the exercises here do not fall into those categories. They are religious exercises, required by the States in violation of the command of the First Amendment that the Government maintain strict neutrality, neither aiding or opposing religion....
>
> The place of religion in our society is an exalted one, achieved through a long tradition of reliance on the home, the church and the inviolable citadel of the individual heart and mind.... In the relationship between man and religion, the State is firmly committed to a position of neutrality.

This decision was met with widespread public debate about the so-called loss of religious values in America.

The issue of whether or not it is constitutional for clergy to offer prayers at graduation ceremonies came before the Supreme Court in 1991 (Lee v. Weisman, 112 S. Ct. 2641). The principal of a middle school in Providence, Robert Lee, invited a rabbi to deliver prayers at the graduation ceremonies and gave him a pamphlet with guidelines for nonsectarian prayer. The father of Deborah Weisman, a student who was graduating, objected. Lee petitioned. The Rhode Island District Court concluded that the practice did lend government endorsement of religion and thus violated the First Amendment. The U.S. Supreme Court also held that these exercises were in violation of the First Amendment. In the Court's opinion:

> The undeniable fact is that the school district's supervision and control of a high school graduation ceremony places public pressure, as well as peer pressure, on attending students to stand as a group or, at least, to maintain respectful silence during the Invocation and Benediction. This pressure, though subtle and indirect, can be as real as any overt compulsion.

In the 1990s, students in different areas of the country have exercised their personal "right" to conduct their own prayers at public high school graduation ceremonies. In 1992 a case on student-led prayer (Jones v. Clear Creek Independent School District, 930 F2d 416) was brought to the Supreme Court, but it denied certiorari. In nonlegal terminology, this means that the Court refused to hear the case, thus letting a lower court decision stand that student-led prayer at graduation ceremonies does not violate the First Amendment so long as it is nonsectarian and not proselytizing. The Court's refusal to hear this case suggests that it is waiting for more lower-court decisions before directly addressing the issue of student-led prayer.

**Religion and Compulsory School Attendance**   The relationship between religion and compulsory school attendance, whether in public or private school, has been examined by both state and federal judiciaries. The basic question in these cases was whether or not the state has jurisdiction in situations where students or their families perceive their religious views as being in conflict with school programs. The answer to this question is that it depends—that is, it depends not only on the religious but also the cultural context of the situation. The following two cases illustrate this point. In the first case, compulsory attendance was not supported; in the second case it was upheld.

The first case involved a religious sect known as the Amish. Jonas Yoder and others were charged and convicted in the Wisconsin Green County Court for violating the compulsory school attendance law. Jonas was a member of an Old Order Amish sect, which views formal education in high school as contrary to their religious beliefs. Their religious convictions seek a simple lifestyle in a community apart from the world. The Amish do support education through the eighth grade in order for their children to be able to read the Bible, to be good citizens, and to interact with non-Amish people when necessary.[2] But they do not want their children to be put into a situation with increasing competition in classes, pressure to conform, and exposure to materialistic and worldly values.

In 1972 the Yoder case came before the U.S. Supreme Court (State of Wisconsin v. Yoder, 406 US 205, 92 S. Ct. 1526). In determining its decision, the Court had the following concerns:

> In evaluating these claims we must be careful to determine whether the Amish religious faith and their mode of life are, as they claim, inseparable and interdependent. A way of life, however virtuous and admirable, may not be interposed as a barrier to reasonable state regulation of education if it is based on purely secular considerations; to have the protection of the Religion Clauses, the claims must be rooted in religious belief.

The Court perceived the Amish lifestyle as more than an individual preference, but rather as a shared religious view affecting daily life. The Court referred to Amish history:

> Aided by a history of three centuries as an identifiable religious sect and a long history as a successful and self-sufficient segment of American society, the Amish . . . have convincingly demonstrated the sincerity of their religious beliefs, the interrelationship of belief with their mode of life, the vital role that belief and daily conduct play in the continued survival of Old Order Amish communities and their religious organization.
>
> The impact of the compulsory attendance law on respondents' (Yoder et al.) practice of the Amish religion is not only severe, but inescapable for the Wisconsin law affirmatively compels them, under threat of criminal sanction, to perform acts undeniably at odds with fundamental tenets of their religious beliefs.

For these reasons, the Supreme Court decided that the state could not compel Amish children to attend public high school. Although culture was not specifically mentioned, it is clear from the following statement that the Court was also interpreting the Amish way of life in a culturally shared context:

> The Amish alternative to formal secondary school education has enabled them to function effectively in their day-to-day life with self-imposed limitations on relations with the world, and to survive and prosper in contemporary society as a separate, sharply identifiable and highly self-sufficient community for more than 200 years in this country.

The Yoder decision has been called the "Amish exception," and therefore is not applicable to other attempts to use it as a precedent. The next case is an example of one of these attempts.

In this case, Peter Duro refused to enroll his children in either public or private school in Tyrrell County, North Carolina, for religious reasons. Peter and his wife were members of the Pentecostal Church, and he was opposed to exposing his children to others who would corrupt them. He was also concerned about "secular humanism." The Duro children were being instructed at home by Mrs. Duro, who did not have any training as a teacher. The Pentecostal religion does not require that children be taught at home, and other children of this faith do attend public school. In 1981 Duro was charged with violating the North Carolina compulsory school attendance law. The district court applied the Wisconsin v. Yoder decision and held that the attendance law was unconstitutional in Duro's case.

In 1983 the case came before the U.S. Court of Appeals (Duro v. District Attorney, Second Judicial District of North Carolina, U.S. Court of Appeals, Fourth Circuit, 712 F.2d 96). This court distinguished the Yoder case from that of Duro, referring to the "unique facts and circumstances associated with the Amish community and religion," and to the fact that Amish children do attend school through the eighth grade and then obtain "informal vocational training to enable them to assimilate into the self-contained Amish community." In the opinion of the Court:

> Duro refuses to enroll his children in any public or nonpublic school for any length of time, but still expects them to be fully integrated and live normally in the modern world upon reaching the age of eighteen.... Duro has not demonstrated that home instruction will prepare his children to be self-sufficient participants in our modern society or enable them to participate intelligently in our political system, which is... a compelling interest of the state.
>
> ... We hold that the welfare of the children is paramount and that their future well-being mandates attendance in a public or non-public school.

Thus the Court judged to override Duro's religious interest in the interests of both his children and the state, which the phrase "participate intelligently in our political system" implies. Clearly, the concern of the Court was preparing children for competent citizenship.

### Language Instruction in School

The issue of language instruction involves the teaching of both English and other languages. Two Supreme Court cases are reviewed in this section; one dealing with the teaching of a "foreign" language, and the other dealing with the failure to provide instruction in English.

In the first case, a teacher in Zion Parochial School in Hamilton County, Nebraska, had been accused, tried, and convicted in the district court for teaching the reading of German to a ten-year-old student, despite a state statute of 1919 that forbade the teaching of foreign languages to students who had not completed the eighth grade. The state supreme court upheld the conviction on the rationale that English should be the "mother tongue" of all children in the state and that enforcement of the statute came within the "police power" of the state. When the case came before the U.S. Supreme Court in 1923 (Meyer v. Nebraska, 262 US 390), the conviction was reversed on the basis of the rights guaranteed by the Fourteenth Amendment. In the opinion of the Court:

> Mere knowledge of the German language cannot reasonably be regarded as harmful.... The protection of the Constitution extends to all, to those who speak other languages as well as to those born with English on the tongue....

No emergency has arisen which renders knowledge ... of some language other than English so ... harmful as to justify its inhibition ... [and] ... the infringement of rights long freely enjoyed.

This decision protected the rights of teachers to teach languages other than English to students before they enter high school. In the 1990s, many students enter schools with a native tongue other than English. When one considers the needs of these students for instruction in other languages, the importance of this Supreme Court decision cannot be overestimated.

In the second case, non–English speaking students were denied English instruction. In 1973 a report by the Human Rights Commission of San Francisco showed that in April of that year there were 3,457 Chinese students who spoke little or no English, and that only 1,707 of those students who needed special instruction in English were in fact receiving it. A suit was brought by non-English-speaking Chinese students against school officials to seek relief against unequal educational opportunity. The students did not specifically request either teaching English to Chinese-speaking students or instruction in Chinese. They asked only that the board of education solve the problem. The district court denied relief. The Court of Appeals upheld the district courst and denied relief on the grounds that students bring different advantages and disadvantages to their educational situation that result from different social, economic, and cultural backgrounds.

In 1974, the U.S. Supreme Court (Lau v. Nichols, 414 US 563) took a different view, based on the California Education Code itself. The code states that:

(a) English shall be the basic language of instruction in all schools; (b) [the state policy is] to insure mastery of English by all pupils in the schools; (c) no pupil shall receive a diploma of graduation from grade 12 who has not met the standards of proficiency in English; and (d) children between the ages of six and sixteen are subject to compulsory full-time education.

In the opinion of the Supreme Court:

Under these state-imposed standards there is no equality of treatment merely by providing students with the same facilities, textbooks, teachers, and curriculum; for students who do not understand English are effectively foreclosed from any meaningful education.

Basic English skills are at the very core of what these public schools teach. Imposition of a requirement that before a child can effectively participate in the educational program, he must already have acquired those basic skills is to make a mockery of public education.

Where inability to speak and understand the English language excludes national origin-minority group children from effective participation in the educational program offered by a school district, the district must take affirmative steps to rectify the language deficiency in order to open its instructional program to these students.

Thus, the Supreme Court decided in favor of the Chinese students. In the 1990s, this decision raises some important questions. Are students merely entitled to instruction in English? Or must they be instructed in English even if they and their families prefer basic instruction in another language? Can a student be exempt from English instruction? Should bilingual education instruct students in their native language only until they learn English? Or should bilingual education maintain students' native language in addition to English? In Chapter 13, these issues in bilingual education are addressed.

Language instruction is a complex issue because language is usually considered a fundamental part of cultural identity. Minority groups fear the loss of their language in succeeding generations of their children. On the other hand, instruction in English has traditionally been viewed by educators as binding the nation's diverse peoples together. A national language does provide cohesiveness in any society. Switzerland, however, has four national languages and a single national identity!

### Public Education for Illegal Immigrant Children

The United States has restricted immigration ever since the nineteenth century, and those who enter illegally are subject to deportation. Nevertheless, people do enter our country unlawfully and live in various states that are obvious ports of entry. One of these states is Texas.

In May 1975, the Texas Legislature revised its Educational Code in order to withhold state funds for the education of children not "legally admitted" to this country. The state also authorized school districts to deny these children enrollment in public schools. Despite this legislation, the schools in Tyler had continued to enroll immigrant children until the 1977-78 year. In July 1977, Tyler adopted a policy requiring undocumented illegal immigrant children to pay a full tuition fee in order to enroll in school. In September 1977, a suit on behalf of these children was filed against the superintendent and board of the Tyler School District in the U.S. District Court for Eastern Texas. The children were of Mexican origin and could not prove that they were legally admitted into the United States. The district court, although recognizing that the increase in Mexican immigrants had caused problems for the public schools, found that excluding these children would save money but not necessarily improve the education of the other students. The court also noted that an illegal immigrant might become a legal immigrant and that if children were denied an education, they would be permanently locked into the lowest socioeconomic status. Therefore, the district court held that they were entitled to equal protection under the Fourteenth Amendment. A court of appeals upheld the district court's finding.

Following this initial case, several similar cases were heard in other district courts in Texas, and were finally consolidated into a case heard before the District Court of Southern Texas in 1980. This court determined that the educational needs of these children were no different from those of other children. In 1981, a Court of Appeals upheld this decision.

When these separate cases reached the U.S. Supreme Court in 1982, they were consolidated into a single hearing (Plyler, Superintendent, Tyler Independent School District et al. v. Doe, Guardian, et al., 457 US 202). In the view of the Tyler School District, people who have entered the United States illegally were considered "not [to be] within a State's boundaries and subject to its laws." The Supreme Court disagreed, referring to the Fourteenth Amendment:

> Nor shall any state ... deny to any person within its jurisdiction the equal protection of the law.

In the opinion of the Court:

> The phrase "within its jurisdiction" was intended in a broad sense to offer the guarantee of equal protection to all within a State's boundaries, and to all upon whom the state would impose the obligations of its laws....
>
>   Use of the phrase "within its jurisdiction" thus does not detract from, but rather confirms, the understanding that the protection of the Fourteenth Amendment extends to anyone, citizen or stranger, who is subject to the laws of a State.... That a person's initial entry into a State ... was unlawful ... cannot negate the simple fact of his presence within the State's (territory). Given such a presence, he is subject to the full range of ... the State's civil and criminal laws ... until he leaves the jurisdiction ... he is entitled to the equal protection of the laws.

Another issue in this case was whether or not the State of Texas violated the equal protection clause quoted above in refusing to reimburse local school boards for the education of undocumented alien children. The Supreme Court took the view that these children are "special members of ... [an] underclass ... [who] can affect neither their parents' conduct nor their own status." The Court interpreted the Texas Educational Code as imposing a discriminatory burden against children on the basis of a legal situation for which they were not responsible. In other words, the children had no control over their parents' actions, which had brought them into their current situation. In the opinion of the Court:

> legislation directing the onus of a parent's misconduct against his children does not (fit) ... with fundamental conceptions of justice.... [E]ducation provides the basic tools by which individuals might lead economically productive lives to the benefit of us all ... denial of education to some isolated group of children poses an affront to ... the goals of the Equal Protection Clause.

The Court also viewed charging tuition for these children as a "ludicrously ineffectual" attempt at reducing illegal immigration, in comparison with the alternative of prohibiting the employment of illegal aliens. The Court's closing statement ended with these words:

> Whatever savings might be achieved by denying these children an education ... are wholly unsubstantiated in light of the costs involved to these children, the State and the Nation.

The allocation of taxpayers' money for educating children of *legal* immigrants has not been questioned, but many people have expressed anger or confusion over public money being spent for educating the children of illegal aliens. A review of this controversial case suggests that perhaps the most important finding in the Court's decision was the view that children are innocent bystanders who cannot be discriminated against for the action of their parents any more than the children of any other lawbreaker can be discriminated against for the actions of their parents, citizen or immigrant alike.

## Testing Standards for Teacher Employment

The issue of testing standards for teachers has been questioned at both the state and federal levels. In 1978 the Supreme Court addressed the issue of states using the National Teachers' Examination (NTE) in hiring and classifying teachers for payment scales (The United States of America v. The State of South Carolina, 445 Fed. Supp. 1094). South Carolina had been using the NTE for both hiring and classifying teachers, although a revision in the test score requirement made in 1976 would disqualify 83 percent of Black applicants, compared with 17.5 percent of White applicants. The United States had brought suit in a South Carolina district court, challenging this use of the NTE. The district court had upheld the state's use of the test for classifying and hiring purposes.

The Supreme Court affirmed South Carolina's use of the test. The Court's rationale was that (a) if applicants for a teaching position had the benefit of information upon which the tests were based, the tests did not violate the Fourteenth Amendment's Equal Protection Clause or the Civil Rights Act of 1964; (b) clear intent to discriminate was not in evidence; and (c) the use of the tests was to establish minimum standards. The fact that the use of the test might result in a disproportionate number of successes or failures among White or Black applicants was not interpreted by the Court as intentional discrimination.

## Testing Standards for Students

A series of court cases, ranging from 1979 to 1984 and dealing with testing standards for students, culminated in a U.S. Court of Appeals decision that had wide legal implications for other states as well (Deborah P. v. R. D. Turlington, 730 F.2d 1405, 1984).

In 1978 the Florida legislature amended its Educational Accountability Act to require public school students to pass a functional literacy exam (the SSAT-II) in order to receive a high school diploma. In 1979 students challenged the use of the test as a graduation requirement, under the Fourteenth Amendment, the Civil Rights Act of 1964, and the Equal Educational Opportunities Act of 1976, arguing that this requirement had a disproportionate impact on Black students, whose 20 percent failure rate was almost ten times greater than that of White students. The district court hearing the case held that the test did violate the Fourteenth Amendment and issued an injunction against using it for diploma granting purposes until the 1982–83 school year. This decision was based on two facts: (a) until the 1982–83 school year, Black students who would be taking the test had attended segregated schools for part of their education; and (b) there had not been sufficient notice before the planned starting date for the test.

The Fifth Circuit Court of Appeals upheld the district court's injunction against using the test, but requested further findings. The State of Florida was asked to demonstrate that the SSAT-II was a fair test of what was being taught in classrooms. Without such proof, using the test as a graduation requirement would violate both the Due Process and Equal Protection Clauses of the Fourteenth Amendment.

On remand in 1983, the district court heard the state's evidence based on information gathered during the 1981–1982 school year. This evidence included (a) a survey distributed to 65,000 teachers, 47,000 of whom replied; (b) a second survey of all sixty-seven Florida school districts that assessed grades in which the skills tested in the SSAT-II were taught, variations in instruction among the school districts, remedial programs, staff development, instructional materials, and special programs designed to help students pass the test; (c) site visits, to verify the accuracy of the reports; and (d) a third survey, given at random in each school district, asking students whether they had been taught the skills in the competency exam. A total of 32,000 students completed this survey. In addition to this evidence, three expert witnesses testified that Florida was in fact teaching what it was testing. The district court concluded that the SSAT-II was a valid exam because students were given an adequate opportunity to learn the skills before the test was used as a diploma requirement.

In 1984, in a second appeal (this time to a U.S. court of appeals), the petitioners (students) objected that the evidence relied on by the district court was invalid because it evaluated only the 1981–82 school year. Basing its finding on the massive amount of information from the teachers' surveys, site visitors' verifications of the district reports, and the student surveys, the Court of Appeals upheld the lower district court's decision that the students were actually being taught what was needed to pass the exams. In regard to a claim by the students that the disproportionate number of Blacks who failed the test was caused by "vestiges" of past discrimination, new evidence revealed that in the class of 1983, 99.5 percent of the Black students passed the communications portion of the test and 91 percent passed the mathematics portion. Considering these percentages, the Court of Appeals held that there was strong evidence that "'vestiges' of past discrimination did not cause Blacks students to fail the test."

Therefore, the U.S. Court of Appeals granted to the State of Florida the right to deny diplomas to students who do not pass the SSAT-II. This court decision that competency testing is not discriminatory, if the skills in the test have been taught in the school program, has given support to testing programs in other states as well.

## Continuing Testing Standards

The practice of teacher and student testing may have a negative impact on minorities seeking to enter the education profession. For example, universities in Illinois require students to pass the Pre-Professional Skills Test (PPST) or other tests of basic skills in order to be admitted into elementary teacher preparation programs (Voelker and Reyes, 1993). (I should mention here that this test is also required in Wisconsin and elsewhere.) A second requirement in Illinois is that students who complete teacher education programs must also pass a certification test before they may practice. A disproportionate number of minorities in Illinois fail these tests. In addition, the number of minority candidates for certification who failed the basic skills test (PPST) exceeded that of White candidates, even though White candidates made up 88 percent of all test takers. Thus, more minorities are screened out of teaching. Data from the Illinois State Board of Education reveals that eventually (students may retake the test), 99 percent of White students pass the basic skills test; 96 percent of Native American students pass; 88 percent of Asian American students pass; 85 percent of "Hispanic" students pass; and 84 percent of Black students pass (Voelker and Reyes, 1993, p. 7). Thus, some minority students were denied admission into the teaching profession at a time when a need for them is increasing. Voelker and Reyes also reported that analyses in other states reveal similar patterns.

Why are students having difficulty with these tests? Teachers are sometimes blamed for failing to prepare students, and students are blamed for a variety of reasons, including lack of motivation or family problems. Nevertheless, questions concerning the validity of these tests when given to culturally diverse students need to be addressed.

For example, one of my Southeast Asian students had trouble with a test I had given. In a follow-up conference, I went over the items on the test that she had missed. I quickly discovered that her problem with the test resulted from the fact that, in creating the test, I had used synonyms for words I had used during class. It became clear that she did not know what some of the words on the test meant. When I inquired why she had not asked me what the words meant, she said that she did not want to be rude! When I told her what the words meant on different questions, she was able to answer correctly. Instead of a failure on the test, her valid grade was a B.

Voelker and Reyes have asserted that "the time is now ripe for ... the substitution of more authentic and valid methods of assessing the potential of an individual to become an effective teacher" (1993, p. 9). I concur.

## CHAPTER SUMMARY

Judicial decisions at the federal level have impacted policies in American education. Cases have involved issues of segregation, gender discrimination, religion, language instruction, and testing standards.

One landmark U.S. Supreme Court decision, Plessy v. Ferguson, upheld segregation in public facilities and, by extension, in education. A second landmark decision, Brown v. Board of Education of Topeka, struck down segregation on the rationale that separate schools for non-White students were inherently unequal.

Judicial decisions involving gender discrimination have included issues of equitable salaries, medical (pregnancy) leave from work, and hiring practices.

The doctrine of separation of church and state has caused confusion and controversy in the minds of the public. Judicial decisions have involved curricular issues, prayer in school, and compulsory school attendance. The Amish have been established as an exception to compulsory school attendance in high school on the basis of their cultural traditions.

Issues regarding language instruction have involved the teaching of English and other languages. One U.S. Supreme Court decision protected the rights of teachers to teach languages other than English before the high school level. Another decision determined that students may not be denied English instruction. With increasing diversity in the United States, the problems of cost and variety in language instruction that a school district may be required to meet have yet to be determined.

Education of the children of illegal immigrants was upheld in the U.S. Supreme Court on the rationale that they cannot be treated on the basis of their parents' illegal action any more than other children are and that to deny them an education violates their rights under the Equal Protection Clause of the Fourteenth Amendment.

Testing standards for hiring and pay scales for teachers have been upheld by the U.S. Supreme Court. Competency testing for students' graduation has also been upheld by a U.S. Court of Appeals, but problems with testing continue.

## IMPORTANT TERMS

Categorical aid

De facto segregation

De jure segregation

The Amish exception

Testing standards

## QUESTIONS FOR DISCUSSION

1. In your educational experience, have you observed or been involved in a situation of de facto segregation? What were the circumstances that caused this?

2. If you have witnessed de facto segregation, what measures do you believe could have been taken to change the situation?

3. How do some of the judicial decisions discussed in this chapter involve the issues of access, quality, and outcomes discussed in chapters 4 and 5?

4. The legality of student-led prayer in schools has yet to be determined. Do you believe that they are in violation of the First Amendment or not? Why do you think so?

5. Do you believe teachers should lose their teaching positions if they fail to pass a national standards exam mandated after they are hired? Why or why not?

6. Do you believe that students should be required to pass a competency test before being granted a diploma? Why or why not?

## NOTES

1. In so saying, the court was actually quoting a decision from a previous case (Kerishian v. Board of Regents, 385 US 589, 1967).

2. The Amish usually refer to all other members of the White race as "English" whether they are or not.

## REFERENCES

Alexander, K., & Alexander, M. D. (1985). *American public school law* (2nd ed.). St. Paul: West.

———. (1992). *American public school law* (3rd ed.). St. Paul: West.

Bennett, L., Jr. (February 1992). "10 most dramatic events in African-American history." *Ebony*.

*Columbia Viking desk encyclopedia,* (1953). New York: Viking Press.

Pfeffer, L. (1967). *Church, state, and freedom.* Boston: Beacon Press.

*The United States Constitution.*

Voelker, A., & Reyes, D. (October 1993). "Some social implications of teacher testing for minorities in education: An Illinois study." Paper presented at the meeting of the Mid-Western Educational Research Association, Chicago, IL.

## KEY TO JUDICIAL CASES

F.2d = *Federal Reporter*. St. Paul, MN: West.

F.Supp = *Federal Supplement*. St. Paul, MN: West.

S.Ct. = *Supreme Court Reporter*. St. Paul, MN: West.

US = *United States Reports*. Washington: US Government Printing Office.

Kan., Mass., Mich. refer to state volumes: West.

## JUDICIAL CASES

This reference system is standard in American legal documentation. The first number refers to volume number, and the second number refers to page number in the volume(s) indicated.

*Brown v. Board of Education of Topeka,* 347 US 483, 74 S.Ct. 686 (1954).

*Cleveland Board of Education v. LaFleur,* 414 US 632 (1974).

*Danzl v. North St. Paul-Maplewood-Oakdale Independent School District No. 622,* US Court of Appeals, Eighth Circuit, 706 F.2d 813 (1983).

*Deborah P. v. R. D. Turlington,* 730 F.2d 1405 (1984).

*Duro v. District Attorney, Second Judicial District of North Carolina,* 712 F.2d 96 (1983).

*Edwards v. Aguillard,* 482 US 578 (1987).

*Epperson v. State of Arkansas,* 393 US 97; 89 S.Ct. 266 (1968).

*Griffin v. County School Board of Prince Edward County,* 377 US 218 (1964).

*Jones v. Clear Creek Independent School District,* 930 F2d 416 (1992).

*Keyes v. School District No. 1, Denver,* 413 US 189 (1973).

*Lau v. Nichols,* 414 US 563 (1974).

*Lee v. Weisman,* 112 S.Ct. 2641 (1992).

*Meyer v. Nebraska,* 262 US 390 (1923).

*North Haven Board of Education v. Bell,* 456 US 512 (1982).

*Plessy v. Ferguson,* 163 US 537 (1896).

*Plyler, Superintendent, Tyler Independent School District et al. v. Doe, Guardian, et al.,* 457 US 202 (1982).

*Roberts v. The City of Boston,* 59 Mass. (5 Cush.) 198 (1850).

*School District of Abington Township v. Schempp and Murray v. Curlett,* 374 US 203, 83 S.Ct. 1560 (1963).

*State of Wisconsin v. Yoder,* 406 US 205, 92 S.Ct. 1526 (1972).

*Swann v. Charlotte-Mecklenburg Board of Education,* 402 US 1 (1971).

*The United States of America v. The State of South Carolina,* 445 F.Supp 1094 (1978).

# PART II

# The Cultural Perspective

# 7

## The Nature of Culture

To understand another person,
it is first necessary to walk a mile in his moccasins.

NATIVE AMERICAN PROVERB

What is culture? How does it affect our lives? Culture is sometimes confused with society, but they are not the same. In common usage, "society" refers to people—a collection of human beings living together within a nation or geographic area.[1] The term "culture" itself does not refer directly to people, although people carry culture. Culture is basically an abstract concept.[2] Years ago an anthropologist, Alfred Kroeber (1948), provided a definition of culture that has become classic:

> Culture … include[s] speech, knowledge, beliefs, customs, arts and technologies, ideals and rules … what we learn from other[s], from our elders or the past, plus what we may add to it. (p. 253)

This definition implies that culture may be the most central factor in all our experience. Indeed it is. Culture gives us language. It sets the standard for our behavior. It shapes our material world. It determines our religion and our views about the divine or spirit world. It influences our relationship with nature and with other species. It defines our views of right and wrong. Culture is the very crucible of our identity.

These influences have a deterministic feel about them. We could believe that we are powerless in regard to our culture—that it controls our lives. Kroeber, however, was quick to point out that people affect culture by "what we may add to it." Social psychologists and sociologists have also taken an interactive view between culture and its members—that culture not only shapes individual values and behavior, but that individuals in turn modify and mold their culture. In the United States, culture exists within a national and ethnic context. There is a dominant mainstream culture (macroculture), and there are subcultures (microcultures) specific to diverse groups.

Kroeber's definition implies that culture exists on two levels: material and nonmaterial; manifest and covert; observable and deduced. Garcia (1991) has compared the visible (manifest) aspects of culture to the tip of an iceberg, the rest of which remains unseen (covert) below the surface of the water.

This chapter reviews the various aspects of nonmaterial culture, including values, mainstream culture, subcultures, cultural attitudes, cultural processes, and cultural types. Also included is an analysis of a culture in the process of being adapted to life in the United States. Finally, material culture is considered with some examples of how it relates to more hidden aspects of culture.

The reader may wonder why I am placing so much emphasis on nonmaterial culture. In school programs, the focus has often been on the material aspects of diverse cultures. This focus has been a problem in multicultural education because, without an understanding of the primacy of nonmaterial culture, there is a real danger of oversimplifying what material culture represents. Seree Weroha (1991), a Thai immigrant to the United States, has remarked that the most serious error in curricular programs has been the failure to connect material culture to the more profound aspects of culture out of which material culture is derived.[3]

# NONMATERIAL CULTURE

Nonmaterial culture is made up of the hidden aspects of culture. Aspects include (a) mainstream values; (b) subcultural values; (c) cultural attitudes; (d) cultural processes; and (d) cultural types.

Cultural values form the essence of any culture. They are the reasons why people act the way they do. Without an awareness of these values, we cannot understand the people who hold them. At first, the idea of learning the values of diverse cultures appears to be an almost impossible goal. After all, there are so many different cultures in the world. How can we hope to understand the "essence" of even a fair number of them?

## Value Orientations

An answer may lie in a concept suggested years ago by the anthropologist Florence Kluckhohn (Kluckhohn, 1956; Kluckhohn & Strodbeck, 1961). She proposed a theory of value orientations as a way of identifying the essential values of diverse cultures. The theory derived from three major assumptions. The first assumption was that there are a limited number of human problems that are common to people everywhere. The second assumption was that the solutions to these problems are not infinite and random but are limited by the variety of solutions that are logically possible. The third assumption was that all possible solutions to the basic human problems are present in all cultures. Thus, every culture has a **dominant orientation** that is believed and followed by most members of the society and, in addition, some alternative or **variant orientations** that are tolerated by the majority so long as they do not appear to threaten the cohesiveness of the society. If they do, they are no longer tolerated, but considered to be **deviant orientations,** which are not acceptable. The most important thing about any value orientation is that it represents a guiding principle for people to follow. Carter (1991) has reported that over the years extensive research in a variety of cultures supports the usefulness of Kluckhohn's theory as a starting point for understanding common viewpoints or values that diverse cultures share.

Kluckhohn originally identified the five following value orientations:

- a human nature orientation or beliefs about the basic character of human nature
- a relationship to nature orientation or beliefs about humanity's relation to the natural world
- a time orientation or a major time focus
- an activity orientation or a view of important human activity
- an orientation to social relationships or a focus on preferred social interaction

I suggest that there is a sixth, or spatial, orientation. A clarification of my use of this term is probably needed here. In psychology, "spatial orientation" generally refers to an individual's ability to interpret space, to perceive objects in it, or to manipulate objects in it. Here I am using the term to refer to a *value placed on location*. A spatial orientation would apply to all cultures. Like the other five value orientations, there is a logical limit to its range of possibilities.

The six orientations and their possible logical alternative solutions appear in Table 7.1. This table is meant to be read *horizontally*. The reader should not assume a fixed vertical relationship within the columns. For example, a present-time orientation is not always found in cultures whose relationship to nature is harmony. It is important to point out that a difference among diverse groups about the major focus for one orientation does not necessarily mean that there will be a difference in the major focus for another orientation. Among diverse groups in the United States, the orientations they share may serve as a starting point for cross-group communication and understanding.

**Mainstream American Value Orientations**  Kluckhohn identified five value orientations of mainstream culture in the United States. There are also variations that are reviewed in the next section. The mainstream orientations are as follows:

### A mutable and neutral human nature orientation
This is a belief that human beings are inherently neither good nor evil, but somewhere in between these two extremes. They may, however, be influenced in one direction or the other. In other words, they may develop in ways that are ethical and "good," or corrupted into cruelty or selfishness. In education, this neutral orientation has been expressed in the concept of tabula rasa, or the belief that a child is born a "blank slate" and that experience "writes" on this slate, thereby determining how the child's character develops. *Mutable* refers to the fact that change is possible, as compared to an immutable or unchangeable character.

### A view of mastery over natural forces
This belief has been expressed historically in the American view that the natural resources of the country are to be used as we wish. Americans also have tried to control nature by constructing dams, channeling rivers, building jetties, clearing forests, or filling in marshlands.

### A future time focus
Planning for the future has been a fundamental American value. Attending college in order to obtain a better job later is a good example of this value.

### A doing activity modality
Americans have had a tendency to equate action with accomplishment. Many teachers and parents tell children to "do something," implying that nonactivity is a waste of time.

### A focus on individualism
The several variations of this value in American culture were reviewed in Chapter 2.

As mentioned above, I suggest a further spatial orientation. A mainstream view in the United States has been one of geographic mobility.

**Table 7.1 Summary of Value Orientations**

| VALUE ORIENTATION | POSSIBLE ALTERNATIVES | | |
|---|---|---|---|
| View of Human Nature | *Evil* Tendencies need to be controlled | *Neutral or Mixed* Neutral at birth of both tendencies | *Good* People are basically good |
| Human Relation to Nature | *Subjugation* People have little control | *Harmony* Nature provides, people preserve | *Mastery* Control and use for own purposes |
| Time | *Past* Focus on tradition | *Present* The present is uppermost | *Future* Focus on planning ahead |
| Activity Focus | *Being* Action based on current situation orientation | *Being-in-Becoming* Focus on personal growth | *Doing* Action/ achievement |
| Focus of Social Relationships | *Lineal* Focus on family or clan | *Collateral* Focus on peer relationships | *Individualistic* Focus on personal goals and needs |
| Space[a] | *Limited* In space | *Shifting* Through space | *Relative* Dual orientation |

[a]Timm, 1995

### A shifting orientation to space

Before the arrival of the Europeans, some Native Americans did move from place to place in accordance with seasons, but their range of land defined their cultural identity. All other Americans obviously relocated here from somewhere else. In Europe, places had contributed to family identity and family names were given to places. With the opening of new opportunities in America, Europeans no longer were bound to their place. They left their cities and towns and country villages to escape war or natural disaster, to seek political or religious freedom, or to pursue individual dreams. Of course, Asians and Latinos also relocated to find new opportunities in America. Before the Civil War, most African Americans had relocation forced upon them by slavery, but a few had voluntarily come to seek new opportunities as so-called freemen or as indentured servants.

Although voluntary mobility was not true for all, it nevertheless gave rise to one of the most American of values—that if circumstances are not good where you are, then you can leave for better opportunities somewhere else. Today, Americans continue to relocate. We move around.

**Variations in American Value Orientations** According to Kluckhohn, variations in value orientation may coexist with the dominant orientation in all cultures. In the United States, some alternative or variant orientations are as follows. I have added some examples:

### An orientation that human beings are basically evil

Some Americans believe that to spare the rod is to spoil the child, which implies a view that children are fundamentally inclined toward evil ways and that they need strong punishment to deter them. This orientation derives historically from Puritanism.

### An orientation toward living in harmony with nature

Native Americans have traditionally held this value. Conservationists have also believed in a more harmonious view of our relationship with nature, including a responsibility to protect our natural environment. For example, the Scottish immigrant John Muir became a well-known conservationist in the late nineteenth century. Muir Woods National Monument in California was named for him.

### A belief that humans live in subjugation to nature

Those who work close to nature, such as farmers and forest rangers, and those who have suffered a natural disaster, are more aware of nature's power and the helplessness of humans in the wake of floods, fire, severe storms, drought, hurricanes, and tornadoes.

### An orientation to the past

Among European Americans, this value is held by those who honor traditions and customs. Sometimes it derives from ancestors' past actions, as for example a forebear who "came over on the Mayflower." Native Americans also value time-honored traditions and beliefs.

### An orientation to the present

This focus is particularly evident among the poor. One can hardly imagine a future filled with opportunities when one is trying to figure out how to meet today's needs. Migrant workers, for example, move from place to place as the jobs arise, and may not know where they will be next month, or even next week if the work is drawing to a close. Middle-class Americans have had a tendency to misunderstand this present-time focus and to characterize the poor as not planning for tomorrow.

### A being activity focus

This orientation may accompany a present-time focus, when people are concerned with their needs of the moment. This is often the case among the poor, but it may also be a value among those who are more economically advantaged. When people advise each other to "take time to smell the roses," they are in fact expressing a belief that we need to spend more time every day on the small joys of life.

### A being-in-becoming orientation

This orientation may be the one that is not readily apparent. Basically, it refers to a focus that may combine a future orientation with a present one. Some hobbies may exemplify this value. When people take college courses

that are unrelated to their work "for the fun of it," they often report that
they enjoy them at the moment and that they are also improving skills for
their future pleasure as well. In other words, they are in the process of "becoming better" at tennis or oil painting, for example.

### An orientation to lineal relationships

Lineal relationships are family relationships. Among European Americans,
those whose families have enjoyed high economic, political, and social status
place a high value on their family membership. On one occasion in South
Carolina, I was informed on first meeting a woman that she was descended
from a United States Senator who had held office over a hundred and fifty
years ago! Asian and Native Americans also place a high value on clan or
family memberships. For example, among the Hmong, clan membership is
extremely important. Among the various nations of the Iroquois Confederation, this clan membership is fundamental.

### A limited orientation to space

Among some European Americans, there are regional orientations that are
important. I have heard New Englanders, Southeasterners, New Yorkers,
Midwesterners, Californians, and others say that they might consider moving
from one city to another within their region, but they would not leave the
area. Once when I invited a couple from another region to visit, one of
them replied that they would probably never take a vacation out of the area
because they had everything they needed in it! Many of my students say that
they hope they would never have to leave the Midwest in order to find a job.
Students said the same thing about New England when I was teaching there.
Poorer people may have fewer options to relocate or even to enjoy vacations
that take them away from their immediate area. Limited resources constrict
the distances we may travel. Among Native Americans, there has traditionally been a strong identification with their land. Enforced relocation onto
reservations far removed from their "place" brought heartbreak with it that
few European Americans understood because they had relocated out of
choice.

### A relative orientation to space

This view is a dual orientation. It may be found in cultural groups that view
the spirit world as being part of this world. For people in these cultures, both
worlds coexist and are equally important.

In addition, this view is not unusual among people who travel between
two or more places. In order to have this view of space, however, the "shift"
must occur on a regular basis. Here, an individual doesn't simply commute
from home to work, but may live or spend extended amounts of time in two
or more places. For example, some friends of mine spend several days a week
in one city, and several days in another. One has said that when she wakes up
in the morning, if she is in a certain city, she knows it is Saturday! Another
friend travels extensively to the same cities on recurring business trips. He
wears two watches, one that he keeps set at his home time and the other that
he adjusts according to his location. He needs to check his "California

watch" when he calls home because he needs to remember that his family is in a different time as well as place. He, like Albert Einstein before him, knows that space and time are relative.

**Value Orientations in Diverse Groups**  Although Kluckhohn suggested the value orientations as a way of understanding culture years ago, her theory has continued to receive attention. Subsequent to Kluckhohn's original reports, extensive cross-cultural research on value orientations has been reported using either an interview schedule developed by Kluckhohn and Strodbeck (1961), which requires respondents to rank-order three value alternatives in response to hypothetical situations, or variations on this instrument (Lengermann, 1971; Carter & Helms, 1990). These studies include Africans, American Blacks, Cubans, Japanese, Native Indians including Navajo and Hupa, Puerto Ricans, Spanish, White middle-class Americans, and various European ethnic groups including Greeks and Italians (Kluckhohn & Strodbeck, 1961; Szapocznik et al., 1978; Carter, 1990; Papajohn & Spiegel, 1975; Bachtold & Eckvall, 1978; Lengermann, 1971; Teffi, 1968; Caudill & Scarr, 1962). A summary of these findings by racial and cultural groups appears in Table 7.2.

Findings in these studies support Kluckhohn's original hypothesis that similarities in these orientations are found across cultural groups. Other studies support Kluckhohn's hypothesis that within cultural groups, value orientations vary and may be influenced by educational level, age, socioeconomic status, and immigrant status (whether first, second, or third generation). Sutcliffe (1974) reported differences in orientations among Palestinians from different social class and educational levels. Lengermann (1972) also reported differences in orientations by social class in Trinidad. Kahl (1968) found differences in orientations by socioeconomic status in Latin American cultures. Caudill and Scarr (1962) reported generational differences between Japanese students and their parents in regard to life situations. In two different studies, Carter and Helms found more preferences for a belief in subjugation to nature, in the basic good in human nature, a being activity modality, and a present-time focus among White women in comparison to White men (1990). They also found more preferences for a belief in subjugation to nature and a present-time focus among Black women in comparison to Black men (1987).

These numerous studies support the value orientation concept as a useful approach to the study of cultural values. It may contribute to our understanding of diverse peoples and their behavior. It may also serve as a basis for communication among diverse groups sharing similar orientations.

## Macroculture

The idea of a mainstream or national culture has also been suggested by Banks (1988), who referred to this "big" culture as the **macroculture.** Because of the predominance of English settlers in the original eastern colonies, it is not surprising that many American institutions are based on English traditions. Our Republican form of government is based partly on the philosophy of natural rights and partly on the structure of the Iroquois Confederation (Chapter 2). Our economic

**Table 7.2  Summary of Cultural Value Orientations for Various Racial/Cultural Groups**

| ORIENTATIONS | ALTERNATIVE | | |
|---|---|---|---|
| **Human Nature** | *Evil*<br>Blacks (3)<br>Puerto Rican (5) | *Mixed*<br>WMCA (1, 2)<br>Chinese (4)<br>Italian (5)<br>Greek (5) | *Good*<br>WMCA (4)<br>Africans (4) |
| **Person/Nature** | *Subjugation*<br>Blacks (3)<br>Africans (4)<br>Chinese (4)<br>Italian 5)<br>Greek (5)<br>Shoshone (6) | *Harmony*<br>Spanish (1)<br>Navaho (1)<br>Cubans (2)<br>Blacks (10) | *Mastery*<br>WMCA (1, 2)<br>Hupa (6)<br>Japanese (9) |
| **Time Sense** | *Past*<br>Blacks (3)<br>Africans (4)<br>Shoshone (6) | *Present*<br>Spanish (1)<br>Navaho (1)<br>Cubans (2)<br>Puerto Rican (5)<br>Italian (5)<br>Greek (5)<br>Hupa (6)<br>Trinidadian (7) | *Future*<br>Texan (1)<br>Mormon (1)<br>WMCA (1, 2)<br>Chinese (4) |
| **Activity** | *Being*<br>Spanish (1)<br>WMCA (3, 4)<br>Puerto Rico (5)<br>Italian (5)<br>Greek (5)<br>Trinidadian (7)<br>Shoshone (8) | *Being-in-Becoming*<br>Blacks (3) | *Doing*<br>Navaho (2)<br>WMCA (1, 2)<br>Africans (4)<br>Chinese (4)<br>Hupa (6)<br>Blacks (10) |
| **Social Relationships** | *Lineal*<br>Greek (5)<br>Japanese (8) | *Collateral*<br>Navaho (1)<br>Cubans (2)<br>WMCA (3)<br>Africans (4)<br>Chinese (4)<br>Puerto Rican (5)<br>Italian (5)<br>Shoshone (8)<br>Japanese (9)<br>Blacks (10) | *Individualistic*<br>Texan (1)<br>Mormon (1)<br>WMCA (1, 2, 4)<br>Hupa (6)<br>Trinidadian (7) |

WMCA = White Middle-Class American

1 = Kluckhohn & Strodbeck (1961); 2 = Szapocznik, et al. (1978a); 3 = Carter (1990); 4 = Sodowsky, et al. (in press); 5 = Papajohn & Spiegel (1975); 6 = Bachtold & Eckvall (1978); 7 = Lengermann (1971); 8 = Teffi (1968); 9 = Caudill & Scarr (1962); 10 = Carter & Helms (1987).

Source: Carter (1991). Reproduced with permission of the American Counseling Association.

system is based on the idea of a free market economy, which developed in England. Our common language has been English.

Gollnik & Chin (1994) have identified several macroculture values in the United States which, in fact, fit with the mainstream American value orientations identified by Kluckhohn. Table 7.3 summarizes these macroculture values in relation to these value orientations.

**Table 7.3  Relationship of United States Macroculture Values to Value Orientations**

| MACROCULTURE VALUE[a] | VALUE ORIENTATION |
| --- | --- |
| a time-oriented and time-regulated life | future time |
| equal opportunity with an expectation of hard work | individualism |
| mass education with an expectation of personal achievement | individualism |
| a "Protestant" work ethic | doing |
| social status based on occupation, education, and economics | individualism |
| an elaborate technology | doing |
| emphasis on manufactured goods | doing |
| achievement judged by material possessions | doing |
| social status based on achievement | individualism |
| achievement valued over inheritance | doing |
| cleanliness | doing |
| emphasis on the new as better than the old | future time |
| emphasis on youthfulness | future time |

[a]Adapted from Gollnick and Chinn (1986, 1994).

## Microculture

The idea of variations within a society has been suggested by others in addition to Kluckhohn. According to Banks, different microcultures "mediate, interpret, re-interpret, perceive and experience these over-arching national values ... differently" (1994, p. 84). Gollnick & Chinn (1994) have identified several microcultures. These are (a) ethnicity; (b) social class; (c) religion; (d) language; (e) gender; (f) age; and (g) exceptionality. (Geographic region may be considered a microculture.) Some of these are subject to change, while others are obviously not. We are born male or female. If our ancestors were Sioux or Japanese, then we are Sioux or Japanese, although the influence of this heritage depends upon the degree of importance we or our parents have given to these traditions. We may, however, choose to embrace a different religion from that of our family. We may move from one area of the country to another. Through education, Americans believe that we may improve our circumstances, but there are limits to this advance that depend not only upon our personal talents, but also on our original socioeconomic level and freedom from discrimination by others. Age is the only microculture in which we may belong to all of its subgroups, if we live long enough to experience life's different stages.

The reader may be surprised that race is not generally considered to be a microculture. There are several reasons for this. All races have ethnic groups or diverse nationalities, with their unique differences. (I stated in Chapter 2 that this is true for more recent African American immigrants who know their nation of origin, in contrast with descendants of former slaves.) Members of all races follow diverse religions. They live in different environments with varying economic circumstances. Because of this, people from different races who share the same economic status, education, religious beliefs, and living environment may have more in common with each other than they have with members of their own race who differ in these ways. Maureen Smith, an Oneida Native American, has stated that there is no "generic Indian culture" and that the confusing and blending of different tribal customs, skills, and artifacts, which happens all too often in schools, not only deprives each group of its true identity but creates stereotypes in the minds of non-Indian peoples (personal communication).

Our personal identity is derived from our individual, group, and national frames of reference (Chapter 2), but it is also derived from the relative importance we place on our various microcultures. For example, two of my students were sisters, and yet their individuality was clear, even though they had grown up in the same home. In class they talked of the different emphasis they placed on their identical microcultures. One said that she considered gender and region of the country as being important to her sense of identity: "I am a Midwestern woman." The other placed more emphasis on age and an exceptional talent: "I am a twenty-two year old athlete."

Some people are **bicultural.** That is, they are equally comfortable within two cultural groups, often with two or more languages. Children may be born into bicultural families and grow up identifying with both cultures. Biculturalism may also occur when people are exposed to and adopt the values of cultures different from their culture of origin. Banks (1994) has described different levels of biculturalism, ranging from superficial cross-ethnic encounters to full assimilation into another culture. These levels are particularly relevant to immigrant groups in America.

## Value Orientations and Microcultures

There is a relationship between value orientations, macroculture, and microcultures. For example, farmers (rural microculture) whose livelihood depends upon the whims of nature may feel more subjugated to natural forces than city dwellers feel. Many older people (age subgroup) orient to the past, while the young orient toward the future. I mentioned earlier that the poor (socioeconomic microculture) are more oriented to the present time in their focus on trying to meet current needs. As children of immigrants become educated in American schools and learn macroculture values, they develop different views from those of their parents, which disrupts both family relationships and cultural traditions.

## CULTURAL ATTITUDES

Following are some definitions of major attitudes concerning culture. In the United States, these attitudes may refer to racial groups or to subcultural groups. The concepts of cultural pride, chauvinism, and degradation are adapted from Garcia (1991).

**Ethnocentrism** is the judgment of another culture according to the values of one's own culture. It is an inability to view other cultures from their point of view, or an attitude that one's own group is superior.

**Cultural Relativism** is the ability to put aside one's own cultural viewpoints and to view other cultures from within their different perspectives.

**Prejudice** is literally a "prejudgment" or preset attitude, which is usually negative, toward both the views and members of other groups.

**Discrimination** is the acting out of negative attitudes toward members of diverse groups. It also refers to legal, economic, political, social, and educational practices that exclude individuals on the basis of race or other factors.

**Stereotype** is an overgeneralized image of and belief about the behavior of members of diverse groups.

**Cultural Pride** is respect and admiration for one's own cultural group and heritage. The group may be defined by nationality, ethnicity, social class, gender, religion, or region.

**Cultural Chauvinism** is a feeling of superiority about one's own group in contrast with those of other groups. People take pride in their culture, but sometimes this pride leads to arrogance and rejection of others. Cultural chauvinism is cultural pride carried to an extreme degree.

**Cultural Degradation** is a view that one's own group is inadequate or inferior, with a resulting low self-esteem, brought about not simply from being discriminated against but also from being overlooked or ignored.

**Ageism** is a belief in the inherent capabilities of individuals on the basis of age. Ageism also refers to discrimination on the basis of age.

**Racism** is a belief in the inherent capabilities of individuals on the basis of race. Racism also refers to discrimination on the basis of race.

**Sexism** is a belief in the inherent capabilities of individuals on the basis of gender. Sexism also refers to discrimination on the basis of gender.

## CULTURAL PROCESSES

How do people learn value orientations and attitudes? There are a several psychological theories about how people learn social attitudes. These are reviewed in Chapter 10, in relation to the development of prejudice. The following are cultural processes involving learning within a cultural context:

**Assimilation** is the process of incorporating one group within another, or the intention of making one group more homogenous in relation to another.

In the United States, official policy has aimed at accomplishing this homo-geneity through education.

**Enculturation** is the process of learning the language, values, traditions, knowledge, and skills of a culture, and accepting these as one's own. This usually occurs in the context of growing up in the culture of one's parents.

**Socialization** is sometimes used as a synonym for enculturation. In the field of anthropology, this process refers to teaching children about rules for be-havior that are expected in the culture of their parents. Socialization includes standards of conduct in regard to eating, sexual behavior (including the ob-servation of taboos), learning how to take care of oneself, and learning how to control aggression. Expectations for these behaviors are usually explicit.

**Acculturation** is the process of becoming acquainted with the language, values, knowledge, and behavior patterns of another culture that are different from those of one's native culture, and adopting these as one's own. Accul-turation also refers to the impact of one culture on another, as occurs in colonization, occupation of another country, or conquest.

**Training** refers to the teaching of skills and knowledge considered necessary to function as an economically independent adult within the social system. This may take place in schools, but it may also occur in apprenticeships or any situation in which an expert teaches a novice.

## CULTURAL TYPES

In spite of the wide variety of cultures in the world, Margaret Mead (1970) iden-tified cultural similarities that are even broader categories than the shared value orientations described by Florence Kluckhohn. She described three basic cultural types, which she labeled as post-figurative, co-figurative, and pre-figurative cul-tures. Interestingly, each of these has its own value orientations.

### Post-Figurative Cultures

Post-figurative cultures are historically preliterate or semiliterate and depend heavily on oral tradition. This type of culture derives authority from the past. Children learn primarily from their elders, who are the transmitters of cultural knowledge, language, skills, customs, traditions, and values. There is a timeless-ness within these cultures. Very few changes occur over the years. Older mem-bers of the society have difficulty with cultural change and wish to maintain the culture as it is, with as little alteration as possible. Even though individuals may come into contact with other cultures or relocate, they find adjustment difficult.

### Co-Figurative Cultures

Co-figurative cultures are those in which individuals within the same generation share their knowledge and skills with each other, simultaneously learning from and teaching their peers. Focused on the present, people attempt to adapt to changing expectations and cultural norms. Conditions for co-figurative cultures arise when one culture comes into contact with another culture or when people immigrate to a new location where the dominant culture is different from their original one. In their struggle to adapt, immigrants learn new ways that are different from those of the past. They develop new behaviors based on their own experience and provide role models for each other. Thus, in Mead's view, members of the same generation teach each other.

### Pre-Figurative Cultures

A pre-figurative culture may also arise when people are conquered or when they immigrate to a new location. This type of cultural situation represents the largest generational gap between the elders and the young, who have grown up in totally different environments. The young realize that their future is not merely an extension of past customs, traditions, and values. They also realize that their parents may not have the knowledge necessary to guide them and that new information and skills are necessary to survive. Although this type of culture may appear to be no different than a co-figurative one, in Mead's view the difference is that in a pre-figurative cultural situation the young impart knowledge to those who are older. The elders must adapt or be left behind, culturally speaking.

Pre-figurative cultural situations may also occur as a result of rapidly expanding technology that renders old ways quickly out of date. Here again, the elders must adapt or be left behind. The microcomputer may serve as an example of this situation. Two older people of my acquaintance took opposite views. A seventy-year-old said to me, "Well, I don't know about computers, but that's all right. I don't need to." An eighty-three-year-old said to me, "Well, I guess I'm going to have to get one of those things so I can know what people are talking about." She then turned to her grandson and asked if he would help her learn how to use it.

Mead suggested that the contrast among these three types of cultures describes the American immigrant experience. Perhaps the need of immigrants to look forward, even as they remembered their original culture, laid the foundation for the dominant American focus on the future. As children are born to immigrant parents, however, their perceptions of society are influenced more by their present situation than by their parents' references to the past. Perhaps the need of immigrant children to reject the old ways, in their effort to find their own way, lays the foundations for the youthful rebel in America.

## A CULTURE IN PROCESS

Over the past several years I have conducted an ethnographic field study among Laotian Hmong in the Midwestern United States (Timm, 1992a; 1992b; 1994). The experiences of these refugees, who have been living in America for less than twenty years, may serve as an example of some of the issues in this chapter. Hmong traditional value orientations are very different from dominant American ones. The Hmong are also moving from a post-figurative into a co-figurative and pre-figurative cultural situation.

## Hmong History

The Hmong trace their ancestry to central Asia over four thousand years ago, from where they migrated into China. In the nineteenth century, they began to move into the highlands of what is now northern Vietnam, Laos, and Thailand. The Laotian Hmong relocation to the United States resulted from political events in Southeast Asia. In 1954, the French protectorate in Indochina ended after sixty-one years, and Vietnam, Cambodia, and Laos were recognized as independent states by the Geneva Accords. A struggle for power erupted in Vietnam and Laos. In the 1960s, the United States increased secret military operations during the Vietnam War and recruited the Hmong, living in villages in the northwestern highlands of Laos, to help support these operations. The Hmong rescued American pilots shot down in combat; they reported North Vietnamese convoys and waged guerilla warfare against them; and they protected the U.S. radar system in Laos. In exchange they were promised that the United States would protect them in the future, regardless of the outcome of the Vietnam War (Podeschi & Xiong, 1992).

When the war ended in 1975, the Pathet Lao (the communist faction in Laos) gained control of the country and began a bloody campaign to exterminate the Hmong in retaliation for their support of both the United States and of the Royal Lao (the political enemies of the Pathet Lao). Hmong villages were bombed and pillaged. Men, women, and children were murdered. The Hmong were forced to flee for their lives. Those who survived hid in the jungle and made their way across the Mekong River into Thailand, where they were interred in relocation camps (Goldfarb, 1982). In the 1970s, American military personnel helped those men who had served the United States to relocate in America, along with members of their families. A few emigrated to Canada and France. Other Hmong also relocated later. In 1994 some remained in relocation camps because a Thai policy forbids their settling in Thailand. In the mid-1990s, those remaining in the camps face repatriation to Laos.

## Hmong Culture

The cultural background of the Hmong stands in sharp contrast to that of mainstream America. In Laos they lived in rural farming villages and practiced slash-and-burn cultivation. Single-walled homes had no heat or water facilities in the mild climate.

Society was organized around patrilineal clans (tracing descent through the father) that guided social relationships. Personal decisions were referred to clan leaders. Ancestor worship was along clan lines. Shamans assisted in both folk medicine and religious rituals. Marriages were arranged between families in different clans. A "bride-price" was paid by the new husband's family as a promise to the bride's family that she would be well treated. Early marriages were considered ideal. The average age of marriage for a girl was between twelve and fifteen years; the average age of marriage for a boy was between fourteen and seventeen. Children were considered as belonging to the husband's clan. A widow often married a brother of her husband as a way of remaining with her children in their clan. Large families were highly valued. The elderly were cared for by younger clan members.

Hmong culture was basically an oral one. Few villages had a school. French missionaries in the 1950s had given a written form based on the Roman alphabet to the Hmong language. Takaki (1989) reported that 70 percent of the first refugees to enter the United States were nonliterate.

### Entering America

The Hmong began arriving in the United States in the late 1970s and early 1980s. Some are still arriving in the 1990s. Coming from a warm climate, many Hmong located in California, but many also located in more northern areas such as Minnesota and Wisconsin, where they found the adjustment to harsh winters very stressful. On first arrival in the United States, many Hmong suffered severe culture shock, which is a response to an abrupt and extreme change in culture. This response has been experienced by people who move from one part of the world to another, from one country to another, or from one region to another. It includes an *emotional* reaction to radically different circumstances from a former situation. When people in the United States move from the seacoast to a location inland, for example, they report that they have a very difficult time adjusting merely to the landscape or climate, even though they are still living in America. (Personally, I have relocated twice, and can understand this mild disorientation.) When an immigrant relocates to an entirely different country and culture, the circumstances can be overwhelming. When a refugee has suffered from the trauma of war, however, a more serious reaction may occur in addition to culture shock. This reaction is known as **post-traumatic stress disorder (PTSD),** and is commonly found among refugees dislocated from their homeland. PTSD has been reported among Cambodian refugees as well (Bemak & Timm, 1994; Chapter 3). Following relocation in the United States, some Hmong men died unexpectedly in their sleep. Medical personnel attributed this to the fact that many of them were suffering from severe stress and depression. In addition, they were desperate to find employment.

### The Hmong in Transition

I interviewed Hmong males and females, ranging from sixteen to over sixty years of age, as well as Hmong clan and community leaders. The interviews ranged in length from two and a half to three hours each. A Hmong research assistant served as translator/interpreter with participants who had a limited mastery of English. Questions included a variety of issues including childrearing practices, marriage customs, clan relationships, gender roles, and views of education. I should mention here that the categories were *suggested by my Hmong assistant.* Traditional Hmong values emerged from this study that may be interpreted in terms of Kluckhohn's value orientations. Table 7.4 presents their traditional orientations. Historically, the Hmong had a neutral view of human nature with some concern about evil spirits, a belief in the powerlessness of humans in regard to natural forces (subjugation to nature), a past-time focus, a lineal (clan) view of social re-

**Table 7.4 Hmong Value Orientations**

| VALUE ORIENTATION | TRADITIONAL ORIENTATION | ACCULTURATED ORIENTATION |
| --- | --- | --- |
| **Human Nature** | Neutral | Neutral |
| **Human Relation to Nature** | Subjugation | Mastery |
| **Time** | Past | Future |
| **Activity Focus** | Being | Doing |
| **Focus of Social Relationships** | Lineal | Individualistic/ Collateral |
| **Space**[a] | Limited | Shifting |

[a]Timm, 1995

lationships, and a formerly limited view of space, arising out of their village life. Generational differences in value orientations appeared in the interviews between the older and younger respondents, who seemed to be adopting more mainstream American values. The acculturating values of these younger Hmong are also presented in Table 7.4.

These generational differences in value orientations reflected the characteristics of post-figurative, co-figurative, and pre-figurative cultural points of view. Those over age thirty-five expressed post-figurative views as they looked to the culture and values they had known in Laos. They feared the loss of their language and traditions and were concerned about the young. *All* of them answered the sixty-five questions on the interview with the words "Well, back in Laos we did...."

Those between their early twenties and age thirty-five expressed a co-figurative point of view. They looked both to the past and to the future and expressed a need for adaptation to American mainstream culture. *All* of them answered the questions with the statement "Well, back in Laos we did..., but we are not in Laos anymore and we are going to have to change a little." They were concerned about the loss of their language and the old traditions, but they also verbalized a need to be "practical." They often added that they had to figure out what to do sometimes, because some of the old ways did not work anymore.

The participants in their teens up to age twenty expressed a pre-figurative point of view. They had respect for their Hmong heritage but also spoke more independently and expressed a wish to make their own decisions, rather than consulting older family and clan members. *All* of them said "Well, my parents [or my grandparents] say so and so, but I can't always do that." A high school student said that no one was going to choose a husband for her. Another student expressed a frustration over wanting to go out with his friends after school, which his parents thought was a waste of time. One college student said it was hard for him to talk to his grandmother and that he felt more American now. He also told me that he has been dreaming in English.

The Hmong experience repeats that of earlier immigrants and refugees. They envision new opportunities that they did not have in their former country. Even as the elders express concern over the loss of their past, they also view education as the hope for their children's future. With great pride, Hmong parents showed me pictures of their children in college. Hmong community leaders recognize that economic and political influence follows educational achievement. These educational advances, however, are causing problems for women, who also are beginning to want to pursue their own way. Relocation in different cities is another problem. Some in their twenties reported that they were conflicted about moving away from their families. A twenty-six-year-old said that when he moved from St. Paul to Green Bay, his father did not understand. A teenage student said she was not going to stay in the same city if a better job was available elsewhere. (She actually said, "No way, Jose!")

Like others before them, the Hmong now live in two cultural worlds. Their future remains uncertain. Yang Dao[4] (1993), a highly respected leader in the United States and the first Hmong to earn a Ph.D., has described the Hmong in the United States as being at "the turning point."

## Hmong Culture and American Education

Carter has suggested that in multicultural programs, it may "not be enough to focus primarily on the history and sociopolitical experience of the culturally different group" (1991, p. 2), and that a knowledge of value orientations may provide meaningful insights. Weroha (1991) has also expressed the belief that educators cannot possibly begin to understand diverse groups without knowledge of their values.

Elsewhere (1992a, 1992b, 1994), I have reported suggestions for teachers and administrators working with Hmong students. From time to time I have presented workshops in various schools. (In 1995 Wisconsin had the second-largest Hmong population in the United States, with only California exceeding it.) When I presented these traditional and acculturating Hmong value orientations to school administrators, counselors, and teachers working with Hmong students, they told me that they found these orientations "enormously useful" in helping them to understand their Hmong students. They also said that they believed knowledge of Hmong values would facilitate their communication with Hmong families. One district supervisor said that "Hmong culture interpreted through Kluckhohn's value orientations actually puts you inside the head of somebody from that culture."

# MATERIAL CULTURE

I have focused on nonmaterial culture in this chapter in order for the reader to be familiar with its pervasiveness in our lives. Some general remarks about material culture are also needed. Two examples illustrate the relationship of material to nonmaterial culture.

Material culture includes the observable and tangible aspects of culture such as dress, architecture, tools, artifacts, foods, music, and dance. These material aspects of culture have been referred to as **cultural expressions** (Weroha, 1991). These tangible aspects of culture have all too often been the major focus of multicultural education programs. Although they are enjoyable, they are not always presented in a way that is conducive to a meaningful awareness of and appreciation for diverse cultures. Material culture, however, can be used in a way that leads to a deeper understanding not only of diverse experiences, but of cultural values as well.

The arts may be particularly suitable for introducing values and nonmaterial culture. The function of art is to portray and embody the most profound beliefs inherent in a culture. A Native American dance symbolizes the relationship between humankind and the spirit and natural worlds. Cultural myths and legends contain profound insights about human experience as viewed within diverse cultures. Chapter 8 examines how popular American culture reflects our cultural values. There are also similarities in stories across cultures that may provide the basis for classroom discussions. Many folktales are humorous, presenting as they do the quirks of human nature by which we can laugh at our human foibles. Drama provides a means of participation and role playing from diverse cultural perspectives. The multicultural comedy in Appendix I was written for school performances and school audiences. Multicultural educational programs can benefit by using these art forms as avenues to deeper awareness.

An example of the relationship between material culture and cultural history appears in Figure 7.1, which shows a Hmong pandeau (or *paj'n taub;* pronounced pan-dow). These stitched "story cloths" arose in this traditionally oral culture as a means of recording important events. This pandeau presents the Hmong refugee experience. In the upper-right corner, planes are bombing a Hmong village. In the upper-left corner, villagers are fleeing. In the second row, Pathet Lao soldiers are pursuing them into the jungle, where they live in a makeshift shelter. In the lower right, they arrive at the Mekong River between Laos and Thailand, which they cross by rafts, inner tubes, or by swimming. In the lower-left corner they arrive safely in Thailand, where a Thai guard greets them.

Figure 7.2 shows a pandeau that I found particularly interesting because it shows the effects of acculturation in the United States. Formerly, pandeaus contained no writing, but here a story line in English is inserted into a traditional Hmong folktale. Here vegetables make their own way to the house, but after they are reprimanded by the farmer, they are "stuck" in the fields. They have lost their feet! The story reads:

A long time ao when
rices corns squashes
and cucumbs knew to
come by themselves

One day the
y came and knocked the
door, "Go back to the field we(')ll c
ome giet you when we needed people s
houted so today we all have
to go get them the field

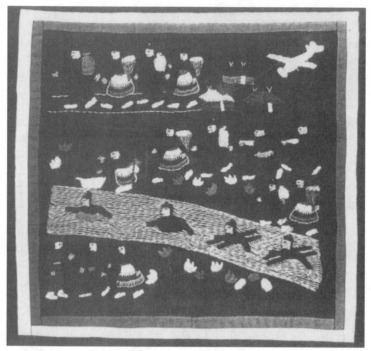

**FIGURE 7.1** Hmong Pandeau Showing History
Photo courtesy of James Labre.

**FIGURE 7.2** Hmong Pandeau Showing Folktale
Photo courtesy of James Labre.

One of the things that is so delightful about this narrative is that it includes the writing style common among all people learning to write in a different language. Examples include (a) the overapplication of plurals as the rule for adding "s" is learned, but not the exceptions to this rule, which have not yet been mastered; (b) misspelled words; (c) punctuation errors; (d) the splitting of letters at the end of the line from the rest of the word at the beginning of the next line; and (e) dropped prepositions. All these represent a stage in the learning of a different language that disappears later, as the language is acquired. This pandeau was made by a woman living in a culture in transition. When I found it at a bazaar, I told her that I really liked it. She was very proud of it.

Material culture need not be "superficial" culture, and multicultural curricula need not be mere "entertainment" or an interesting diversion. By relating material culture to cultural history, values, and processes, both the artifacts and the culture may become more meaningful to students of all ages. Chapter 12 examines more issues in relating material culture to nonmaterial culture in the classroom.

## CHAPTER SUMMARY

Culture is an abstract concept that refers to the knowledge, customs, technologies, rules, and values of various groups. It consists of nonmaterial and material aspects.

Nonmaterial culture includes value orientations, including those of the American mainstream (macroculture) and diverse groups (microcultures). Nonmaterial culture also refers to cultural attitudes about diverse groups and cultural processes or ways in which people learn the ways of their group's culture.

There are three cultural types: post-figurative, co-figurative, and pre-figurative. The Hmong experience in the United States represents these three types of culture in its process of adapting to American ways.

Material culture refers to tangible things, such as art, music, literature, and technology. It may be used in multicultural curricula so long as it is integrated with the deeper values of nonmaterial culture, in order for it not to be merely an entertaining diversion.

## IMPORTANT TERMS

Bicultural

Nonmaterial culture

Value orientations

Dominant orientations

Variant orientations

Deviant orientations

Material culture

Macroculture

Microculture

Post-figurative culture

Co-figurative culture

Pre-figurative culture

Cultural expressions

## QUESTIONS FOR DISCUSSION

1. Compare the mainstream American value orientations with those of a subgroup with which you are familiar. How do they differ in regard to their views about human nature, our relationship to the natural world, time, social relationships, and space or location?

2. Which value orientations do you personally believe in and follow in your life? Why?

3. Do you believe that the microcultures identified in this chapter are true "cultures," or are they simply a collection of people within a specific category? Is there a "culture" by geographic region, urban or rural area, age, gender, or religion?

For example, among young adults, what would be the dominant values in terms of Kluckhohn's value orientations? What would be some variations? What would be some deviant views? Do college students share the same values as others who are not attending college?

4. Does anyone you know hold a post-figurative, co-figurative, or pre-figurative view of the world? How?

5. Give some examples of how material culture from your diversity group may be used in the classroom, and describe how you would relate it to your cultural history or values.

## NOTES

1. Society has been defined as (a) "an enduring and cooperating social group whose members have developed organized patterns of relationships through interaction with one another"; (b) "a community, nation, or broad grouping of people having common traditions, institutions, and collective activities and interests" (*Merriam-Webster's Collegiate Dictionary,* 10th Ed., 1993, p. 1115); (c) "the collective body of persons composing a community" (*Funk & Wagnalls New "Standard" Dictionary of the English Language,* 1962, p. 2311).

2. Culture has been defined as "the concepts, habits, skills, arts, instruments, institu-

tions, etc., of a given people in a given period" (*Webster's New World Dictionary,* 1955, p. 359).

3. This problem is not limited to schools. In Chapter 11, I refer to an exhibit at the Museum of Modern Art in New York City that committed this error. By including artifacts from Africa without providing the context out of which they were created, the exhibit presented a superficial and Western interpretation of them.

4. Yang Dao appears in the reference list under Yang, his clan name. In Hmong, the clan name appears first as an identification of that membership.

## REFERENCES

Bachtold, L. M., & Eckvall, K. L. (1978). "Current value orientations of American Indians in northern California: The Hupa." *Journal of Cross-Cultural Psychology* 9, 367–75.

Banks, J. A. (1994). *Multiethnic education: Theory and practice* (3rd ed.). Boston, MA: Allyn and Bacon.

Bemak, F., & Timm, J. (1994). "Case study of an adolescent Cambodian refugee: A clinical, developmental and cultural perspective." *The International Journal for the Advancement of Counselling* 17, 47–58.

Carter, R. T. (1990). "Cultural value differences between African Americans and White Americans." *Journal of College Student Development* 31, 71–79.

————. (September/October, 1991). "Cultural values: A review of empirical research and implications for counseling." *Journal of Counseling and Development* 70, 164–73.

Carter, R. T., & Helms, J. E. (1990). "White racial identity attitudes and cultural values." In J. E. Helms (Ed.), *Black and white racial identity: Theory, research and practice.* Westport, CT: Greenwood Press.

Caudill, W., & Scarr, H. A. (1962). "Japanese value orientations and cultural change." *Ethnology* 1, 53–91.

*Funk & Wagnalls new "standard" dictionary of the English language* (1962). New York: Funk & Wagnalls.

Garcia, R. L. (1991). *Teaching in a pluralistic society: Concepts, models and strategies* (2nd ed.). New York: HarperCollins.

Goldfarb, M. (1982). *Fighters, refugees, immigrants: A story of the Hmong.* Minneapolis: Carolrhoda Books.

Gollnick, D. M., & Chinn, D. C. (1986). *Multicultural education in a pluralistic society* (2nd ed.) Columbus, OH: Charles E. Merrill.

Gollnik, D. M., & Chinn, D. C. (1994). *Multicultural education in a pluralistic society* (4th ed.). Columbus, OH: Charles E. Merrill.

Kahl, J. A. (1968). *The measurement of modernism: A study of values in Brazil and Mexico.* Austin: University of Texas Press.

Kluckhohn, F. R. (1956). "Dominant and variant value orientations." In C. Kluckhohn, H. Murray, & Schneider, D. M. (Eds.), *Personality in nature, culture and society.* New York: Alfred A. Knopf.

Kluckhohn, F. R., & Strodbeck, F. L. (1961). *Variations in value orientations.* Evanston, IL: Row Peterson.

Kroeber, A. (1948). *Anthropology.* New York: Harcourt, Brace.

Lengermann, P. M. (1971). "Working-class values in Trinidad and Tobago." *Social Economic Issues* 20, 151–63.

————. (1972). "The debate on the structure and content of West Indian values: Some relevant data from Trinidad and Tobago." *British Journal of Sociology* 23, 298–311.

Mead, M. (1970). *Culture and commitment: A study of the generation gap.* Garden City, NY: Natural History Press/Doubleday.

*Merriam-Webster's collegiate dictionary,* 10th ed. (1993). Springfield, MA: Merriam-Webster.

Papajohn, J. C., & Spiegel, J. P. (1975). *Transactions in families.* San Francisco: Jossey Bass.

Podeschi, R., & Xiong, V. (1992). *The Hmong and American education: The 1990s.* Milwaukee, WI: University of Wisconsin-Milwaukee, Educational Policy and Community Studies.

Sutcliffe, C. R. (1974). "The effects of differential exposure to modernization on the value orientations of Palestinians." *The Journal of Social Psychology* 93, 173–80.

Szapocznik, J., Scopetta, M. A., Arannadle, M. A., & Kurtines, W. (1978). "Cuban value structure: Treatment implications." *Journal of Consulting and Clinical Psychology* 46, 961–70.

Takaki, R. (1989). *Strangers from a different shore.* Boston: Little, Brown.

Teffi, S. K. (1968). "Intergenerational value differences and family structure among the Wind River Shoshone." *American Anthropologist* 70, 330–33.

Tiedt, P. L., & Tiedt, I. M. (1990). *Multicultural teaching: A handbook of activities, information and resources* (3rd ed.). Boston, MA: Allyn and Bacon.

Timm, J. S. (1992a). "Hmong values and American education." *FORWARD: Wisconsin Journal for Supervision and Curricular Development* 16 (2), 1–11.

————. (1992b). "Research and pedagogy in the Hmong community." Paper presented at the Association for Moral Education Conference: Power Within Diversity. Toronto, Canada, November 14.

————. (1994). "Hmong values and American education." *Equity and Excellence in Education* 27 (2), 36–44.

*Webster's new world dictionary of the American language.* (1955). New York: World.

Weroha, S. (March 1991). "Southeast Asian culture: Implications for the classroom." Paper presented at Super Seminar II, Conference on Cultural Diversity. Milwaukee, WI.

Yang, D. (1993). *Hmong at the turning point.* Minneapolis, MN: WorldBridge.

# 8

∽

# Popular Culture

## American Myths and Icons

The films of a nation reflect its mentality in a more direct way
than any other artistic media for two reasons:
First, films are never the product of an individual....
Second, films address themselves, and appeal, to the anonymous multitude. Popular films—or, to be more precise, popular screen motifs—
can therefore be supposed to satisfy existing mass desires.

SIEGFRIED KRACAUER
*FROM CALIGARI TO HITLER: A PSYCHOLOGICAL*
*HISTORY OF THE GERMAN FILM*

In common use, the term *myth* refers to an idea that is not true or to a story that never happened. In the field of cultural anthropology, however, myths refer to *psychological and spiritual truths,* and to legends that contain powerful insights into different cultures by reflecting their deepest belief systems (Campbell, 1988). Both interpretations apply in American culture. On one hand our "myths" do appear as stories in popular films and television. On the other hand, these media do reflect some American values. Indeed, our myths may be interpreted "as a paradigm for making sense out of life" (Wright, 1975, p. 193).

An **icon** may be defined as "an image or a likeness ... (of) a monumental figure" (*Funk & Wagnalls New "Standard" Dictionary of the English Language,* 1962, p. 1218). The characters in films and television are icons or images with which audiences identify. They are monumental figures because, as heroes, they appear larger than life. They also elevate ordinary men and women to the status of hero. These characters reveal startling insights about how we Americans see ourselves and our society.

Plots in popular culture include the themes of freedom, success, and justice, which were discussed in Chapter 2. These themes appear in stories both about individuals and diverse groups.

It is important to point out here the fact that the entertainment industry is *market driven*. Perceptions by those in the industry of what they believe will sell to the mass market determine which films and television programs are produced (except for a few independent producers who cater to particular groups). In other words, the determining factor is the potential size of the audience. Not everyone has the same taste, but producers' decisions depend on how large an audience they think will respond.

In Chapter 4, I referred to a hidden curriculum in schools by which students learn behavior considered by educators to be appropriate for their future place in American society. There is a hidden curriculum in popular culture as well. If American children in fact spend as many hours or more watching movies and television as they spend in school, as educators we must also address this hidden curriculum and the lessons it teaches.

This chapter examines ways in which popular culture is, in fact, an American mythology in the way it embodies our beliefs about individualism, about our relationships with each other, about our diversity, and about issues that affect all of us as a nation.

## INDIVIDUALISM IN
## AMERICAN POPULAR CULTURE

The theme of individualism pervades American popular culture. This is not surprising, given the values of Protestant, Republican, utilitarian, economic, and expressive individualism in our society (Chapter 2). These various views of individualism appear in different combinations in the characters depicted in films and television. Bellah (Bellah et al., 1985) referred to these expressions of individualism in popular culture as **mythic individualism**. The characters are mythic because they do provide insights into American values.

Bellah identified a romantic mythic hero, **the loner,** who as an individual is never completely a part of society. Two character types, the cowboy and the "hard-boiled detective," represent this type of hero, who serves society by standing alone, "not needing others, not depending on their judgment, and not submitting to their wishes" (Bellah et al., 1985, p. 146). Remaining alone is a form of selflessness and heroism. Thus these characters display an ambivalence about their relationship to society. They are good guys who restore justice, but they ultimately choose to avoid entangling relationships.

These insights are fine so far as they go, but there is another side to the loner. Bellah's description assumes that the loner is essentially good and acts to serve society, but in history and in fiction a loner may function *on behalf of, against, or in a neutral position in relation to society.* In other words, the individual may work to repair the fabric of society, tear it apart, or simply choose to live independently from it as much as possible. Historically, the cowboy, the outlaw, and the trapper were all loners. In popular culture the cowboy and detective work to restore order and justice in the society, while the outlaw or criminal tears at its foundations. To designate "loner" itself does not define whether or not the individual in history or legend works to benefit society.

I suggest that there are two additional mythic character types: the so-called self-made man (or woman) and the rebel, who pursue their own way as well. These also represent individual values in American society, but they appear to be more self-oriented than the cowboy or the detective. Taken as a whole, these four character types of the cowboy, detective, self-made individual, and rebel are represented in four different American myths: (a) the Western myth; (b) the detective myth; (c) the Horatio Alger myth; and (d) the rebel myth. If the reader is not familiar with some of the films in the following review, many of these classics are available on videotape.

## The Western Myth

In its emphasis on individual liberty, this myth reflects both Republican and utilitarian individualism. In a provocative analysis of Western films, Wright (1975) has suggested four different "opposites," or dichotomies, that appear in Western film plots. These dichotomies set the individual hero apart from everyone else in very symbolic ways. The dichotomies are (a) between those who are outside and those who are inside the society; (b) between good and evil; (c) between the strong and the weak; and (d) between wilderness and civilization. In general, the hero is outside the society, good, strong, and associated with the wilderness, or the pure and natural world. He is of the West. He has no apparent relationship with the East, education, or "culture," in the sense of refinement. He is, so to speak, "his own man." He represents individual as compared to communal values. Wright cited *Shane* as the quintessential classic Western film. Shane is good, strong, and rides out of the wilderness and an ambiguous past. Through his bravery, he saves the situation for a group of homesteaders who represent society and, although wounded, rides back again into the wilderness. He will survive on his own. More recently, *Rambo* appears to be an extreme variation on this loner. He is strong, fighting for justice, located basically outside of society, and associated with the wilderness. His violence, however, is more extreme than that of Shane. *High Plains Drifter* is the account of a stranger who rides out of the wilderness to avenge his brother's death, but there is an ambiguity in this film as to whether the stranger is really the brother of the murdered man or his ghost. Either way, the theme is the same: the stranger appears from outside society and fights for justice, although in the form of revenge.

According to Wright, a variation on this classic Western myth occurs when the hero starts out "in" society but is virtually abandoned by those less courageous than himself. He must stand alone against a common danger that threatens both him and others. An example of this variation is *High Noon*, which may well contain the most famous gunfight in film. In the end, the hero and his wife go off together to where? Inside society or apart from it? Another plot variation is one in which the hero also starts out "in" society but suffers an injustice by a villain, against whom he swears personal revenge, or he is forced out of society due to unusual circumstances. If he becomes an outlaw, working against the society, he ultimately dies. Historically and in legend, Billy the Kid is shot down by Marshal Pat Garrett.

A variation on the hero who functions absolutely alone is one who meets the criteria of being outside conventional society—good, strong, and natural—but who has a friend or sidekick who assists him. In the classic *Lone Ranger* series, the ranger had Tonto, a Native American, as his companion, played by actor Jay Silverheels, the first Native American to play an "Indian" in films.[1] A more recent variation is *Pale Rider,* which meets all of the requirements of the classic Western in that the hero, another loner, is strong, good, and rides out of the wilderness. He joins "society" for a while and overcomes all of the villains except one. At the end of this film, a new friend saves him from being shot by the last villain. Thus, the hero is depicted as also being vulnerable in his humanity. The hero's vulnerability appears clearly in *Unforgiven,* a Western which presents the moral theme that violence is wrong even when it is used to attain justice.

An interesting development in the Western myth has been the emergence of the "professional" heroes who are no longer fighting to defend social values: "They are fighting for themselves, for money, and they enjoy it as professionals" (Wright, 1975, p. 170). In this version of the narrative, there are several heroes, or at least companions, who find identity in their relationships. Wright considers them to be "corporate men"—experts in what they do best but operating beyond the restrictions of society, which are irrelevant to them. They depend on each other's abilities, defeat their opponents or villains, and then move on together or go down together. *The Magnificent Seven* is an example.

A satiric variation on the Western hero is the con man. He also is a loner, but he works not only by himself but for himself, rather than for the good of society. *Elmer Gantry* is ostensibly the story of a traveling religion show, but the heroine, a fundamentalist preacher, dies in a fire. The hero walks away indifferently at the end of the film to seek new opportunities. *The Great Imposter* is the true story of a man who posed as a priest, a professor, and other characters. Sometimes, two friends are con men together. In *The Sting*, the two heroes engage others to help them in their scheme. A more recent film, *Maverick,* has four principal cons: a father and son, a lady gambler, and a Native American friend of the son. There is also a plethora of supporting cons, each looking out for their own gain.

## The Detective Myth

Like the Western myth, the detective myth reflects Republican individualism. Bellah (1985) described the detective as a loner who works marginally in relation to society (law enforcement agencies) and identified Sam Spade as an example of this type of hero who, like the cowboy, defends the weak and pursues justice. A more recent example is the detective (or private eye) in *Chinatown*. An important theme throughout both the Western and detective myths is that society is sometimes depicted as weak, ineffectual, and unable to solve the problem of justice. Society may also be portrayed as corrupt, and the villains are part of the established culture. Examples are ruthless business tycoons or dishonest officials (Wright, 1975). In the detective myth as well as in the Western myth, sometimes it takes someone who is not a private eye to solve the problem. Frequently on television, amateur detectives solve the mysteries or crimes while the police arrest the wrong suspect or remain totally confused. In *Diagnosis Murder,* a doctor solves the crimes with help from his medical assistants. The idea of this "outsider" is not limited to males. The detective in *Murder She Wrote* is a not-so-hard-boiled middle-aged widow, who lives alone and rejects any serious emotional entanglements.

There is, however, another type of detective who does work within society's law enforcement agencies and, therefore, within "the system." The hero may be perceived as being "on the fringe," however, like the detective in the *Lethal Weapon* series. On television, police lieutenant *Columbo* works alone, but many detectives, like cowboys, have their buddies or sidekicks. *Miami Vice, Cagney and Lacey, The X Files,* and *Walker, Texas Ranger* come to mind. My point here is that these "loners" may function outside, on the edge, or inside the social system.

## The Horatio Alger Myth

This myth is named for Horatio Alger (1834-1899), the American writer of stories for boys. In over one hundred books, his plots showed "success gained by exemplary living, heroic deeds, [and] struggle against odds" (*Columbia-Viking Desk Encyclopedia*, 1953, p. 27). Perhaps the American Creed has been most clearly expressed in this myth, which depicts the loner who succeeds through his or her own efforts with little or no help from anyone. He has "pulled himself up by his own bootstraps." In its focus on the pursuit of happiness, this myth expresses Republican and utilitarian individualism in the achieved aspirations of its heroes. Also contained in this myth is the idea that the hero deserves success—a reflection of Protestant individualism's view of personal effort deserving reward. This myth reverses the Western hero theme, because the hero begins "outside" society and yearns for success "inside" it. Success, however, does not necessarily bring a happy ending. In *Giant,* for example, the character played by James Dean starts out as an outsider, literally strikes oil, gains vast wealth, and builds a huge empire, but psychologically he remains a loner throughout the film.

A popular variation on the Horatio Alger myth is the successful athlete who makes good through special talent and/or hard work. As in the classic Western myth, it is because of the hero's unique ability that he or she becomes recognized and accepted. In *The Natural,* a fictional hero maintains his integrity at the end by refusing to be "bought" by crooked corporate executives and to throw the pennant-winning game to the other team. His final hit may be the most dramatically and beautifully depicted home run in films. *Rocky* is another success story in professional sports. A favorite of mine is *Breaking Away*, in which the adolescent hero, a cyclist, wins the race after great determination and sustained effort.

Another variation on the Horatio Alger myth might be identified as the "loser redeemed," in which the hero achieves enormous success, almost by accident, as in *The Jerk,* and most recently, *Forrest Gump.*

### The Rebel Myth

Another type of hero that has recurred in American films is the rebel—a loner who shows a generalized discontent. A prevailing theme in the rebel myth is the search for personal identity, which is found in opposition to established values in the society. Another theme is that one's personal feelings are of primary importance—reflecting expressive individualism. In the 1950s, *Rebel Without a Cause* depicted adolescent rebellion as a rite of passage. For adult rebels, however, rebellion is not simply a rite of passage. Like the Western hero, the adult is self-reliant and usually a loner but, unlike the Western hero, does not work to solve social problems. Society and personal entanglements are interpreted as being restrictive of personal freedom. An example is *Five Easy Pieces,* in which the hero abandons both personal entanglements and material possessions. In the final scene he leaves his girlfriend, coat, and car at a gas station, and rides off down the highway after hitching a ride. This ambiguous ending is a variation on the cowboy leaving society behind and returning to the wilderness by riding off alone into the sunset. This hero, however, also leaves his wallet behind. The implication is that even his identity no longer matters, and that he is escaping from it. The question the viewer is left with is this: Is he "free," or is he "lost?"

In some rebel narratives, two friends may link up together. Sometimes their rebellious actions become a pathway to self-destruction. *Butch Cassidy and the Sundance Kid* is based on the true story of two outlaws who finally ran into a barrage of bullets. In popular culture, these rebel "heroes" are not limited to men. *Thelma and Louise* is an example of two friends who follow this adult rebel path, even to the degree of driving over a cliff together, without telling the police that their crime had been an act of self-defense.

### Freedom, Success, and Justice in Individualistic Myths

The themes of freedom, success, and justice routinely appear in films and television. Our mythic heroes enact these themes in popular culture in accordance with the various interpretations of them contained in the different views of individualism (Chapter 2).

In the Western and detective narratives, *freedom* is portrayed as the right to act on one's own according to one's personal judgment, as long as it does not interfere with the rights of others. If, however, a character expresses a view of per-

sonal rights as simply following personal desires or pursuing personal gain, regardless of the rights of others, this character is presented as the villain. *Success* is
depicted as settling the score, thus achieving *justice,* which of course restores order
to the community. This restoration of harmony in the society is at the core of
the Western and detective myths.

In the Horatio Alger myth, *freedom* is presented as the opportunity to strive
toward a goal, and *success* is depicted as the achievement of that goal. *Justice* appears in the form of fairness on the part of those competing for the same goal
and fairness by those in positions to judge performance and to award success on
the basis of merit.

In the rebel myth, *freedom* is presented as having the courage to follow one's
personal desires, feeling little or no obligation to society, and avoiding entanglements and the claims of others within personal relationships. *Success* is depicted as
attaining a sense of personal fulfillment, even if members of society would not
interpret the final outcome as "successful"—again a reflection of expressive individualism. *Justice* is portrayed as being left alone to pursue one's personal choices.

### Myths of Individualism Reconsidered

Whichever mythic heroes appeal to us personally, the romanticizing of the individual appears to be a fundamental aspect of popular culture. Judging from the
popularity of some of these films and television programs, it appears that Americans admire and identify with heroes who repair our social problems, succeed by
their own efforts, or escape from the problems of our society. The underlying
message in the portrayal of individualism is that "heroes" of both genders should
be strong and autonomous.

At the beginning of this chapter, I referred to an icon as an image of a monumental figure. There is another definition of an icon, however, which is "an object of uncritical devotion" (*Merriam-Webster's Collegiate Dictionary,* 10th ed., 1993,
p. 574). This definition is a thought-provoking one within the context of American popular culture because it raises this question: Do we Americans unthinkingly
admire the focus on personal goals that some of these heroes represent? True, the
cowboys and detectives work for social justice, but what about the Horatio Algers
and the rebels? All four characters are loners, but the first two are concerned with
larger social issues, while the latter two are more focused on personal desires. How
conducive are some of these images to the fostering of an ethics of care?

## DIVERSITY IN POPULAR CULTURE

Diversity is also depicted in popular culture, but European Americans are overrepresented in comparison with other groups. The reader may not always agree
with some of my observations about the films included here, which is fair
enough. I believe, however, that what is important about these films is that they
bring social issues into the public's mind and offer a starting point for debate.
Some films present experiences that diverse groups have shared.

## African Americans

African Americans have been depicted in some films that break stereotypes and present important images of Black life and Black issues in America. My favorite film concerning African Americans is *Glory,* the true account of the heroism of the first African American military regiment, the 54th Regiment Massachusetts Infantry, in which Blacks fought and died in a battle with Confederate soldiers on a beach in South Carolina during the Civil War.

*Bird* is the story of Charlie Parker, the great saxophone player known by that nickname, whose innovative style redefined modern jazz. This film received critical acclaim for its sensitive portrayal of a major American artist. *The Josephine Baker Story* is another film about a musical great, the singer who achieved international success in Europe yet was discriminated against at home in the United States. In *The Jackie Robinson Story,* Robinson portrayed himself in a true-life account of the first African American to break through the racial barrier in big-league baseball. These three films contain the Horatio Alger story of individuals who achieved success through their talents and efforts, even as they encountered prejudice and discrimination.

Some films depict various levels of socioeconomic status. *Sounder* offers a view of the life of poverty in the rural South. Also set in the rural South, *The Color Purple* has recently been criticized for presenting a negative image of Black men. It does, however, present a variety of characters, including landowners, a minister, and a businessman, in different degrees of socioeconomic success.

*Mississippi Burning* may overrepresent the importance of two White FBI agents in solving the murder of three freedom riders during the Civil Rights Movement in 1964. In so doing, it overlooks the Black activism of the period. It does, however, present the tragedy of the victims and the terror of the time. The recent television program *I'll Fly Away* perhaps was more true to life in its depiction of events surrounding the Civil Rights Movement in the South in the 1960s.

Educational issues appear in *Lean on Me,* the true story of Joe Clark, the African American principal of Eastside High School in New Jersey, who inspired his students from diverse backgrounds to achieve academic success by holding them to high standards.

*The Ernest Green Story* is a film that recounts the experience of the first Black student to graduate from Central High School in Little Rock, Arkansas, in 1958. The events surrounding the integration of this school brought national attention when President Eisenhower sent federal troops to enforce the Supreme Court decision of Brown v. Board of Education of Topeka.

Interracial concern for justice appears in *To Kill a Mockingbird,* when a White lawyer defends an African American, and more recently in *Philadelphia,* when a Black attorney defends a White colleague dismissed from his law firm because he has AIDS. *Mississippi Masala* is a poignant love story about an African American businessman and an East Indian woman who encounter bigotry in a Southern town.

## Asian Americans

Films about Asian Americans are more rare. The theme of acculturation is sometimes portrayed. *Dim Sum: A Little Bit of Heart* is an engaging story of Chinese American families in San Francisco. *The Joy Luck Club,* based on the book by Amy Tan, unfolds in layered narratives about the relationships of Chinese mothers and daughters. This film has been criticized for presenting a stereotyped view of Chinese men and women. If one looks deeper, however, it becomes clearer that the experiences of four Chinese women with their mothers in China are different from their daughters' experiences with them in the United States. The film depicts acculturation of Chinese traditions in America. It is not the same story told over again four times, as one critic remarked to me, but rather a subtle narrative about the experiences of changing attitudes that are common between first and second generations living in America. In my own research with Hmong refugees, I have encountered similar changes in attitudes between the mothers and daughters whom I interviewed. The more recent *Picture Bride* concerns the former custom among Japanese men in Hawaii of importing wives chosen from photographs, discussed in Chapter 3.

There are a few films presenting the experiences of Southeast Asians, especially during the Vietnam War. A motion picture that vividly portrays the excruciating experiences in this war of both Vietnamese civilians and American troops is *Platoon,* which won the Academy Award for Best Picture of the Year in 1986. *Heaven and Earth* is the story of the struggles of a Vietnamese woman during the Vietnam War. *The Killing Fields* presents a horrifying account of genocide in Cambodia under the Khmer Rouge during the Pol Pot regime and the efforts of an American reporter to locate his Cambodian friend caught in that war. This film enables viewers to understand the horror that Cambodian refugees experienced before they were able to leave their country (Chapter 3). The brutal images in this film still linger in my mind.

## European Americans

By far the majority of films are about White Americans, but ethnicity is not usually identified. The hero, heroine, and other characters are presented simply as "Americans." Films about White immigrants, however, do identify ethnic background. Some of these films depict the dreams of immigrants who saw in America the hope for economic opportunity and personal happiness. An example is the story of Scandinavian farmers in Minnesota in *The Emigrants. Far and Away* is about a young Irish man and woman who seek their dreams in America. Some films portray the injustice that immigrants encountered. An example is the betrayal of Irish coal miners in Pennsylvania in *The Molly Maguires.* Some films present the desperation of those who fear deportation. *Green Card* is the story of the hopes of an illegal French immigrant to remain in New York City. At the end of this delightful film, the hero is ordered to leave the country by the immigration authorities, but because he has found love, the audience walks away with the impression that everything will turn out all right in the long run.

Some films are about religious issues. *The Chosen* is a powerful story about the friendship between two young Jewish men in New York, one the son of a Zionist working for the creation of the State of Israel following World War II, and the other the son of a Hasidic rabbi who is opposed to the formation of a secular Jewish state. This film clarifies religious and philosophical differences in values within the Jewish community. *A Stranger Among Us* presents Hasidic culture to a non-Jewish woman detective investigating a murder. Religious bigotry among Whites in the form of anti-Semitism is investigated by the journalist hero in *Gentlemen's Agreement* from the 1940s. He succeeds in uncovering Gentile prejudice by presenting himself as Jewish. The more recent *School Ties* reveals similar anti-Semitism toward a Jewish student by other students at an elite prep school.

## Latino Americans

Stereotyped images, particularly about Mexican Americans, have been a continuing problem in films about Latino Americans. There are a few films that do run counter to old stereotypes. Exploitation of Latinos appears in *The Milagro Beanfield War.* This story is about Mexican Americans' dislocation from some of their land by indifferent White business tycoons who want the land for their own economic gain. Clever planning, however, thwarts the villains.

A Horatio Alger type of hero appears in *La Bamba.* This film recounts the phenomenal success of Ritchie Valens, the extremely talented teenage pop singer who died tragically in an airplane crash while on a concert tour. Anglo prejudice appears in *Stand and Deliver,* the true story of Jaime Escalante, a mathematics teacher at Garfield High School in Los Angeles. When eighteen students in his calculus class achieved top scores on the College Advanced Placement Test, representatives of the Education Testing Service, creators of the test, questioned the validity (or accuracy) of their scores on the basis of the students' Latino background. In other words, the students were suspected of having cheated. When the students were reexamined, they repeated their high scores. This film not only presents the prejudgments of test makers about students' abilities; it presents similar biases on the part of some teachers as well.

## Native Americans

Films with Native American characters have been plagued with White actors cast in these roles. An early exception to this pattern was the old *Lone Ranger* series, which did cast Jay Silverheels in the role of Tonto. As I mentioned earlier, Silverheels was the first Native American to play an "Indian" in the movies. Throughout his life, he worked assiduously for authentic casting in Native American roles.

Recently, films that are free from stereotyped images of Native Americans have been increasing. *Map of the Human Heart* is the story of an Eskimo boy, befriended by a Canadian officer, who grows up to enlist in the Canadian Air Force during World War II. This film is also the love story between the hero and a Canadian Native American whom he meets as a child. *Thunderheart* deals with the themes of exploitation and dislocation of indigenous peoples by indifferent

White business tycoons who pursue their own economic self-interest. In other words, it deals with the same issues as *The Milagro Beanfield War.*

Issues of injustice and cruelty appear in *Dances with Wolves,* which has been popular with the general public. This film attempts to depict Indian life shattered by White settlement and the brutality inflicted on Native Americans by the United States Army. It is not free of stereotypes, however, including the image of the beautiful maiden as an "Indian princess" in her white ceremonial dress. A better film is *Geronimo* (1993 version), which recounts the true story of the broken promises and betrayal by the United States Army both toward Geronimo and toward the Apache scouts who served the Army. This film presents the shame and anger of two White officers involved in the "Geronimo Campaign." After resigning his commission from the army in disgust, one of these officers reflects:

> Days of bravery and cruelty, of heroism and deceit, and I'm still faced with an undeniable truth—a way of life that endured a thousand years was gone. This desert, this land that we look out on, would never be the same.

### Freedom, Success, and Justice in Films of Diversity

The issues of freedom, success, and justice in films about diverse groups are presented in relation either to individuals or to groups taken collectively. For example, the freedom to pursue one's dreams is depicted in *The Jackie Robinson Story,* but his breakthrough into major league baseball also represents a breakthrough for other African Americans. His success paved the way for other talented athletes to enter a field formerly closed to them. The issue of freedom in terms of civil rights is more somber in such films as *Mississippi Burning* or *Geronimo.*

The issues of economic power, legal power, and social power discussed in Chapter 3 appear in some of these films in narratives of the struggle of diverse groups for economic justice (*The Milagro Beanfield War, Thunderheart,* and *The Molly Maguires*), legal justice (*Mississippi Burning, Philadelphia,* and *Stand and Deliver*) and social justice (*Gentleman's Agreement* and *The Josephine Baker Story*). Success in these films occurs when justice is achieved. Films about diverse groups present their unique experiences and make clearer the struggles that they have shared.

## AMERICAN SOCIETY
## IN POPULAR CULTURE

The Founding Fathers who established our Republican form of government believed that American citizenship carries with it not only personal rights, but civic responsibilities as well (Chapter 2). These responsibilities are sometimes viewed as inconvenient or not personally important, but in fact they are the foundation upon which our nation depends. Bellah has observed that "without such virtues as responsibility and care, ... autonomy itself becomes ... an empty form without substance" (Bellah et al., 1991, p. 12). Individuals may become self-absorbed and indifferent toward others.

How does popular culture depict the value our Founding Fathers placed on citizens' involvement in public affairs and responsibility for each other's welfare? The emphasis in American society on individualism means that fewer filmmakers are interested in stories about national issues and common concerns. It is far more difficult to find examples that focus on themes of the common national good than it is to find stories extolling the various interpretations of individualism or narratives about members of diverse groups.

There has been a shift in storytelling in the United states from that of older societies. In other societies, the condition of *society* was the major concern. In classical drama, such as *Oedipus Rex* by Sophocles or *Macbeth* by William Shakespeare, the important question was "What was the effect of social leaders' actions on the collective good?" For example, in the social-problem plays of Henrik Ibsen, such as *The Enemy of the People* or *Pillars of Society,* those in positions of power are depicted as the enemies of the common good. In *Pillars of Society,* shipping magnates sell passage on rotten ships to emigrants leaving Norway and insure the ships. When the ships sink and the passengers are lost, the magnates beat their breasts and collect the insurance money. A comparison could be made here between this fictional dramatic narrative and some resistance in 1994 on the part of commuter airline companies in the United States to tighten safety measures on their planes because of the costs. How many "ships" are unsafe?

A focus on national cohesion, personal social responsibility, and social justice is scant in American popular culture. The issue of the commonweal and a concern for the continuance of the principles of democracy have been portrayed in a few films about elected officials, especially in Washington, D.C. The same type of greed and indifference in *Pillars of Society* is depicted in *The Distinguished Gentleman.* Here, Washington politicians and lobbyists are indifferent to the hazards of electric powerlines to children's health. The hero, who originally seeks public office for personal gain, ultimately reveals this corruption. This film is a more recent statement on the theme of the hero elected to Congress and the responsibilities of that office; this theme also appeared in the classic *Mr. Smith Goes to Washington* in the 1930s. Both of these films place the hero in a confrontation with the collusion between government and powerful business interest groups. In both cases, the hero acts as a catalyst for correcting the corruption and bringing about a solution in line with the common good. In *Keeper of the Flame,* another classic from the 1940s, the politician-hero maintains his integrity by choosing to remain true to the principles of democratic government rather than capitulating to pressure from party politicians and a desire for his own personal gain.

*The Candidate* is the story of the struggle of a candidate for the United States Senate to maintain his integrity in spite of his campaign managers' marketing of his public image. The disturbing issue in this film is the fact that the candidate has not yet been elected when the pressure on his integrity begins. This film also raises other issues about the "selling" of a candidate to the American public through the production of television commercials, the creation of "sound bites" that contain merely vacuous phrases, and the unwritten rule that a candidate should never say what he or she truly believes because it may cost votes. A cynicism about candidates' seeking public office is expressed in this film by one of the characters, who says, "Any man running for the Senate has to want something." The role public leaders should serve for the common good of the nation is expressed by the hero near the end of the film:

> No candidate can have all the answers. All a man can say is "Here I am and I'm willing to give it all I've got."

If all those who serve in public office shared this view, could we ask for more?

*All the President's Men* presents a chilling account of the abuse of power in government with its narrative of the investigation of the events surrounding the break-in of the Democratic National Headquarters preceding the 1972 presidential election. The film reveals the conflict between the power that comes with elected office, individual interpretations of that power, and responsibility in government. Until this series of events, corrupt politicians were depicted as caricatures in American films. Here, however, the narrative was *true.* This devastating account of corruption in government left its legacy. Historically, of course, there has been a public suspicion of officials, but today an assumption that politicians are, by definition, not to be trusted is pervasive. The question raised by the Watergate affair is "What almost happened to the democratic process were it not for an accident of discovery by a night watchman and the efforts of two investigative reporters, Carl Bernstein and Bob Woodward of the *Washington Post?*" The Watergate affair highlights the importance of the "Fourth Estate" (journalism) and freedom of the press with its responsibility as the watchdog of our commonweal.

The theme of the role of private individuals within the context of human decency issues has also appeared in American films. During World War II, for example, many actors who portrayed gangsters in the 1930s were recast into more responsible social roles. Such was the case when Humphrey Bogart was cast as Rick Blaine in *Casablanca.* In this famous film, the "hero" is the quintessential classic American loner. He is "outside" American society, even to the extent of living in a foreign and exotic land. At the end of the film, he walks not into the sunset with his newfound friend or sidekick but into the fog. Before he does so, however, he rejects a selfish decision and utters one of the best-known lines in the movies. It is about the insignificance of personal desires in contrast with more important social concerns. He turns to the heroine and says:

> I'm no good at being noble, but it doesn't take much to see that the problems of three little people don't amount to a hill of beans in this crazy world.

## POPULAR CULTURE IN EDUCATION

Educators often take popular culture lightly. It is a mistake to do so. The hidden curriculum in films and television influences viewers' attitudes with positive or negative outcomes. For example, *The Harvard Education Newsletter* reported in April 1985 that 80 percent of White students in a Midwestern town expressed favorable views toward African Americans. After they saw the silent film *Birth of a Nation,* only 45 percent continued to express these positive feelings.

The impact of radio and films on public attitudes has been recognized by officials in these industries for a long time. In 1922 Will Hays, President of the Motion Pictures Producers and Distributors of America (MPPDA), spoke at the annual meeting of the National Education Association (NEA). Hays expressed a commitment to high moral standards and to the educational as well as the entertainment value of movies. Recognition of the impact of movies on public attitudes was also reflected in state licensing laws in the 1920s. By the 1930s, in order to avoid government censorship, the MPPDA established a code to monitor values in American movies. A debate over government regulation versus industry regulation grew out of the recognition of the extreme influence of movies and radio on viewers' and listeners' lives (Spring, 1994b).

The idea of using popular culture in classroom discussions is not new. In 1933 the National Council of Teachers of English and the MPPDA cooperated in writing and distributing to schools study guides for three films: *Emperor Jones, Little Women,* and *Alice in Wonderland.* (It should be mentioned here that *Emperor Jones* contains several negative stereotypes about "Africans."). The following year, the National Education Association's Department of Secondary Education took over this task of producing and distributing study guides for films. By 1937, English, history, geography, and science teachers were receiving these guides for films relevant to their courses (Spring, 1994b). The guides were seen as helping the teachers. They certainly benefited the film industry by increasing attendance at certain movies.

With the advent of television, which became available to the general public following World War II, concerns over the effects of popular images on viewers' attitudes followed the earlier concerns about movies and radio. Since the 1950s there have been literally hundreds of studies investigating the impact of television viewing on children and adolescents. With the creation of The Corporation for Public Broadcasting in 1967 came the notion that television could be designed as a means of education. Another new idea was that television could reach preschool audiences and help prepare young children for school. Out of this concept, the Children's Television Workshop (CTW) was created in 1968; it produced *Sesame Street* the following year. Ironically for a public television program, the commercial success of *Sesame Street* was phenomenal. Gerald Lesser, Bigelow Professor at the Harvard Graduate School of Education, became CTW's chief academic advisor. An educational psychologist, Lesser believed that much of children's learning occurs through observation of role models (Spring, 1994b). Lesser believed in **pro-social television,** where children could observe a world in which people of all social classes and races treat each other with respect. (Even Oscar the Grouch, who lives in a garbage can on Sesame Street, receives this courtesy.) Lesser also believed that *"television could create myths to guide children's actions"* (Spring, 1994b, p. 336; italics mine). The "myth" (in the sense of a cultural value) that *Sesame Street* presented was the expressed American belief in the dignity of all people.

Children and adolescents identify with popular figures as part of their development. This identification takes on a critical intensity when it is applied to real-life celebrities, rock stars, and sports heroes. In their own way, these "icons" represent the theme of individualism in American society. When they achieve success, these stars symbolize real-life Horatio Algers in their fulfillment of the American Dream. Sometimes these popular heroes express a belief in personal and social responsibility. Not all sports and film stars appear in television commercials that advertise name-brand products and promote consumerism. Some of these stars appear on television with messages against the use of drugs, in support of safe and responsible sexual behavior, and in favor of less violent stories and role models in the media.

The use of American popular culture in education is not new. What may be new is a critical examination of its "hidden curriculum," which is relevant to students of all ages. (The hidden curriculum behind the stereotypes in popular culture is addressed in Chapter 12.) Popular culture is a powerful expression of American values. The actions of its heroes reflect these values. The care of Shane for the welfare of strangers, the success of Rocky, the indifference to personal commitment of the hero in *Five Easy Pieces* all offer examples of different views of individualism. Interracial compassion appears in *Philadelphia*. Greed is transformed to social responsibility in *The Distinguished Gentleman*. Examining American myths and icons in the classroom may enlighten our students about American society. The irony is that in using stories as examples, the issues become more real.

## CHAPTER SUMMARY

Popular culture offers important insights into American values through its characters and stories. There are four basic American myths: (a) the Western myth; (b) the detective myth; (c) the Horatio Alger myth; and (d) the rebel myth. All of these reflect various views of individualism. They also contain the themes of freedom, success, and justice.

Films about diverse groups also reflect the themes of freedom, success, and justice.

There are fewer films about national issues. These generally pertain to the responsibility of elected officials in relation to justice and the common good.

Using popular culture in educational settings is not new. Analyzing its hidden curriculum is a new approach.

## IMPORTANT TERMS

| | |
|---|---|
| Myth | The Western myth |
| Icon | The detective myth |
| Mythic individualism | The Horatio Alger myth |
| The loner | The rebel myth |
| The Fourth Estate | Pro-social television |

## QUESTIONS FOR DISCUSSION

1. Identify some individualistic values in the actions of the hero or heroine in films you have seen.

2. How are individualistic values contained in Western, detective, Horatio Alger, and rebel films you have seen?

3. Identify a film about a diversity group and explain how it presents the issues of freedom, success, and justice.

4. Identify a film concerned with national issues.

5. How would you use some of the films discussed in this chapter in your classroom?

## NOTES

1. In spite of the authentic casting in this series, it is extremely disturbing to consider the fact that Tonto means "silly" or "foolish" in Spanish (Smith, Davies, & Hall, 1989, p. 462).

## REFERENCES

Bellah, R. N., Madsen, R., Sullivan, W. M., Swidler, A., & Tipton, S. M. (1985). *Habits of the heart: Individualism and commitment in American life.* New York: Harper and Row.

———. (1991). *The good society.* New York: Alfred A. Knopf.

Campbell, J., & Moyers, B. (1988). *The power of myth.* New York: Doubleday.

*Columbia-Viking desk encyclopedia, The.* (1953). New York: Viking Press.

*Funk & Wagnalls new "standard" dictionary of the English language.* (1962). New York: Funk & Wagnalls.

Kracauer, S. (1960). *From Caligari to Hitler: A psychological history of the German film* (2nd Noonday Paperbound Ed.). New York: Farrar, Straus & Cudahy.

Lears, T. J. J. (1984). "From salvation to self realization: Advertising and the therapeutic roots of the consumer culture." In R. W. Fox & T. J. J. Lears (Eds.), *The culture of consumption: Critical essays in American history, 1880–1980.* New York: Pantheon Books.

*Merriam-Webster's collegiate dictionary,* 10th ed. (1993). Springfield, MA: Merriam-Webster.

Smith, C. C., Davies, G. A., & Hall, H. B. (1989). *Langenscheidt's Compact Spanish Dictionary.* New York: Langenscheidt.

Spring, J. (1994b). *The American school: 1642-1993.* New York: McGraw-Hill.

Wright, W. (1975). *Sixguns & society: A structural study of the western.* Berkeley, CA: University of California Press.

# PART III

# The Psychological Perspective

# 9

ಀಀಀ

# Cultural Styles
# or Learning Styles?

A trifling matter, and fussy of me, but we all have our little ways.

EEYORE SPEAKING TO WINNIE-THE-POOH

A. A. MILNE, *THE HOUSE AT POOH CORNER*

Obviously, students differ from each other in many ways. Thus far in this text, I have reviewed ways in which diverse students' experiences have varied in accordance with their race, ethnicity, gender, and social class. I have also reviewed ways in which culture, including popular culture, impacts their attitudes and values. There are obviously psychological differences among students as well. Educators have been concerned with identifying these psychological differences for a long time.

A view that prevailed in education for many years is the concept of intelligence. Slavin has pointed out that "intelligence is one of those words that everyone thinks they understand until you ask them to define it" (1994, p. 134). A current view is that intelligence includes the ability to learn and to solve problems (Slavin, 1994). The practice of testing students to measure their intelligence began in France in 1904, when Alfred Binet devised a test to assess a range of skills. This test yielded a score, known as the *intelligence quotient,* or IQ. The concept of IQ, or general intelligence level, became widespread. Since Binet's time, numerous tests have been constructed and routinely used in schools. Similar tests have also been used in the military services. One problem with the idea of a general intelligence level, however, is that people have different abilities and talents, and that while one person may excel in one area, he or she may have less skill in another. Furthermore, tests of so-called intelligence may not measure some of these capacities because of an emphasis on linguistic and mathematical abilities. Over the past several years, a debate has centered around the question of how many different types of intelligence there are. Howard Gardner has suggested that there are "multiple intelligences," and has recently conducted research on these different abilities (1983, 1990).

Another problem with the notion of a generalized intelligence is a cultural experiential one. When students from diverse backgrounds perform differently on standardized tests, what does that mean? Are the test scores a result of differences in abilities, or are the tests simply not testing some students' knowledge? The idea of "culture bias" in testing became a widely debated issue in the 1960s and 1970s. Culture bias may result from items on a test that reflect the vocabulary of White, middle-class America. Bias may also result from test items that are unrelated to students' experience or based on information that they may never have learned.

The best example I have encountered of this type of test bias is the experience of a friend of mine. After graduating from a liberal arts college and earning a master's degree, she applied to a doctoral program at a state university. She was required to take one of the standardized exams often required for admission into an upper-level degree program. (The test was not a test of analogies.) She failed the test. When her application was rejected, she had a conference with the dean of admissions. She asked whether her high grades in college and her master's degree program counted. The dean replied that they were fine, but that her score on the test was the reason for her rejection. My friend responded that there were almost no items on the test that were based on information she had learned in her major area of study in college, which had been a foreign language, or in her minor area of study, which had been the history and culture of a different area of the world. She had, in fact, spent a portion of her time in college studying abroad. The dean said that he was sorry, but there was nothing that could be done. I should mention here that this friend was a graduate of one of the most academically prestigious colleges in the United States.

Recently, the notion of *cultural styles* has become an important concept in education. This view maintains that psychological differences among students may be a result of cultural influences that impact their approach to learning and to problem solving. There has, however, also been a notion in education of differences in *learning styles* in reference to students from diverse groups, and to individuals within diverse groups. As in the case of the concept of IQ, there were tests devised to determine students' so-called learning styles. There are some problems with these tests, just as there had been with some of the measures of mental ability.

This chapter reviews cultural factors that contribute to a "cultural style" of learning, describes the multiple intelligences suggested by Gardner, and examines an approach to learning style that may be partially culturally determined, known as the field independent/dependent style. The chapter also reviews the long history behind the notion of learning styles. Some empirical findings about different styles in diverse students are included. The reader may wonder why I devote some attention to the problems associated with learning styles. After all, if there are so many problems, why not simply dismiss the concept? Many of the difficulties that I review here have not always been taken into account when educators refer to learning styles or use the learning style approach with their students. I believe that it is important for teachers to be aware of these problems.

## CULTURAL STYLES

In the 1970s and 1980s, reports began to appear of different "styles" among students from different cultural groups. The styles were perceived as being characteristic of these groups. Workshops appeared at educational conferences that offered ways for teachers to work with diverse group styles. One such workshop I attended was based on the assumption that children within particular cultural groups used a cognitive style characteristic of their group. Variables within their cultural group, such as urban or rural environment, parents' educational level, differences in parental teaching styles, or socioeconomic level, were not taken into account. The problems with the tests for learning styles were not considered. Such a generalized approach does not address the issue of style differences of individuals within cultural groups.

Nevertheless, some observable differences in the way students from diverse groups approach a learning or problem-solving situation have been reported. Perhaps cultural style would be a more appropriate term than learning style. Obviously, all humans cognitively process information, but "cultures differ with respect to the processes used to deal with various situations" (Springer & Deutsch, 1981, p. 188). In other words, *learning styles may be learned through cultural experience.*

## Cultural Influences on Learning

How does culture affect the way people approach a learning situation? The first way is through **socialization,** or the process by which parents transmit cultural expectations to their children. Socialization includes ways of learning and solving problems. Gollnick and Chinn have suggested that "the individual differences in learning and teaching styles develop from early and continuing socialization patterns" (1994, p. 307). Witkin (1979) also recognized the influence of family structure and parental roles on cognitive style. Thus, parental roles may be interpreted as **teaching styles.**

The second way that culture influences learning style is in its amount of **pressure for conformity** (Worthley, 1987). Conformity, of course, requires people to follow traditional ways of doing things. In cultures that use an approach to learning known as field dependent (or field sensitive), the emphasis is on following the proper procedure in order to solve a problem or learn a skill. In cultures that use an approach known as field independent, people are freer to try new possibilities in solving problems. In other words, they may focus on the nature of the problem rather than on the ways that others have solved it.

The third way that culture affects learning style is known as **ecological adaptation** (Worthley, 1987). In some areas of the world, human survival depends on keen observation. In some environments there is an emphasis on visual and auditory perception. Hearing a rustle in the underbrush and reacting quickly, for example, can enable the listener to prevent a snakebite, or perhaps serious injury when a rhinoceros charges out of the woods toward the light of a campfire. Knowing how to find a root in the Kalahari Desert during the dry season can provide a source of water. The child of the Bushman watches his father find roots in the desert. In preliterate cultures, skills were often demonstrated rather than described.

The fourth way that culture affects learning is through **language** (Worthley, 1987). Literate cultures transmit large amounts of important knowledge in written form. In preliterate cultures, important information is learned through verbal instruction and demonstration. Years ago, the linguist Benjamen Lee Whorf suggested that language shapes the way people in any culture understand the world around them (1956). Language is a means by which people organize the world by classifying objects and events into linguistic categories. The degree of elaboration of terms suggests the importance of a concept within the culture. For example, in English there is a single word, "snow," to describe frozen water crystals, but in the Aleut language, there are several terms for snow that connote different types. In the climate of the Aleuts, knowing what to do in response to these different types is important. In contrast, cultures may have less elaborate linguistic codes as well. Years ago in a graduate class, the anthropologist Charles Frake reported that in some cultures in the South Pacific there are only two color terms. The first refers to green, blue, and purple on the color spectrum, and the second refers to red, yellow, and brown. In a climate with a wet and dry season, this designation is sufficient for knowing how to respond to the environment, for the vegetation changes color during the seasons. No further elaboration is necessary. Humans classify things because they need to know how to act. Language enables them to do so and provides guidelines for actions in response. Children learn about these categories and appropriate actions in the process of socialization.[1]

Pressure for conformity, ecological adaptation, and language account for similarities among members of the same cultural group, but socialization can vary within families. In other words, both culture and personal environment influence the ways in which children learn. Children from the same family may also vary among themselves. When teachers consider how children approach learning situations, they need to take culture and family influences into account, and at the same time allow for individual differences.

## Culture and Logical Operations

Jean Piaget, the Swiss psychologist who is well known in education, identified a series of mental abilities, or "logical operations," that children develop as they grow older (Chapter 10). One of these operations is the ability to classify or categorize. Culture affects logical operations. A good example is a case that a teacher in a Wisconsin elementary school reported to me. Many of her Hmong students chose incorrect responses among an array of pictures in a sorting test. The directions for the test were to "draw a circle around the object which does *not belong*." One task included pictures of a hatchet, a saw, a hammer, and a fire. The Hmong students circled the hammer. The "correct" answer is the fire, because it is not a tool. Fortunately, the teacher asked the students why they chose the hammer. They replied that a hatchet and a saw can be used to cut the wood to make a fire, but that you don't use a hammer to do that! The lesson is obvious. In working with students from diverse cultures, teachers must ask the reasons why students answer the way they do, rather than assuming that students do not understand the concepts behind the questions on the task.

## THE THEORY OF MULTIPLE INTELLIGENCES

Howard Gardner (1983) has suggested a theory of multiple intelligences. This theory evolved out of his concern over the emphasis that schools place on two kinds of symbolic processes: the use of language and logical-mathematical analysis. It was Gardner's contention that other abilities such as those in the arts, in different kinds of experimentation, *or those valued in different cultures,* were not considered relevant to the concept of intelligence. Gardner derived a list of "intelligences" from an array of data including (a) the development of cognitive abilities in normal individuals; (b) the abilities of people who deviate from the norm (child prodigies, idiot savants);[2] (c) the loss of abilities due to organic factors; (d) factor analysis of studies of cognitive transfer; and (e) forms of intelligence valued in different cultural groups.

Gardner identified several different types of intelligence, which are listed below, followed by their essential capacities:

### Linguistic Intelligence
This includes a sensitivity to word meaning and word order, an ability for grammatical rules, and an awareness of the fact that communication has or

has not occurred between people. Writers, journalists, and poets use this ability. (Teachers do, too!)

### Logical–Mathematical Intelligence

This includes an ability to classify, reclassify, follow long sequences of logical thinking, and pursue complex procedures. Scientists, mathematicians, and inventors use this ability. (Teachers do, too!)

### Musical Intelligence

This includes a perception of rhythm, pitch, and timbre, an ability for performance, and perhaps for composition. It also includes an ability for improvisation. Performers, composers, and conductors use this ability. (So do music teachers!)

### Interpersonal Intelligence

This includes an awareness of emotion and mood in oneself and in others and the ability to respond appropriately to the views of others. Therapists and counselors use this ability. (So do teachers!)

### Bodily-Kinesthetic Intelligence

This includes an ability for small and large muscle control, body control, and manipulation of objects. Athletes, dancers, musicians, artists, surgeons, and mechanics use this control. (So do teachers of these subjects!)

### Spatial Intelligence

This includes an ability to perceive the world accurately, to remember those perceptions, to modify, transform, or recreate them, to manipulate space, and to understand tension and balance. Engineers, architects, artists, sculptors, designers, and mechanics use this ability. (Teachers of these subjects do, too!)

The theory of multiple intelligences has been questioned on the basis of difficulties in assessment. Gardner and Hatch (1990) have attempted empirical research to investigate if in fact these intelligences are independent of each other. In two studies (twenty participants in the first, fifteen participants in the second), children were assessed on ten different activities, as well as on the Stanford Binet Intelligence Scale. In the first study, fifteen of the twenty children showed ability in at least one activity, and twelve of the twenty children showed a weakness in one or more activities. In the second study, the children did not perform comparably across activities, which suggested that they did have different abilities. Further research could prove very exciting. A fable of multiple intelligences appears in Box 9.1.

## FIELD INDEPENDENT/DEPENDENT STYLE

Another view of the way individuals differ is how they approach a learning or problem-solving situation. A concept known as **field independence/dependence** has received some attention in relation to cultural diversity. It is based on the research of Herman Witkin. Witkin was interested in the psychology of perception and designed a study to determine the degree to which people are de-

---

**BOX 9.1** Multiple Intelligences at the Animal School: An Old Tale Retold

The students at the animal school were very diverse. The wise old owl, who was the principal of the school, decided that in order to receive their diploma the students should pass a test that measured their ability in different skills. The eagle received the top score in flying, but he failed climbing, crawling, and running. He didn't even try to swim. The turtle excelled at crawling and swam all right, but he could not run or climb too well. He didn't try to fly. The tiger surpassed all the others in running and climbing. He passed swimming, he refused to crawl, and flying was too much for him. The crocodile outperformed everyone in swimming and she crawled all right, but she could not manage climbing and running. She refused to try flying. Finally it was the snake's turn. She excelled at crawling, could climb pretty well, and managed to swim. She also hurled herself a short distance through the air. She just couldn't run. The wise old owl decided that the eagle, the turtle, the tiger, and the crocodile did not have the competencies to graduate, but the snake received her diploma even though she was a little weak in flying. And the owl was convinced that he was the wisest of animals, even though he himself had failed crawling, climbing, running, and swimming when he went to school.

---

pendent upon visual and kinesthetic cues (derived from the effect of gravity on the body) in their perception of the upright position. In other words, Witkin was investigating the relative use of visual cues and internal cues on people's perception of their spatial position. His first experiment "set out to separate the gravitational standard of the upright position from the standard provided by the visual field, with the aim of evaluating the importance of each" (Witkin, 1959, p. 187). In this experiment, participants sat in a chair, which the experimenter tilted to the right or left, within a room that the experimenter also tilted to the right or left. This room also contained decorative elements, such as pictures on the wall, that accentuated its vertical and horizontal lines. The participants were asked to align themselves in the true upright position regardless of the tilt of the room. A second study aimed at studying the accuracy of participants' perceptions about the degree of straightness of external objects. In other words, kinesthetic cues were not involved. In this experiment they sat in total darkness, facing a luminous rod inside a luminous frame that was tilted to varying degrees. They were then asked to direct the experimenter to adjust the rod until it appeared upright to them inside the tilted frame. Results of these two experiments produced an unexpected finding. People differed greatly in their perception of the upright. In the first experiment, some people were always able to align their chair in an upright position no matter how far the room was tilted. Others reported that they were upright when in fact they were tilted as much as 35 degrees in alignment with the room. In the second experiment, some people were consistently able to align the rod to a true vertical position despite the tilt of the frame, while others perceived the rod to be straight when it was tilted in alignment with the frame. In other words, some participants appeared to be more dependent on the surrounding visual field, while others were not so influenced by these adjacent cues. In summarizing the results of these experiments, Witkin reported that instead of discovering whether visual or kinesthetic cues were more important, what was discovered was the extent of individual differences in perception. Witkin then set out to investigate the nature of these individual differences.

His subsequent studies did not involve body position but required people to separate an item from its surrounding field. It was in the context of these studies that the **Embedded Figures** Test was developed. In this test, people are asked to locate a simple geometric figure within a larger complex figure or design. An example problem appears in Figure 9.1.

In testing the same participants who had participated in the two previous experiments, Witkin discovered that the people who required more time to find the hidden figures were those who tended to align their bodies with the tilt of the room and to align the rod with the tilt of the frame. Witkin (1959) described his choice of terms as follows:

> We designated as **"field–independent"** those who showed a capacity to differentiate objects from their backgrounds. Conversely, the **"field–dependent"** subjects were those whose performance reflected...submission to the domination of the background, and inability to keep an item separate from its surroundings. In the general population, perceptual performances reflecting the extent of field-dependence or field-independence are ranged *in a continuum rather than constituting two distinct types.* (p. 189, italics mine)

Witkin soon realized the value of his research findings for educational settings. He described people who were more inclined toward field-independence as excelling at problems that require the isolation of essential elements from a context and the recombining of these elements in new relationships. He further pointed out that *standard intelligence tests* focus on this type of analytical logic. Witkin also reported that students with a tendency toward field-independence do not score better than field-dependent students on items dealing with vocabulary, information, and comprehension. Finally, Witkin associated field-independence with an ability to function "with relative autonomy...in everyday life" (1959, p. 189).

A concept of *learning style* based on field independence/dependence subsequently emerged. Tests similar to the Embedded Figures Test were developed for different ages, including measurements for preschool children (Coates, 1972) and elementary age children (Karp and Konstadt, 1971).

## Empirical Studies of Field Independence/Dependence

Research on this approach to learning style has been extensive. The studies I have included in this section are some that offer possibilities for future study in three areas: (a) general student characteristics; (b) students' styles in relation to parents' child-rearing practices and parents' employment; and (c) changes in style over time. Studies reporting different results for diverse groups are discussed later in this chapter, because these studies also related to other learning style issues.

Within educational settings, the characteristics of a field independent style have been described as (a) an inclination to work independently; (b) motivation

INSTRUCTIONS: This is a test of your ability to find a simple form when it is hidden within a complex pattern.

Here is a simple form which we have labeled "X":

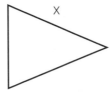

This simple form, named "X", is hidden within the more complex figure below:

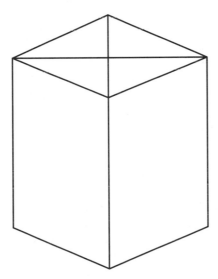

Try to find the simple form in the complex figure and trace it *in pencil* directly over the lines of the complex figure. It is the SAME SIZE, in the SAME PROPORTIONS, and FACES THE SAME DIRECTION within the complex figure as when it appeared alone.

**FIGURE 9.1** Example Problem: Group Embedded Figures Test

from within (intrinsic motivation), with a lower need for external reinforcement; (c) an orientation to the assigned task; (d) an analytic approach; and (e) a preference for personal recognition. Some of the characteristics of a field dependent style are (a) a preference to work with others; (b) a need for reinforcement in the form of encouragement and guidance (extrinsic motivation); (c) an awareness of social cues with an orientation to the environment along with a sensitivity to others' views and feelings; (d) a global approach; and (e) an appreciation of social rewards (Witkin et al., 1973; Witkin et al., 1977). The term *field sensitive* has recently been used to describe this type of learner. More recently, Heppner and Krauskopf (1987) have reported that field independent learners perform well in situations conducive to intrinsic motivation, persevere longer, and are more self-directive and systematic in their learning. Field dependent learners, on the other hand, are better at incidental learning and at adapting to new situations.

There have also been studies of field independence and dependence in regard to family situations. There has sometimes been an assumption in regard to parental roles that *parents' discipline* is related to their children's learning style. The belief has been that lenient child rearing is associated with field independence, and that strict child rearing is associated with field dependence. A report by Britain and Abad (1974) *assumed* a strict discipline style in Cuban culture when they reported differences between Cuban and American children.

Liao and Chiang (1993) investigated field dependence and independence among Chinese fifth graders, eleventh graders, and college students in Taiwan. Although these students were not Asian Americans, the results of this study raise some intriguing questions that might be considered in regard to diverse racial and ethnic groups in the United States. For this reason, I have included their study here. Liao and Chiang found significant differences in scores on the Group Embedded Figures Test among fifth graders *in relation to parents' employment*. (The eleventh graders and college students were not included in this part of the study.) The students whose parents both worked outside the home were more field independent than those with only one parent who worked. This finding is particularly interesting in light of Witkin's (1979) recognition of the influence of family structure and parental roles on cognitive style. Liao and Chiang suggest that assumptions about the effect of cultural influences (in the form of traditional child-rearing practices) on cognitive style may not be valid if situations in the home are changing. This line of inquiry into parents' employment patterns and their children's "style" warrants further investigation.

Liao and Chiang further found significantly higher scores on the Group Embedded Figures Test (indicating field independence) among eleventh graders in comparison with *both* the fifth graders and the college students. It has generally been assumed that field independence is cumulatively affected by exposure to the analytical skills emphasized in school programs. These results, however, suggest (a) that cognitive style may not progress in a linear relation with schooling, and (b) that cognitive style may fluctuate over time. Witkin himself (1959) reported that results of a longitudinal study indicated that children tend to be field dependent early in their development and to become more field independent between ages eight to thirteen, after which there appeared to be a leveling off or even a return to more field-dependent thought. More research could shed light on individual variations in cognitive style over time.

## LEARNING STYLES

In addition to the field independent/dependent approach, the concept of learning styles derives from two other areas in psychology: personality and cognitive theory. Personality theory has sought to understand, explain, and predict differences in people's *behavior* by identifying different types of people. In this context, the term "type" refers to differences in personality. Cognitive theory has sought to understand, explain, and predict differences in people's *thinking*. In this context, the term "style" refers to variations in perceiving, conceptualizing, analyzing, and problem solving.

In the field of education, the distinction between the personality and the cognitive approaches to individual differences has not always been maintained. Both are contained in popular conceptions of learning styles. In order for the reader to have a perspective on how the concept of learning styles evolved, a review of the history leading up to it is important here.

### Psychological Types

The idea of different types of personalities began in ancient Greece, when the physician Hippocrates first described four types of people.[3] Carl Jung, a Swiss psychiatrist, offered a more modern theory of personality types in the early twentieth century. A former pupil of Sigmund Freud, Jung was interested in the subconscious reasons why people respond to situations differently. In his book *Psychological Types,* published in 1921, he suggested the term **psychological types** to describe different personalities.[4]

Jung also described another aspect of personality—that of extroversion and introversion. An extrovert is outgoing and enjoys interacting with people. An introvert is more reserved and reticent with others. All people, of course, interact with others, but in Jung's view, people are simply more comfortable in one mode or the other. He also asserted that problems may arise when people of different modes must live and work together. The concepts of extroversion and introversion have been used in education. Recently, Lazarus (1991) suggested that in problem-solving situations, extroverts may have difficulty encoding problems and that introverts may have difficulty perceiving them in the environment.

In the early 1940s, Isabel Briggs Myers and her mother, Katherine Cook Briggs, created the well-known Myers-Briggs Type Indicator (MBTI), based on Jung's theory.[5] Myers designed this test to identify individuals' psychological types as a test for personnel selection. This test has been popular in business, education, and counseling. It is still widely used (in a revised version) on college campuses. There are questions, however, concerning the MBTI's validity and usefulness as a means of understanding behavior (Pittinger, 1993). It is important to point out here that items on later learning style tests were based on Jung's theory and partly derived from the Myers-Briggs test, in spite of its validity problems.

## Hemispheric Differences in Cognitive Processing

In addition to the personality or psychological types identified by Jung and extended by Myers and Briggs, the concept of learning style also derives from clinical evidence that some cognitive processes are differentiated within the two hemispheres of the brain.[6]

In the 1960s, research on hemispheric processing began to be reported on so-called split-brain patients who had undergone surgery that severed the neural pathways between the two hemispheres of the brain (Sperry, 1967). This radical surgery was done in order to reduce the possibility of recurring grand mal epileptic seizures, which can be life threatening. From a psychological point of view, this surgery provided a unique opportunity to study, under controlled laboratory conditions, the cognitive processing in each hemisphere of the patients who had the operation.[7] The patients were asked questions, and their answers revealed previously unknown data about differences in cognitive processing within the two hemispheres. The major findings may be summarized as follows. Specialization in cognitive processing in the left hemisphere appeared to include (a) speech production and interpretation; (b) verbal or linguistic thinking; (c) time-related or sequential logic; (d) calculation; and (e) an ability to focus on details, including item analysis. Specialization in cognitive processing in the right hemisphere appeared to include (a) perception of spatial relationships and patterns; (b) some limited language ability; (c) interpretation of tone of voice; (d) correlational (as contrasted with sequential) logic; and (e) emotional reactions (Sperry, 1967; Springer & Deutsch, 1981).

Reports of these findings hit both the general public and the field of education like a bomb. The findings were overgeneralized, oversimplified, and even distorted, not only by the public but by educators. During the 1970s the so-called left-brained/right-brained concept came into fashion, even to the degree of becoming a fad. The left brain was described in the popular press as verbal, logical, rational, and dull. The right brain was described as visual, imaginative, and creative. There was a flurry of activity to develop tests to identify whether people were "left brained" or "right brained." Numerous books were published with tests that people could take to discover which "brain" they were. In education, suggestions appeared for teaching "left-brained" or "right-brained" students. The problem was that both the tests and the educational procedures were based on the popular view of hemispheric processing with little understanding of the clinical data itself.

There were three *serious* errors in the popular view of hemispheric specialization. The first error was the failure to realize that data obtained from split-brain patients tested under controlled laboratory conditions have limited application to the general population. In normal subjects, information is rapidly exchanged between the two hemispheres, which function in conjunction with each other.

The second error in the public mind was the notion that the left hemisphere is dull and the right hemisphere is imaginative and creative. This view fails to consider the contributions of the left hemisphere's linguistic thinking, attention to details, and sequential logic to creative thought. This view also fails to recognize the importance of the right hemisphere's correlational logic and recognition of relationships among ideas.

The third error was the failure to understand that people use both hemispheres' cognitive processing *simultaneously*. A visual example would be that of looking at the face of a clock. Most people notice the details and read the numerals, whether they are Arabic or Roman, and at the same time notice the spatial relationships, including the position of the hands in reference to the numbers. Thus, they are interpreting the face of the clock (and therefore the time) through processing in both hemispheres. A verbal example would be a conversation. People are usually aware of both the meaning of the words and the tone of voice, which together may or may not convey the same message. When tone of voice conveys a different message from the words, most people recognize the contradiction. Therefore, they are interpreting the conversation in both hemispheres. People are not "left brained" or "right brained," although they may have a preference for the processes in one or the other hemisphere when they approach a problem.

By the early 1980s, educators began to recognize the problems in the popular, oversimplified, and distorted interpretations of hemispheric processing. Unfortunately, this realization led some to question the usefulness of the information about hemispheric differences. Some doubted the validity of the laboratory research findings altogether. The clinical findings became confused with the fashion and, like all fashions, began to go out of style. For example, many textbooks in educational psychology that formerly included a description of hemispheric differences no longer do so in recent editions. (The descriptions that they formerly included were all too often based on the oversimplified and overgeneralized interpretations of the clinical findings.) The concept of hemispheric differences, however, has not altogether disappeared in education. Hohn has reported that recent studies indicate "that the two cerebral hemispheres do contribute in different ways to cognitive functioning" (1995, p. 44). In addition to the concept of the field-independent/dependent approach and a recognition of personality differences, *hemispheric processing has also become incorporated into the definition of learning styles.*

**Culture and Hemispheric Processing**   Studies of cultural differences in hemispheric processing have been limited. One study by Bogen and his associates (1972) compared the performance of 1,220 people, including Hopi Indians, urban Blacks, and rural and urban Whites, on two tests. The first test was the Street Gestalt Completion Test, which involves primarily right-hemisphere processing. The second test was the Similarities Subtest of the Wechsler Adult Intelligence Scale, a verbal test that involves primarily left-hemisphere processing. Results showed the highest ratio of right- over left-hemisphere processing among the Hopi Indians, followed by urban Blacks, rural Whites, and urban Whites. The researchers concluded that Hopis and urban Blacks rely more on right-hemisphere thinking. In a critique of this study, Zook and Dwyer (1976) suggested an alternative interpretation. The scores for right-hemisphere processing showed no appreciable difference across the groups, but the scores of the Hopi and the urban Blacks were lower on the Weschler verbal subtest. There is a cultural bias, however, in the Weschler verbal subtest. Therefore, in Zook and Dwyer's view, an argument could be made that development of left-hemisphere (verbal) processing is depressed by lack of educational opportunities that provide the vocabulary necessary to attain higher scores on this type of verbal test.

## Learning Styles in Education

In the 1970s and 1980s, the notion of **learning styles** became a fashionable trend in educational and business settings. According to Curry (1990), learning style has been related in education to (a) curriculum design; (b) methods of instruction; (c) assessment; and (d) guidance. The concept of learning styles, however, has been challenged recently for several reasons. Curry has pointed out that problems include (a) the ambiguity in definitions of learning styles; (b) the questions concerning validity and reliability in the tests for learning style; and (c) the issue of what learning style actually means in terms of classroom application. In addition to these problems, I suggest that there are three more: (a) the confusion of cognitive processes with the notion of psychological types; (b) assumptions that people have a habitual or fixed rather than an adaptive approach to learning and problem solving; and (c) a tendency in multicultural education to confuse students' thinking with culturally learned approaches to learning (and problem solving).

**Problems in Definition**  Although the term *learning style* has been widely used, exactly what it means has not always been clear. As early as 1945, Lowenfeld described a difference between visual and haptic types, with vision and touch as the primary modes of experience. Royer and Feldman (1984) defined learning style as a personality trait. Nieto described learning style as "the way in which individuals receive and process information" (1992, p. 111). Rita and Kenneth Dunn (1979), developers of the Learning Style Inventory (LSI), defined learning style as the way in which environmental, emotional, sociological, and physical stimuli affect the ability to absorb and retain information. Shade (1989) distinguished between an analytic style and a synergetic style. Analytic learners are independent, focus on one task at a time, and work in a step-by-step sequence. Synergetic learners prefer to work cooperatively, are stimulated by multiple activities, and prefer active or hands-on involvement in the learning process. As early as 1964, Kagan distinguished between an impulsive and a reflective approach to learning. Hunt (1979) described students' varying needs for external structure in the learning situation as an aspect of learning style. Cornett (1983) considered learning styles to be consistent patterns of behavior along cognitive, affective, and physiological dimensions.

Perhaps the most comprehensive definition of learning style has been that of the National Task Force on Learning Style and Brain Behavior (in Keefe & Languis, 1983):

> Learning style is that consistent pattern of behavior and performance by which an individual approaches educational experiences. It is the composite

of characteristic cognitive, affective, and physiological behaviors that serve as relatively stable indicators of how a learner perceives, interacts with, and responds to the learning environment. It is formed in the deep structure of neural organization and personality [that] ... is molded by ... the cultural experiences of home, school, and society. (p. 1)

A careful reading of this definition reveals implications that it is derived from concepts about psychological types, cognitive processing, and cultural influences.

As if this variety of definitions was not confusing enough for teachers trying to understand individual differences in ways that their students learn, Curry (1990) has identified another problem. The differences between **style, strategy,** and **tactic** have not always been clear. Some educators have suggested that style refers to information processing that functions in individuals like personality traits (Entwistle, 1981). Educators have also suggested that strategy refers to consistency in how students approach learning in different situations (Entwistle, 1988; Ramsden, 1988). Others have proposed that tactic refers to the observable activity or habitual responses of students in a variety of learning situations (Snowman, 1989). In view of these different interpretations of what learning style means, it is clear that different people use the term to refer to different concepts. A further problem develops when educators use the term *learning style,* when in fact they may mean *strategy* or *tactic.*

**Problems in Learning Style Tests**   Along with the notion of learning styles came a proliferation of tests designed to identify learning styles in both children and adults. Bennett (1990) has reported a total of thirty learning style instruments. These may be classified as (a) multidimensional instruments; (b) cognitive style instruments; (c) affective style instruments; and (d) perceptual modality instruments. Learning style tests consist of rank-order or forced-choice type questions. Some questions were designed to identify the psychological type of the test taker. Some questions were based on popular interpretations of hemispheric processing. Responses were then interpreted as the test-taker's "style."

Both the validity and the reliability of tests for learning style have been questioned (Curry, 1990). Early tests were created and marketed quickly without due consideration of procedures commonly expected in the construction of valid tests. The statistical reliability of these tests varied widely, and in some cases was based on only a few test items. Reliability was not reported for some tests. Educators using a learning style test should have information about the test's reliability in order to have confidence in the test results. Curry (1990) has reported serious omissions and other problems with the reliability of information supplied with some of these tests.

Another problem common to these tests is the forced-choice format, which requires the test taker to select an answer that describes how he or she "usually" responds in a learning or problem-solving situation. This format assumes that people always take the same approach and fails to take into account the fact that *people's approach to a problem is often determined by the nature of the problem.* Therefore, they may choose answers on the basis of the kind of problem they were thinking about when they were taking the test. For example, a friend of mine who is a teacher was required to take a widely marketed learning style test by her school administrator. During the test she considered how she approached the task of writing a report, and answered the test items accordingly. Being suspicious of the test's validity, she asked to retake the test immediately. Because her hobby was sewing, this time she considered how she approached the task of constructing a dress of her own design. The results of her two tests indicated two totally different learning styles! The lesson is clear. Creators of learning style tests have proceeded on the assumption that people have a predominant "style" and have focused on trying to identify that style. They have not taken into consideration the fact that people may use a variety of approaches and employ different cognitive processes that best suit the task at hand. Furthermore, the creators of the tests have assumed that results of these tests among diverse cultural groups indicate a style for that group. Perhaps if different types of problems were presented, the tests might elicit more information about how members of diverse groups approach different situations.

**Problems with Application**   New approaches to curricular planning that take students' learning styles into account followed shortly after the appearance of the learning style tests. One approach sought to integrate left/right hemispheric processes with psychological types (McCarthy, 1980; McCarthy & Lafler, 1983). Several educators suggested the idea of systematically matching the learning styles of students with teachers' cognitive styles and curricular methods (Barbe & Swassing, 1979; Dunn & Dunn, 1975; Witkin, 1977). Did this match produce optimal learning? Others suggested that students could benefit from becoming familiar with alternative learning strategies (Shipman & Shipman, 1985). In other words, there might be a benefit in "mismatching" learning and teaching styles to facilitate more flexibility in learning. An approach that incorporates both views was offered by Snow and Lohman (1984), who suggested matching students' learning styles with teaching methods in the initial stages of learning, and then mismatching them later in the process. Reports on the effects of these methods have been mixed. Snider suggests that it is "good practice to present information in a variety of ways through more than one modality" (1990, p. 53). O'Neil (1990) has reported that debates over classroom procedures in relation to style have continued. Students may have a predisposition toward one modality, but they may also benefit from a variety of approaches in a learning or problem-solving situation.

## CULTURAL DIVERSITY AND STYLE

Guild (1994) has called attention to the fact that, in general, three types of information have been reported about the relationship between culture and learning styles. These are (a) observational descriptions of diverse cultural groups of learners or students; (b) data-based descriptions that use assessments including the Myers-Briggs Type Indicator, from which learning styles are inferred (in spite of its validity problems); and (c) direct discussion. Studies have revealed some patterns in relation to diverse groups.

Even before the concept of learning styles evolved in education, cultural patterns in different mental abilities were investigated in an important study by Stodolsky and Lesser (1967). In this study, test scores of six- and seven-year-old Chinese, Jewish, Black, and Puerto Rican children from both middle-class and poor homes revealed different patterns for each ethnic group *in spite of social class background*. Stodolsky and Lesser concluded that ethnicity appeared to have more influence than social class on the mental abilities tested. The young age of these children was an important factor because it implied a shorter period of time in which formal schooling could affect their test scores. In a review of studies some twenty years later, Banks (1988) also reported that ethnicity appeared to influence cognitive style more than social class and that the ethnic differences remained even when social class changed for the better.[8]

Studies with diverse groups have been reported in regard to field-independent/dependent styles and other approaches to learning. Among African American students, Hilliard (1976) reported a more relational (or field-dependent) style, a preference for inferential reasoning, and a proficiency in nonverbal communication. Perney (1976) reported that African American females were more field dependent than males. Shade (1989, 1990) reported that African American students are inclined toward learning cooperatively, and through observation, group discussion, and hands-on or kinesthetic activities. Bennett (1990) summarized findings which indicate that African Americans are inclined toward a global approach to learning, a preference for inference, and a focus on people. In a review of the literature, Shade (1982) reported mixed findings for "Afro-Americans." Importantly, Shade called attention to the fact that differences in personality style among groups are sometimes reported as a racial rather than a socioeconomic difference. Shade further pointed out that African American cognitive or perceptual style preference focuses on a person rather than an object orientation (which would fit with a field-dependent orientation and a cooperative learning approach). Shade (1982) described this orientation as follows:

> An examination of the culture or lifestyle and world view of Afro-Americans … portrays strategies designed to foster survival and therefore tends to be rather universalistic, intuitive, and, more than that, very person-oriented. (p. 238)

Asian students have a reputation for being conscientious, highly motivated, and conforming to teachers' expectations. Reports on Japanese American students appear to support this view (Yoshiwara, 1983). Suzuki (1983) has called attention to the fact that teachers may stereotype Asian students as hard working and conforming, with the result that students may not develop the ability to express their feelings. There is also a danger that teachers may overgeneralize their perceptions to other Asian students, including recent Southeast Asian refugees. Hmong students tend to be field dependent and use a global approach, rather than an analytic approach, to problem-solving situations. They also tend toward a receptive learning mode, depend upon memorizing, and are oriented toward group cooperation (Worthley, 1987). In a study of Hmong students that Berttram Chiang and I conducted in the spring of 1995 (which we are reporting here for the first time), results indicated that these students were highly field dependent. We administered the Group Embedded Figures Test to a total of ninety students in upper elementary and middle school (fifth through eighth grade) in two Wisconsin communities. Of these students, only seven boys and no girls were field independent. (Eighty students fell within the first quartile range of scores; three in the second quartile; three in the third quartile; and four in the fourth quartile.) A field-cooperative orientation was evident in the fact that during the administering of the test, we continuously had to stop both boys and girls from trying to help each other. Interestingly, the four students whose scores fell within the fourth quartile were intently focused on the test.

Ramirez and Casteneda (1974) reported that Mexican American students are inclined toward a field-sensitive learning style in comparison with Anglo American students, who tend to be more field independent. Dunn and Dunn (1978) reported that Mexican American students were peer oriented, and more likely to perform well in small, cooperative group learning situations. They also reported that the boys were more motivated by their parents. More recently, Vasquez (1990) suggested that Hispanic American students' orientation of loyalty to family and groups may predispose them toward cooperative learning situations.

Phillips (1978) reported that Native American students show a preference for learning by observation before they attempt to perform a task themselves. Traditionally, Indian children frequently learned through observation and role modeling. According to More (1987), these students prefer visual to verbal modes, use images to learn concepts, and are reflective (in contrast to impulsive) learners. A holistic approach to learning and a preference for cooperation have been reported among Native American students (Caldwell, 1989; Kasten, 1992). Caldwell has suggested that Native American teaching is based on (a) examples rather than on precepts or rules, and (b) cooperative rather than competitive social values.

## STYLES AND EDUCATION

What do the different intelligences that Gardner identified—field independence or dependence, psychological types, hemispheric processing—and the various notions of learning styles have to do with multicultural education? The answer is a great deal, so long as educators use them with caution. There appears to be considerable agreement about the need to avoid overgeneralizing and overapplying these concepts. Witkin (1977) himself cautioned against using cognitive style to perpetuate self-fulfilling prophecies regarding the field-independence or dependence approach. Pittinger (1993) has referred to dangers in the overinterpretation of test results. Although he was referring to test scores on the Myers-Briggs Type Indicator, his advice also may apply in a broader context. Pittinger described the problem as follows:

> The research on self-fulfilling prophecies … suggest that people will develop expectations when they are given basic descriptive information about another person. These expectations can dramatically alter the nature of the interactions between the individuals, and they may be self-perpetuating be-

cause people will selectively remember and interpret the behavior of another using the stereotype as a ... filter. (pp. 482–83)

Educators also need to bear in mind the past zeal that led to absurd overgeneralizations about the clinical data on hemispheric processing. In attempting to "classify" different types of learners, educators need to remember that different approaches to teaching and learning may be used in different learning situations involving different types of problems. Twenty years ago, Ramirez and Casteneda (1974) suggested that a major goal of democratic education should be **bicognitive** development. In other words, students should become familiar with and be able to use different approaches to learning and problem solving. While continuing to prefer one style, they may have the flexibility of other styles as well.

There *are* different cultural influences on students' approaches to learning, but there are different intelligences and abilities as well. There are different personalities. Guild has suggested that "generalizations about a *group* of people often lead to naive inferences about *individual* members of that group" (1994, p. 17; emphasis Guild's). In automatically assuming similarities among members of any group, we may inadvertently stereotype our students and thereby rob them of their unique individual qualities.

## CHAPTER SUMMARY

There are several ways that students and people differ. The first is cultural. Culture influences the way people learn through (a) socialization; (b) pressure for conformity; (c) ecological adaptation; and (d) language.

Another way people differ is in varying abilities. Howard Gardner has suggested that there are multiple intelligences. These are (a) linguistic intelligence; (b) logical-mathematical intelligence; (c) musical intelligence; (d) interpersonal intelligence; (e) bodily-kinesthetic intelligence; and (f) spatial intelligence.

People have different ways in orienting to the environment. Herman Witkin identified a field-independent and a field-dependent style that people use in learning and problem-solving situations.

Psychological types refer to different kinds of personalities. In addition to these types, there are also extroverts, or people who are outgoing, and introverts, or people who are more reserved.

The two hemispheres of the brain function in conjunction with each other. Each contributes to cognitive processing.

The concept of learning styles has been popular in education. There have been problems of definition, test construction, and application of learning styles in classroom settings. There has also been an assumption that people have a habitual approach to learning and problem solving, when in fact their approach may depend on the nature of the problem.

Studies of students from diverse groups suggest that there are cultural differences in the way people approach learning and problem-solving situations. Educators need to be cautious to avoid overgeneralizing individuals in terms of their group.

## IMPORTANT TERMS

Cultural style

Ecological adaptation

Multiple intelligences

Field-dependent learning

Field-independent learning

Psychological types

Bicognitive

Bicognitive development

Hemispheric processing

Learning style

Learning strategy

Learning tactic

Teaching style

Embedded Figures Test

Pressure for conformity

## QUESTIONS FOR DISCUSSION

1. Give an example of ecological adaptation in your cultural experience.

2. In which of the different "intelligences" do you excel? With which do you have trouble?

3. Are you a field-independent or a field-dependent type of person? Why do you think so?

4. Have you ever taken a learning styles test or styles indicator such as the Myers-Briggs test? If so, what "type" were you? Do you believe that it is an accurate assessment of your personality? Do the results fit with your perception of being field independent/dependent?

5. Have you ever had difficulty working with someone who was a different "type" from yourself? How did you resolve the problem? If you were hired to work with a person who is a different type, how would you handle the situation?

6. Do you believe that heredity or environment has more impact on the types of people we are?

## NOTES

1. A more complex example of the relation between language and behavior may be offered here. In English, we have a single short word, "cousin," to denote the daughter or son of an aunt or uncle on either our mother's or father's side of the family. In Hmong, however, specific terms such as "father's sister's daughter" or "father's brother's daughter" denote very different behaviors that are expected, allowed, and considered appropriate regarding these two kinds of cousins. From the point of view of a young Hmong man, the daughter of his father's sister is viewed as an ideal potential marriage partner, while the daughter of his father's brother is strictly taboo as a potential bride. Why? It is because marriage outside one's patrilineal family clan is required, and marriage within it is forbidden. For example, let us take the situation of our young man, who is a member of the Vue clan. When his father's sister married, she became a member of her husband's clan—let us say, in this case, the Lee clan. Her daughter's birth clan is Lee and therefore different from the clan of the potential groom. His father's brother, however, would retain his own clan name when he married—that is, he would remain a Vue. Therefore, his daughter would be a Vue, of the same clan as the potential groom, and therefore forbidden as a wife.

2. A popular film that portrayed an idiot savant was *Rainman*.

3. Hippocrates believed that these types derived from the four body humors: black bile, yellow bile, phlegm, and blood. Too much black bile resulted in a melancholic or sad type of person. Too much yellow bile resulted in a choleric or irritable and bad-tempered type of person. Too much phlegm resulted in a phlegmatic or apathetic type of person. Too much blood resulted in a sanguine type of person who was prone to shifts of mood, sometimes buoyant and sometimes cruel (Bootzin & Acocella, 1980). Today there is still a recognition of bad-tempered, depressed, lethargic, euphoric, and sadistic aspects of personality.

4. Jung suggested that there are four psychological "functions" through which people interpret their experiences. These are (a) sensation, by which they observe their environment and gather information; (b) intuition, by which they induct and interpret subtle information such as implication or tone of voice; (c) thinking, by which they logically analyze information available to them; and (d) feeling, by which they use a more subjective approach in deciding their actions. Jung believed that people use all of these approaches, but that they have personal preferences. These preferences constitute the types.

5. Myers and Briggs also added a perceptive function and a judging function to those of Jung.

6. The first report of such possible differentiation occurred in 1836 when Marc Dax, a French physician, observed difficulties in speaking among forty patients who had suffered cerebral strokes. In every case, post mortem examination revealed damage in the same area of the left hemisphere. When Dax suggested that speaking ability was located in the left hemisphere, his fellow doctors ignored him. In 1861 Paul Broca, another French physician, reported a similar case of a man who lost his speaking ability after a stroke. Again, post mortem examination revealed damage in his left hemisphere. When the medical community was skeptical, Paul Broca did not give up and continued to collect clinical data. Two years later he presented substantiating post mortem evidence of damage in the same area of the left hemisphere among stroke victims who

had lost the ability to speak. In 1870 the German scientist Karl Wernicke reported another area in the left hemisphere that apparently was specialized for speech interpretation. Today these regions of the brain are known as Broca's Area and Wernicke's Area. These discoveries suggested at least some specialization within the two hemispheres. Except for a few isolated reports of effects on behavior following head injuries, further research on hemispheric specialization was not undertaken for nearly ninety years (Springer and Deutsch, 1981).

7. This surgery severed the corpus callosum, or the nerve fibers connecting the two cerebral hemispheres. It is the primary pathway by which information is transmitted from one hemisphere to the other. Laboratory procedures were developed by which information was presented to a patient's left or right hemisphere only, following surgery. Because the corpus callosum was severed, there was no transmission of information to the alternative hemisphere. In other words, each hemisphere had its own information, which was inaccessible to the other. These procedures are described in detail elsewhere (Springer & Deutsch, 1981).

Other clinical evidence came from patients who had suffered damage to one hemisphere only as a result of injury or strokes.

8. These studies focused on differences in abilities and cognitive style. Their results do not contradict other research findings that indicated social class differences in the way parents teach their children. Years ago, for example, Hess and Shipman (1965) studied the interactions between middle-class and lower-class mothers and their young children. Middle-class mothers were more verbal, gave clearer directions, provided suggestions, and encouraged their children to solve problems themselves. Lower-class mothers gave directions that were less clear and did not explain the reasons or procedures for a task. Hess and McDevitt (1984) reported a relationship between differences in social class parenting styles and children's scores on achievement tests (not to be confused with tests of cognitive abilities). Scores on *achievement* tests are based on knowledge of specific items of learned information and not on different approaches to problem solving.

The social class differences in performance on achievement tests may derive from the difference between a focus on thinking problems through and a focus on getting the task done without a consideration of concepts. In the first approach, comprehension involves a deeper level of cognitive processing, which would predict more meaningful retention of knowledge. In the second approach, the emphasis on task completion would predict shorter retention. It may be that these two approaches establish a "mindset" toward understanding or memorizing. Merely memorizing would predict more rapid decay of information.

# REFERENCES

Banks, J. A. (1988). "Ethnicity, class, cognitive and motivational styles: Research and teaching implications." *Journal of Negro Education* 57 (4), 452–66.

Barbe, W. B., & Swassing, R. H. (1979). *Teaching through modality strengths: Concepts and practices.* Columbus, OH: Zaner-Bloser.

Bennett, C. I. (1990). *Comprehensive multicultural education: Theory and practice* (2nd ed.). Boston: Allyn and Bacon.

Bogen, J. E., DeZare, R., TenHouten, W. D., & Marsh, J. F. (1972). "The other side of the brain IV: The A/P ratio." *Bulletin of the Los Angeles Neurological Societies* 37, 49–61.

Bootzin, R. R., & Acocella, J. R. (1980). *Abnormal personality: Current perspectives* (3rd ed.). New York: Random House.

Britain, S. D., & Abad, M. (August 1974). "Field-Independence: A function of sex and socialization in Cuban and American adolescents." Paper presented at the American Psychological Association Convention, New Orleans, LA.

Caldwell, A. J. (1989). *Cultural learning styles: American Indian students in the classroom.* Madison, WI: Wisconsin Department of Public Instruction.

Coates, S. (1972). *Preschool embedded figures test.* Palo Alto, CA: Consulting Psychologists Press.

Cornett, C. E. (1983). *What you should know about teaching and learning styles* (Fastback 191). Bloomington, IN: Phi Delta Kappa.

Curry, L. (1990). "A critique of the research on learning styles." *Educational Leadership* 48 (2), 50–56.

DeVos, G. (1973). *Socialization for achievement: Essays on the cultural psychology of the Japanese.* Berkeley: University of California Press.

Dunn, R., & Dunn, K. (1975). "Finding the best fit: Learning styles, teaching styles." *NASSP Bulletin* 59, 37–49.

———. (1978). *Teaching students through their individual learning styles: A practical approach.* Reston, VA: Reston Publ.

Dunn, R., Dunn, K., & Price, G. E. (1975). *Learning style inventory.* Lawrence, KS: Price Systems.

Entwistle, N. (1981). *Styles of learning and teaching.* Chichester: Wiley.

———. (1988). "Motivational factors in students' approaches to learning." In R. R. Schmeck (Ed.), *Learning strategies and learning styles.* New York: Plenum Press.

Gardner, H. (1983). *Frames of mind.* New York: Basic Books.

Gardner, H. & Hatch, T. (1990). "Multiple intelligences go to school: Educational implications of the theory of multiple intelligences." *Educational Researcher* 18 (8), 4–10.

Gollnick, D. M., & Chinn, P. C. (1994). *Multicultural education in a pluralistic society.* New York: Merrill.

Gregorc, A. (1978). *Gregorc style delineator.* Maynard, MA: Gabriel Systems.

Guild, P. (May 1994). "The culture/learning style connection." *Educational Leadership* 51 (8), 16–21.

Heppner, P., & Krauskopf, C. (1987). "An information processing approach to personal problem solving." *Counseling Psychologist,* 15 (3), 371–447.

Hess, R., & McDevitt, T. (1984). "Some cognitive consequences of maternal intervention techniques: A longitudinal study." *Child Development* 55, 1902–12.

Hess, R. D., & Shipman, V. C. (1965). "Early experience and the socialization of cognitive modes in children." *Child Development* 36, 869–86.

Hilliard, A. (1976). *Alternatives to IQ testing: An approach to the identification of gifted minority children*. Final report to the California State Department of Education, Sacramento, 39.

Hohn, R. L. (1995). *Classroom learning and teaching*. White Plains, NY: Longman.

Hunt, D. E. (1979). "Learning style and student needs: An introduction to conceptual level." In *Student learning styles: Diagnosing and prescribing programs*. Reston, VA: National Association of Secondary School Principals.

Jung, C. G. (1971) *Psychological types*. Princeton, NJ: Princeton University Press. (Originally published in 1921).

Kagan, J. (1964). "American longitudinal research on psychological development." *Child Development* 35, 1–32.

Karp, S. A., & Konstadt, N. (1971). *Children's embedded figures test*. Palo Alto, CA: Consulting Psychologists Press.

Kasten, W. C. (1992). "Bridging the horizon: American Indian beliefs and whole language learning." *Anthropology and Education Quarterly* 23 (2), 108–19.

Keefe, J. W., & Languis, M. (Summer 1983). (Untitled article). *Learning Stages Network Newsletter* 4 (2), 1.

Kolb, D. (1976). *Learning style inventory*. Boston, MA: McBer and Company.

Lazarus, R. S. (1991). "Cognition and motivation in emotion." *American Psychologist* 46 (4), 352–67.

Liao, L. H. M., & Chiang, B. (October 1993). "Cognitive style and culture: An analysis of Chinese students' field dependence/independence among three age groups." Paper presented at the meeting of The Mid-Western Educational Research Association, Chicago, IL.

Lowenfeld, V. (1945). "Tests for visual and haptic aptitudes." *The American Journal of Psychology* 58 (1), 100–11.

McCarthy, B. (1980). *The 4Mat system: Teaching to learning styles with right/left mode techniques*. Barrington, IL: EXCEL.

McCarthy, B., & Lafler, S. (1983). *4Mat in action: Creative lesson plans for teaching to learning styles with right/left mode techniques*. Barrington, IL: EXCEL.

More, A. J. (1987). "Native-American learning styles: A review for researchers and teachers." *Journal of American Indian Education* 27 (1), 17–29.

Myers, I. B., & Briggs, K. C. (1943, 1976). *Myers-Briggs type indicator*. Palo Alto, CA: Consulting Psychologists Press.

Nieto, S. (1992). *Affirming diversity: The sociopolitical context of multicultural education*. New York: Longman.

O'Neil, J. (1990). "Making sense out of style." *Educational Leadership* 48 (2), 4–9.

Perney, V. H. (1976). "Effects of race and sex on field dependence-independence in children." *Perceptual and Motor Skills* 42, 975–80.

Phillips, J. C. (January 16, 1978). "College of, by and for Navajo Indians." *Chronicle of Higher Education,* 10–12.

Pittinger, D. J. (Winter 1993). "The utility of the Myers-Briggs type indicator." *Review of Educational Research* 63 (4), 467–88.

Puthiyottil, C. C. (1991). *Welcoming strangers to a new land: A model for successful refugee sponsorship*. Minneapolis: Augsburg Press.

Ramirez, M., & Casteneda, A. (1974). *Cultural democracy, biocognitive development and education*. New York: Academic Press.

Ramsden, P. (1988). "Context and strategy: Situational influences on learning." In R. R. Schmeck (Ed.), *Learning strategies and learning styles*. New York: Plenum Press.

Royer, J., & Feldman, R. (1984). *Educational psychology: Applications and theory*. New York: Alfred A. Knopf.

Shade, B. J. (Summer 1982). "Afro-American cognitive style: A variable in school success?" *Review of Educational Research* 52 (2), 219–44.

————. (1989). *Culture, style and the educative process*. Springfield, IL: Charles C. Thomas.

————. (November 1990). "Engaging the battle for African American minds." A Commissioned Paper for the Charles Moody Research Institute. National Alliance of Black School Educators.

Shipman, S., & Shipman, V. C. (1985). "Cognitive styles: Some conceptual, methodological and applied issues." In E. W. Gordon (Ed.), *Review of research in education*. Washington, DC: American Educational Research Association.

Slavin, R. E. (1994). *Educational psychology: Theory and practice*. Boston: Allyn and Bacon.

Snider, V. E. (1990). "What we know about learning styles from research in special education." *Educational Leadership* 48 (2), 53.

Snow, R. E., & Lohman, D. F. (1984). "Towards a theory of cognitive aptitude for learning from instruction." *Journal of Educational Psychology* 76, 347–76.

Snowman, J. (1989). "Learning tactics and strategies." In G. D. Phy & T. Andre (Eds.), *Cognitive instructional psychology: Components of classroom learning*. New York: Academic Press.

Sperry, R. W. (1967). "Split brains: Hemisphere deconnection and unity in conscious awareness." In D. Kolak & R. Martin (Eds.), *Self and identity: Contemporary philosophical issues*. New York: Macmillan.

Springer, S., & Deutsch, G. (1981). *Left brain, right brain*. San Francisco: W. H. Freeman.

Stodolsky, S. S., & Lesser, G. (1976). "Learning patterns of the disadvantaged." *Harvard Educational Review* 37 (4), 546–53.

Suzuki, B. H. (1983). "The education of Asian and Pacific Americans: An introductory overview." In D. Nakanishi & M. Hirano-Nakanishi (Eds.), *The education of Asian and Pacific Americans: Historical perspectives and prescriptions for the future*. Phoenix, AZ: Oryx Press.

Takaki, R. (1990). *Strangers from a different shore*. Boston, MA: Little, Brown.

Vasquez, J. A. (1990). "Teaching to the distinctive traits of minority students." *The Clearing House* 63, 299–304.

Whorf, B. L. (1956). *Language, thought, and reality*. Cambridge: M.I.T. Press.

Witkin, H. A. (February 1959). "The perception of the upright." In S. Coopersmith (Ed.) (1966), *Frontiers of psychological research: Readings from Scientific American* (187–92). San Francisco: W. H. Freeman.

————. (1979). "Socialization, culture and ecology in the development of group and sex differences in cognitive style." *Human Development* 22, 358–72.

Witkin, H. A., Moore, C. A., Goodenough, D. R., & Cox, P. W. (Winter 1977). "Field dependent and field independent cognitive styles and their educational implications." *Review of Educational Research* 47, 1–64.

Witkin, H. A., Oldman, P. K., Cox, P. W., Ehrlichman, E., Hamm, R. M., & Ringler, R. W. (1973). Field-dependence-independence and psychological differentiation: A bibliography. Princeton, NJ: Educational Testing Service.

Worthley, K. M. E. (1987). *Learning style factor of field dependence/independence and problem solving strategies of Hmong refugee students*. Master's Thesis, University of Wisconsin (Stout), Menomonie, WI.

Yoshiwara, F. M. (1983). "Shattering myths: Japanese-American educational issues." In D. T. Nakanski & M. Hirano-Nakanski, (Eds.), *The education of Asian and Pacific Americans: Historical perspectives and prescriptions for the future*. Phoenix, AZ: Oryx Press, 23.

Zook, J. A., & Dwyer, J. H. (1976). "Cultural differences in hemisphericity: A critique." *Bulletin of the Los Angeles Neurological Societies* 41, 87–90.

# 10

ༀ

# The Development of Prejudice

You've got to be taught to hate and fear
You've got to be taught from year to year
It's got to be drummed in your dear little ear
You've got to be carefully taught.

"CAREFULLY TAUGHT," FROM *SOUTH PACIFIC*
LYRICS BY OSCAR HAMMERSTEIN II

The words on the previous page express the most common view about the way prejudice develops—that children learn the attitudes of their parents and other role models. In fact they do, but there is more to the development of prejudice than this simple formula. This chapter reviews the major theories about ways prejudice may occur. These theories are (a) social learning theory; (b) social reflection theory; (c) inner state theory; and (d) cognitive theory, which includes information processing, dissonance theory, Piaget's learning sequence, and cognitive developmental theory. A summary of some surprising research findings about children's changing attitudes toward others as they grow older is also included. Finally, the relationship between social attitudes and levels of moral reasoning is considered.

## SOCIAL LEARNING THEORY

The lyrics quoted at the beginning of this chapter reflect the viewpoint of social learning theory, which is the most popular explanation about how prejudice develops. In this view, children are not "naturally" prejudiced, but they learn it from others. According to social learning theory, children learn by observing and imitating the actions of role models (Bandura, 1977; Bandura et al., 1963a; Bandura & Walters, 1963b). Bandura's early research involved young children who watched the actions of adult models in a controlled laboratory setting. Subsequently, the children did imitate the behavior that they had seen. In everyday situations, however, whether or not children actually reproduce the behavior they have witnessed depends upon three factors: (a) their motivation under specific circumstances; (b) whether or not the situation is favorable; and (c) whether or not they have been rewarded or punished for imitating the actions in the past. Parents are obviously both role models and the dispensers of rewards and punishments. In social situations, when parents or other role models express prejudiced views or act in discriminatory ways toward others, children learn these attitudes and behaviors.

Although this theory seems plausible enough, it fails to take some age-related changes in children's thinking into account. These changes are considered later in this chapter. Social learning theory also fails to address the confusion that children may feel when behavior they have observed does not match what they have been taught. When parents' actions are inconsistent with their teaching, they send a mixed message. The old adage "Do what I say and not what I do" expresses this contradiction. Children may recognize this discrepancy between what adults say and how they sometimes act. Children may also be confused under other circumstances, when their personal experience with people is different from what they have been taught by their parents to expect. In psychology, when a person recognizes a contradiction between different information, he or she is said to be in a state of **cognitive dissonance.** Social learning theory does not address this problem, but dissonance theory does.

## SOCIAL REFLECTION THEORY

Like social learning theory, social reflection theory suggests that young children are not prejudiced and that they learn the attitudes and behavior of their parents (Allport, 1979). Unlike social learning theory, however, this theory considers the issue of social class. People learn attitudes that reflect the economic status and political power of diverse groups. This theory does not apply to children before they reach age ten or so, because before then they are too young to understand the concepts of socioeconomic status and social power. Younger children may parrot the ideas or mimic the actions of their parents without fully understanding them. Once children understand differences in socioeconomic status, their views may begin to reflect their parents' attitudes, and prejudice may result.

Social reflection theory appears to explain why groups that lack economic, political, and social power are disdained by those with greater affluence, political influence, and higher social position. The poor may be regarded as "shiftless" or "lazy," and the extent of their powerlessness is overlooked. Social reflection theory may explain the fear of competition that occurs during hard economic times. Workers become prejudiced against members of diverse minority groups, including new immigrants, when they believe that their jobs are in jeopardy (Chapter 3).

Social reflection theory offers a logical explanation for prejudice in adults, and a seemingly logical explanation for prejudice in adolescents and perhaps older children. Cognitive developmental research about the origins of prejudice, however, suggests that the attitudes of younger children are not simple reflections of those of their parents, and that age developmental issues are more complex than accounted for by social reflection theory.

## INNER STATE THEORY

This theory is based on a psychodynamic view of childhood. It explains prejudice in terms of unresolved conflicts (Aboud, 1988). According to this theory, children experience frustration in their relationships with their parents, especially when they cannot have their own way or do what they want to do. This frustration causes children to act, sometimes aggressively, in ways that are not tolerated by parents, who then punish their children for behaving this way. The children learn a lesson that they are not allowed to act aggressively, but the lesson results in anxiety. They may still be angry, but they are also afraid of further punishment. The combination of these conflicting emotions of anger and anxiety is heightened when parents do not help their children learn how to express their frustration and anger in conversations that work through these problems. When children do not learn how to work through their frustrations or when parents are especially punitive, several psychological processes—usually subconscious—may result. Sigmund Freud identified several such processes, which he labeled **defense mechanisms.** Three of these processes are relevant to the inner state theory of how prejudice develops. These are **denial, displacement,** and **projection.**

At first, children *deny* their negative feelings or anger against their parents because they have learned that these feelings are not acceptable. They then *displace* their anger and frustration onto a safe neutral target, usually people who lack the authority and power that their parents represent. In most family situations, of course, the nearest "target" may be a sibling, but children quickly learn that releasing their frustrations on a brother or a sister leads to further punishment. They then may seek a safer target in the neighborhood or at school. These "safe" targets may be weaker members of their own group, but if prejudice is also being learned at home, then the chances are increased that members of other groups will be selected. Finally, they *project* their anger and frustration onto these targets and come to believe that others have the same negative feelings toward them. The level of severity of the parents' child rearing is related to the degree of negative feelings that are eventually felt toward people of diverse groups. People's frustrations become projected onto minority groups, which become scapegoats for their hostility. In economic hard times, both fear and insecurity form the basis of the hostility that is characteristic of both the social reflection and the inner state theories of prejudice.

The inner state theory has several strengths. It explains the intensity of emotions in some people's prejudice. It accounts for different levels of prejudice, as well as the persistence of prejudice, even under changing personal circumstances. Aboud (1988) has stated that:

> Prejudice is viewed as one aspect of the person's personality structure, and … it does not readily change … attitudes seem to be based on something more ego-involving than simply imitation or conformity. They [prejudiced persons] appear to be energized by a strongly personal force involving conflict and intense emotions. (p. 21)

In addition to the strengths of inner state theory cited above, Aboud has identified two weaknesses. First, it does not adequately account for which targets are selected, because it claims that all minority groups are perceived and treated similarly. The only requirements are that a group is (a) different from the parents; (b) of low status; and (c) relatively powerless. A second weakness in the theory is that it does not adequately explain different patterns of prejudice in children because it fails to take developmental changes in thinking into account.


## COGNITIVE THEORY

Cognitive theory refers to the way in which knowledge is learned and altered through experience. There are four main cognitive theories that are relevant to the issue of prejudice: (a) information processing theory; (b) dissonance theory; (c) Piaget's learning sequence; and (d) cognitive developmental theory, also described by Piaget.

## Information Processing Theory

This theory describes learning as a sequence of mental operations (Atkinson & Shiffrin, 1968). First, the learner perceives a stimulus in the environment through the sensory system. The learner then focuses or concentrates on this information long enough to pass it along from mere impression into so-called short-term or working memory, which in turn organizes and rehearses the information long enough to "encode" it or store it in long-term memory. Once stored in long-term memory, the information is semipermanent and may remain for years, ready to be "retrieved" into conscious thought whenever a situation or event brings it to mind. The relevance for multicultural education is obviously that information learned about diverse groups and memories of past experiences may continue for a very long time.

## Dissonance Theory

Years ago, Festinger (1962) described a theory of cognitive dissonance, which explains what happens when a person recognizes an inconsistency or contradiction between different items of information, including people's behavior, events, or other information. When a person realizes the inconsistency, he or she tries to fit the information together. Changes in thinking that restore consistency or integrate the information are *dissonance-reducing* changes. In social situations, people may attempt to bring new and contradictory information about others more into line with their previous views. For example, when a person behaves differently from our expectations (including stereotyped views), we may disregard this discrepancy with our previous attitude by regarding it as "an exception," and continue to hold our old views. According to Watts (1984), when personal experience with other people does not match a person's preconceptions about them, there must be an adjustment in attitude to reduce feelings of tension or confusion. In encounters with people from diverse groups, if one expects a member of that group to behave in a certain way and he or she behaves differently, this experience must be taken into account. People then have a choice between maintaining their former attitude or adopting a new attitude. If the experience is pleasant, then a positive change in attitude might occur. Unfortunately, however, if the experience is unpleasant, then prejudice may begin or increase. Thus, the *type of interaction* becomes the determining factor in subsequent attitudes toward members of other groups.

Dissonance theory offers an explanation about why children's attitudes and behaviors toward others do not always match the attitudes and behaviors of their parents. It also accounts for changes of attitude at any age.

## Piaget's Learning Sequence

The Swiss psychologist Jean Piaget used the term **assimilation** to describe the way in which information is learned (Piaget, 1969; Inhelder & Piaget, 1958). In other words, it was Piaget's term for the same sequence of receiving information and encoding it into long-term memory that information processing theory describes.

A **scheme** (or schema) was Piaget's term for information that has been learned and stored in long-term memory. Schemes may include specific information, a procedure or skill, or a recollection of an event. (In educational psychology, these different types of knowledge are referred to as declarative, procedural, and episodic knowledge.) People refer to their "schemes" in social situations, in responding to their environment, or in solving problems. The sum total of a person's schemes is in fact the sum total of his or her knowledge. Schemes, therefore, are the basis for people's behavior.

Sometimes a person's knowledge or schemes are not adequate to deal with a new situation, in which case the individual must learn (or assimilate) new information in order to be able to respond more appropriately. Sometimes, however, new experiences or information conflict with past knowledge. Piaget used the term **cognitive dissonance** to describe the state of mental confusion that people experience when this happens. Thus, Piaget's view of dissonance was similar to that of Festinger (1962) and Watts (1984). Because confusion is painful, Piaget believed that people make adjustments in their thinking in order to cope with it. Most people's first tendency is to reject new information that does not fit with what they already know. They tend to think of it as untrue or invalid. The example I use in class is the situation in which a teacher or professor provides information that does not agree with information students have learned in another class. I reassure my students that when they don't believe some information I have given them, it is "OK"—they are in a state of cognitive dissonance! In social situations, however, a tendency to hold on to old attitudes may account for continuing biases in spite of new experiences that run counter to old ones.

Sometimes, however, people may feel a need to adjust their thinking in order to take the new information or experience into account. Piaget used the term **accommodation** to describe this adjustment. When the old and new information are brought into harmony or balance (Piaget used the term **equilibrium**), a new scheme has been created. In social situations, accommodation accounts for a change of attitude. The problem is that accommodation requires mental effort. We have to work at changing our minds.

## Cognitive Developmental Theory

The cognitive processes described above (in information processing theory, dissonance theory, and Piaget's learning sequence) all function within a social context and continue throughout a person's lifetime. Babies, children, teenagers, and adults all perceive, encode, and store knowledge. They all assimilate information, form schemes, become confused, and make adjustments in their thinking.

Cognition, however, also changes with age. Piaget described the changes in children's thinking that occur in relation to age (Inhelder & Piaget, 1958; 1969). His views were known as **cognitive developmental theory.** Following is a brief review of these stages. I have not included all of the cognitive characteristics of these stages, only those *that are relevant to an understanding of the relationship between these stages and children's attitudes about themselves and others.*

**Pre-Operations** Piaget used the term **pre-operations** to identify this stage because children have not yet acquired the reasoning ability necessary to form logical conclusions about their experience. (In other words, they cannot perform logical operations.)

In the early phase of pre-operations, the emotions of happiness and fear influence children's thinking. They are happy when their wishes are satisfied. They are unhappy when their wishes are denied. They may also be afraid of adults, primarily because of their size. I have always found it interesting that tales of fairy godmothers and wicked witches reflect children's views of people who gratify their wishes as "nice" and people who deny their wishes as "mean."

Visual perception dominates children's logic. (Tales of giants reflect a child's perspective of some people as being very tall.) They arrive at conclusions based on this visual evidence alone. For example, when my daughter was five years old and lost her first tooth, she was convinced that the tooth fairy had in fact visited during the night because the old tooth was gone and a prize was there under her pillow in the morning. Children also have a limited ability to classify objects into categories and do so on the basis of their visual experience. For example, when a teacher of my acquaintance compared hills to mountains and asserted that mountains were bigger, a boy in her class waved his hand wildly and said, "No, no, no! Garbage hill is *huge!*"

Piaget and others have observed that very young children have a limited understanding of social interactions. Piaget described this limitation as **naive egocentrism,** whereby children focus primarily on their own point of view. They may be somewhat aware of others' views, but they usually assume that others share their own perceptions and emotions. A few studies suggest that young children may have a partial understanding of another point of view. For example, they may turn a picture away from themselves toward another person, thus giving that person a better view (Lempers, Flavell & Flavell, 1977). They may modify their speech by talking louder to a person farther away (Johnson et al., 1981). They may use shorter and simpler sentences when talking to an even younger child, in contrast with talking to older people (Sachs & Devin, 1976). (The question here is whether or not they are imitating adults.) These behaviors suggest that young children are to some extent aware of others' needs, but their interpretation is limited.

**Concrete Operations**   Piaget used the term **concrete operations** to describe this stage because children become less dependent on visual perceptions and more able to arrive at *logical* conclusions in relation to physical events. For example, when my daughter was eight years old the following conversation occurred:

> You know, I figured it out. There can't possibly be a Santa Claus for three reasons. Do you want me to tell you what they are? [I nodded.] Well, first, reindeer can't possibly fly. That's dumb. Second, no one can fit in a chimney, unless it's in a factory. And third, there is *no way* that anyone could have time to visit all of those places in one night. I mean not even in a jet plane could you do that. But don't worry, Mom. I'm not going to tell Annie [her four-year-old sister]. I won't spoil it for her. I'll let her figure it out for herself.

Another characteristic of this stage is that children develop more adequate sorting and classifying skills and they begin to understand categories. These categories may include categories of *different kinds of people.* They also become able to follow visual transformations, or changes in appearance, and are not so easily misled by them.

The ability to consider another person's point of view becomes more consistent during this stage. This ability is known as **cognitive reversibility.** As they grow older, children extend this to **social perspective-taking,** which means that they are not only aware of another person's viewpoint but consider it in their social actions. For example, when my daughter was ten, she told me that she had been invited to go somewhere with a friend and she did not really want to go, but that she was going because she did not want to hurt her friend's feelings.

**Formal Operations**   Piaget used the term **formal operations** to refer to this stage because logical conclusions are more formally reached by means of more adequate reasoning abilities. Adolescents and young adults develop the ability to bring a new range of logical capacities into solving a problem or analyzing a situation. They become able to (a) understand deductive and inductive logic; (b) consider several issues simultaneously; (c) understand implication; and (d) extend logical analysis into hypothetical situations. One of the most important capabilities that develops at this stage is that of being able to consider factors that are not directly observable. Considering the fact that in pre-operations, judgments were based on visual appearances, these abilities represent a *major* advance in cognition. An example comes from an occasion when a friend of mine and I narrowly missed being hit by an oncoming car, which was halfway into our side on a curve of the road. My friend said, "I can't believe that driver cut that corner so close. Didn't he think there might be a car around the corner that he couldn't see?" (No gender bias intended!) In social relationships, this ability to look beyond appearances leads to an awareness of people's inner qualities.

Piaget placed the onset of formal operations at around age fourteen, but recent research suggests that many of the logical operations of this stage are not attained until age sixteen or later. Several studies (Killian, 1979; Kolodiy, 1974; Reyes, 1986; Silverman & Creswell, 1982; Thornton & Fuller, 1981; Timm & Gross, 1990) indicate that even traditional-age college undergraduates do not consistently employ these higher order reasoning skills.

## THE DEVELOPMENT OF PREJUDICE
## AND COGNITIVE STAGE

Cognitive developmental theory is the least-known theory about how personal identity, social attitudes, and prejudice occur. Extensive research findings suggest that children's perceptions and attitudes do reflect their cognitive stage. Aboud (1988) has suggested the following developmental theory of racial or ethnic identity and attitudes, which coincides with the cognitive stages:

At any particular age the child's way of relating to ethnic groups will be determined by his/her present level… by the process and focus of attention that dominate at [the] time. (p. 23)

In order to make it easier for the reader to understand Aboud's theory, I am going to review children's attitudes in relation to the cognitive stages.[1]

## Attitudes on Diversity and Cognitive Stage

**The Pre-Operational Stage**   The dominance of visual perception during this stage affects children's views of themselves and of others in relation to themselves. Therefore, any biases that they may have are based on how similar or dissimilar others appear in comparison to themselves. Children notice the most obvious features of skin color, hair texture, clothing, and language, and judge accordingly. These perceptions form the basis of self-identification, by which children begin to realize their own group membership. For example, in a study of ethnic awareness, an Italian child who put on native Indian clothing was seen as being an Indian by most children under the age of eight (Aboud, 1984).

Earlier I mentioned that children are strongly influenced by their emotions during this stage. Friendships may be based on benefits to the self. For example, when my stepson was four, he told me that he liked one of his friends because "he has the best trike [tricycle] on our street."

**The Concrete Operational Stage**   During this stage, children's ability to classify objects and to understand categories helps to solidify their concepts about their own ethnic group. Aboud (1988) has suggested that so long as children are preoccupied with classifying people by groups, their social attitudes are to a great extent determined by their own group membership. The ability to classify objects and *people* into categories or groups leads children to become focused on their own group and on the differences between it and other groups. Sometimes they form a strong identification with their own group, and unfavorable attitudes toward other groups. In other words, they may develop prejudice against members of other groups, simply on the basis of their differences. Aboud (1984) reported that elementary-age children may at first exaggerate dissimilarities in order to clarify their understanding of groups. Their focus on external (perceptual) attributes actually increases between age five and nine, while the consideration of internal (psychological) attributes remains low. Even eight- and nine-year-olds do not apply internal psychological qualities to other ethnic groups (Aboud and Skerry, 1983). As their ability to understand cognitive reversibility improves and they become more aware of the psychological similarities between themselves and members of other groups, children may ultimately outgrow this prejudice based on group memberships.

As I mentioned earlier, children become able to follow visual **transformations** and are not easily misled by changes of appearance. They begin to understand that race, ethnicity, or gender is a more permanent quality than surface attributes such as dress. In the study of ethnic awareness mentioned above, children over eight years of age exhibited their ability to follow transformations by concluding that the Italian boy who put on native Indian clothing did not become an Indian (Aboud, 1984).

**Transition to Formal Operations**   As children become more aware of inner psychological qualities, they begin to take these qualities into account. In other words, they shift their attention and the basis for their acceptance of others from people's membership in groups to accepting them as individuals. Friendships with children from diverse backgrounds may enhance this process of moving beyond the earlier focus on groups per se.

I would like to point out here that sharing common interests, participating in extracurricular activities, playing on the same team, and performing in a play are important avenues for the development of meaningful friendships between members of diverse groups. When public officials cut funding for in-school or out-of-school organizations, they fail to realize that these do not simply "keep children off the streets." They fail to understand that these organizations enhance the kind of friendships that I referred to in Chapter 2, whereby people share their joys and learn to care about each other.

## Attitudes Among Children of Diverse Groups

Extensive studies support the view that among children of diverse groups, both perceptions of identity and attitudes toward others are related to the cognitive stages. Table 10.1 shows the relationship between the characteristic thinking of the cognitive stages and the social attitudes found by Aboud and others.

**Studies with White Children**   I am reviewing these studies first, because more research has been done with White children. Results indicate that by age four or five, White children express a predominance of negative attitudes toward children of other groups and that they prefer other Whites in comparison to African, Asian, Hispanic (Aboud's term), or Indian Americans (Aboud, 1977, 1980; Brown & Johnson, 1971). Between ages five and seven, White children expressed negative attitudes toward Asian, African, or Native Indian children, and between ages six and eight, they expressed a preference for photographs of children from their own group over children from other groups, including Asians, Hispanics, and Native Indians (Aboud, 1977; 1980). After age seven or eight, these negative attitudes begin to decline (Brown & Johnson, 1971; Asher & Allen, 1969; George & Hoppe, 1979). Interestingly, Marsh (1970) reported that White children who had a Black foster sibling preferred a Black child over a White one. Between age seven and twelve, a decline in prejudice has been reported (Aboud, 1980; George & Hoppe, 1979).

In a more recent study, Bigler and Liben (1993) reported findings for White children between the ages of four and nine. On a Piagetian-type classification task, children who exhibited a limited ability to sort a set of photographs according to different variables (such as African and European males and females of different ages and facial expressions) also gave more stereotyped responses to a test based on the Preschool Racial Attitudes Measure II (PRAM II). (See Doyle et

**Table 10.1 Similarities of Focus Among Cognitive Stage, Social Attitudes, and Moral Level**

| COGNITIVE STAGE | SOCIAL ATTITUDES | MORAL LEVEL |
| --- | --- | --- |
| *Pre-operations* <br> naive egocentrism <br> logic based on <br>    visual perception <br> focus on emotions <br> limited awareness of <br> others' views | *Early Childhood* <br> identity of self and <br>    others based on <br>    appearances | *Pre-conventional* <br> focus on own wishes <br> focus on physical <br>    results of acts <br> unawareness of <br>    group values |
| *Concrete Operations* <br> ability to classify <br>    objects <br> logic based on <br>    plausibliity <br> cognitive reversibility | *Middle Childhood* <br> identity and social pref- <br>    erences based on <br>    group membership | *Conventional* <br> values derived from <br>    groups <br> conformity to group <br>    values <br> attempt to please others |
| *Transition to Formal Operations* <br> deductive logic <br> inductive logic <br> consideration of mul- <br>    tiple issues <br> implication | *Preteen or Later* <br> awareness of inner <br>    psychological qualities <br> recognition of shared <br>    interests | *Post-conventional* <br> values logically derived <br> awareness of relative <br>    values <br> scrutiny of cross-group <br>    values |

al., 1988, and Williams et al., 1975.) The children also tended to remember stories better with culturally/racially stereotyped images of African or European American characters than they remembered stories with counter-stereotypes. As their ability to classify according to more characteristics or variables increased, the children's stereotyped responses decreased and they remembered better the stories with counter-stereotyped images.

In a survey of 151 first-grade students' preferences in trade books, Lambert (1994) reported that student diversity within schools had an effect on students' choices. Children in heterogeneous (culturally diverse) classrooms expressed a significantly greater interest in books *without* multicultural themes in comparison with multicultural ones. Children in White homogeneous classrooms did not rate the multicultural books significantly differently from the nonmulticultural ones. These findings are interesting in light of the cognitive developmental findings on children's social attitudes. It could be that the culturally heterogeneous classes enhanced the process at this age of identification with the children's own group by reinforcing their perceptions of their "category." Therefore, mainstream books without multicultural themes would reinforce this identity for White children. Preferences for books with or without multicultural themes were not reported for the minority students, however.

**Studies with Black Children** Studies of Black children suggest that they also begin to develop social attitudes by age three or four, but that they show less rejection of other groups before age seven than White children do (Asher & Allen,

1969; Kircher & Furby, 1971). After age seven they more closely identify with their own group and show more negative attitudes toward other groups (Cross, 1980). Between ages seven and ten, they become even more in-group oriented. For example, Spencer (1982) reported a higher degree of pro-Black preferences at age nine than at age five. A preference for Blacks, however, does not necessarily imply prejudice toward Whites. Aboud (1980) reported that Black children, while preferring other Blacks, expressed neutral attitudes toward Whites.

**Studies with Asian Children**  The few studies reported for Asian children indicate that in early childhood their attitudes are mixed or positively oriented toward Whites. After age seven their views become more pro-Asian, but also more biased against Blacks (Aboud, 1977; Davey, 1983; Milner, 1973).

**Studies with Latino Children**  Reports on the attitudes of Latino children are inconclusive but appear to be similar to those of Black children. Two studies reported that young Hispanic (Newman's term) children preferred a Hispanic child to a White child (Newman et al., 1983; Rohrer, 1977), but two other studies reported a preference for a White child over a Hispanic (Rice et al., 1974; Weiland & Coughlin, 1979). Aboud (1988) has suggested that perhaps contact with White teachers may be an influencing factor for young non-White children. After age seven, Hispanic children appear to become more Hispanic oriented (Newman et al., 1983; Rice et al., 1974; Stephan & Rosenfield, 1979).

**Studies with Native American Children**  The few studies reported for Native American children indicate that three- and four-year-olds showed no clear ethnic preferences (Rosenthal, 1974), but that after age four they showed a preference for Whites (Corenblum & Annis, 1987; Corenblum & Wilson, 1982; George & Hoppe, 1979; Hunsberger, 1978). Aboud (1977) reported that after age six, they liked their own plus one other group, but also disliked one or two other groups when asked about Asian, African, Native American, Hispanic, and White children.

### Summary of the Cognitive Developmental Research

These findings run counter to popular ideas about the way prejudice develops. According to these findings, children may in fact *outgrow* prejudice as they grow older. The findings do not support social learning theory, which would predict a steady *increase* in prejudice with age. Evidence from these studies indicates that children's prejudice toward other groups increases between the ages of four and seven, and then begins to decline after age seven or eight. Furthermore, even if *preferences* for their own group increase around age seven, while children are classifying groups and establishing their identify by group, these preferences decline by age twelve, as children develop more social perspective-taking ability and an awareness of more psychological and internal qualities in others.

The findings fail to support social reflection theory because negative attitudes toward other groups were found to decrease at just the age when children would have been able to begin to understand the issues of social power and social class stratification.

The findings do not address the relationship between parents' child-rearing practices and children's attitudes, so central to inner state theory, but they do suggest that children's contact with members of other groups provides opportunities for them to learn about the qualities of diverse individuals, which in turn could decrease any tendencies they might have to project their personal frustrations with parents or other adults onto others. There is an obvious danger, however, in situations where personal encounters are unpleasant. In this case, prejudice may increase through overgeneralization of the experience.

What conclusions may be derived from these studies? As children grow from early childhood to adolescence, their perceptions and attitudes do reflect the kinds of thinking characteristic of the cognitive stages. Aboud has asserted that the main conclusion to be derived from children's descriptions of themselves and others is that they are "overwhelmingly concerned with external attributes" (1988, p. 106), or visual characteristics—at least until late childhood. As they shift to a focus on internal and psychological factors, children's attitudes toward others become more flexible and empathic.

## SOCIAL ATTITUDES AND MORAL REASONING

The cognitive-developmental sequence, which focuses first on self, then on groups, and finally on individuals has also been reported by Lawrence Kohlberg, whose research on moral reasoning provided new insights into the relationship between ways in which people think about moral issues and their cognitive level.[2] Others have reported similar findings in studies of moral reasoning, not only in the United States but in other countries as well (Kohlberg 1969; 1984; Colby, Kohlberg, Gibbs & Lieberman, 1983; Nisan & Kohlberg, 1982; Walker & Moran, 1991).

Basing his theory on his research findings, Kohlberg described three levels of moral reasoning.[3] It is important to mention here that moral reasoning reflects the kind of thinking characteristic of the Piagetian stages of cognitive development.

Children do not abruptly move from one level of moral reasoning to another. At any given time, their reasoning may include the logic of two levels, for they are in the process of transition. It is important to point out here that the term *moral* refers to issues of fairness, and that *to children, fairness is the equivalent of social justice.* Finally, moral reasoning is not merely an abstract concept unrelated to real-life situations. Perhaps some of the examples that follow will clarify the centrality of moral reasoning in our lives.

### Level I: The Pre-Conventional Level

This level is called **pre-conventional** because personal values are not yet derived from the groups with which people are associated. In other words, children are not aware of the values of their family and friends. Reasoning at this level begins with the *naive egocentrism* typical of pre-operational thinking. Early in this phase, decisions and actions are based on consequences to the self. Right and wrong are seen in terms of physical consequences, including rewards and punishments. Children may be motivated by the emotional considerations of happiness and fear that were described above in relation to pre-operational reasoning. A four-year-old once told me that he would take another child's toy if he liked it. Toward the end of this phase, children are sometimes motivated to take chances in order to get something they want. For example, during a moral judgment interview I was conducting, a student told me that cheating on a test was OK if you got a good grade and did not get caught, but if you got caught it was wrong.

## Level II: The Conventional Level

This level is called **conventional** because people reasoning at this level derive their values from the groups with which they are associated. These groups include family and friends. A major advance at this level is that children develop the cognitive reversibility characteristic of concrete operational logic. In other words, they begin to understand other points of view. In their realization of these views, however, they also realize that other people have thoughts about *them*. Their decisions and actions become based on others' attitudes. The problem at this level is that a need for social acceptance, along with a fear of being socially rejected, leads to a high degree of conformity. As educators, we are familiar with the pervasive need to conform to their friends' opinions and styles that older children and teenagers feel. For example, a ten-year-old reported to me that she agreed with a friend about liking a certain rock star when she really did not, only to find out later that her friend did not like him either, but was trying to agree with her!

Some people never grow beyond this phase. For them, behavior continues to be based on whether or not it conforms to the views of family or friends. To be disloyal to the values of family and friends is seen as letting them down. People may also be fiercely loyal to wider groups, based on a religion or a nationality. To question prevailing attitudes within one's religion may be considered by others in the group as a loss of "values." To question a prevailing political attitude may be considered treasonous. The frightening aspect about this conformity is that judgments about *right and wrong* are based on how well they conform to the views of others. If those views are prejudiced or unjust, what then? As some people grow older, they may move beyond a focus on conforming to group values that comes from a need to be socially accepted or a fear of being rejected.

## Level III: The Post-Conventional Level

This level is called **post-conventional** because people derive their moral beliefs from logical analyses of issues rather than the values of groups. They are no longer dependent upon the opinions of others in their assessment of what "moral" means. That does not mean, however, that their moral reasoning is egoistic in the sense that pre-conventional reasoning is. Before adolescents progress to this level, the social perspective-taking ability associated with later concrete operations enables them to be more aware of inner psychological qualities in others. They may begin not only to consider these qualities but also to empathize with others' views. The poem in Box 10.1 illustrates this ability.

---

**BOX 10.1** Prejudice

---

As once along a street I walked
I saw some men and heard their talk.
A house was for sale or so it seemed
An offer was made and the owner beamed.
But after a moment he stopped his grin
His customer had a different skin.
"You cannot buy this house of pine—
Your skin is unlike that of mine."

"But that's not fair," the buyer cried.
"You said it was for sale. You lied!"
"I cannot help the way things are.
To buy a house you must go far."
The man turned sadly and walked away:
He's looking for a house today.

JEANNE THROWER, AGE 13

---

At the post-conventional level, formal operational logic provides a more adequate analysis of social issues. The ability to consider several issues simultaneously enables people to consider the multiple viewpoints of individuals and diverse groups at the same time. People reasoning at this level scrutinize the values and traditions of diverse groups and societies, *including their own,* with a realization that traditions may not always be logical or just. There is an awareness of relative values arising out of different environments and cultures, but there is also a recognition of values that different groups share.[5] In addition, there is recognition of a responsibility to strive for justice for others, regardless of whether they are members of one's own group. This recognition is the logical extension of the social perspective-taking ability that enables people to recognize their own role in response to others. Issues of social justice and human rights are perceived not only in relation to groups, but in regard to every human being. Kohlberg used the writings of Martin Luther King, Jr. as an example of this type of reasoning. The sense of obligation to another's needs extends to everyone, regardless of whether a person is a friend or stranger.[6] Box 10.2 provides an example of this view that I designed to use in my classes.

Extensive research in the field of moral development indicates that not all adults attain post-conventional moral reasoning, and therefore they never recognize the inherent dangers in conforming to social conventions of any group merely for tradition's sake.

## Prejudice and Moral Reasoning

Of particular interest for multicultural education is a study conducted by Davidson (1976). Although this study was done almost twenty years ago, its results still have important considerations for multicultural contexts. Davidson reported *lower* levels of prejudice in children with *higher* levels of moral reasoning. A group orientation was associated with higher levels of prejudice.

In her investigation of the relationship between moral judgment and social attitudes, Davidson also found that children reasoning at lower levels of moral

---

**BOX 10.2**  A Modern Good Samaritan

---

Once upon a time, a driver encountered an accident as he was driving down a highway. Apparently a car had skidded off the road, and was disabled in a ditch. A man was lying along the side of the road next to his damaged car. Other drivers were whizzing by and disregarding him. The driver pulled over to the side of the road and stopped. As he approached the other man, the driver saw that he was of a different race. The driver leaned over him and instructed him to stay still, in case he might have a serious injury. Returning to his car, the driver called for an ambulance on his car telephone. He waited with the injured man until the ambulance arrived. The driver asked where they were taking the man, and said that he would stop there later in the day.

On his way back home, the driver did stop at the hospital and visited the injured man, who was now lying in a hospital room. The driver assured him that he would do all he could. On leaving the hospital, the driver stopped at the business office. The receptionist informed him that there was a question about whether or not the injured man's insurance was valid because he was from a foreign country and he had been driving a rented car. The driver responded by taking out his checkbook and writing a check to cover the costs of the first couple of days.

Later, the driver returned to the hospital to find the accident victim, who was now recovered from his minor injuries, sitting on the edge of the bed with the telephone in his hand.

"I was just trying to call you to tell you that I am being discharged. I want to thank you for everything you did. I talked to my wife back home, and she is very grateful to you. When I get my insurance straightened out, I will send you a check as soon as I can. Is there anything I may do for you?"

The driver shook his head. "Reimburse me if you feel the need, but perhaps you could pass the favor on to someone else who needs help instead."

---

judgment were more likely to describe members of ethnic groups in terms of appearance, while those reasoning at higher levels used more psychological attributes, thus indicating the same cognitive developmental sequence later described by Aboud and others.

## DEVELOPMENTAL LEVELS, PREJUDICE, AND MULTICULTURAL EDUCATION

The lesson to be derived from the research of Aboud, Kohlberg, Davidson, and others is that children apparently need experiences by which they can learn *not* to be prejudiced! Bigler and Liben's study (cited above), in which children remembered stories with stereotyped images better than they remembered counter-stereotyped stories, suggests that children need to have educational experiences that would help them to move beyond stereotyped perceptions. In the classroom, lessons in diversity may not be enough. A more effective approach may be lessons that directly combat stereotypes. This approach uses cognitive dissonance, which forces students to accommodate or to make adjustments in their thinking. This approach also promotes students' ability to move beyond conventional perceptions.

Another method of combating prejudice is by using literature and popular culture to present images and narratives either free of stereotypes, or even running counter to them. There are ways of using literature that stimulate discussions of social justice. There are ways of using drama that promote the ability to take another person's point of view.

A third approach is through the use of multicultural curricular materials that are appropriate for students' cognitive stage (Kehoe, 1988). A resource for some materials is Pacific Educational Press.

A fourth approach is through students sharing their interests with each other. This approach focuses on inner psychological qualities that may help children to outgrow their focus on groups. I referred to this approach in Chapter 2 in connection with the development of friendships that lead to caring. These possibilities are discussed in Chapter 12.

## CHAPTER SUMMARY

There are several different theories that attempt to explain how prejudice develops.

According to social learning theory, children learn to be prejudiced by observing and imitating the actions of parents and other role models.

According to social reflection theory, prejudice is based on perceived differences in social power and inequities on the basis of social class. Those with social power may disdain those lacking it.

The inner state theory accounts for prejudice on the basis of child-rearing practices. When parents are overly punitive, their children may displace their anger and frustration onto safe targets or scapegoats.

Information processing theory focuses on learning information and storing it in long-term memory. Once stored, these memories may last for years. In the social realm, pleasant or unpleasant experiences may result in persistent memories that are conducive to social attitudes, either positive or negative.

Dissonance theory focuses on the need to reduce tension when different knowledge conflicts or when experience does not match expectations. Adjustments in thinking are determined by the nature of social interactions, with positive experiences resulting in positive changes in attitudes, and negative experiences resulting in negative ones.

Piaget's learning sequence is similar to information processing. People store information that affects their subsequent behavior in both problem-solving and social situations. Piaget's learning sequence is also similar to dissonance theory because adjustments in attitudes are possible when new information conflicts with old knowledge.

Cognitive developmental theory explains social attitudes on the basis of different kinds of logic that are characteristic of different stages of development.

Research on children's perceptions of ethnic identity, their preferences for friends, their attitudes toward groups, their moral reasoning, and their biased views all support the notion of cognitive developmental differences in their thinking about these issues.

## IMPORTANT TERMS

Social learning theory

Social reflection theory

Inner state theory

Information processing theory

Dissonance theory

Cognitive developmental theory

Denial

Displacement

Projection

Pre-conventional

Conventional

Post-conventional

Defense mechanisms

Assimilation

Scheme

Cognitive dissonance

Accommodation

Equilibrium

Pre-operations

Concrete operations

Formal operations

Cognitive reversibility

Transformations

Naive egocentrism

Social perspective-taking

## QUESTIONS FOR DISCUSSION

1. Give examples of viewpoints you have heard that reflect the different theories of ways in which prejudice occurs.

2. Give examples from conversations you have had with children, teenagers, or adults that reflect the different kinds of thinking characteristic of the different cognitive levels.

3. Give examples of conversations you have had with children, teenagers, or adults that reflect the different kinds of thinking characteristic of the different social attitudes reported by Aboud and others.

4. Give examples of conversations you have had with children, teenagers, or adults that reflect the different kinds of thinking characteristic of the different moral levels.

5. As an educator, what do you believe could be done to enhance the development of children's ability to understand another point of view?

6. Do you believe that there are any modern Good Samaritans? Why or why not? Should financial considerations affect a person's actions? Why or why not? How would you feel if you were the victim?

## NOTES

1. Aboud described the development of children's perceptions about themselves and others in two overlapping sequences: (a) an affective, perception, cognition sequence; and (b) a focus-of-attention sequence. My students have informed me that it is easier to understand the development of children's

attitudes if these two sequences are described in accordance with the cognitive stages.

2. Kohlberg's theory has been questioned on the basis of gender differences in moral development (Gilligan, 1982; Baumrind, 1986), but an extensive review of moral development in both boys and girls suggests

that these gender differences may have been overestimated (Walker, 1984; 1986).

3. Each level has two substages, and there are actually six stages of moral development. The subtle differences between the substages within levels are not critically relevant to the analysis of moral reasoning in this chapter. Therefore, I have chosen to review the basic logic of the pre-conventional, conventional, and post-conventional levels. In this chapter I have derived the summaries of the moral levels from the writings of Kohlberg and others, including my dissertation (Thrower, 1971).

4. Some research evidence indicates that those who progress to this level may not do so until their twenties.

5. These shared values may include the value orientations discussed in Chapter 7.

6. In the sense "obligation" is used here, it does not refer to intrusion into others' lives, but a realization of a situation in which one may be of genuine help. See Box 10.2.

# REFERENCES

Aboud, F. E. (1977). "Interest in ethnic information: A cross-cultural developmental study." *Canadian Journal of Behavioral Science* 9, 134–46.

———. (1980). "A test of ethnocentrism with young children." *Canadian Journal of Behavioral Science* 12, 195–209.

———. (1984). "Social and cognitive bases of ethnic identity constancy." *Journal of Genetic Psychology* 184, 217–30.

———. (1988). *Children and prejudice.* New York: Basil Blackwell.

Aboud, F. E., & Skerry, S. A. (1983). "Self and ethnic concepts in relation to ethnic constancy." *Canadian Journal of Behavioural Science* 15, 14–26.

Allport, G. (1979). *The nature of prejudice* (25th anniversary ed.). Reading, MA: Addison-Wesley.

Asher, S. R., & Allen, V. L. (1969). "Racial preference and social comparison processes." *Journal of Social Issues* 25, 157–67.

Atkinson, R. C., & Shiffrin, R. M. (1968). "Human memory: A proposed system and its control processes." In K. W. Spence & J. T. Spence (Eds.), *The psychology of learning and motivation* (Vol. 2). New York: Academic Press.

Bandura, A. (1977). *Social learning theory.* Englewood Cliffs, NJ: Prentice-Hall.

Bandura, A., Ross, D., & Ross, S. (1963a). "Imitation of film-mediated aggressive models." *Journal of Abnormal and Social Psychology* 41, 586–98.

Bandura, A., & Walters, R. (1963b). *Social learning and personality development.* New York: Holt, Rinehart and Winston.

Baumrind, D. (1986). "Sex differences in moral reasoning: Response to Walker's (1984) conclusion that there are none." *Child Development* 57, 511–21.

Bigler, R. S., & Liben, L. S. (1993). "A cognitive-developmental approach to racial stereotyping and reconstructive memory in Euro-American children." *Child Development* 64 (5), 1507–18.

Brown, G., & Johnson, S. P. (1971). "The attribution of behavioural connotations to shaded and white figures by Caucasian children." *British Journal of Social and Clinical Psychology* 10, 306–12.

Colby, A., Kohlberg, L., Gibbs, J., & Lieberman, M. (1983). "A longitudinal study of moral judgment." *Monographs of the Society for Research in Child Development* 48 (1-2, Serial No. 200).

Corenblum, B., & Annis, R. C. (1987). "Racial identity and preference in Native and White Canadian children." *Canadian Journal of Behavioural Science* 19, 254–65.

Corenblum, B., & Wilson, S. E. (1982). "Ethnic preference and identification among Canadian Indian and White children: Replication and extension." *Canadian Journal of Behavioural Science* 14, 50–59.

Cross, W. E. (1980). "Models of psychological nigrescence: A literature review." In R. L. Jones (Ed.), *Black Psychology.* New York: Harper & Row, 81–98.

Davey, A. G. (1983). *Learning to be prejudiced: Growing up in multi-ethnic Britain.* London: Edward Arnold.

Davidson, F. N. (1976). "Ability to respect persons compared to ethnic prejudice." *Journal of Personality and Social Psychology, 34,* 1256–67.

Doyle, A., Beaudet, J., & Aboud, F. (1988). "Developmental patterns in the flexibility of children's ethnic attitudes." *Journal of Cross-Cultural Psychology* 19, 3–18.

Festinger, L. (October 1962). "Cognitive dissonance." In S. Coopersmith (Ed.), *Frontiers of psychological research: Readings from Scientific American* (1966: 207–13). San Francisco: W. H. Freeman.

George, D. M., & Hoppe, R. A. (1979). "Racial identification, preference, and self-concept." *Journal of Cross-Cultural Psychology* 10, 85–100.

Gilligan, C. (1982). *In a different voice: Psychological theory and women's development.* Cambridge, MA: Harvard University Press.

Hunsberger, B. (1978). "Racial awareness and preference of White and Indian Canadian children." *Canadian Journal of Behavioural Science* 10, 176–79.

Inhelder, B., & Piaget, J. (1958). *The growth of logical thinking from childhood to adolescence.* New York: Basic Books.

Johnson, C. J., Pick, H. L., Jr., Siegel, G. M., Cicciarelli, A. W., & Garber, S. R. (1981). "Effects of interpersonal distance on children's vocal intensity." *Child Development* 52, 721–23.

Kehoe, J. W. (1988). *A handbook for enhancing the multicultural climate of the school.* Vancouver, BC: Pacific Educational Press.

Killian, C. R. (1979). "Cognitive development of college freshmen." *Journal of Research in Science Teaching* 16 (4), 347–50.

Kircher, M., & Furby, L. (1971). "Racial preferences in young children." *Child Development* 42, 2076–78.

Kohlberg, L. (1969). "Stage and sequence: The cognitive-developmental approach to socialization." In D. A. Goslin (Ed.), *Handbook of socialization theory and research* (347–480). Chicago: Rand McNally.

———. (1984). *Essays on moral development: 2, The psychology of moral development.* San Francisco: Harper & Row.

Kolodiy, G. (April 1974). "Piagetian theory and college science teaching." *Journal of College Science Teaching,* 261–62.

Lambert, J. C. (1994). "Teacher perceptions of student interest in multicultural trade books." Paper presented at the Midwestern Educational Research Association, Chicago, IL.

Lempers, J. D., Flavell, E. R., & Flavell, J. H. (1977). "The development in very young children of tacit knowledge concerning visual perception." *Genetic Psychology Monographs* 95, 3–53.

Marsh, A. (1970). "Awareness of racial differences in West African and British children." *Race* 11, 289–302.

Milner, D. (1973). "Racial identification and preference in Black British children." *European Journal of Social Psychology* 3, 281–95.

Newman, M. A., Liss, M. B., & Sherman, F. (1983). "Ethnic awareness in children: Not a unitary concept." *Journal of Genetic Psychology* 143, 103–12.

Nisan, M., & Kohlberg, L. (1982). "Universality and variation in moral judgment: A longitudinal and cross-sectional study in Turkey." *Child Development* 53, 865–76.

Pacific Educational Press. Faculty of Education. University of British Columbia, Vancouver, B.C. V6T 1Z4.

Piaget, J., & Inhelder, B. (1969). *The psychology of the child.* New York: Basic Books.

Reyes, D. (1986). "Cognitive development of teacher candidates: An analysis." *Journal of Teacher Education* 18 (2), 18–21.

Rice, A. S., Ruiz, R. A., & Padilla, A. M. (1974). "Person perception, self-identity, and ethnic group preference in Anglo, Black, and Chicano preschool and third-grade children." *Journal of Cross-Cultural Psychology* 5, 100–8.

Rohrer, G. K. (1977). "Racial and ethnic identification and preference in young children." *Young Children* 32, 24–33.

Rosenthal, B. G. (1974). "Development of self-identification in relation to attitudes toward the self in Chippewa Indians." *Genetic Psychology Monographs* 90, 43–141.

Sachs, J., & Devin, J. (1976). "Young children's use of age-appropriate speech styles in social interaction and role-playing." *Journal of Child Language* 3, 81–98.

Silverman, F., & Creswell, J. L. (1982). "Preservice teachers: A profile of cognitive development." *Texas Tech Journal of Education* 9 (3), 175–85.

Sleeter, C. E., & Grant, C. A. (1988). *Making choices for multicultural education: Five approaches to race, class, and gender.* Columbus, OH: Merrill.

Spencer, M. B. (1982). "Personal and group identity of Black children: An alternative synthesis." *Genetic Psychology Monographs* 106, 59–84.

Stephan, W. G., & Rosenfield, D. (1979). "Black self rejection: Another look." *Journal of Educational Psychology* 71, 708–16.

Thornton, M. C., & Fuller, R. G. (1981). "How do college students solve proportion problems?" *Journal of Research in Science Teaching* 18 (4), 335–40.

Thrower, J. S. (now Timm). (1971). *Effects of orphanage and foster care on development of moral judgement.* Unpublished doctoral dissertation, Harvard University, Cambridge, MA.

Timm, J., & Gross, J. (1990). *Cognitive levels of reasoning among traditional and non-traditional age college students.* ERIC Document #ED 332 619.

Walker, L. J. (1984). "Sex differences in the development of moral reasoning: A critical review." *Child Development* 55, 677–91.

———. (1986). "Sex differences in the development of moral reasoning: A rejoinder to Baumrind." *Child Development* 57, 522–26.

Walker, L. J., & Moran, T. J. (1991). "Moral reasoning in a communist Chinese society." *Journal of Moral Education* 20 (2), 139–55.

Watts, W. A. (1984). "Attitude change: Theories and methods." In R. L. Jones (Ed.), *Attitudes and attitude change in special education: Theory and practice.* Reston, VA: Council for Exceptional Children.

Weiland, A., & Coughlin, R. (1979). "Self-identification and preference: A comparison of White and Mexican-American first and third graders." *Journal of Cross-Cultural Psychology* 10, 356–65.

Williams, J. E., Best, D. L., Boswell, D. A., Mattson, L. A., & Graves, D. J. (1975). "Preschool Racial Attitude Measure II." *Educational and Psychological Measurement* 35, 3–18.

# PART IV

೫ಂಡ

# The Educational Perspective

# 11

# Politics and Multicultural Education

Revolutions never go backwards.

WILLIAM HENRY SEWARD

Over the past few years, debates about multiculturalism and multicultural education have become highly political in nature. Diverse views on multicultural education have taken conservative, liberal, and radical positions (Sleeter, 1994). In the conservative view, multicultural education is perceived as too great a departure from traditional mainstream education, which has historically been based on Western European culture and philosophy. Those with this view see multicultural education as a threat to the cohesion of American society and to the quality of education. In the liberal view, multicultural education is seen as making important contributions to students' knowledge and understanding about diverse groups in the United States. In the radical view, multicultural education is seen as being too conservative because of its failure to reject a primarily Western European focus in course content, and because it has not seriously improved inequities in American education. Thus, critiques of multicultural education include conservative charges that the field is too radical and radical charges that the field is not radical enough. There is also a critique from cultural anthropologists that many educators use the concept of "culture" in a simplistic way and miss important insights about diversity that anthropology could give (Coughlin, 1992).

This chapter reviews the conservative, liberal, and radical views of multicultural education and the ideologies contained within them. The reader may agree or disagree with these opposing views, but knowledge of them is essential in order to understand the issues in the current political debate over multiculturalism and multicultural education.

## CONTROVERSY OVER DIVERSITY IN EDUCATION

Controversy over diversity in education in the United States is not new. Glazer (1994) has reported the following:

> To its critics, multiculturalism looks like a very new thing in American education.... However, viewed in the long stretch of the history of American public schooling, we can recognize it as a new word for an old problem: how public schools are to respond to and take account of the diversity of backgrounds of their students—religious, ethnic, racial. American public education ... has rarely been free of this issue. (p. 6)

Glazer has cited "public disputes" such as the objection of Catholic religious leaders to readings from the Protestant King James Bible in public schools in the 1840s and the rights of children of German immigrants to receive instruction in German in the 1880s. Banks (1988) has reported that as new immigrants from southern, central, and eastern Europe arrived toward the end of the nineteenth century, those in the United States from northern Europe viewed these newcomers as a threat to "American tradition." A movement known as **nativism** developed, with a distrust of these "foreigners ... because of their Catholicism, cultural differences, and competition for jobs" (Banks, 1988, p. 3). During World War I, the teaching of German was forbidden in many public schools. In 1919 Nebraska forbade the teaching of any foreign language before the eighth grade. Glazer (1994) has pointed out that in the 1940s, an attempt was made to include "intercultural education" in the schools, but this movement did not last long, primarily due to three issues in the 1950s: (a) Soviet achievements in space technology, which redirected educational efforts toward the sciences; (b) the U.S. Supreme Court ruling in Brown v. Board of Education of Topeka, which redirected national attention to the issue of desegregation in the nation's schools; and (c) hostility from new American nativists, who saw it as a threat to established education. In the 1960s, the Civil Rights Movement set the stage for a new emphasis on diversity in education.

## CONSERVATIVE VIEWS OF MULTICULTURAL EDUCATION

The most visible critiques of multicultural education in the 1980s and 1990s have been conservative, because these critiques are often written for popular audiences. Conservatives focus on the rights of individuals within America's free market economy and minimize the legitimacy of diverse group claims of inequities in the system. The society is seen as being best protected by historical institutions such as schools that preserve democratic traditions in a country led by those with talent or ability (Hoover, 1987). Because individuals differ, conservatives believe that inequality results naturally from differences not only in ability but also in effort. There is a hint of the old Protestant work ethic in this view that hard work is the pathway to success. Also contained in this view is the notion that social problems can be solved best by encouraging the development of knowledge and talent in so-called disadvantaged children and by refusing to focus on the history of diverse groups, which has inhibited their successful inclusion into the American mainstream. There is also a notion that schools may have failed at times to maintain academic rigor, but they have not failed in preparing students for the responsibilities of citizenship in a multicultural society (Balch, 1992). (The fact that less than half of the population eligible to vote usually does so in national elections throws this view into question.) Some conservatives recognize the fact that education should be "multicultural" in light of America's increasing diversity, but they disagree over what that education ought to be (Sleeter, 1994).

Although there have been many conservative critics of multicultural education, the review that follows is intended to focus on those writers whose views have received the most public attention as well as exposure in the media. For example, in an essay published in *Time* magazine (July 8, 1991), the historian Arthur Schlesinger, Jr. viewed multiculturalism as threatening "the ideal that binds America." His argument was based on the crises and fragmentation resulting in countries such as the former Soviet Union, Cyprus, and Yugoslavia when ideological differences among ethnic and racial groups tore these countries apart.

In Schlesinger's view, the United States has been unique among nations in its successful achievement of creating and maintaining a unified culture in a multi-ethnic and multiracial society. He referred to the historical assimilation of diverse groups into a "new national identity." He did acknowledge that increased diversity has had "many healthy consequences," but he claimed that diversity contains the possibility of "unhealthy" consequences as well. He saw a danger in multiculturalism that "crystallizes the differences, magnifies tensions, [and] intensifies hostilities," and he maintained that a focus on the ideals of a common culture is "urgent" for the continuance of national cohesion. Elsewhere, Schlesinger (1992) has asserted that ethnic ideologies have imposed ethnocentric, Afrocentric, and bilingual programs on public schools that are designed to hold minority children out of American society—in other words, condemning them to a caste system in America.

In a similar vein, others have vigorously defended a traditional curricular "canon" based on Western European culture. In 1987, three books were published that were directed at the general public. These were *Cultural Literacy* by E. D. Hirsch, *The Closing of the American Mind* by Allan Bloom, and *What Do Our 17-Year Olds Know?* by Chester E. Finn and Diane Ravitch. These volumes received considerable attention in the media. A review of them follows.

E. D. Hirsch (1987a) called for a return to "cultural literacy," even in the early grades. In the book *Cultural Literacy* (1987b), his approach for older students was based on the premise that in order to be educated, Americans must share a common literate culture, including a vocabulary of a few thousand common words and facts that he viewed as important in regard to the nation's culture. His concern was for the creation of a common frame of reference among all Americans. He argued that, historically, great nations have shared a national language and culture. His goal was the achievement of both. In the long run, his approach was pedantic and focused on simplistic learning skills, including memorizing. It failed to address the development of critical-thinking and problem-solving skills in students of all ages—in other words, those skills that promote communication among individuals.

In *The Closing of the American Mind,* Allan Bloom (1987) derived his defense of the traditional curricular **canon** from the philosophical principles of our Republican form of government and the doctrine of natural rights. In Bloom's view, our government was "an entirely new experiment in politics" that brought with it a new form of education:

> Democratic education, whether it admits it or not, wants and needs to produce men and women who have the tastes, knowledge, and character supportive of a democratic regime.... The old view was that, by recognizing and accepting ... natural rights, men found a fundamental basis of unity and sameness. Class, race, religion, national origin or culture all disappear or become dim when bathed in the light of natural rights.... The recent education of openness ... pays no attention to natural rights or the historical origins of our regime.... But when there are no shared goals or vision of the public good, is the social contract any longer possible? (pp. 26, 27)

Bloom advocated a curriculum of Western European culture on the basis of individualistic conceptions of democratic principles. There are problems with his argument, however. First, he committed the either/or logical fallacy, which interprets situations as being one alternative or the other, without considering (a) that there is a possibility for a third alternative, or (b) that both alternatives may coexist. In other words, students may learn about both Western studies *and* diverse groups' history and culture, and be the richer for it. Second, Bloom disregarded the fact that differences in class, race, religion, and national origin (ethnicity) have not disappeared as a result of a Eurocentric focus in education. Third, he overlooked achievements in the extension of "natural rights" through the courts in the twentieth century. In other words, the concept of natural rights did not originally include women and non-White males.

In *What Do Our 17-Year Olds Know?* Finn and Ravitch (1987) presented their argument for a return to the canon in a report of the results of an objective (multiple-choice items) test on American literature and history. This test was administered to high school juniors across the nation. The questions included items about famous people, historical events, and literature. Correct answers averaged 54.5 percent for the history questions and 51.8 percent for the literature items. In a critique of the Finn and Ravitch study, Walker (1990) called attention to the fact that students' low scores on (so-called) common cultural knowledge are not new, but that difficulties in testing are rarely taken into account. These include errors in entering responses on the test sheet, time restrictions, internal factors such as hunger or fatigue, and external factors such as distracting events during testing. I would add here that the length of time between the material being taught and the taking of the test could also affect test results. Walker also criticized the study for its failure to address the question as to how the traditional academic curriculum that Finn and Ravitch advocated, but which is unrelated to current social issues, will better prepare students for life in America.

Elsewhere, Ravitch addressed the question of how a nation should "school its people." She pointed out that "for most of the United States' existence there has been no national policy of education" (1985, p. 185), but that there have been two basic approaches: the common school and state subsidy of private schools. The common school theoretically represented an attempt at egalitarian reform, because it was open to all children in a community. (In many situations, however, "all children" was interpreted to be all *White* children. This "egalitarian" approach did not include African and Native American students except on a very limited and local basis.) For Ravitch, an important question was "Do we want schooling that accentuates awareness of cultural differences, or do we want schooling that minimizes them?" (1985, p. 207) Ravitch viewed American schools as being caught ever since the nineteenth century in a "politicization" process involving a variety of issues, including the teaching of foreign languages, resistance to desegregation, and the demands of diverse groups with different religious and political ideologies to have their views imposed on the curriculum. Her concern was with this politicization process and with the "increased power of the federal government and the courts to intervene in educational institutions" (1985, p. 273). Ravitch was also concerned with the following:

We need the courts as vigilant guardians of our rights; we need federal agencies that respond promptly to any violations of those rights. But we also need educational institutions that are free to exercise their responsibilities without fear of pressure groups and political lobbies. Decisions about which textbooks to use, which theories to teach, which books to place in the school library, how to teach, and what to teach are educational issues. They should be made by appropriate lay and professional authorities on educational grounds. In a democratic society, all of us share the responsibility to protect schools, colleges, and universities against unwarranted political intrusion into educational affairs. (p. 274)

Ravitch, however, not only failed to define just who "appropriate" lay and professional authorities are but also assumed that these groups would automatically select appropriate texts, library books, course content, and teaching procedures that would be effective for most if not all students. In so doing, she overlooked both psychological and culturally determined differences in the way students learn. She also assumed that lay groups are without bias and failed to address the issue of school authorities being subject to pressure by those who would seek to limit educational materials to conform to their point of view. She ignored the possibility that pressure might come from both individuals and community groups to censor materials in public schools. Interestingly, a survey of attempts at censorship in both schools and public libraries I conducted revealed that the reasons parents and community members gave for wanting to censor books represented conservative political views far more often than liberal views. Conservative reasons for wanting books removed included religious and "personal" values, while liberal reasons included racism and sexism in the reading materials (Timm, 1989).

More recently, Dinesh D'Souza has addressed the departure from the canon on college campuses. In his book *Illiberal Education,* published in 1991, he reviewed curricular changes such as increases in culturally diverse courses at prestigious campuses like the University of California at Berkeley, Duke, and Harvard. D'Souza refers to the subversion of "academic standards" and the politicizing of university curricular programs by minority groups seeking to have courses in the history, culture, and literature of diversity groups added to traditional course offerings. In D'Souza's view (1991), adding these courses somehow undermines the quality of a university education:

Among university professors, there are many qualms about the academic revolution under way because it challenges traditional norms of scholarship and debate. But these doubts are dissipating with time, as the composition of the body of American faculty rapidly changes. Older, traditionally liberal professors are retiring and making way for a new generation, weaned on the assorted ideologies of the late 1960s. (p. 17)

There is an assumption here that the content of multicultural courses is somehow inferior to traditional (Western European) courses. The achievements of scholars and writers from diverse groups are overlooked. Recognition for distinctions such as the Nobel Prize for Literature (African American Toni Morrison) and the Pulitzer Prize (Native American N. Scott Momaday) awarded to people of color is ignored. There is also an implication that those concerned with the history, culture, and social issues in regard to race and gender are somehow less "scholarly." D'Souza was concerned with what he perceived to be a lowering of academic standards on American campuses, but he failed to consider that the newer diversity-oriented courses may in fact broaden students' perspectives and provide information that they would otherwise not receive. Courses in diversity are especially important for students coming from racially homogenous communities and hometowns. It is my impression that those who support the traditional canon and criticize courses in cultural diversity believe that the students in American colleges are all exposed to the same information when they fulfill general education requirements. A student, however, may select one history course, or one social science course, or one literature course out of a range of course offerings within these various academic departments. Obviously, in doing so, what students learn about "Western culture" is not all the same.

Ironically, students in my multicultural education classes have reported that studying the history of diverse groups in the United States has in fact provided them with new information about United States history that they had not studied before. Others have said that they now thought about the events covered in traditional American history courses with a new perspective. Even history majors have said that studying the experiences of diverse groups has helped them to integrate information they had previously learned. For example, one student said:

> I never stopped to think about the fact that if the Treaty of Guadalupe Hidalgo had not resulted in the United States acquiring all that land from Mexico in 1848, then when gold was discovered in California in 1849, it would have been in Mexico! The Spanish were right. There was gold here. It's also interesting to think that probably fewer Chinese might have come to the United States because would we have needed to build the transcontinental railroad to connect the eastern part of the country to Mexico? I never thought about all this in this way before we studied the history of the Mexican and Chinese Americans in this course. All this information puts a new perspective on American history for me.

Perhaps those educators on college campuses who are so opposed to multiculturalism should consider the possibility that courses with multicultural content broaden students' understanding of diverse groups and their perspective of our nation as well. Another one of my students, also a history major, said:

> You know, I just realized that the history of every group is the *real* history of the United States. It's all our history put together. I never knew about the Iroquois Confederation before. Wow.

# LIBERAL VIEWS
# OF MULTICULTURAL EDUCATION

Liberals share conservatives' view of individual competition, but liberals also consider diverse groups' claims of unfair opportunity within American society and recognize past inequities and discrimination (Sleeter, 1994). They believe that the government should address these problems and see the process as a mechanism for social change. They believe that schools can bring about social change and equalize opportunities for diverse students through special programs such as bilingual education. Liberals also believe that prejudice and stereotyping can be reduced through education.

One educator who has recently shifted his position from a conservative to a more liberal view is Nathan Glazer. Writing in 1981, Glazer questioned the effectiveness of both bilingual and bicultural education in regard to educational achievement and was concerned about their impact on "divisiveness" in relation to national "loyalty." He viewed a common language as "binding a nation" and its economic interests, but went on to add that Switzerland's prosperity did not seem to be affected by having four official languages!

Ten years later, Glazer (1991) had shifted his position somewhat. He continued to hold the view that national unity is an important focus in education, but he also saw some benefits in incorporating diverse perspectives into the traditional curriculum:

> Demographic and political pressures change the history that is to be taught. They direct us to look for things we could not have noticed before.... Yes, there is another side to the story of the expansion of Europe and imperialism.... Yes, there is a Mexican perspective on the Mexican American war.... Yet another development bears on the multicultural problem. This is the push for more choice in the public school system.... Choice bears upon this [multicultural] debate because it implies diversity of curricula, because there should be something to choose among. It implies that quite a range of emphases may be offered. (p. 20)

By 1994, in an article published in *Multicultural Education,* Glazer had adopted an even more supportive view of multicultural education. He stated that multiculturalism has reappeared as a public issue because of rapidly changing racial and ethnic demographics and the failure of civil rights reforms of the 1960s to achieve their objectives:

> America's population is changing in its racial and ethnic composition. Its values are changing. Its notions of the proper relation of groups and individuals to the national society are changing. As hard as it may be for veterans of the educational system of earlier decades to wrench free of their own schooling, it is even harder to see how such a (former) system can be defended in the face of these changes. (p. 9)

Unlike the conservatives who perceive multicultural education as being a threat to "national interests," James Banks has been a long-time proponent of multicultural education. Banks (1993) has identified five different types of knowledge. These types are personal/cultural, popular, mainstream academic, transformative academic, and school knowledge. In Banks's view, *transformative academic knowledge* challenges mainstream knowledge, expands students' perceptions of diversity, and facilitates understanding among groups by including discussions of America's social problems such as racism, sexism, and poverty.

## RADICAL VIEWS
## OF MULTICULTURAL EDUCATION

Radical critiques of multicultural education have not been written to influence public opinion but to further a debate among multicultural theorists. This limitation is unfortunate because as a result, their arguments for collective advancement in equity in American society are not being heard by the general public or adequately covered in the media. According to Sleeter (1994), the U.S. public tends to dislike radical arguments and views them as un-American. In doing so, they are overlooking or discounting inequities in American society.

Radical proponents reject an emphasis on individual competition in America's free market economic system. Unlike the conservatives, radicals do not view individual "success" as necessarily resulting from differences in ability and effort but rather depending upon inequities in opportunity that place members of oppressed groups at a disadvantage. Radicals view these inequities as being controlled by those in positions of economic and political power who protect their own interests. In other words, radicals are concerned about the differential status of diverse groups in relation to access to the economic, political, and social power, as discussed in Chapter 3. Radicals view membership in diverse groups as a source of strength. They also tend to focus on three forms of social inequity based on gender, race, or social class (Sleeter, 1994).

Some radical critics fault multicultural education for supporting individual rather than group gains in America's economic and political system. They also criticize multicultural education for minimizing social problems. One of the frustrations radical critics have regarding multicultural education is the superficial way in which White teachers avoid discussions about inequity issues in the classroom and thereby fail to address prejudice and discrimination in American society. In Sleeter's view (1994), multicultural education should direct more attention to racism, patriarchy, and capitalism, since these impact race, gender, and socioeconomic level.

Radical critics perceive a tendency by teachers to focus on cultural "contributions" and on material culture without addressing the deeper values that are reflected in material culture. Popkewitz (1988) has reported that multicultural programs can decontextualize material culture and reformulate it according to

Western (European) concepts. This problem is not limited to multicultural education. Popkewitz described an exhibition at the Museum of Modern Art in New York City in 1984–85 in which tribal objects from Africa were juxtaposed with paintings by early twentieth-century artists such as Picasso and Leger. The exhibit was intended to illustrate the common qualities in these works. In focusing on these "qualities," the show ignored the historical context of the tribal objects and imposed Western design concepts of shape, line, and color, which were used to explain the relationship between the objects and the paintings. The result was both an omission and a distortion of African cultural concepts.

One advocate of "radical education" has been Henry Giroux. Unlike some radical critics, however, he has expressed a belief that schools may, in fact, address the nation's social problems. In his view, the focus on the traditional education called for by conservative critics (such as Bloom, D'Souza, and Hirsch) represents a **new American nativism** that puts pressure on schools to maintain the status quo in American society and thereby serve conservative political interests. Giroux's (1992) concern has been that the conservative (he refers to it as "reactionary") political agenda enhances the fortunes of a privileged few. He has criticized the conservatives' emphasis on traditional education as follows:

> Accountability, in current mainstream discourse, offers no insights into how schools should prepare students to push against the oppressive boundaries of gender, class, race, and age domination. (p. 7)

Giroux has asserted that "pedagogy is always related to power" (1988, p. 97). In a reference to a different vision of public life, he has expressed a concern about the role schools play in the formulation of democracy. In his view, public schools have a choice between uncritically perpetuating the status quo or enhancing a culture based on justice in American society. In preparing tomorrow's teachers, "schools of education need to inspire their students … to find ways to get involved, to make a difference" (Giroux, 1992, p. 8). Giroux is referring to both academic and social responsibility here, but his words are not far from the ethics of care described in Chapter 2. This vision, this inspiration, and this involvement need not be limited to students in the public schools and the colleges of education to which Giroux refers.

This dream may be more than rhetoric. It has happened in many communities, but one person may serve as an example. While still an undergraduate at Harvard University, Wayne Meisel found a way to involve fellow students in community service work in Cambridge, Massachusetts (personal communication). In 1984 he trekked 1,500 miles from Maine to Washington to launch other community service projects. The Campus Outreach Opportunity League (COOL), involving over 700 colleges and universities, grew out of his efforts. In 1994, at age thirty-five, he was head of the Bonner Foundation, which grants 1,600 scholarships annually to students who are involved in community service work (*Time*, December 5, 1994, p. 60). Sometimes a vision can make a difference.

## CHAPTER SUMMARY

The political debate over multicultural education has increased over the past fifteen years. There are basically three points of view: (a) the conservative, (b) the liberal, and (c) the radical.

The conservative viewpoint advocates a "traditional" curriculum based on the history and culture of Western Europe. This curriculum is sometimes referred to as "the canon." In this viewpoint, curricular programs that focus on or include the study of diverse groups are seen as either divisive to American society or not meeting the needs of students in order for them to succeed in American society.

In the liberal viewpoint, inequity in American society may be alleviated through education. There is also a view that recognizing American diversity in educational programs is not divisive for the society but rather in the national interest.

In the radical viewpoint, differential power in the United States is seen as the cause of inequity across groups. Strength is perceived in terms of groups. There is also a concern that multicultural education may focus on the superficial aspects of cultural diversity, which decontextualizes material culture from deeper cultural values.

## IMPORTANT TERMS

Nativism

New American nativism

The conservative right

Liberalism

The radical left

The canon

## QUESTIONS FOR DISCUSSION

1. Create a debate team. Have one member argue the conservative view, one member argue the liberal view, and one member argue the radical view of multicultural education. Be sure to follow the rules of debate, including (a) a time limit for remarks; (b) no interruptions when another is speaking; (c) logical supporting evidence for all statements; and (d) logical supporting evidence for rebuttals. Keep in mind that a debate (unlike television talk shows) is not merely stating or exchanging opinions, but an effort to convince others by means of the logic of viewpoints.

2. If you met Dinesh D'Souza, what would you like to say to him?

3. If you met Henry Giroux, what would you like to say to him?

4. If you met someone who had a negative opinion of multicultural education, what logical arguments would you make to persuade that person differently?

# REFERENCES

Balch, S. A. (1992). "Political correctness or public choice?" *Educational Record* 73 (1), 21–24.

Banks, J. A. (1988). *Multiethnic education: Theory and practice.* Boston: Allyn & Bacon.

———. (June-July 1993). "The canon debate, knowledge construction, and multicultural education." *Educational Researcher* 22 (5), 4–14.

Bloom, A. (1987). *The closing of the American mind.* New York: Simon & Schuster.

Coughlin, E. K. (1992). "Anthropologists ask how they wound up in the wings of multicultural debate." *Chronicle of Higher Education* 39 (17), A8.

D'Souza, D. (1991). *Illiberal education: The politics of race and sex on campus.* New York: The Free Press.

Finn, C. E., & Ravitch, D. (1987). *What do our 17-year olds know?* New York: Harper & Row.

Giroux, H. A. (1988). "The hope of radical education: A conversation with Henry Giroux." *Journal of Education* 170 (2), 91–101.

———. (1992). "Educational leadership and the crisis of democratic government." *Educational Researcher* 21 (4), 4–11.

Glazer, N. (November/December 1981). "Pluralism and the new immigrants." *Society* 19, 31–36.

———. (September 2, 1991). "In defense of multiculturalism." *The New Republic,* 18–22.

———. (1994). "A new word for an old problem: Multicultural 'school wars'

date to the 1840s." *Multicultural Education* 1 (5), 6–9.

Hirsch, E. D. (1987a). "Restoring cultural literacy in the early grades." In J. Wm. Noll (Ed.), *Taking sides: Clashing views on controversial educational issues* (7th ed.). Guilford, CT: Dushkin.

———. (1987b). *Cultural literacy: What every American needs to know.* Boston: Houghton Mifflin.

Hoover, K. R. (1987). *Ideology and political life.* Monterey, CA: Brooks/Cole.

Popkewitz, T. S. (1988). "Culture, pedagogy, and power: Issues in the production of values and colonization." *Journal of Education* 170 (2), 77–90.

Ravitch, D. (1985). *The schools we deserve: Reflections on the educational crises of our times.* New York: Basic Books.

Schlesinger, A. M., Jr. (July 8, 1991). "The cult of ethnicity." *Time* 138 (1), 21.

———. (1992). *The disuniting of America: Reflections on a multicultural society.* New York: W. W. Norton.

Sleeter, C. (1994). "An analysis of the critiques of multicultural education." In J. A. Banks & C. M. Banks (Eds.), *Handbook of research on multicultural education.* New York: Macmillan.

Timm, J. (1989). "Censorship challenges in Wisconsin schools and libraries." *FORWARD: Wisconsin journal for supervision and curriculum development* 14 (1), 10–19.

Walker, D. F. (1990). "Back to the future: The new conservatism in education." *Educational Researcher* 19 (3), 35–38.

# 12

ॐ

# The Multicultural Classroom

## Putting It All Together

There is no absolute knowledge, and those who claim it,
whether they are scientists or dogmatists, open the door to tragedy.

J. BRONOWSKI

The question, of course, is how are all the issues addressed in this text brought together in the classroom? How do the historical perspective, the cultural perspective, and the psychological perspective interface in practice? Is it possible to integrate the various topics in a way that makes sense? I believe that it is.

Others have identified various approaches to multicultural education, provided important insights, and described strategies to follow. All of their views have made important contributions to a field that sometimes seems overwhelming. It is not my intention to review here all of their contributions and suggestions for implementing multicultural education. They are all valuable.

This chapter offers a "bird's-eye" view of the various perspectives in this text that fits the pieces together. Some broad guidelines for selecting resources that are relevant across curricular areas are reviewed. Other curricular issues are also considered. Ultimately, however, the task is up to each and every one of us. There is no best way to achieve the goals that we all hope for in multicultural education—there are only possibilities. Teaching and learning are creative processes. When we as teachers enter our classrooms, we become a dynamic part of that process.

# A SCHEMA FOR
# MULTICULTURAL EDUCATION

In order to facilitate the integration of the many issues emerging out of the multicultural approach to education, I propose a "schema" or concept of organization based on three major areas of focus: (a) cultural information; (b) social issues; and (c) interrelationships. Table 12.1 presents the relationship of these three areas to the issues so far addressed in this text.[1]

## The Cultural Information Area of Focus

In multicultural education, **cultural information** refers to *curricular content*. This focus encompasses the history and experiences of diverse groups, nonmaterial culture, macroculture, microcultures, and material culture (Chapters 3, 4, 5, 6, and 7). Curricular materials in this area include reference books, histories, biographies, autobiographies, literature, artifacts, sciences, technology, and diverse customs of any given cultural group. The arts and popular culture (Chapter 8) provide a rich source of materials for classroom use. Films and the media present values held by some members of the society on a day-to-day basis. Literature, which by its nature is frequently reflective, may present a broad scope of cultural information including values, historical context, and descriptions of lifestyles and material culture. Drama may do so as well.

When educators and teachers select materials for this area of focus, there are three important considerations that should be taken into account. These are (a)

**Table 12.1 Areas of Focus in Multicultural Education**

| CULTURAL INFORMATION (Curricular Content) | SOCIAL ISSUES (Combating Bias) | INTERRELATIONSHIPS (Behavioral Processes) |
|---|---|---|
| history | attitudes | home/school |
| biographies | ageism | teacher/student |
| nonmaterial culture | bias | student/student |
| values | discrimination | self-esteem |
| macroculture | equity | multiple intelligences |
| microculture | ethnocentrism | field independence/dependence |
| material culture | prejudice | cultural styles |
| technologies | racism | learning styles |
| sciences | sexism | role playing/drama |
| cultural customs | social power | ethics of care |
| popular culture | stereotypes | |
| the arts | | |

the cognitive developmental level of the students; (b) the accuracy, quality, and objectivity of the materials in reference to historical events and to culture; and (c) the presentation of material culture within its cultural context. Later in this chapter some guidelines for assessing the quality of materials are reviewed.

### The Social Issues Area of Focus

In multicultural education, **social issues** refer to a curriculum that goes beyond cultural information and aims specifically at *combating bias.* In other words, this focus actively and directly addresses inequities in the American society, either past or present. This focus deals with the issues of economic, political, and social power (Chapter 3). It considers the differential access, quality, and outcomes of education that students of diverse groups have experienced on the basis of their race, ethnicity, gender, or socioeconomic status (Chapters 4 and 5). It considers legal issues in relation to social justice (Chapter 6). It deals with social attitudes, prejudice, and bias (Chapter 10). Curricular materials in this area include histories, biographies, autobiographies, literature, and popular culture that deal specifically with these social issues. Literature and artifacts may also be used to present stereotypes that can be identified and discussed.

When educators and teachers select materials for this area of focus, there are also important concerns that should be taken into account. These are (a) the cognitive developmental level of the students; (b) the quality and accuracy of the materials in reference to historical events; and (c) portrayals of characters in fiction, film, or the media that present a basis for analysis and discussion. The guidelines for assessing the quality and appropriateness of materials presented later in this chapter also pertain to materials for this antibias focus. In early childhood education, selecting materials also includes play materials. Teachers need to be able to recognize stereotypes in these materials.

In planning lessons for combating stereotypes, it is crucial that teachers provide the historical background about how these notions and images evolved. Later in this chapter, the origins of stereotypes about Native Americans and their continuing impact on children today are considered. Knowing the history behind these images helps students to recognize them for what they are. Becoming aware of stereotypes provides a strong base from which to combat them.

## The Interrelationships Area of Focus

In multicultural education, **interrelationships** refer to psychological and cultural factors and their effect on individual and group *behavior*. *Interrelationships* refer not only to students' relationships with each other, but also to relationships between the school and parents. An example of a cultural misunderstanding appears in Box 12.1. When expectations by parents are different from those of teachers, these culturally based differences in perceptions need to be addressed in conversations between educators and parents from diverse groups. For example, in my conversations with over a hundred teachers having Hmong students in their classrooms, I realized that educators need to *explain* to parents their reasons for their classroom procedures and to *listen* to parents' concerns.

The interrelationship area of focus also refers to students' self-esteem. Self-images are often determined by the way students perceive themselves in reference to others. When students encounter inequities on the basis of race, ethnicity, gender, or socioeconomic status, these experiences have a devastating impact on their perceptions of their future in American society. Garcia (1991) has referred to this situation as cultural degradation (Chapter 7).

Finally, this focus considers the unique qualities that individual students bring to a learning situation, as well as the cultural influences that they bring into the classroom. Here is where teachers need to consider the effects of both individual differences and culture on their students' perceptions, performance, and interactions with each other (Chapter 9). What value orientations do students bring with them? Which students are living in a co-figurative cultural situation in comparison with their elders at home (Chapter 7)? What languages do they speak? What are their different "intelligences" and strengths? Which students appear to be more field independent and prefer to set their own course when they are working? Which students are more field sensitive and oriented toward social cues in the classroom? What happens when students are assigned to work together and one prefers a more independent approach, while another prefers a cooperative, problem-solving situation? How aware are teachers of a tendency to overgeneralize students on the basis of their cultural group in relation to their "style"? How much faith is placed in learning style tests in spite of their problems? Do teachers assign students to cooperative learning groups on the basis of their cultural groups? Do they intentionally mix or match students' field-independent/dependent styles?

When teachers select materials for this area of focus, there are issues that should be taken into account. These are (a) the cognitive developmental level of the students, and (b) *ways in which these materials may enhance students' ability to take another point of view.* Drama and an ethics of care approach may be especially relevant here.

---

**BOX 12.1** Why Doesn't the Teacher Teach?

The scene is an urban second-grade classroom. The teacher, Mrs. A., is sitting at her desk and helping one student with a lesson. Other students are engaged in various activities. Four are playing a math game. Some are working in pairs. Others are working individually at their desks. A cluster of children are reading on the patch of carpet in the reading corner. A boy is watering the plants. A girl is feeding the gerbils.

Mrs. L., the Hmong mother of one of the students, slowly enters the classroom. She ap-

proaches the teacher and hands her a small bag with the comment that she is sorry to interrupt, but her son forgot his lunch. Mrs. A. smiles and thanks her.

A few minutes later Mrs. A. happens to glance out of the window that overlooks the parking lot. Mrs. L. is looking toward the school. She is slowly shaking her head back and forth. Mrs. A. realizes that her visitor expected a more formal approach to teaching.

---

# SOME PROCEDURES
# FOR THE DIFFERENT AREAS OF FOCUS

## Selecting Materials for the Cultural Content and Social Issues Areas of Focus

One of the most confusing decisions educators encounter is choosing materials—reference books, biographies, history, storybooks, and fiction—for school libraries and classroom use. How do you decide? In multicultural education this question seems almost overwhelming. For example, there are literally thousands of books in print in reference to Native Americans alone (Kuipers, 1991). You see an advertisement in a professional magazine announcing a new publication that looks interesting. Should you send for it? You read the book section in the Sunday newspaper. There are six new storybooks for children your students' age. Which one should you order? You go shopping after school and stop in a bookstore that has a display of fifty books about diverse peoples and cultures. How do you choose which to buy? What "catches" your eye? The illustrations? The story? The author? The publisher? Should teachers purchase books for their students' use? Anyone who teaches faces these decisions constantly.

I learned at a library conference last year that most books purchased for school and public libraries are selected on the basis of announcements or reviews in professional or library publications without being seen or evaluated by the person ordering them. This practice is understandable in light of the scope and number of publications produced yearly. I also learned that many librarians select materials on the basis of the author's reputation or the publisher's reputation in the subject area of the book. But what about the rest of us? What if the books are not what they appear to be? Some guidelines are necessary in order to know which possibilities are better than others.

**Library and Information Science Guidelines** There are several criteria for selecting reference books, according to *The Encyclopedia of Library and Information Science* (ELIS, as cited in Kuipers, 1991). These criteria include (a) the author's qualifications and experience; (b) the focus and range of the work or text; (c) the accuracy of the information; and (d) the objectivity or freedom from bias in the presentation of information. These guidelines also apply to the selection of fiction.

Kuipers (1991) has suggested three basic criteria for assessing the treatment of Native Americans in literature, but in a multicultural context these may be applied to other groups as well. The criteria are (a) accuracy, (b) authenticity, and (c) objectivity. Whether a resource meets these standards can be determined by asking some basic questions, which I have rephrased in order to make them applicable to all groups. Accuracy depends on four issues that the following questions consider. I have added some parenthetical considerations to Kuipers' issues.

1. Are the sources used in gathering background information accurate?
2. Was the background research carefully done by the author?
3. Is there careful documentation of any historical events referred to in the plot or story line?
4. Is the factual information referred to in the story correct?

Authenticity depends on eight issues, which the following questions address:

1. Is the culture portrayed in the book presented from the point of view of that culture, or from someone outside of it? If it is presented from another point of view, is that crucial to the plot or the recalling of events? Is a biography carefully documented?
2. Does the work refer to contributions of the cultural group to culture in the United States?
3. Does the literature (or reference) recognize the diversity within the broad group portrayed? If the story is about characters within a subgroup, a broader perspective may not be relevant, but it should be clear that the story is limited to a certain location, time, and place.
4. Are members of the cultural group portrayed as individuals with their own unique qualities, or simply as representatives (or tokens) of the group?
5. Does the literature (or the reference) recognize the group as unique and valuable?
6. If there are languages other than English in the story, are these accurately portrayed without stereotyped phrases? (If the language deviates from standard English, is there a historical reason for this? Is the deviation accurate?)
7. Does the story present a realistic view of the life of its characters?
8. Are women (and also men) portrayed as individual characters, or in stereotyped roles?

Objectivity depends on issues that may be addressed through the following questions:

1. Is the story presented in a way that is free of biases in the form of overgeneralization or clichés?
2. Is the portrayal of characters free of stereotypes?
3. Does the story present positive values of the group? (Does it include different value orientations of the group?)
4. Is the lifestyle of the characters accurately represented and realistically described?
5. Are the characters presented as unique individuals with their own strengths and weaknesses?

To the above criteria, I would add one more question:

Does the story enable students to appreciate the unique qualities of the culture described?

At first, these issues may seem too extensive for educators to be able to consider in their busy schedules. It may, however, be better to build a collection of reference works and literature slowly in order to do it well.

**Guidelines for Early Childhood Education**   Derman-Sparks (1991) has suggested a checklist for teachers of early childhood education. Her criteria are similar to many of those listed above, but with some considerations that are especially relevant to books for young children. I have added some parenthetical issues to her list.

1. Check the illustrations. Are they free from stereotyped images? Are they free from stereotyped gender- or racial- (or age-) biased activities? (Are they authentic?)
2. Check the story line. Is success represented according to White mainstream standards? Are different (diverse cultural) lifestyles free from stereotypes? (Are relationships among individuals accurate in terms of the group's value orientation? For example, in groups that place a high value on family relationships, is that lineal orientation reflected in the story?)
3. Check the author's point of view. (Is the story presented from the point of view of the cultural group being portrayed or from an outsider's view? Is there a reason for this?)
4. Check the language for offensive or stereotyped words. Is the language sexist?
5. Check the copyright date. Publications prior to the early 1970s tend to have more stereotyped images and plots.

**Other Considerations**   In science or mathematics, information about the work of individuals from diverse groups is obviously important. This type of information comes under the focus area on curricular content, and the guidelines for assessing accuracy of reference books, biographies, and fictional accounts obviously apply here. A caveat may be in order, however. In incorporating information about the "contributions" of individuals from diverse groups, teachers need to avoid tokenism and disconnecting these contributions as "interesting" additions. These contributions must be incorporated into the main context of the subject. There are extensive references for diverse peoples' work in the sciences and mathematics. Before the Dark Ages in Europe, so-called Western science and philosophy derived many of its concepts from cultures in Africa. When Europe was in the Dark Ages, cultures in the Middle East and Asia were making significant advances in knowledge. What can we learn from them? Pharmacology, for example, owes much to the ancient wisdom of Native Americans and other groups.

### Relating Material Culture to Nonmaterial Culture

Material culture must be presented within its cultural context in order for students to learn the values and meaning of cultural products. Figure 12.1 shows a Medicine Wheel, which may serve as an example of the importance of this approach.

The Medicine Wheel symbolizes both concepts and values sacred to many Native Americans from a wide variety of tribes (Bopp, Bopp, Brown, & Lane, 1989). It symbolizes the idea that all things are interconnected. Its four directions symbolize the four elements: earth, air, water, and fire. Taken together, these stand for the wholeness of the earth.

The medicine wheel stands for the four aspects of human nature: spiritual, emotional, physical, and mental. Taken together, these represent the wholeness of our being and each person's potential for growth and learning. These four aspects of humanity are strikingly similar to Carl Jung's four aspects of personality (Chapter 9).

The medicine wheel represents the four aspects of the universe (or world): human beings, animals, plants, and minerals. These are all interconnected realities.

The medicine wheel represents the four cardinal directions: East, South, West, and North. Each of these carries its own symbolic lesson in relation to the four seasons of life. The East indicates spring, the dawn of a new day, renewal, and hope. For humans it connotes the beginning of life—of birth and rebirth. The South denotes summer, the season of fullness. For humans, it symbolizes youth and the time of physical strength. It also represents passion and love, but love without a need to control others. This view reminds me of a remark Carl Jung once made that where love rules, there is no will to power. The West is the time of autumn. It implies the spiritual aspect of human nature and middle age. It looks back to the innocence of childhood and the passion of youth, and forward to the wisdom of old age. The lesson of the West is that for those things we take from the world, we must give something in return. The North denotes winter and old age. Thus it represents the beginning of true wisdom, which embraces all knowledge.

Finally, the medicine wheel symbolizes the four races, or the Red, Yellow, Black, and White embodiments of humanity and our interconnectedness with each other. There is a teaching about the four races. In the beginning, the Creator gave *instructions* to the different races about guardianship for the four elements. The Red race was given guardianship of the earth, its food, and its minerals. The Yellow race was given guardianship of the air and space, with

**FIGURE 12.1** A Medicine Wheel

Photo courtesy of James Labre.

knowledge of meditation and spirituality. The Black race was assigned the guardianship of water. The White race was given guardianship of fire. After the Creator assigned these guardianships, the four races went their separate ways in four different directions with different ways of life, but today they are coming together again. The White race did enter the world of the Red race, forced the Black race to come also, and the Yellow race followed them into the land of the Red race.[2]

I have a medicine wheel hanging in my office. Whenever I look at it, I am reminded of something Mathew King, a Lakota elder, has said (cited in Wall & Arden, 1990):

> I know why you're here! White Man came to this country and forgot his original Instructions. We have never forgotten our Instructions. So you're here looking for the Instructions you lost. I can't tell you what those were, but maybe there are some things I can explain. It's time Indians tell the world what we know … about nature and about God. (p. 29)

## Using Literature in the Social Issues Focus

Class discussions involving literature may be used with students of all ages. Literature may obviously present cultural content, historical information, and cultural values, but it may also articulate social issues. It seems logical that literature concerning social issues would be directed toward older students, but there are a few books for younger children. *You Look Ridiculous* (Waber, 1966) addresses self-image. *A Look at Prejudice and Understanding* (Anders, 1976) addresses prejudice. A resource for teachers is *Anti-Bias Curriculum: Tools for Empowering Young Children,* which includes a reference list for early childhood education (Derman-Sparks, 1991).

One author who addressed social issues over the years was Theodor Geisel, otherwise known as Dr. Seuss. Although Geisel claimed he never wrote to convey a moral message, nevertheless some of his stories contain important lessons (Moje & Shyu, 1992). *The Sneetches* is about a kind of animal, some with stars on their bellies and some without. The star-bellied sneetches believe that they are the best kind of sneetches and will have nothing to do with the "plain bellied sort." When Sylvester McMonkey McBean arrives with a machine to put stars on bellies, the plain sneetches eagerly line up, but then those who had stars originally want their stars taken off in order to remain different—and therefore better. (McBean also has a machine to remove stars.) The sneetches continue to have stars added or removed until they realize that it doesn't matter whether they have stars or not—that they are all sneetches together. Obviously, the moral of this tale is that prejudice and segregation based on physical appearance are ludicrous. Other Dr. Seuss stories that deal with issues of equity and mutual respect include *Yertle the Turtle* and *Horton Hears a Who!*

There is also another consideration in regard to literature in early childhood education. In light of the findings reported by Bigler and Liben (1993, Chapter 10) that younger children remembered stories with racially stereotyped images better than they remembered stories with counterstereotyped images, it is important for early childhood teachers to present more stories with counterstereotyped images.[3]

In my own teaching experience, I have witnessed the impact of literature on older students. A poignant example is *Roll of Thunder, Hear My Cry* by Mildred Taylor. Elizabeth Fitzgerald Howard (1991) has described the power in this book as follows:

> Some years ago I read *Roll of Thunder, Hear My Cry* and I knew. I did not grow up in Mississippi, I never had to undergo any kind of prejudice like that the Logan family experienced, but the story struck a chord, a wrenching chord. I knew Mildred Taylor was writing my history. A Euro-American in a suburban school might not know any of the history, but that reader would feel with Cassie and Little Man, in their hurt, and would be touched by Jeremy's efforts to be their friend. This experience could make a difference in how such a reader might respond to real life African-Americans. In Taylor's stories of a particular time and place, the plight of Blacks becomes imaginable, tangible, and true because her art evokes feelings. (p. 92)

A few years ago, a European American student walked into my office with a book. It was *Roll of Thunder, Hear My Cry.* The student said:

> I brought you a present. I thought you might like it. As a matter of fact, I thought you might want to consider using it in multicultural education. It made me wake up and smell the coffee. I understand now what it must have been like for Black Americans. This book has changed my life.

I have adopted *Roll of Thunder, Hear My Cry* in my multicultural classes. The story takes place during the Depression. In discussing the book, however, I relate it to the continuing issues of economic, political, and social power, or the lack of them, in American society (Chapter 3). I also relate it to the issues of access, quality, and outcomes in education (Chapter 4). When my multicultural students ask me if the events in this book seem authentic to me, I tell them that during the 1960s, as a young wife, I moved with my husband to the South for a few years. I describe what it was like to observe people's reactions to events like the integration of lunch counters in the downtown stores. I compare the picket lines to the scenes of the picket lines in the television program *I'll Fly Away* (Chapter 8). I describe hearing a White person comment "Isn't that disgusting," when a preadolescent Black girl carried a sign for equal rights in public facilities. I describe the experience of turning a corner in a country road at twilight and coming upon a group of people dressed in hooded white robes. When they saw the car approach, they quickly convened in the road, thus forcing my husband to stop. Men crowded around the car, and peered inside. When they saw a White couple, the apparent leader walked around to the back of the car to check our license plate. We had just a few weeks before changed it to the local area. The head man turned back to my husband and waved us on. Oh, yes, it was all too real. For my students, the book takes them back to see for themselves.

### Assessing Bias in Curricular Materials

Teachers need to identify biases in reference books, biographies, literature, and even cultural products in order for students to become more aware of them. In Chapter 7, various microcultures in the United States were reviewed. Several years ago Gollnick and Chinn (1986), in addition to discussing these microcultures, identified six types of bias in educational materials. These biases were (a) fragmentation, (b) imbalance, (c) invisibility, (d) language, (e) stereotyping, and (f) unreality.[4] (Gollnick and Chinn [1994] have continued to refer to these biases.)

About the same time, Sleeter (1986) commented that the issues of race, gender, and social class had received attention in education. I agreed with Sleeter, but I also believed that bias was not limited to these issues and that age, religious affiliation, and rural/urban environment had been largely ignored and needed to be added to a study of stereotyping and bias. For this reason, I conducted an analysis of 167 children's storybooks for which I tabulated the occurrences of these six biases across microcultural groups (Timm, 1988; originally there were 200 books in the sample, but for various reasons 33 of these were dropped from the data analysis). The results of this study appear in Table 12.2. The reason that the total N (727) exceeds 167 is that *multiple biases* were found in many of these storybooks.

**Table 12.2  Frequency of Bias Categories by Different Groups in Children's Storybooks**

| Bias Category | GROUP | | | | | | |
| | Age | Gender | Race | Religion | SES* | Urban/rural | Totals |
|---|---|---|---|---|---|---|---|
| **Fragmentation** | 1 | 1 | 3 | 1 | 2 | – | 8 |
| **Imbalance** | 15 | 28 | 26 | 2 | 23 | 5 | 99 |
| **Invisibility** | 18 | 38 | 79 | 31 | 36 | 6 | 208 |
| **Language** | 4 | 45 | 15 | – | 4 | 1 | 69 |
| **Stereotyping** | 53 | 117 | 41 | 9 | 49 | 12 | 281 |
| **Unreality** | 10 | 12 | 17 | 2 | 16 | 5 | 62 |
| | 101 | 241 | 181 | 45 | 130 | 29 | 727 |

Source: Timm, 1988.

*socioeconomic status

What is the connection between these results and multicultural education? I suggest that educators construct a grid for individual books similar to that in Table 12.2. Although such a grid would not assess a collection of books, it would clearly lay out which biases are occurring in reference to different groups within any given book. It is a simple matter to assess the illustrations, story line, and language, as Derman-Sparks (1991) suggested, but a grid provides an at-a-glance view that is not so readily apparent otherwise. For teachers of early childhood education and the lower grades, this is not such a time-consuming exercise as it may at first appear to be. Many of the books that are developmentally appropriate for younger students do emphasize pictures. In light of the research findings about children's attitudes being so influenced by their perceptions of others (Chapter 10), the visual information conveyed in illustrations makes it all the more imperative for teachers to assess the messages these illustrations convey. For teachers of older students, a class project could engage the students in identifying biases in books designed for them. Thus, teachers may use a classroom strategy that would not only help them in their assessments of the materials, but enable their students to learn how to identify biases at the same time. In other words, it may provide an opportunity for teachers and students to coexplore these issues.

## Dealing with Stereotypes

Stereotypes about different groups are pervasive in American society. No group escapes these images. The African American mammy. The Asian American laundryman. The German American girl with her blond braids. The Mexican American with his sombrero and mustache. The Native American with a tomahawk or feathered headdress.

Where do these images come from? When do they begin in children's minds? Popular culture contributes mightily to their persistence. How many films and television programs can you remember with these images? Advertising and product symbols contribute their share, although some have improved lately. Aunt Jemima has evolved since 1910, but only last year did she lose her red bandana. Mascots for sports teams also perpetuate stereotyped images, along with the names of the teams themselves. The Braves. The Cowboys. The Redskins. The Vikings. There is obviously a history behind the stereotypes of diverse groups. The origins of a stereotype about Native Americans may serve as an example of the way past events have created these images and influenced our perceptions.[5]

**The History of a Stereotype**   The image of the Plains Indian as that of the "Indian" has had several foundations in history (Ewers, 1982). These were (a) the work of George Catlin and other artists; (b) the Plains Indian Wars; (c) the Wild West Show; and (d) the Plains Indian as a symbol of the United States. In 1832 and 1834, the American artist George Catlin traveled among the tribes of the Upper Missouri and the Southern Plains, where he gathered information and prepared pictures for an exhibition in several American cities. In 1840 he took his exhibit to London, and later to Paris. Along with his paintings he included costumes, a Crow tipi, and reenactments of ceremonies by Chippewa Indians. Anyone who has seen Catlin's paintings knows the powerful images of Native Americans that he recreated. In addition to the exhibit, his book, *Manners, Customs, and Condition of the North American Indians,* further extended the image of the Plains Indian as the "Indian." Artists' illustrations in other publications further advanced these images. Another artist who should be mentioned here was John Gilbert, who first illustrated Henry Wadsworth Longfellow's epic poem "Song of Hiawatha". I mentioned in Chapter 2 that Longfellow confused the historical Hiawatha with a legendary Ojibwa hero. In illustrating Longfellow's poem, Gilbert based his drawings on Catlin's paintings. Thus, he portrayed an Iroquois leader as an Objibwa from the region of Lake Superior, but who was in fact presented in the image of a Plains Indian of the Upper Missouri! His drawing of "Paw-puk-keewis" is recognizable as Catlin's Mandan hero, "Four Bears" (Ewers, 1982, p. 24). One final artist whom I will mention here is Jennie Brownscombe, who placed nineteenth-century Plains Indians in the Plymouth, Massachusetts, of 1621 in the painting *The First Thanksgiving,* which hangs in Pilgrim Hall.

Reports in the popular press of the Plains Indian Wars also contributed to the dominance of the image of Plains Indians. Another perhaps surprising source was that of the so-called dime novels, which began to appear in 1860. These paperback books presented stories of European heroes battling Native Americans in the West. These publications became enormously popular with boys and contributed to the image of the Indian as a violent warrior.

The third contributing factor to the widespread image of Plains Indians was the Wild West Show. In 1883 William F. Cody, otherwise known as "Buffalo Bill," created a traveling show that reenacted episodes from frontier history. These included a buffalo hunt, war dancing, horse racing, and Indian attacks on a pioneer's cabin and on a stagecoach, which Cody "rescued." The show ran for three decades, was seen by millions, and toured not only in the United States but in Canada and Europe as well. Even Sitting Bull himself traveled with the show in 1885. The show's contribution to the image of the Plains Indian and the Indian warrior was far reaching.

The fourth contributing factor to the prevailing image of the Plains Indian was its use as a national symbol. The Indian-head penny, originally minted in 1859, and the $10 gold piece in 1907, both represent Liberty wearing a feathered bonnet. The famous buffalo nickel, minted in 1913, depicts an Indian profile. Two of the three models were Plains Indians. A Sioux from South Dakota was the model for the fourteen-cent stamp issued in 1923. Ewers' (1982) review of the history behind these images of the "American Indian" makes clear a need for teachers to research the origins of stereotypes and to explain them in multicultural discussions, in order for students to understand where, why, and how they developed.

**Children's Perceptions of Stereotypes**　A study conducted among 238 suburban kindergarten and 239 fifth-grade children (League of Women Voters, New Brighton, MN, 1975) found that the children viewed Native Americans as living in a faraway place, hunting and shooting their food, wearing skin clothing and feathers. Only sixteen of the fifth graders referred to tribal differences. It might be easy to dismiss these findings, which are twenty years old, but students in my multicultural classes report that they also believed these same images in their own childhood.

**Sources of Stereotypes**　Where do children learn these stereotyped views? The first source is obviously in books written expressly for children. Some of these books contain images of Native Americans dressed in loin cloths and feathered headdresses, living in Plains Indian tipis, and carrying tomahawks. Moore and Hirschfelder (1982) have listed several categories of children's books that have in the past included stereotyped images of Native Americans. These categories are (a) books with pictures of children "playing" Indian; (b) books with animals depicted as Indians; (c) alphabet and dictionary books ("I is for Indian"); and (d) counting books ("Ten little, nine little, eight little Indians ..."). In the survey mentioned above that I conducted of children's storybooks in school and public libraries, I found these images repeatedly (Timm, 1988).

Another source contributing to stereotypes is one so common that it may be a surprise. *Toys* have a powerful influence. Hirschfelder (1982) has reported on a variety of toys produced by different manufacturers that embody Indian stereotypes, including feather headdresses, tomahawks, and so forth. The Playmobile System, for example, offered a Discovery Set with figures and accessories for a variety of roles, including cowboys, farmers, and *Indians*. (Is it an occupation?) Figure 12.2 shows a play set combining elements from very distinct areas. The Plains Indian tipi is packaged along with a Northwest Coast totem pole.

Earlier I referred to the names of teams, but names are not limited to teams. Ironically, as I was writing this section, an advertisement appeared in a national magazine for a miniature model motorcycle. Described as "wild, defiant, free,"

**FIGURE 12.2** A Sample "Indian Play Set"
Reprinted by permission of Leslie Frank McKeon, The Scarecrow Press, Inc.

its name is *The Indian 442*! In the same issue, another advertisement for collector plates included one entitled *Princess of Wisdom,* with a picture of a Sioux maiden on it. The beautiful "Indian princess" is another stereotyped image. Indian princess dolls are widely available in mail-order catalogs. Toys with stereotypes are not limited to children.

A different type of toy appears at Halloween. It is a costume. The Indian costume is easily recognized. If it didn't have a headdress and a tomahawk, would children see it as "Indian"? Would their parents purchase it? Are we back to the market economy issue discussed in Chapter 3? These toys, after all, are manufactured for profit. The issue of toys is particularly relevant to early childhood education because they are often included among classroom materials. Teachers need to evaluate these materials for the hidden lessons they may convey.

Another source contributing to stereotypes is one that continues beyond childhood. Team mascots are currently a controversial issue.[6] Many Native Americans are offended by the depictions of "Indians" and Indian themes in athletics. Phrases also may be offensive. What does a "tomahawk chop" or the phrase "scalp the..." (other team) connote about some Americans' views toward Native Americans?

The fifth source of stereotypes is popular culture. Stereotypes may be found for all diverse groups. Even though some recent films and television programs may be working against old images, their recurrence is extensive. Furthermore, reruns on television of old films and cartoons continue to present these images and social roles.

Even films from the Disney studio contain stereotypes. Because some of these films are based on old fairy tales, ugly older women are portrayed as cruel stepmothers or witches, and young heroines are portrayed as needing help from fairy godmothers or young heroes (*Snow White, Cinderella, The Little Mermaid, Aladdin*). Male villains are depicted as darker than the heroes (*Aladdin*), including animals (*The Jungle Book, The Lion King*). In *Pocahontas,* the dress of the Native American maiden is not culturally authentic and Captain John Smith is depicted according to the romantic stereotype of the blonde northern European hero. He was in fact dark-haired and considerably older than Pocahontas, who was approximately 15 years old when Smith landed in Virginia. Pocahontas in fact married John Rolf, another Englishman.

**Combating Stereotypes** In the preceding section, Figure 12.2 illustrated a play set that not only scrambled elements from different cultures, but presented stereotyped images as well. Figure 12.3 shows a collection of figures, toys, and other items teachers may use in class discussions as a way of combating stereotypes of Native Americans. Obviously, collections of figures and toys of other groups may be equally effective.

These items include figures with feather headdresses, tomahawks, and loin cloths. There is even a troll dressed as an Indian. The tomahawk and shrunken head were marketed for Halloween.[7] This collection belongs to Maureen Smith, an Oneida Native American. She discussed these materials in my multicultural classes as a way of confronting stereotypes. The next day a student walked into my office and made the following comment:

> I just want you to know that Dr. Smith's presentation last night was a wake-up call for me. I have never thought about some of those things before. I played with those toys when I was a kid. I dressed up like that one Halloween. I have pennants in my room at home with Indians on them. I didn't even think about the tomahawk chop. And I couldn't understand what this whole mascot issue was about. Well, I do now.

**FIGURE 12.3** Stereotyped Items of American Indians

Courtesy of Maureen Smith.

Teachers may also combat the stereotypes in films and television by examining these images in classroom discussions similar to those involving storybooks and literature.

### Focusing on Relationships

In early childhood education, Derman-Sparks (1991) has suggested that teachers need to set limits, address confrontations between students directly, and determine the real reason for interpersonal conflicts. Among young children, conflicts over possession of toys or play equipment are common, and the best way to enhance interpersonal relationships is to establish firm rules for cooperation. It is also important to explain to a young child how another child *feels.*

At the elementary, middle school, and high school level, there are ways for teachers to help their students develop an awareness of other points of view. In so doing, students may begin to realize the inner qualities in others. In other words, there are ways to facilitate students' growth out of the kind of prejudice based on the concrete operational reasoning common in middle childhood (Chapter 10).

**Using Drama**  Drama is especially conducive to developing social perspective-taking (Chapter 10). Several years ago my husband and I presented a workshop at an educational conference in which we demonstrated how this process works. Rather than simply assigning roles in a play and having the participants act them out, we assigned roles in the script that participants read aloud for twenty minutes, after which we reassigned the roles. Altogether, each participant read the parts of three different characters, and then we discussed their reactions. Everyone in the group commented how differently they felt as they identified with their role of the moment, and that in being forced to change roles (which they all resisted at first), they were also forced to change their points of view.

My husband has used this method in directing theatrical productions with students ranging from eight years through college age. In producing children's theater, he frequently required cast members to read each other's roles together as a group, in order for them to understand better the points of view of other characters in the play. He required boys to read girls' parts, and the other way around. Their comments included "I didn't like that character until I had to be that part, then I tried to understand it," and "Do we always have to be the same person [character] every time [in performance], or can we switch around? I don't mind learning more than one part. It's more interesting." We have found that this expanded use of drama works well in helping children to understand the *interrelationships* of characters in a play. I should emphasize the fact that the follow-up discussions are *crucial to the process.* It is during these discussions that children express their feelings and perceptions about the different characters' points of view.

**Integrating an Ethics of Care into the Curriculum**   In Chapter 2, I referred to four forms of pluralism in an ethics of care: (a) a pluralism of coexistence; (b) a pluralism of cooperation; (c) a pluralism of coexploring; and (d) a pluralism of coenjoyment (Diller, 1992). I also described the processes of these pluralisms within the context of the larger society. In educational settings, some of these pluralisms have been around for a while.

The pluralism of coexistence has depended on the diversity of students within individual schools. Some schools, communities, and even states resisted coexistence by segregating students into different schools on the basis of race, or into different educational tracks on the basis of race, ethnicity, gender, and socioeconomic status (Chapters 4 and 5). When students of diverse backgrounds have shared the same classes, was this coexistence acknowledged only on the basis of tolerance?

The pluralism of cooperation has also been around for a long time. Long before the current interest in cooperative learning, students were paired as laboratory partners in science classes or grouped together to work on projects. Their cooperation sometimes led to mutual discovery, not only about curricular content but sometimes about each other as well.

The pluralism of coexploring teaches the value of diverse viewpoints. An example of coexploring comes from a research study by Johnston (as cited in Diller, 1992). A fable about moles and porcupines was presented to a group of children. In this fable, a family of moles takes in a porcupine who needs a home for the winter, but soon the porcupine's size and quills present problems. Questions about the story allowed for multiple solutions. Used in a classroom setting, this type of problem offers opportunities for coexploring solutions. It further offers opportunities to take different points of view, similar to the procedure described above for using drama. In addition to enhancing social perspective-taking, this type of dilemma teaches the lesson that there is more than one way of looking at a situation and more than one solution to a problem. With younger students, fables and folktales may be used to elicit different perceptions. With older students, literature does this as well, but it also provides a basis for discussions of diverse values and viewpoints at more advanced levels of cognitive and moral reasoning (Timm & Timm, 1982).

The pluralism of coenjoyment offers some new possibilities in education by enhancing interrelationships when students share their interests with each other. Because this approach is not dependent upon academic content, my concern is that educators may perceive it as not inherent to the educative process, but simply as an extra to be included if there is time. In fact, this pluralism also offers opportunities for enhancing cognitive processing and problem-solving skills. One way to integrate the pluralism of coenjoyment with these skills is through *games.* Games offer challenges at the same time that they promote friendships. There are games related to a wide variety of subjects: math games, science games, geography games, language games, even games about economics. Athletics is another way. When students share a passion for soccer, for example, they see each other as team members—in other words, *as members of the same group.* Extracurricular activities provide another avenue for coenjoyment. When school boards cut funding for these activities, they fail to understand the opportunities for interrelationships that these activities offer. Finally, any mutually shared interest may bring students from diverse backgrounds together, whether that interest is baseball cards or rock music. When we as educators overhear students talking together about their favorite music CD or film star, we sometimes think they are "off the track" from more serious concerns. Perhaps they are more on track than we realize, and we should take another look at that track.

## CHAPTER SUMMARY

Three major areas of focus in multicultural education are the cultural information area, the social issues area, and the interrelationships area.

The cultural information area includes all knowledge relating to historical events, biographies, cultural values, mathematics and science, technology, customs, popular culture, and the arts of diverse peoples.

The social issues area involves attitudes about and behavior toward people of diverse groups. This area also refers to issues of bias; equity; economic, political, and social power; and stereotypes.

The interrelationships area includes home-school relationships and relationships among teachers and students. (Interrelationships in the larger society come under the social issues area.) This area also refers to cultural and psychological factors that students bring with them into the classroom.

Criteria for selecting curricular materials include accuracy, authenticity, and objectivity. In addition to providing cultural and historical information, some curricular materials may serve as a basis for discussing social issues. Literature and popular culture may do so as well.

Drama may enhance students' ability to understand other points of view. Procedures in the ethics of care may foster the development of meaningful relationships among diverse students.

## IMPORTANT TERMS

The cultural information area of focus

The social issues area of focus

The interrelationships area of focus

Ethics of care

## QUESTIONS FOR DISCUSSION

1. How would you apply the criteria for selecting materials to your teaching area?

2. What materials could you use in your teaching area that would serve as a basis for discussing social issues?

3. What procedures would you use to foster an ethics of care among your students?

4. Research and report on the cultural context of an artifact related to your teaching area.

5. Research and report on the historical background of the stereotypes for a diverse group of your choice.

6. Bring materials into the classroom that illustrate stereotypes in items currently being sold.

7. How would you introduce the process of coenjoyment into your classes?

## NOTES

1. The areas of knowledge that others have suggested are contained within these areas of focus. I have simply organized them differently. I shall address two other approaches here as examples.

I. Banks (1993) has referred to five types of knowledge: (a) personal/cultural; (b) popular; (c) mainstream academic; (d) transformative academic; and (e) school knowledge.

In the areas of focus that I am suggesting, personal/cultural would be included under interrelationships because this knowledge refers to culturally based perceptions about and reasons for behavior.

Popular knowledge (culture) would be included within cultural information and

social issues, depending upon the values and issues portrayed.

Mainstream academic knowledge would be included within cultural information *if* the information is accurate and objective. If it is inaccurate, subjective, and biased, then it would fall within the social issues area and should be addressed as such. In my view, the criteria for accuracy, objectivity, and freedom from bias should apply across all cultural groups, including European culture, history, and the experiences of diverse ethnic groups. Stereotypes about European Americans should be included with an examination of stereotypes of other racial groups.

Transformative academic knowledge that expands students' perceptions and appreciation for non-European cultures would come within the cultural information area. If information about non-European cultures is not accurately and objectively presented, then its Eurocentric bias should be challenged.

School knowledge would be included in the social issues area of focus, because teachers need to be aware of inaccuracies and biases in texts, teachers' guides, and media materials in order to combat them. School knowledge, however, also includes expectations for behavior in the school, which would place it within the interrelationships area as well. For example, Anyon's (1980) findings of schools' "hidden curriculum" for behavior based on social class indicates that school knowledge is not limited to information in texts or other materials, but part of the fabric of the school (Chapter 4).

II. Sleeter and Grant (1993; Sleeter, 1993) have suggested five approaches to multicultural education: (a) teaching the exceptional and culturally different; (b) human relations; (c) single-group studies; (d) multicultural; and (e) multicultural and social reconstructionist.

In the first approach, education is based on the assumptions of the American Dream—that limitless opportunity is a social reality. In other words, this view does not take inequities in the social system into account. It does recognize students' differences, including learning styles, and attempts to address diverse students' "needs," but it does not hold that there are reasons to alter the traditional (Western) curriculum. This approach relates to my interrelationships area of focus in its recognition of different styles. In curricular content it is the same as Banks' mainstream academic knowledge category, and the same criteria for accuracy and lack of bias in curricular materials about Western culture would apply here. I should mention that I agree with Sleeter and Grant's identification of the problems in this approach.

The human relations approach is similar to my interrelationships area of focus. Sleeter and Grant, however, include lessons about stereotyping in their human relations category. Learning about stereotypes clearly affects behavior, but I have included it in my social issues area of focus.

Single-group studies would fall under my cultural information area of focus. Sleeter and Grant have asserted that at times teachers have unwittingly failed to correct misinformation about diverse groups. Following the criteria for selecting materials offered in this chapter will help to correct this problem.

The multicultural approach takes students' cultural learning styles into account, infuses cultural content into the course of study, and reorganizes the curriculum in regard to race, ethnicity, gender, and social class. Therefore, it contains elements of all three of my areas of focus.

The multicultural and social reconstructionist approach includes the above, but with more emphasis on social issues that pertain to all groups. This approach also pertains to all three of my areas of focus.

In summary, I believe we are concerned about the same issues. We simply have arranged them slightly differently.

2. This "teaching" was told by Nick Hockings, a Lac de Flambeau Ojibwa, at a meeting in Oshkosh, Wisconsin, on January 30, 1995.

3. As early as 1932, Bartlett reported that subjects were more likely to remember information that was consistent with or "fit" with their previously established schemes, and that they were also more likely not to remember information that was inconsistent with these schemes. Bartlett also reported that when they remembered information that was inconsistent with their schemes, they tended to distort it.

4. **Fragmentation** is the separation of information about different groups, with a resulting lack of clarity.

**Imbalance** refers to the overrepresentation of members of one cultural group in comparison to other groups or to an emphasis on one cultural viewpoint.

**Invisibility** is the absence of members of various groups.

**Language** bias may be either stereotyped representations of speech or gender-biased terms.

**Stereotyping** is the presentation of individuals in accordance with overgeneralized attributes or traditional roles. These apply to all groups, but I should add that they also apply to the handicapped and disabled.

**Unreality** is an inaccurate or distorted presentation of the lifestyles of various groups.

Not all of these apply to all books. If a story is focused on a particular group or character within a historical context, it would not be fair to accuse the author of fragmentation, imbalance, or invisibility, if other groups are not germane to the narrative.

5. The origins of African American stereotypes may be traced from the early nineteenth century (Riggs & Rolle, 1987). Black stereotypes include several different images, all of which are caricatures. The sambo, a simple, happy Black man, derived from T. D. Rice, a White entertainer who blackened his face and imitated on stage the dance of a tattered and crippled Black man in the 1820s. This portrayal of a happy Black man evolved into the minstrel show, a popular entertainment in the nineteenth century. (In *The Jazz Singer,* the first talking American film in the 1920s, Al Jolson blackened his face as well.) Zib Coon, a buffoon, was another caricature presented on stage by White actors in blackface. It was a ludicrous image of a Black man trying to adapt to White education and culture. The responsible and loyal mammy was an image of a servant who protected the White home and cared for White children. The uncle was a virtuous and servile older Black man, referred to in popular songs and stories. The message in these last two stereotypes was that Blacks were happy to serve Whites. Collectively, these images have been referred to as the great-grandparents of modern images of Blacks (Riggs & Rolle, 1987).

Another stereotype was the violent Black man. In early films, such as *Birth of a Nation,* White men portrayed violent Black men, just as they did Native Americans in Western movies.

6. Dartmouth College, Marquette University, and Stanford University are among those that have dropped their Indian mascots.

7. This is another example of confusing cultures. Some shrunken heads, which were found among the Jivaro tribe (pronounced Hee-var-oh) in South America, have been on display in the Smithsonian in Washington, D.C. There is no evidence that this practice occurred in North American tribes.

# REFERENCES

Anders, R. (1976). *A look at prejudice and understanding.* Minneapolis, MN: Lerner.

Anyon, J. (1980). "Social class and the hidden curriculum of work." *Journal of Education* 162 (1), 67–92.

Banks, J. A. (June-July 1993). "The canon debate, knowledge construction, and multicultural education." *Educational Researcher,* 22 (5), 4–14.

Bartlett, F. C. (1932). *Remembering.* Cambridge: Cambridge University Press.

Bigler, R. S., & Liben, L. S. (1993). "A cognitive-developmental approach to racial stereotyping and reconstructive memory in Euro–American children." *Child Development,* 64 (5), 1507–18.

Bopp, J., Bopp, M., Brown, L., & Lane, P. (1989). *The sacred tree* (3rd ed.). Twin Lakes, WI: Lotus Light.

Derman-Sparks, L., & the A.B.C. Task Force. (1991). *Anti-bias curriculum: Tools for empowering young children.* Washington, DC: National Association for the Education of Young Children.

Diller, A. (1992). "What happens when an ethics of care faces pluralism? Some implications for education." In F. C. Power & D. K. Lapsley (Eds.), *Education, politics, and values: The challenge of pluralism.* Notre Dame: University of Notre Dame Press.

Ewers, J. D. (1982). "The emergence of the Plains Indian as the symbol of the North American Indian." In A. B. Hirschfelder (Ed.), *American Indian stereotypes in the world of children: A reader and bibliography* (16–32). Metuchen, NJ: Scarecrow Press.

Garcia, R. L. (1991). *Teaching in a pluralistic society: Concepts, models and strategies* (2nd ed.). New York: HarperCollins.

Gollnik, D. M., & Chinn, D. C. (1986). *Multicultural education in a pluralistic society.* Columbus, OH: Charles E. Merrill.

————. (1994). *Multicultural education in a pluralistic society* (4th ed.). Columbus, OH: Charles E. Merrill.

Hirschfelder, A. B. (1982). "Toys with Indian imagery." In A. B. Hirschfelder (Ed.), *American Indian stereotypes in the world of children: A reader and bibliography* (145–80). Metuchen, NJ: Scarecrow Press.

Howard, E. F. (1991). "Authentic multicultural literature for children: An author's perspective." In M. V. Lindgren (Ed.), *The multicolored mirror: Cultural substance in literature for children and young adults* (91–99). Fort Atkinson, WI: Highsmith Press.

Kuipers, B. J. (1991). *American Indian reference books for children and young adults.* Englewood, CO: Libraries Unlimited.

League of Women Voters, New Brighton, MN. (1982). "Children's impressions of American Indians." In A. B. Hirschfelder (Ed.), *American Indian stereotypes in the world of children: A reader and bibliography* (7–14). Metuchen, NJ: Scarecrow Press.

Moje, M. B., & Shyu, W. R. (May 1992). "Oh, the places you've taken us; RT's tribute to Dr. Seuss." *The Reading Teacher,* 670–76.

Moore, R. B., & Hirschfelder, A. B. (1982). "Feathers, tomahawks and tipis." In A. B. Hirschfelder (Ed.), *American Indian stereotypes in the world of children: A reader and bibliography* (46–79). Metuchen, NJ: Scarecrow Press.

Ralbovsky, M. (November 14, 1971). "An Indian affair: American Indian students concerned about nicknames, mascots in sports." (Article in *New York Times,* p. 9.) In A. B. Hirschfelder (Ed.), *American Indian stereotypes in the world of children: A reader and bibliography* (212–14). Metuchen, NJ: Scarecrow Press.

Riggs, M., & Rolle, E. (authors). (1987). "Ethnic notions" [Videorecording].

Berkeley, CA: California Newsreel. (KQED-TV: San Francisco).

Seuss, Dr. (1954). *Horton hears a who!* New York: Random House.

————. (1958). *Yertle the turtle and other stories.* New York: Random House.

————. (1961). *The sneetches.* New York: Random House.

Sleeter, C. E. (1986). "Race, class, and gender in educational research: An argument for integrative analysis." *Review of Educational Research* 56 (2), 195–211.

————. (March 1993). "Multicultural education: Five views." *The Education Digest,* 53–57.

Sleeter, C. E., and Grant, C. A. (1993). *Making choices for multicultural education: Five approaches to race, class, and gender* (2nd ed.). New York: Macmillan.

"Stanford removes Indian symbol; student petition gains support." (Spring 1972). *The Indian Historian* 5 (1), 21–11. In A. B. Hirschfelder (Ed.), *American Indian stereotypes in the world of children: A reader and bibliography* (215–19). Metuchen, NJ: Scarecrow Press.

Taylor, M. D. (1991). *Roll of thunder, hear my cry.* New York: Puffin Books.

Timm, J. (1988). "Cultural bias in children's storybooks: Implications for education." Paper presented at The American Educational Research Association, New Orleans, LA.

Timm, J., & Timm, H. C. (1982). *Athena's mirror: Moral reasoning in poetry, short story, and drama.* Schenectady, NY: Character Research Press.

Waber, B. (1966). *You look ridiculous.* Boston: Houghton Mifflin.

Wall, S., & Arden, H. (1990). *Wisdom Keepers: Meetings with Native American spiritual elders.* Hillsboro, OR: Beyond Words.

# 13

ॐ

# Bilingual Education

Now the whole earth had one language and the same words.
And as they migrated from the east, they came upon a plain
in the land of Shinar and settled there. And they said to one another,
"Come, let us make bricks, and burn them thoroughly."
And they had brick for stone, and bitumen for mortar.
Then they said, "Come, let us build ourselves a city,
and a tower with its top in the heavens, and let us make a name
for ourselves; otherwise we shall be scattered abroad
upon the face of the whole earth." The Lord came down
to see the city and the tower, which mortals had built.
And the Lord said, "Look, they are one people,
and they have all one language; and this is only the beginning
of what they will do; nothing that they propose to do
will now be impossible for them. Come, let us go down,
and confuse their language there, so that they will not understand
one another's speech." So the Lord scattered them abroad
from there over the face of all the earth, and they left off
building the city. Therefore it was called Babel,
because there the Lord confused their language
of all the earth; and from there the Lord scattered them abroad
over the face of all the earth.

GENESIS, CHAPTER 11, VERSES 1–9

Any discussion of language and bilingualism should begin with a profound appreciation for the importance of language in the definition of the self. Language is not simply the vehicle through which human beings exchange ideas. Language is the primary means through which we present our interpretations of our experience. Furthermore, as our perceptions of who we are become associated with our experiences with our family, clan, tribe, and other groups, language becomes a highly symbolic issue that is frequently tied to our deepest understanding of our identity. We see this fact institutionalized in other countries where ethnic groups focus their claims for recognition on the acceptance of their language. Norway, for example, has two official languages. In Belgium, Flemish and French exist side by side. In Canada, language and culture (English and French) are embedded in a national debate that appears to be threatening the unity of our northern neighbor.

In 1968 the United States Congress decided to take action concerning the neglect of children with limited proficiency in English. **The Bilingual Education Act** (Public Law 90-247) represented a change in federal attitude toward Americans whose native language was not English. Until then, minority languages in the United States had been dealt with in three ways. *They have been accommodated, ignored, or resisted* at the federal, state, and local levels during different times in our history. Accommodation to minority languages in the United States has been intermittent and has depended upon both political and educational attitudes in different locations, as well as the prevailing number of students needing instruction. When minority languages were ignored, immigrant and Native American students were placed in classes with instruction in English, in a sink-or-swim situation. Resistance to the teaching of minority languages has fluctuated in relation to prevailing political attitudes and national events.

This chapter reviews these three reactions to the instruction of diverse languages in the United States within the historical context in which they occurred. The stages of normal language acquisition are considered, because these stages have important implications for bilingual education. Finally, some alternative approaches to language instruction in American education are examined.

## ATTITUDES TOWARD LANGUAGE
## INSTRUCTION IN AMERICA

Bilingualism is by no means new in America. Diverse Native American tribes spoke different languages, but they also communicated freely with each other. When European colonists arrived, they brought their diverse languages with them. Federally supported programs in bilingual education, however, are a relatively recent innovation. I see four different eras in language instruction in the United States, with changing and even contradictory attitudes within some of them.[1]

## The Colonial Era

In the beginning of the colonial era, language education was used for religious purposes. Formal language instruction began in the Southwest when Jesuit and Franciscan missionaries first taught Christianity to Native Americans *in their own dialects* (Garcia, 1991). In colonial Massachusetts, the Old Deluder Satan Law required that children be taught English literacy in order to be able to read the Bible (Chapter 4). In New England, colonists recognized Native American dialects. One could say without exaggeration that from the beginning America was a patchwork quilt of enormous linguistic variation. Dutch, French, German, and Swedish coexisted in New York, New Jersey, Pennsylvania, and Delaware. Bilingualism was not unusual among the educated and in the working class as well. Newspaper advertisements for the return of runaway servants reveal that many of these servants were bilingual or even trilingual (Allen Walker Read [1937], *Bilingualism in the Middle Colonies;* cited in Crawford, 1991). German Americans had their own schools in Philadelphia before 1700 (Crawford, 1991). Eventually, however, once the French were defeated in the French and Indian Wars and the Spanish were confined to the Southwest, English was taken to be the language of the Eastern colonies and eventually of the whole United States. Interestingly, after the American Revolution there was no attempt by the newly formed federal government to adopt an official national language. In other words, even though English was taken for granted, personal choice of language was regarded as a political "natural right."

## The Nineteenth Century

In the nineteenth century, several factors contributed to contradictory views of bilingualism. In spite of the dominance of English, there were communities of people where English was a second language, as for example among the Italians in Boston, the Polish in Chicago, the Germans in Milwaukee, the Norwegians, Swedes, and Danes in Minnesota, the Chinese and Japanese in California, and the Spanish in Texas. The dialects of Gullah in the Sea Islands off the South Carolina coast and Cajun in the bayous of Louisiana also attest to the diversity of language in the United States. Newspapers in languages other than English were common and continue today. These attempts to maintain language diversity occurred in areas with large numbers of language minority groups *who had the political influence necessary to implement this diversity.* For example, in 1834 Pennsylvania enacted a free school law that provided for instruction in German and English for students whose primary language was German. Altogether, eleven states and one territory allowed bilingual education. These were Pennsylvania (1834); Ohio (1839); Territory of New Mexico (1850); Wisconsin (1855); Illinois (1857); Iowa (1861); Kentucky and Minnesota (1867); Indiana (1869); Oregon (1872); Colorado (1887); and Nebraska (1913) (Garcia, 1991, p. 161). In 1847 Louisiana provided for instruction in French. In addition, various cities such as Baltimore, Cleveland, and Milwaukee also offered bilingual instruction (Crawford, 1991).

On the other hand, in the nineteenth century three other factors contributed to a view that was not so accepting of instruction in languages other than English. First, a focus on the new United States after the American Revolution brought with it a concern for national cohesiveness. Even though Congress had not made English the official language of the United States, English was viewed as contributing to national unity.

Second, Noah Webster's efforts contributed greatly to a perception of a distinctly American English as distinguished from British English. In his famous dictionary, Webster standardized American spelling as well as American pronunciation as compared with British. For example, the compound word *waistcoat* was to be pronounced "waist coat," with equal emphasis on both parts, rather than pronounced "westcut" as it was in the British Isles (Cran, McCrum, & MacNeil, 1988).

The third factor contributing to a resistance to non-English languages came from the assimilationist view of the purpose of American education. The focus on both teaching English and teaching in English dates to the educational philosophy of absorbing the rapidly increasing number of immigrant children into American society. The prevailing attitude was that they would do "just fine" without special instruction and that "immersion" in English would hasten their enculturation and by implication their chances for success in American society. The evidence has not supported this view. Immigrants' children may have achieved fluency in English, but it was their grandchildren who were usually the first to complete high school (Crawford, 1991). (Even by the 1960s, high dropout rates persisted among students whose native language was not English.) In addition to immigrant children, Native American children were included in this English-only policy. The Indian Boarding Schools set out to remove children from their culture and their language. The fact that these boarding schools resulted in a pan-tribal identity was an unforeseen outcome (Chapter 3).

Disputes arose in the nineteenth century with these clashing pro and con views over instruction in languages other than American English. As one example, disputes arose over whether or not the children of German immigrants should receive instruction in German in the public schools in several areas of the Midwest in the 1880s. Mandates for instruction in English as the basic language were passed in Illinois and Wisconsin, where the German population was high.

## The Early to Mid-Twentieth Century

At the end of the nineteenth century, as more immigrants from southern, central, and eastern Europe arrived in the United States, these newcomers were regarded as a threat to the country because of their religion, cultural differences, and competition for employment. The movement of nativism was antithetical to their ways Chapter 11). An organization known as the **American Protective Association** was instrumental in this movement. Its impact affected education in languages other than English. In 1915 the **National Americanization Committee** began an "English first" project in Detroit, with the support of local business. Resistance to German increased during World War I when German was removed from the curriculum. Legislation also banned the speaking of German in church, at public meetings, and even on the telephone (Crawford, 1991). Increasingly, a nationalistic political view equated English with patriotism. Instruction in other languages also diminished or disappeared in public schools. In American high schools, modern language instruction dropped steadily until the late 1940s. United States involvement in the Spanish-American War, two World Wars, and the Korean War added to the strong nationalistic values during this time (Garcia, 1991). Instruction in languages other than English rose again in the 1960s and 1970s due to the passage of the Bilingual Education Act.

## The 1960s to the Early 1990s

In 1959 Cubans began to flee from the revolution against the Batista regime and to arrive in Miami. More than 20,000 Cuban Spanish-speaking students enrolled in the Dade County schools (Garcia, 1991). Two bilingual programs were implemented to serve these students. In the Coral Way's program, first, second, and third graders received their lessons in Spanish in the morning and in English in the afternoon (Crawford, 1991). Results were encouraging, for the students progressed in both languages. Both federal and local funds financed this and other school projects. This marked the first time that the federal government supported bilingual education in the public schools (Garcia, 1991).

When the Bilingual Education Act was passed by Congress in 1968, it was in fact the seventh amendment to the Elementary and Secondary Education Act of 1965 (Title VII). By providing funding assistance to local education agencies, it was intended to meet the needs of students who came from backgrounds with non-English languages. There was a view, however, that these students were "educationally disadvantaged" because of their inability to speak English. The Civil Rights Movement resulted in parents in other parts of the country beginning to file lawsuits against school districts to meet their children's needs. These included Mexican Americans and Native Americans. In San Francisco, Chinese-speaking students were being denied access to special instruction in English. When their case reached the U.S. Supreme Court in 1974, the Court ruled in their favor (Lau v. Nichols, 414 US 563) by its decision that special educational programs were necessary in order to provide equal educational opportunity to these students (Chapter 6). This decision received little public notice at the time. Although it did not mandate bilingual education, it gave legal endorsement to bilingual education. In 1973 the Bilingual Education Act came up for renewal in Congress. It was changed to the Comprehensive Bilingual Education Amendment Act of 1973 and expanded to include the training of bilingual education teachers (Garcia, 1991). In addition, the political climate of the 1970s and into the 1980s made clear the need for foreign language instruction in an increasingly worldwide perspective.

All was not well with bilingual education, however. In the 1980s, during the Reagan administration, support for these programs decreased. Not only was funding for bilingual education cut, but Education Department data indicated in 1986 that "school districts were nine times less likely to be monitored for *Lau* compliance under the Reagan Administration than under the Ford and Carter administrations" (Crawford, 1991, p. 45), and that federal investigators found violations in 58 percent of their reviews.

The problems were not limited to Washington. In November 1986, a referendum in California (Proposition 63) was directed to public officials to preserve English as the common language of the state. The referendum passed by a three-to-one vote. It resulted in the destruction of California's bilingual education law. Many believed that the national group known as **U.S. English** had created a public climate that affected the outcome of this election. The group had spent over $700,000 to support the referendum, which was in agreement with its **English Only** viewpoint (Crawford, 1991).

In order to combat the English Only movement, in 1985 the League of United Latin American Citizens and the Spanish American League Against Discrimination began to support a movement known as **English Plus.** This group affirmed English, but also sought to preserve language diversity (Crawford, 1991). By the beginning of the 1990s, public debate over bilingual education was intensifying.

### Back to the Future?

I mentioned at the beginning of this chapter that minority languages in the United States have been accommodated, ignored, or resisted at different times in our history. There are signs that all of these policies are being practiced in the 1990s.

Accommodation with programs for minority language students continues to be implemented. Many school administrators speak with pride of their bilingual education programs, although the types of programs constitute a wide range of offerings.

The practice of placing minority language students in regular classes was not abandoned after 1968 with the enactment of the Bilingual Education Act. For example, one of my Hmong students told me that this was precisely what happened to him in the 1980s in a school in Illinois. He described sitting in a class and not understanding one word the teacher said. The first English word that he learned was "TV," and he learned that from other students. Indeed, ignoring the needs of these students remains to this day. This year a former student of mine who is now a teacher came to see me. She reported that she had three Hmong students in her kindergarten class and that they did not know any English. She was desperately trying to find ways to help them. She was teaching in a school district that had no bilingual education teacher, even on a part-time basis.

In the 1990s, resistance to bilingual education is apparently increasing with the American public. Ironically, as I was writing this section, I received a telephone call asking whether I would talk to a newspaper reporter about "the return to English only and a swing away from bilingual education" in American schools. This call may have been due in part to the fact that a U.S. Congressman from a district in Wisconsin has been highly vocal in his opposition to bilingual education. I replied that I would be happy to tell the reporter why I believe that this swing is wrong-headed. As of this writing, no one has called me back.

One reason for the current public resistance to bilingual education is the **new American nativism** and its call for a focus on Western culture in American education (Chapter 11). Another reason is the increased immigration since the 1960s, and with it more linguistic diversity, which is perceived by some as un-American and divisive to the society. A third reason for the increased resistance to bilingual education is that school administrators believe that their facilities and resources in their districts may be inadequate to deal with this increased need for specialized instruction. Recently, a principal reported to me that in her school there was only a "handful" of Spanish-speaking students a few years ago, but that today her students represent *seven* different non-English languages and that she feels overwhelmed in terms of how best to meet their needs.

## LANGUAGE ACQUISITION

Although language is not innate, the capacity for language is part of every infant's human potential.[2] Noam Chomsky (1965) has referred to this capacity as a **Language Acquisition Device (LAD).** Extensive research in different cultures around the world has shown that children progress through the same stages of language development the world over. Although this developmental sequence may not seem directly relevant to instruction in bilingual education, there are cognitive considerations in this sequence that have important implications for the way in which language is presented to students at different ages.

In the course of their language development, children move through various stages: (a) babbling; (b) echolalic babbling; (c) holophrases or one-word sentences; (d) two-word sentences or telegraphic speech; (e) three-word sentences; (f) awareness of grammatical rules; and finally (g) mastery of the structure of the language (Etaugh & Rathus 1995; LeFrancois, 1992).

During **babbling** (birth to 6 months), the baby tries out speech sounds. At this stage, the baby has the full range of vocalization that is possible for humans to utter. I used to marvel at the perfect guttural "r" that my children produced at this time. Later, when they studied French, they had to struggle to try to master this sound.

During **echolalic babbling** (6 to 12 months), the baby imitates the pitch and emphasis patterns of its parents' speech. My daughter commented once that the baby of a friend of hers was babbling perfectly in French. Once this stage is reached, the baby loses the capacity to produce the full range of vocalizations.

With **holophrases** (12 to 18 months), the baby begins to vocalize words. (A holophrase is a one-word sentence.) It is at this time that the baby begins to form *cognitive schema* between speech sound and the fact that a certain sound has meaning. This starts by accident. As the baby experiments with putting sounds together, a combination of sounds may produce a word in the native language. For example, in English, if the baby says "Da, ba, ga, ma, ma," the mother is very likely to give a strong response to "ma, ma." The baby learns to associate this sound with *her.* (In the case of my Hmong student whose first English word was "TV," he realized that the sound of those two letters in fact meant a particular object.) Soon, the baby is pointing to objects, and as the parents name the object, the baby names the object as well. A wonderful example of this awareness was described by Helen Keller. She was normal when she was born, but an illness in late infancy left her both blind and deaf. For years her family tried in vain to teach her to communicate. Finally, when she was nearly seven years old, they hired Anne Sullivan to teach her to communicate by touch. Keller (1905) described her experience as follows:

> I was at once interested in this finger play and tried to imitate it.... But my teacher had been with me several weeks before I understood that everything has a name.... We walked down the path to the well-house, attracted by the fragrance of the honeysuckle.... Some one was drawing water and my teacher placed my hand under the spout. As the cool stream gushed over one hand she spelled into the other the word water.... I stood still, my whole attention fixed upon the motions of her fingers. Suddenly...the mystery of language was revealed to me. I knew then that "w–a–t–e–r" meant the wonderful cool something that was flowing over my hand. That living word awakened my soul, gave it light, hope, joy, set it free! I left the well-house eager to learn. Everything had a name, and each name gave birth to a new thought. (pp. 22, 23–24)

This realization that the different feelings of touch in her hand communicated concepts freed Helen from her dark prison. She went on to college when she was older and became internationally known for her brilliance and her courage.

There is an extremely important lesson here for language acquisition: that children learn language *within the context of its meaning. Without schema, speech is only babbling. The connection must be made between vocalization (or signs) and meaning for language to occur.*

During the two-word sentence stage (18 to 24 months), toddlers convey the meaning of full sentences in two words. This is known as **telegraphic speech** because it conveys meaning in a shortened form similar to that used in telegraph messages. The range of children is amazing. For example, "Mama, milk" means "Mother, give me milk." "Red ball" is obviously descriptive. "Go out" means "Take me out" or that someone has just gone out. The problem is that children's pronunciation sometimes makes it difficult for those not familiar with their "code" to understand them. Once when my mother was baby-sitting with my daughter, she met me at the door as I came into the house. "Joan, what in the world does 'Lil' bobbie' mean? She cried for ten minutes when I put her to bed because I didn't understand her." I replied that it meant that she wanted her little bottle. I also felt guilty that I had forgotten to tell my mother this! I got the bottle and went to the baby's room. Tone of voice also connotes different meanings for the same words. The baby was awake, stood up in her crib, looked at me, and said, "Lil' bobbie?" with a clear accent on the question. I gave her the bottle, she laughed joyously, murmured "Lil' bobbie" in a contented tone of voice, and lay down to drink it.

During the three- to four-word stage (24 to 30 months), children begin to put sentences together with subject, verb, and object in that order if the language is English. At twenty-six months, my daughter was able to say to me, "I want more juice."

Around age three, children start to make mistakes in grammar that they never made when their speech was purely imitative of their parents. This stage is known as **overregularization** because children overregularize irregular forms in the language. For example, they say things such as "We goed to the store" when six months old before they say "We went." This pattern is confusing to adults who are unfamiliar with the fact that these errors actually represent a growing awareness of rules of grammar. If the plural of cat is cats, then the plural of foot is foots—right? It takes several years for children to master the exceptions to the rules. The amazing aspect of this stage is that no one is telling three- or four-year-olds about the rules for past tense or plurals. They have figured out that the sound for "s" means more than one. In Chapter 7, I described a pandeau made by a Hmong woman who was learning English. Her errors reflect this overregularization, which people also go through in learning a *new* language.

## ALTERNATIVES IN SECOND LANGUAGE INSTRUCTION

Learning a second language depends upon four factors: (a) the quality of instruction; (b) the motivation of the learner; (c) the cognitive stage of the learner; and (d) the student's level of communicative competency and basic literacy in the native language before the second language is introduced.[3] These are by no means minor considerations, but all four of them have not generally been taken into account in evaluations of second language programs. All too often the primary issues considered have been the outcomes of learning and the length of time that students have been in a program. In focusing on the time factor, educators may be addressing the wrong issue and overlooking more important considerations.

Language instruction in the United States has followed different approaches, which are reviewed below.

### The Grammar-Translation Approach

Many European Americans have learned a second language through courses in high school and college in which they were taught basic grammar and were given passages to translate. In this approach, known as **grammar-translation,** students conscientiously memorized vocabulary lists, learned the rules, and tried to place the words into a context. These students, however, were learning at a formal operational level of cognition (Chapter 10). They were able to reason through all the information being presented to them. Even then, the process was often slow and arduous for some students. Many achieved **receptive language** and understood what the teacher was saying, but felt awkward when it came to speaking. They had not yet mastered **productive language.** Those who were fortunate enough to travel abroad reported that only then were they able to master speaking in a foreign tongue. The point is that in this situation they were actually relating language to experience. In other words, they were able to conceptualize within a meaningful context. At this stage of language acquisition, the person is forming a new identity of the self as an active participant in a new milieu.

## The Audio-Lingual Approach

Commercial programs specializing in languages have taken a different approach, known as **audio-lingual.** For example, Berlitz emphasizes speaking and listening from the beginning. Those who have taken these courses report that they are at least able to communicate within specific contexts when they travel abroad. I was able to manage in the former Soviet Union because I had acquired some practical speaking ability in Russian. At least I could ask for directions when the need arose.

## The Direct-Natural Approach

But what about children? Opponents of bilingual education programs often do not realize the cognitive issues involved. The practice of placing language minority students in a classroom with instruction in English used the **direct–natural approach** to language instruction, which includes the use of gestures to add meaning. Whether or not this approach is actually language instruction is questionable. This approach was in fact **language immersion,** based on the assumption that if the student was forced to adjust, the student would. This approach has been considered developmental (Garcia, 1991), but in fact it failed to take into account the process of schema building in regard to culture. The attempt to instruct students in a language that they do not understand assumes that along with the acquiring of vocabulary comes understanding of *cultural concepts.* Classroom instruction often assumes cultural knowledge, including classification concepts, which students may not have. The case of the Hmong student who classified the saw, hatchet, and fire together and omitted the hammer illustrates this point (Chapter 9). Familiarity with cultural referents is essential before students are able to understand lessons and to build schema from them. The psychological effect of this experience can produce a sense of alienation from the second language, which has the opposite effect intended by this type of program.

## The Bilingual Approach

True bilingualism refers to full literacy in two languages. Language literacy involves four abilities: (a) listening comprehension; (b) speaking; (c) reading; and (d) writing. A truly bilingual person is able to do all of these at the same level of competence as someone who is native to *both* languages. Most bilinguals achieve varying degrees of proficiency in combinations of these four abilities.

In education, the question of whether learning a second language interferes with language development or enhances it has been of some concern. The answer is that it depends. That is, it depends upon *the degree of competence in communication and elementary literacy that students have achieved in their first language, before being introduced to a second.* If a second language is introduced after these skills have been acquired, the effect may be one of two possibilities. The first is that students will achieve equal competency and literacy in both languages. This result is known as **additive bilingualism.** The second possibility is that students will achieve full competency in their first language and some degree of competency in their second. This result is known as **dominant bilingualism.** If, however, the second language is introduced before students have achieved competency in communication and some literacy in their native language, the second language will interfere with the development of these skills in both languages. This is known as **subtractive bilingualism** (Cummins, 1979). The important point here is that evaluations of the success of bilingual education programs may be meaningless if students' competency level in their *first language* is unknown or not taken into account. Merely noting the length of time students spend in a program and assessing the results overlooks this basic entrance-level factor.

Bilingual education programs in the United States have generally followed one of three methods, depending upon the intended goals. They are as follows:

**Transitional Bilingual Education (TBE)**  This approach provides instruction in students' native language only long enough for them to make the transition to English (Edelsky, 1992). In other words, this approach uses the first language as a bridge to the second. The goal in this approach is to displace the original language with English. Another term for this approach is **monolingual-remedial,** because contained within it is the belief that students are educationally "disadvantaged" because of their lack of the dominant language (Crawford, 1991).

**Maintenance Bilingual Education (MBE)**  This approach offers both the native language and the target language throughout the school years, with a goal of preserving the native language (Edelsky, 1992). This approach is in line with the English Plus view of valuing diversity languages in addition to the learning of English. Instruction is maintained in both languages, which is seen as a **bilingual enrichment** approach. Maintenance programs build upon the culturally related cognitive schema acquired in the first language and at the same time enhance the development of schema with the second.

**English as a Second Language (ESL)**  Some programs have been referred to as ESL, but this is something of a misnomer, because all programs in the United States are aimed at students' acquiring English. In practice, ESL has frequently been used to refer to so-called pull-out programs, in which students are placed in regular classes with instruction in English, and "pulled out" for a portion of the day for special instruction that relates English to their native languages. Whether or not curricular content is offered in the students' native language often depends upon the school. The goal is usually for students to learn English. Perhaps the most disturbing report about this type of program was told to me at a convention by a teacher who said that the principal in her school directed the teachers to dismiss their minority language students for their ESL classes only if they had completed all of their work. This administrator expressed the belief that the program should be used as a *reward* for conscientious students!

ESL programs should not be confused with true bilingual education. In some situations, ESL programs are in fact transitional programs in which the goal is to help students transfer to English as quickly as possible. In other cases, ESL may be closer to maintenance programs in which students are instructed in both their native language and in English with a view toward competency in both.

## PLACEMENT OF MINORITY LANGUAGE STUDENTS

Recently, a disturbing practice in regard to minority language students has evolved. These students are sometimes identified as having special needs (or being learning disabled). This judgment is based on their limited ability to communicate, read, and write in English. Apparently educators are still determining "intelligence" by means of culturally and linguistically biased assessments (Chapter 9). These students are then provided with special instruction for a portion of the day, but this is not necessarily in bilingual education. A teacher reported to me that in her district these students with **limited English proficiency (LEP)** are included in special education programs, but the help they are given is no different from that provided for students whose only language is English! Trueba et al. (1990) have articulated the issues in this practice:

> If we start with the assumption that in general all … [minority] children are competent enough to handle difficult learning tasks in the home and out-of-school settings, including the acquisition of their language and culture, then we are pressed to search for more rational explanations that lead to individual attributes of deficiencies such as "learning disabilities." We must also assume that the acquisition of English literacy is not an intrinsically difficult task, but it becomes difficult in the social and cultural context in which children are expected to obtain it. Because English literacy will continue to affect the future educational level and socioeconomic status of large numbers of minority students, it is important to explore ways of optimizing the sociocultural context of English literacy acquisition. (pp. 91–92)

Labeling these students as having learning disabilities on the basis of limited proficiency in English makes little sense. Failing to provide them with programs that build on their cognitive skills in their native language could result in subtractive bilingualism, in which case the programs designed to help them would prove detrimental instead.

A review of the effectiveness of various bilingual programs is beyond the scope of this text. Cziko (1992) has reported on the evaluation of bilingual education programs and described a bilingual program in which majority language and minority language students learn from each other. This type of program has also been reviewed by Crawford (1991). Educators should consider the consequences of the types of programs and placements that they provide for minority language students. Diversity in the United States is greater than ever before in our history, yet minority language students are one and a half times more likely to drop out of school before the twelfth grade (Crawford, 1991). How we provide for them impacts our future as well as theirs.

In the past we have wasted the language diversity in the United States. We have allocated federal funds to add courses in language diversity for European Americans at the same time that we have allocated federal funds to wean minority language students away from their native tongues. This contradictory practice makes no sense. It is important for minority language students to learn English, but their linguistic heritage is also a national treasure. How long are we going to continue to waste it?

## CHAPTER SUMMARY

Minority languages have been accommodated, ignored, or resisted at different times in United States history. In colonial times, bilingualism was prevalent among many people of diverse social classes.

In the nineteenth century, conflicting attitudes either supported diverse languages or were antagonistic toward them. Some states implemented instruction in languages other than English. At the same time, assimilationist educational policies aimed at teaching the children of immigrants English as quickly as possible. At the end of the century, the nativist movement strongly resisted the languages, religion, and culture of immigrants from southern, central, and eastern Europe.

In the early twentieth century, proficiency in English was associated with patriotism. Courses in foreign language instruction decreased steadily until the 1960s, when political events—including the Civil Rights Movement—brought about demands for language diversity in the schools. The U.S. Congress passed the Bilingual Education Act in 1968.

In the 1980s, federal support for bilingual education declined. A new emphasis on English only appeared in connection with the rise of more politically conservative public attitudes. Today minority languages continue to be accommodated, ignored, or resisted.

The stages of language development have important implications for learning a second language. Language instruction in the United States has taken several approaches. These are the grammar-translation approach, the audio-lingual approach, the immersion approach, and bilingual education.

Bilingual education has focused on transitional programs or on maintenance programs. ESL programs have often involved pulling students out of regular classes for a portion of their instruction.

Recently, a practice of assessing minority language students in terms of their proficiency in English has resulted in their being placed in programs to address their special needs, but cognitive issues in relation to language have not always been considered in these programs.

## IMPORTANT TERMS

The Bilingual Education Act

American Protective Association

National Americanization Committee
Holophrases

U.S. English

English Only

English Plus

Language Acquisition Device

The grammar-translation approach

The audio-lingual approach

The direct-natural approach

Transitional bilingual education

Maintenance bilingual education

Limited English proficiency (LEP)

ESL programs

Echolalic babbling

Telegraphic speech

Overregularization

Receptive language

Productive language

Monolingual-remedial

Bilingual enrichment

Additive bilingualism

Dominant bilingualism

Subtractive bilingualism

Language immersion

## QUESTIONS FOR DISCUSSION

1. Have you ever studied a foreign language? Which approach did your program of study follow? How successful do you believe it was?

2. Discuss the contradictory attitudes toward bilingualism in educational policy in the United States.

3. Discuss the English Only viewpoint in relation to the English Plus viewpoint in the United States today.

4. If you were planning a bilingual education program, what issues would you take into account and how would you proceed?

## NOTES

1. Ricardo Garcia (1991) also identified four time periods, but mine have a slightly different range. Basically, however, mine overlap with his.

2. There is a critical period for the development of language. Children who have been isolated from human contact during their earliest years have exhibited severe difficulties in learning language later.

3. Garcia (1991) has identified the first two of these four factors. The issue of motivation raises interesting questions about students who have a second language forced upon them.

## REFERENCES

Chomsky, N. (1965). *Aspects of the theory of syntax*. Cambridge, MA: M.I.T. Press.

Cran, W., McCrum, R., & MacNeil, R. (1988). "Pioneers o! pioneers." In Mac-Neil/Lehrer (Producers), *The Story of English*. New York: WNET.

Crawford, J. (1991). *Bilingual education: History, politics, theory, and practice* (2nd ed.). Los Angeles: Bilingual Education Services.

Cummins, J. (1979). "Linguistic interdependence and the educational development of bilingual children." *Review of Educational Research* 49, 222–51.

Cziko, G. A. (1992). "The evaluation of bilingual education: From necessity and probability to possibility." *Educational Researcher* 21 (2), 10–15.

Edelsky, C. (1992). *With literacy and justice for all: Re-thinking the social in language and education.* New York: Falmer Press.

Etaugh, C., & Rathus, S. A. (1995). *The world of children.* New York: Harcourt Brace.

Garcia, R. L. (1991). *Teaching in a pluralistic society: Concepts, models, strategies* (2nd ed.). New York: HarperCollins.

Keller, H. (1905). *The story of my life.* New York: Grosset & Dunlap.

LeFrancois, G. R. (1992). *Of children: An introduction to child development* (7th ed.). Belmont, CA: Wadsworth.

Trueba, H. T., Jacobs, L., & Kirton, E. (1990). *Cultural conflict and adaptation: The case of Hmong children in American society.* New York: Falmer Press.

# 14

ဩ

# Toward the Future

Think not forever of yourselves,
O Chiefs, nor of your own generation.
Think of continuing generations of our families,
think of our grandchildren and of those yet unborn,
whose faces are coming from beneath the ground.

THE PEACEMAKER
FOUNDER OF THE IROQUOIS CONFEDERATION

At the beginning of this text, I referred to a question asked by Paul Gauguin: "Where do we come from? What are we? Where are we going?" I have examined the question of "Where do we come from?" in terms of our separate and collective histories. I have also examined the question of "What are we?" in terms of our diversity. The question "Where are we going?" still remains.

In no time at all, not only is a new century upon us, but also a new millennium. At the beginning of the century we are about to leave, horse-drawn carriages jostled for position on city streets with newfangled contraptions called automobiles. A few city dwellers had telephones. Such luxuries were rare and limited to the economically advantaged, however. The fact that twentieth-century technology would bring into our homes electronic images of events from halfway around the world and put humans on the moon remained for history to reveal. The fact that technology would produce the means to obliterate life on earth as we know it also remained for history to reveal. The century we are about to leave also continued the mind-set of the nineteenth century's industrial revolution with its preoccupation with production and consumption of material goods. As we near the end of the twentieth century, third-world nations are increasingly joining a **global marketplace.** Apparently, nations of the world have recognized the fact that it is better to compete in the marketplace than to destroy each other because of fear of differing ideologies.

At the beginning of the millennium we are about to leave, a small band of people known as Normans, living on the northwest coast of France, were about to cross the English Channel to an island domain off the coast of continental Europe in the year 1066. The fact that their regional dialect would evolve into English, the international language of trade and commerce, remained for history to reveal. The fact that these Normans would set Britain on a course of growth that would result in a colonialism exceeding that of the Roman Empire also remained for history to reveal. Even so, colonialism was by no means limited to the country that became known as England. The Spanish, Dutch, French, and Portuguese participated in this process as well. They not only fractured the lives of those living in a hemisphere yet to be entered by Europeans when the millennium began, but also forced people living on the continent of Africa to come along with them. We are about to leave a millennium during half of which Europeans held sway over peoples around the globe.

There is a lot of speculation these days about what the twenty-first century will bring. I have also wondered what the next millennium will bring. What, if any, signs appear in our crystal ball? Will we be able to outgrow our ethnocentrism? Will diverse peoples be able to look at each other and say "We're different, but that's OK"?

I see three current trends that have implications for the future. The first trend is that we are leaving the industrial age and entering the information age. Computer and telecommunications technologies offer more flexible working schedules and settings whereby commuting to work, whether it be office, school, or factory, may not be necessary for all workers. The tools of this technology are purported to be new "knowledges" available on the **information highway.** On the surface, this new technology sounds beneficial to all. But is it really? Who will be empowered in this system? Those who have the resources to buy the equipment? Furthermore, if education increasingly follows the current trend of "distance learning," who will be cut out of the loop? The answer is obviously those who cannot afford to purchase the technology or to buy new models as "state of the art" improvements render older equipment obsolete. Thus, empowerment remains in the control of those with at least some economic power to begin with.

The second trend is the extension of a global economy. Recent international trade agreements were designed to break down protective barriers and to increase equal opportunity for nations in the world to compete in the global market, but who actually benefits? Obviously, the corporate investors, but what about the workers who make the production possible? We hear more about profit sharing these days, but how widespread is it? My concern here is that the future appears to belong to those with access to both the information highway and the global market, and that as a consequence the old industrial-age gulf between management and labor based on social class across all racial and ethnic groups could become intensified with these trends, rather than diminished.

The third trend is a contradictory one and concerns cultural diversity. On one hand, resistance to cultural diversity is intensifying both abroad and in America. The rekindled antipathy among Muslims, Croats, and Serbs dates back, ironically, to the early days of this millenium. In the United States there is a view among conservatives that cultural diversity could become equally devisive here, and for this reason some are opposed to including courses in multiculturalism in schools and colleges (Chapter 11). This view perceives multiculturalism as working against national interests. I view this trend as a continuation of the new American nativism, with its drive toward uniformity in American society. This view fails to understand that it is possible for people to have more than one loyalty and one identity (Chapter 2). For example, a Hmong refugee, now living in Green Bay, Wisconsin, said to me "I am concerned about my clan responsibilities, but I also love this new country of mine." The current conservative call for an emphasis on the "canon," with its Eurocentric curriculum, fails to consider the fact that a curriculum including diverse materials in our schools and universities may enrich rather than weaken our educational programs. As one student remarked to me, she was unaware of the fact that Toni Morrison had won the Nobel Prize for Literature until she took a multicultural course.

Chapter 12 presented three areas of focus in education that may combat this new American nativism. The first is to familiarize students with the rich variety of diverse cultural information that is not being included in Eurocentric curricular programs. The second is to address social issues directly in the classroom by selecting curricular materials that provide examples of these issues. The third way is through procedures that focus directly on helping students develop the ability to take different points of view.

The alternative trend regarding cultural diversity is an increasing awareness that knowledge about diverse cultures is important in surprising ways. For example, an executive friend who is scheduled for an assignment in Japan told me that American business firms have not been effective in retaining employees in foreign work assignments. Like other managers given overseas assignments, she does not feel adequately prepared for the cultural differences. She also reported that cross-cultural training may relieve this problem, but that the average amount of time devoted to this training for overseas personnel is only one or two days. In some cases, less than a half day is given to it, or no time at all. Furthermore, if managers return to the United States before the allotted time, it can still cost the company thousands of dollars (personal communication).

I see these trends—the information highway, the growing global market, and the impact of diverse cultures on politics and the global market—as leading us into a new era in history. We are living in what is now being referred to as the **postmodern era**—a time when one age is being replaced by another.

In post-figurative traditional cultures (Chapter 7), the function of education was to transmit to the young the skills that they would need for survival. The function of education in the United States served a similar purpose. In other words, it sought to prepare students for their anticipated roles in society by teaching the skills they would need to qualify for employment. Educators determined what "place" students would have in the society and assigned them to educational programs accordingly. Thus, from colonial days through the nineteenth and twentieth centuries, access to school programs was determined on the basis of race, ethnicity, gender, and social class. A hidden curriculum in schools serving different social classes continues today (Chapter 4). In post-figurative cultures, however, values included an awareness of humans' relationships with each other, with the natural world, and with the spirit world.

When industrial cultures collided with traditional cultures, co-figurative cultures emerged. The traditional skills for survival were no longer sufficient. In situations where colonialism disrupted the lives of indigenous peoples around the world, those peoples were forced to learn new skills and languages in order to survive. At the same time, they tried to hold on to their values about their relationships with each other as well as with the physical and spiritual world. When immigrants and dislocated peoples (whether through slavery or war) found themselves in new environments, they were forced to learn new skills and languages in order to survive as well. Some of them maintained their values, but in the United States, assimilationist educational policies resulted in deculturalization for many students. This process continues today. A Hmong youth said to me that he can no longer really communicate with his grandmother because he thinks better in English now and also because their two lives are so different.

In entering the postmodern era, we have already entered a pre-figurative cultural situation. Technology is now merged with the global corporate marketplace. Those lacking either the equipment or skills are already at a disadvantage. Is the function of education in the twenty-first century merely to teach students the skills for this technology? Is the function of education to be essentially no different from that of the industrial age? What effect does this kind of education have on our individual and diverse identities?

On the Fourth of July, 1994, Vaclav Havel, President of the Czech Republic, spoke in Independence Hall in Philadelphia on the occasion of his being awarded the Philadelphia Liberty Medal. This honor is bestowed for leadership in the pursuit of freedom from oppression, ignorance, or deprivation.

Havel referred to our postmodern time as one in which a new world culture is evolving, where old solutions no longer serve us, where everything is possible, and where almost nothing is certain. He viewed cultural diversity as being a central issue in the future. He pointed out the fact that, in spite of the emergence of a transnational, global sort of culture, diverse peoples are also clinging to ancient tribal and ethnic certainties. When cultural conflicts arise, Havel views them as more dangerous today than at any other time in history because antagonists are armed with the same super weapons purchased from the same suppliers (Havel, 1995).

It is true that with the collapse of the Soviet Union, the artificial world order that dominated the twentieth century has also collapsed, but a new world order has not yet emerged with guidelines to deal with conflicts within and between nations and tribes. Havel views the central political task of the final years of this century to be the creation of a new model of coexistence among the various peoples, races, and nations of the world.

There is a ray of hope. In turning to the heritage, culture, and values of their past, diverse peoples are rediscovering their identities. They are also rediscovering that survival is not good enough. There is more to life.

I believe there is a lesson here for education in the twenty-first century. Therefore, I believe that all education should be multicultural. Multicultural education helps students to affirm their identity. It embraces our collective heritages, which are the real wealth of our nation. It strives for equity and justice. It teaches us that in embracing our diversity we embrace our humanity.

Havel believes that our decisions about the path to peaceful coexistence must be based on the conviction that our common human destiny is not dependent on what we do for ourselves, but rather for the planet and for future generations to come. This view, spoken by one at the end of this millennium, is strikingly similar to that of the Iroquois Peacemaker quoted at the beginning of this chapter.

Multicultural education enables us to hear this wisdom of the peacemakers and the elders. If we remember those yet unborn, we may truly enter not only a new century, but also a different kind of millennium.

## IMPORTANT TERMS

Information highway          Global marketplace

Postmodern era

## REFERENCES

Havel, V. (January/February 1995). "A time for transcendence." *Utne Reader*, 53, 112, 113.

ဢ

# The Sultan's Jester

## A Multicultural Comedy

Adapted by Henry C. Timm* from
*Tales from the Arabian Nights*

### Cast of Characters

The Narrator

The Jester

The Chinese Tailor

The Tailor's Wife

The Jewish Doctor

The Servant

The Muslim Merchant

The Christian Sea Captain

Policeman One

Policeman Two

The Sultan

The Barber

The Hangman

A Crowd of Townspeople

### Production Notes

To balance the cast, many of these roles may be played by males or females. In *The Sultan's Jester* there are several explanations that should be delivered as asides to the audience—like those in a nineteenth-century melodrama. These asides and exaggerated gestures heighten the feelings of farce which should permeate the play.

---

*Henry C. Timm has written over 75 original plays, which have been produced in the United States and abroad.

## THE SULTAN'S JESTER

**SCENE ONE:** *A street in an Arabian City. The* **Narrator** *enters.*

**The Narrator:** Once upon a time, in the Kingdom of Kashgar, there lived a little hunchback. Now it happened that this little hunchback was the great friend and court jester of the King, or Sultan, as he was called in that country. The Sultan was very fond of his little Jester, whose intelligence, wit, and humor helped to brighten the Sultan's day and keep his thinking straight.

One day the jester stopped at the door of a Chinese tailor's shop, on his way to the palace. His wit amused the tailor no end, so the tailor invited the jester to stay for dinner. He wanted his wife to meet this amusing fellow.

*(The* **Jester***, the* **Tailor***, and the* **Wife** *enter and sit down to eat, but they can hardly get a bite, they are laughing so hard at the Jester's jokes. This is played with gestures.)*

**The Narrator:** Now the Tailor's Wife had prepared a delicious meal, for she was an excellent chef. Fish was her specialty, and she had cooked a stuffed flounder that could have been served to the Sultan himself. The Jester loved stuffed flounder, but the Sultan hated it—so it was never served at the Palace. The Jester didn't know whether to talk or eat—they were the two things he liked to do best in the world—so, unwisely, he did both at once until—

*(The* **Narrator** *sits to one side.* **The three** *are feasting happily until suddenly the* **Jester** *stops, his mouth open, his eyes wide. His hands fly up to his mouth and throat, he staggers away from the table and falls to the floor. The* **Wife** *screams. The* **Tailor** *runs to the Jester to find out what's wrong.)*

**The Wife:** What's wrong with him?

**The Tailor:** Oh, no. Oh, my stars!

**The Wife:** What's happened? What's wrong?

**The Tailor:** Oh, woman…oh, wife! I think he's dead!

**The Wife:** Dead?

**The Tailor:** Dead.

**The Wife:** A curse upon our heads! The man is dead.

**The Tailor:** That's what I said. The jester is dead!

**The Wife:** What will we do? What's to be done?

**The Tailor:** *(Aside—to the audience.)* This is terrible. We are Chinese and Buddhists as well. If we tell the Sultan, he will think we have killed his jester, and then we ourselves will surely be put to death. We are outsiders in this country. *(To the Wife.)* No one will believe this was an accident. We have to get rid of him.

**The Wife:** How? Where?

**The Tailor:** I know. Next door.

**The Wife:** The Doctor?

**The Tailor:** The Doctor. *(Aside—to the audience.)* He is a clever Jew. He will know better than we what to do with him.

(**They both** *pick up the Jester and carry him next door. They lean him against the house and knock at the door. The* **Servant** *answers the door.)*

**The Tailor:** This man is very sick. The Doctor will know what to do. Here, take this money—for the Doctor's trouble.

*(The* **Tailor** *and the* **Wife** *start to leave.)*

**The Servant:** Wait! Who is he?

**The Tailor:** He is the Sultan's Jester. He fell down in front of our house.

**The Wife:** We brought him here as soon as we found him.

*(The* **Tailor** *and the* **Wife** *leave.).*

**The Servant:** *(Calling inside the door.)* Master, come quickly. There is a sick man at the door.

**The Doctor:** *(Appearing in the doorway.)* A patient? At last. *(Aside—to the audience.)* It's about time. I've just completed my medical studies, so I have no patients. You can't practice medicine without patients!

**The Servant:** He's very weak—he cannot walk.

**The Doctor:** Who is he? Where did he come from?

**The Servant:** The Chinaman and his wife from next door brought him. They said they found him in the street. They also said he is the Sultan's Jester.

**The Doctor:** The Sultan's Jester! *(Aside—to the audience.)* What luck! Just what I need to start a reputation at court. *(The Doctor starts to examine the Jester.)* Now then, my good man, let's just have a look here. Come, let me help you into my examining room. *(To the Servant.)* He looks a little rickety.

*(The* **Doctor** *and the* **Servant** *try to get the Jester into the house, but the Jester keeps slipping out of their grasp like a rag doll and falls down the steps of the house. The Doctor and the Servant run to the Jester. The following is said with wide gestures and waving of arms.)*

**The Doctor:** Oh, no!

**The Servant:** What's wrong with him?

**The Doctor:** Oh, no. Oh, my stars!

**The Servant:** What's happened? What's wrong?

**The Doctor:** I think he's dead!

**The Servant:** Dead?

**The Doctor:** Dead.

**The Servant:** A curse upon our heads! *(Aside—to the audience.)* The man is dead.

**The Doctor:** That's what I said. *(Aside—to the audience.)* The jester is dead!

**The Servant:** What will we do? What's to be done?

**The Doctor:** This is terrible. *(Aside—to the audience.)* We are Jews. If we tell the authorities, they will think we have killed the Sultan's jester, and then we will surely be put to death, for we are outsiders in this country. No one will believe that this was an accident. *(To the Servant.)* We have to get rid of him.

**The Servant:** How? Where?

**The Doctor:** I know. Next door.

**The Servant:** The Camel Merchant?

**The Doctor:** Yes. *(Aside—to the audience.)* He is a Muslim. He will know better what to do with him, and at least they won't assume he is guilty. He is not a foreigner.

*(The **Doctor** and the **Servant** pick up the Jester and carry him next door to the Camel Merchant's warehouse. They lean him up precariously against the wall. Just as they are about to leave, they hear the Camel **Merchant** coming back.)*

**The Servant:** Hurry. I hear him coming.

*(They scurry off as the Camel **Merchant** enters, carrying some sacks.)*

**The Merchant:** *(Aside—to the audience.)* It was ever thus: if you want things done right, you have to do it yourself. I know that I received twenty sacks of sorghum yesterday, and I know they are all around here somewhere. Where did my clerk put them? *(Seeing the Jester.)* What's this? Some one is here? Hello? I know you're there. Speak up, fellow, or I will take you for a thief and deal with you likewise. *(He waits for an answer.)* I'm telling you, I know how to deal with thieves. If you have come to steal, you have come to the wrong place. *(Again, silence.)* Very well, I warned you.

*(The **Merchant** takes a small sack, sneaks behind the Jester and drops it on him. The **Jester** falls forward.)*

**The Merchant:** *(Aside—to the audience.)* Well, that was easier than I thought it would be. Some thief! He must have been asleep. *(He examines the Jester.)* Now, let's just see who we have here before I call for the police. What's this? Oh, no! This is the Sultan's Jester, Achmed Ababalah! I recognize him from the palace. How did he get here? Achmed. *(Shakes him.)* Achmed Ababalah! Wake up! *(He puts his head against the Jester's chest.)* What's this? What's this?! Oh, no. Oh, my stars! I think he's dead!

*(The **Merchant** starts walking around in circles, talking to himself, looking at the audience, shaking his head, looking at the ground, looking at the sky, looking at his hands, holding his head as he says these lines.)*

**The Merchant:** Dead? Dead. A curse upon my head! The man is dead. That's what I said. The Jester is dead! What will I do? What's to be done? This is terrible. *(Aside—to the audience.)* Achmed Ababalah is the Sultan's favorite Jester. When he finds out that I have killed him, he will have me shot—or maybe hanged for sure. *(He grabs his throat with both hands.)* That is the custom of our country: to punish murder without mercy, even if the death was an accident. I have to get rid of him. I'll just move him away from here. Let the authorities deal with him.

*(The **Merchant** drags the **Jester** and leans him up against another building and goes back into his house. Just as he disappears, the **Sea Captain** comes along, singing his sea song. He is a little drunk. When the noise starts, all the others peer out of their windows to watch what happens.)*

**The Sea Captain:**  *(Singing.)*
  I sail on every ocean.
  I sail from sea to sea
  But the shores I like the best
  Are the shores of Araby—

*(The **Sea Captain** sees the Jester lying in the street and goes over to him. As he does so, **Two Policemen** enter and watch, unnoticed by the Sea Captain.)*

**The Sea Captain:**  Well now, my friend, you look a little gray around the gills. What seems to be the matter? Here, try a little of this.

*(The **Sea Captain** offers the Jester a sniff from a flask of brandy that he carries. He tries to help the Jester to drink, but the **Jester** slides down sideways to lie flat on the ground.)*

**The Sea Captain:**  This just won't do. Here, try to get this down. It'll do you good.

*(The **Policemen** come over to the Sea Captain.)*

**Policeman One:**  Here now, what's going on here?

**The Sea Captain:**  I'm just trying to help this poor fellow.

**Policeman Two:**  *(Who has been inspecting the Jester.)* Help him? I should think so. But the man is beyond help. He is dead.

**The Sea Captain:**  Dead?

**Policeman One:**  Let me see that flask in your hand. What is that?

**The Captain:**  This? Why, it's only brandy. I thought it might perk him up.

**Policeman One:**  Brandy? What is this brandy? I think it is a poison.

**Policeman Two:**  It is surely a poison. We saw you feeding it to this man.

**Policeman One:**  You are a stranger. Where do you come from?

**Policeman Two:**  He is a Christian, that's clear enough. And he has done harm to a Muslim.

**The Captain:**  I...I was only trying to help.

**Policeman One:**  Look here, I think I know this poor dead man. Is he not Achmed Ababalah, the Sultan's favorite Jester?

**Policeman Two:** I believe so. That makes matters even worse. Not only have you, a Christian, done harm to a Muslim, you have done harm to the Sultan's favorite. You will surely die for this.

**The Captain:** But I...

**Policeman One:** Come with us. And pray to your Christian God for mercy. You will surely meet him before the day is out. We must take this matter to the Sultan himself.

**The Sea Captain:** *(Aside—to the audience.)* He is right. This may well be the day of reckoning for me. These Muslims can be very strict and evidently the poor dead man was a person of some importance. I must indeed pray for the fate of my soul and wish that the whole world saw everything the same way. Only that would put an end to mishaps like this.

*(The **Policemen** carry out the **Jester**, followed by the **Sea Captain**. The **Tailor**, the **Tailor's Wife**, the **Doctor**, the **Servant**, and the Camel **Merchant** leave their windows, come out of their houses, and follow the Policemen and the Sea Captain offstage.)*

**SCENE TWO:** *The Sultan's Palace. The **Sultan** is sitting on a pillow while his **Barber** is trimming his hair. The others arrive. It is a long procession: first the two **Policemen**, carrying the **Jester**, then the **Sea Captain**, the Camel **Merchant**, the **Doctor**, the **Servant**, the **Tailor**, and the **Tailor's Wife** followed by a small crowd. The Sultan recognizes Achmed, who is laid on the ground in front of him.*

**The Narrator:** Now as I said at the beginning, the Sultan was very fond of this little Jester, whose intelligence, wit, and humor helped to brighten his day and, as I said before, helped to keep the Sultan's thinking straight. *(The Narrator looks on.)*

**The Sultan:** Achmed? Achmed!! My Jester! Is he dead?

**Policeman One:** *(With proper gestures of respect.)* Oh, Most Noble Star of all of Allah's skies—it is our misfortune to tell you: Achmed Ababalah is dead—

**Policeman Two:** Foully murdered by this Christian Sea Captain here. We caught him in the act!

**The Sea Captain:** I was only trying to help. I thought he was sick. I was giving him a sniff to wake him up.

**The Sultan:** That is the way with you Christians; no matter where you are, you take your ways with you and think they are the best. But here you have done more harm than good, and you shall pay for that harm with your life. Give him to the rope!

*(The **Hangman** appears, puts a noose around the **Captain's** neck, and is about to drag him off when the Camel **Merchant** steps out from the crowd.)*

**The Merchant:** Stop! This is not right. There is no justice in this execution. This man could not have murdered the Jester!

**The Sultan:** What do you know about this?

**The Merchant:** Oh Prince of the Sun, I know that this Christian did no harm to this poor Jester of yours. I know this because it was I who killed him. I found him and mistook him for a thief, so I knocked him dead with a sack of sorghum. It was I who left him in the street, hoping the problem would go away.

**The Sultan:** A sack of sorghum?! That is even worse than before. Oh, my poor Achmed, what a terrible way to die. *(He turns to the Barber.)* Here, take him out of the way before someone trips over him. *(To the Hangman.)* You there, take the innocent man out of the rope and give it to this man. You are a Muslim and you kill your own kind out of anger! That is a terrible thing and you shall die for it.

*(The **Hangman** puts the noose around the **Merchant's** neck and begins to take him away, but the **Doctor** stops him.)*

**The Doctor:** Stop! Stop! *(He runs up to the Sultan.)* This is not right. There is no justice in this execution. This man could not have murdered the Jester!

**The Sultan:** What do you know about this?

**The Doctor:** Oh Most Gracious One, I am a Doctor, and a Jew, and I must tell you, someone brought this man to me this evening and left him at my doorstep, saying that he was already ailing and in need of help. But when I went to treat him, he fell down my steps. That's what killed him, and I am the one responsible. This Camel Merchant is my neighbor. My servant and I left the Jester by his house, fearing for what would happen to us.

**The Sultan:** That was a cowardly fear, and if the crime were not so serious, it might be forgiven by your admission now. But alas, I cannot be so lenient. You there, this is the rightful murderer. Take him, Hangman.

*(The **Hangman** takes the noose off the Camel **Merchant**, puts it around the Doctor's neck, and starts to lead him away. The **Tailor** steps forth.)*

**The Tailor:** Oh Most Noble and Wise Leader, release this poor Jew! Of all the murderers here, I am the worst of them and the worst guilt is mine.

**The Sultan:** Yet another murderer? Is this the season for mayhem? Then tell us your part of this mystery.

**The Tailor:** Of all of us, my wife and I were the last to see the poor Jester alive. I invited him to dinner and then and there he died—just up and died! We didn't know what to do and we thought the Doctor might know best— so we took him to the Doctor and left him there.

**The Sultan:** He died at dinner?

**The Tailor:** Well, he kept talking with his mouth full.

**The Sultan:** But he always did that. Is there anyone else here who has some confession surrounding the death of Achmed Ababalah, the greatest Jester of them all?

*(There is no answer to his question.)*

**The Sultan:** Good. Then we have come to the bottom of things. And I begin to soften on this crime. Although the four of you are almost murderers, you have all redeemed yourselves a little by coming forward as you did. I will not have you put away, but you will all be whipped a hundred lashes each for your miserable cowardice. Take them away.

(*The* **Hangman** *begins to march the* **Tailor**, *the* **Doctor**, *the Camel* **Merchant**, *and the* **Sea Captain** *away while the Barber examines the* **Jester's** *body.*)

**The Sultan:** I will remain here to mourn my beloved friend. It will be a long time before he will be replaced. (*Looking at the Tailor.*) By the way—what did he eat?

(*The Tailor starts to reply. The Barber answers.*)

**The Barber:** Fish.

**The Sultan:** Fish?

**The Barber:** He was eating fish. Observe, Oh Favorite Son of the Full Moon.

(*The* **Barber** *positions himself with his back to the audience, leans over the* **Jester**, *"removes" a huge [metal or cardboard] skeleton of a fish, and holds it high in the air. The Barber then moves to the side of the Jester. The Jester begins to quiver, and gurgle for a moment, then sits up and looks around.*)

**The Sultan:** Allah be praised, he is not dead at all! My friend, my companion in truth, you are alive after all!

(*The* **Jester** *tries to talk but cannot.*)

**The Sultan:** And for the first time in your life you are at a loss for words!

**The Barber:** It will take a little time, but he will speak again. Oh Flower of the Sun, there was no murder at all. Should you really punish them nonetheless?

**The Sultan:** Surely not for murder. But these four, coming from the four corners of humanity as they do, have shown one thing: all men are silly and afraid, and though they confessed when they did, they should have done so sooner and not put a fellow human being in danger.

**The Jester:** But a hundred lashes, Oh Blossom of the Desert?

**The Sultan:** He speaks. My Achmed speaks.

**The Jester:** I do, Oh Blossom of the Desert.

**The Sultan:** And what have you to say after so long a silence among such fools?

**The Jester:** Only that the distance between a Sultan and a fool can sometimes be no greater than a spider's filament, Oh Favored One of Allah.

**The Sultan:** And what is the sting of wisdom in thy spider's tongue?

**The Jester:** Only this poor wisp of a thought, Oh Wisest of Sultans. That a Sultan's life is measured in his thoughts as well as his deeds, for the thoughts are the parents of the deeds. If you truly see each of these foolish people as bearing the single face of humanity, regardless of the corners of the earth from which they come, then you must teach them how to think before they act, and never let the color or the shape of another's face cause one to leap like a silly child to a foolish deed. That is what the Wind of Allah whispers to my ear. Surely such a whispering is worthy of a Sultan's ear as well. That is all I think to tell you, Oh Wisest of the Wise.

**The Sultan:**  Achmed, beloved of your Sultan, you are indeed a wise little spider. I am chastised by your wise words. *(The Sultan turns to the Tailor, the Doctor, the Camel Merchant and the Sea Captain.)* Just as Achmed Ababalah has rightly chastened me, so you will have to taste a little pain. Let this be the last of this affair. *(To the Hangman.)* Take each one of these over your knee and give them a spanking for their foolishness.

*(The* **Tailor***, the* **Doctor***, the Camel* **Merchant***, and the* **Sea Captain** *line up and each receives a comic spanking in turn. The Hangman uses exaggerated gestures and each wriggles and squirms, makes faces, and yells "Ouch!" and "Ow!" and "Stop!")*

**The Sultan:**  Now be on your way home, and in the morning bless each other as friends and neighbors for the brotherhood which lies beneath your different skins.

**The Narrator:**  So saying, the Sultan waved them on their way. And now you have heard the moral of our tale. They were a Buddhist, a Jew, a Muslim, and a Christian, but they cared about each other after all, and that is the way things ought to be.

**CURTAIN**

ᔕᓂ

# Glossary

**Access** refers to whether or not school programs are open to students regardless of their race, ethnicity, gender, social class, or other factors.

**Acculturation** may be used in three different ways. First, it refers to the process of becoming acquainted with the language, values, knowledge, and behavior of a culture. In this sense, it is a synonym for enculturation. Second, it may connote the adoption of cultural customs and values from another culture than one's native culture. Third, it may refer to the impact of one culture on another as a result of colonization or conquest.

**Additive bilingualism** is the achievement of equal competency and literacy in one's native language and in a second language.

**Ageism** is a belief in the inherent capabilities of individuals on the basis of age. Ageism also refers to discrimination on the basis of age.

**Assimilation** is the process of incorporating one group within another or the intention of making one group more homogenous in relation to another. In the United States, official policy has aimed at accomplishing this homogeneity through education.

**Asylees** are people in the United States who have entered the country under temporary visas but who would face persecution in their homeland if they were forced to return. They seek political asylum in order to remain here.

**Autonomous minorities** are groups having distinct ethnic, religious, linguistic, and cultural identities. Within these groups may be families whose forebears go back several generations, or newcomers, as in the case of Jewish immigrants from Europe or the Middle East.

**Bias** is an inclination or predisposition in attitude. Bias is often assumed to be negative, but it is equally possible to be biased in favor of certain groups, values, and viewpoints.

**(The) canon** is a traditional curricular approach to education based on Western European culture, history, philosophy, science, and thought.

**Castes** are groups that have been incorporated into American society involuntarily and permanently and who in the past have lacked economic, political, and social power. In the United States, castes have been delineated along racial lines, including African and Native Americans.

**Co-figurative culture** is focused on the present. People in the same generation share their knowledge and skills with each other and attempt to adapt to changing circumstances. Co-figurative cultures arise when one culture comes into contact with another culture, or when people move to a new location where the dominant culture is different from their original one.

**Contextualizing** in multicultural education refers to presenting material culture within the context of its cultural background, including history and values.

**Culture** is an abstract concept that includes knowledge, skills, customs, arts, technologies, values, rules about behavior, and language, which are passed from one generation to another.

**Cultural chauvinism** is a feeling of superiority about one's own group in contrast with other groups. Cultural chauvinism carries cultural pride to an extreme degree.

**Cultural degradation** is a view that one's own group is inferior, with a resulting low self-esteem brought about by discrimination or being dicounted by others.

**Cultural information** in multicultural education refers to curricular content. It includes the history and experiences of diverse groups, cultural values, literature, science, technology, and the arts.

**Cultural interrelationships** in multicultural education refers to the effect of psychological and cultural factors on individual and group behavior. It includes students' relationships with each other and relationships between the school and parents.

**Cultural myths** refer to legends that contain powerful psychological and spiritual insights into different cultures by portraying their most profound belief systems and values.

**Cultural pride** is respect and admiration for one's own cultural group and heritage. The group may be defined by nationality, ethnicity, social class, gender, religion, or region.

**Cultural relativism** is the ability to put aside one's own cultural viewpoint and to view other cultures from within their own perspectives.

**Deculturalization** refers to the exclusion of the language and culture of minority students in educational settings.

**De facto segregation** is separation not by law but resulting from a variety of local practices or circumstances, such as racially unbalanced neighborhoods.

**De jure segregation** is segregation by means of law.

**Discrimination** is the acting out of negative attitudes toward individuals or groups. It refers to legal, economic, political, social, and educational practices that exclude individuals on the basis of race or other factors.

**Diversity** usually refers to variation among groups. It is an umbrella term that may apply to a wide spectrum of people.

**Dominant bilingualism** is the achievement of full competency and literacy in one's first language and some degree of competency in a second language.

**Enculturation** is the process of learning the language, values, traditions, knowledge, and skills of a culture. This usually occurs in the context of growing up in the culture of one's parents.

**English as a second language (ESL)** has been used to refer to "pull-out" programs, in which students are placed in regular classes with instruction in English, and "pulled out" for a portion of the day for special language instruction.

**Ethnicity** refers to national or tribal origin.

**Ethnocentrism** is the judgment of another culture according to the values of one's own culture. It is an inability to view other cultures from their point of view, or an attitude that one's own group is superior.

**Female paradox** refers to the fact that higher education for women appeared to be out of harmony with their traditional social roles.

**Field-dependent style** refers to a cognitive style that includes a preference to work with others, a need for encouragement (extrinsic motivation), a sensitivity to the social or learning environment, and a wholistic or global approach to learning. This style is sometimes referred to as field sensitive.

**Field-independent style** refers to a cognitive style that includes a preference to work independently, internal (intrinsic) motivation, task orientation, and an analytic approach to learning.

**Glass ceiling** refers to the fact that advancement to upper-level positions in the professions and in business is limited to members of American society on the basis of race, ethnicity, and gender.

**Hidden curriculum** refers to educational policies and procedures based on students' social class.

**Horizontal diversity** refers primarily to race, ethnicity, and gender (or variables that are predetermined). Sometimes, however, it may refer to geographic region or different environmental backgrounds.

**Horizontal socialization** refers to the process by which children are instructed in the knowledge, customs, traditions, and values of their particular group of origin. Traditional expectations about gender-related roles are included in this socialization process.

**Immigrant minorities** are those who have moved voluntarily to the United States from their native countries.

**Limited English proficiency (LEP)** refers to minority language students with limited ability in understanding, speaking, reading, and writing English.

**Macroculture** in the United States is the mainstream national culture.

**Maintenance bilingual education (MBE)** provides instruction in both students' native language and English throughout the school years, with a goal of preserving the native language.

**Material culture** refers to the observable and/or tangible aspects of culture, such as clothing, architecture, tools, artifacts, food, and music.

**Microculture** refers to variations in cultural knowledge and values held by people of diverse subgroups within American society.

**Minority** generally refers to non-Whites. It is a term that some people use interchangeably with "people of color." It may, however, also refer to groups with little or no economic, political, or social power. In this sense, it could include some European Americans who have suffered discrimination in the United States on the basis of their ethnicity, gender, or social class.

**Multicultural** refers to distinct and identifiable cultures within and across diverse groups and societies. It includes both differences and similarities in beliefs, experiences, values, and behavior across groups.

**New American nativism** is a political viewpoint that emphasizes mainstream thought, usually Western European, in the United States.

**Nonmaterial culture** refers to the hidden aspects of culture, including the knowledge and values of diverse groups.

**Outcomes** refer to the end result of educational programs for students of all diverse groups.

**People of color** refers to non-White peoples.

**Pluralism** may be simply a synonym for diversity. Recently it has been defined as the holding of two or more viewpoints simultaneously.

**Post-figurative culture** is focused on the past and depends heavily on tradition. Children learn primarily from their elders, who are the transmitters of cultural knowledge, language, skills, customs, traditions, and values.

**Pre-figurative culture** is focused on the future. When the older members and younger members of a group have grown up in totally different environments, parents may not have the knowledge necessary to guide their children, who must find a new way for themselves. This often occurs with immigrants in a new location.

**Prejudice** is literally a prejudgment or preset attitude, which is usually negative, toward both the views and members of other groups.

**Racism** is a belief in the inherent capabilities of individuals on the basis of race. Racism also refers to discrimination on the basis of race.

**Refugees** are dislocated persons, forced to emigrate from their native countries by circumstances such as war or political or religious persecution.

**Segregation** is the separation of people on the basis of race, ethnicity, gender, religion, social class, or any other identifiable criterion.

**Sexism** is a belief in the inherent capabilities of individuals on the basis of gender. Sexism also refers to discrimination on the basis of gender.

**Social issues** in multicultural education refers to a curriculum that aims specifically at combating bias. It directly addresses inequities in the American society, either past or present.

**Socialization** refers to teaching children about rules for behavior that is expected in the culture of their parents.

**Society** refers to a collection of people, living together within a nation or geographic area, who have common economic, social, and political institutions and organized interactions with each other.

**Stereotype** is an overgeneralized image of and belief about the behavior of members of diverse groups.

**Subtractive bilingualism** is the interference of a second language with the development of competency and literacy in one's native language, with resulting problems in both languages.

**Transitional bilingual education (TBE)** provides instruction in students' native language only long enough for them to make the transition to English.

**Vertical diversity** refers to differences in socioeconomic status, educational level, and age. Greater social power accrues to higher social status and education. In the United States, social power increases until middle age, and then declines, depending upon factors such as equity and opportunity. Some societies venerate the elders for their wisdom.

**Vertical socialization** is the process by which children are instructed in the expectations that parents and others have for their behavior in reference to age and social class.

# Index